Accounting for the Holocaust

Accounting for the Holocaust: Enabling the Final Solution reveals how accounting practices allowed the attempted annihilation of Jews by the German Nazis and the Italian Fascists to be carried out with machine-like efficiency and devoid of any moral considerations.

This largely hidden aspect of the Holocaust will allow a wide range of readers, both academic and across many sectors of the general population, to understand how the systematic murder of more than six million Jews was expedited by accounting practices and the information that these produced by allowing the humanity of those killed to be denied when they became mere numbers in a process. Readers will gain a new understanding of how the enactment of the scale of the Holocaust was made possible by the way in which accounting practices as "technologies of death" were used to reduce Jews to a life without value. The numerical calculations, techniques, and reports that constitute accounting practices allowed the systematic murder of Jews to be drained of any considerations that would imply that the numbers and costings were related to prescient human beings. These technologies of death also allowed those who managed and organised the murder of Jews to absolve themselves of the actual killings.

Warwick Funnell is Emeritus Professor of Accounting and Public Sector Accountability at Kent Business School, University of Kent, Canterbury, UK.

Michele Bigoni is a Reader in Accounting at Kent Business School, University of Kent, Canterbury, UK.

Erin Twyford is a Senior Lecturer in Accounting at the University of Wollongong, Gwynneville, NSW, Australia.

Routledge New Works in Accounting History
Series Editor: John Richard Edwards, Richard Fleischman, Garry Carnegie, Salvador Carmona

This innovative series contains volumes on accounting history, auditing, bibliography, development of accounting principles and standards, education and ethics, financial reporting, law and regulations, management accounting, and the theoretical works of leading scholars. Providing students, teachers and researchers with the opportunity to learn more about the discipline of accountancy and its past, this series is a vital addition to any accounting library.

49. **Memorial Articles for 20th Century American Accounting Leaders**
    Edited by Stephen A. Zeff

50. **The Italian and Iberian Influence in Accounting History**
    The Imperative of Power
    Edited by Michele Bigoni and Warwick Funnell

51. **The Origins of Accounting Culture**
    The Venetian Connection
    Edited by Massimo Sargiacomo, Stefano Coronella, Chiara Mio, Ugo Sostero, and Roberto Di Pietra

52. **Accounting for Alcohol**
    An Accounting History of Brewing, Distilling and Viniculture
    Edited by Martin Quinn and João Oliveira

53. **Accounting Thought and Practice Reform**
    Ray Chambers' Odyssey
    Frank Clarke, Graeme Dean, and Martin Persson

54. **Accounting for the Holocaust**
    Enabling the Final Solution
    Edited by Warwick Funnell, Michele Bigoni and Erin Twyford

Accounting for the Holocaust

Enabling the Final Solution

Edited by Warwick Funnell, Michele Bigoni, and Erin Twyford

Routledge
Taylor & Francis Group
LONDON AND NEW YORK

First published 2024
by Routledge
4 Park Square, Milton Park, Abingdon, Oxon OX14 4RN

and by Routledge
605 Third Avenue, New York, NY 10158

Routledge is an imprint of the Taylor & Francis Group, an informa business

British Library Cataloguing-in-Publication Data
A catalogue record for this book is available from the British Library

Library of Congress Cataloging-in-Publication Data
Names: Funnell, Warwick, editor. | Bigoni, Michele, editor. | Twyford, Erin, editor.
Title: Accounting for the Holocaust : enabling the Final Solution / edited by Warwick Funnell, Michele Bigoni and Erin Twyford.
Description: Abingdon, Oxon ; New York, NY : Routledge, 2024. | Series: Routledge new works in accounting history | Includes bibliographical references and index.
Identifiers: LCCN 2024001297 (print) | LCCN 2024001298 (ebook) | ISBN 9781032685274 (hardback) | ISBN 9781032685311 (paperback) | ISBN 9781032685328 (ebook)
Subjects: LCSH: Accounting--Germany--History--20th century. | Accounting--Moral and ethical aspects--Germany. | Holocaust, Jewish (1939-1945)--Economic aspects.
Classification: LCC HF5616.G3 A23 2024 (print) | LCC HF5616.G3 (ebook) | DDC 940.53/1813--dc23/eng/20240224
LC record available at https://lccn.loc.gov/2024001297
LC ebook record available at https://lccn.loc.gov/2024001298

ISBN: 978-1-032-68527-4 (hbk)
ISBN: 978-1-032-68531-1 (pbk)
ISBN: 978-1-032-68532-8 (ebk)

DOI: 10.4324/9781032685328

Typeset in Sabon
by KnowledgeWorks Global Ltd.

Contents

List of Figures

List of Tables

List of Contributors

Valerio Antonelli
Department of Management & Innovation Systems
University of Salerno
Italy

Michele Bigoni
Kent Business School
University of Kent
United Kingdom

Emanuela Mattia Cafaro
Department of Management & Innovation Systems
University of Salerno
Italy

Raffaele D'Alessio
Department of Management & Innovation Systems
University of Salerno
Italy

Enrico Deidda Gagliardo
Department of Economics and Management
University of Ferrara
Italy

Warwick Funnell
Kent Business School
University of Kent
United Kingdom

Ellen Lippman
Pamplin School of Business
University of Portland
United States

Roberto Rossi
Department of Management & Innovation Systems
University of Salerno
Italy

Erin Twyford
Faculty of Business and Law
University of Wollongong
Australia

Stephen P. Walker
University of Edinburgh Business School
University of Edinburgh
Scotland

Paula Wilson
University of Puget Sound
School of Business
United States

1 Accounting and the dehumanisation of the Jewish "Other"

Warwick Funnell, Michele Bigoni, and Erin Twyford

Jewish condemnation

The Holocaust has been referred to as a "gigantic, murderous operation" (Muller-Hill, 1994, p. 68) that involved the systematic annihilation of more than 6 million Jews[1] (Wellers, 1978, pp. 139–143). It is recognised as one of the most momentous events in the 20th century, if not in recorded history (Dawidowicz, 1975; Hilberg, 1980, p. xi; Katz, 1989, p. 354). According to Pois (1989, p. 1938), "the Holocaust is the single most important phenomenon associated with a movement which … attempted to end history". It is widely seen as creating a watershed not only in Jewish history but in what had been understandings of the nature of humanity. After the Holocaust, there would never be the same level of innocence and faith in the inherent goodness of humankind or a similar understanding of the way in which social institutions worked (Hilberg, 1980, p. 102; Rosenberg, 1983, pp. 8, 9, 14; Browning, 1988, p. 173). Wiesel (1988, p. 11) refers to the Holocaust as "a kind of black hole in history … Man's attitude towards heresy and faith, language and silence, science and political science is no longer the same …". The scale and intent of the horror and misery during the Holocaust, declares Habermas, creates an obligation always to remember those who were murdered (Talmon, 1989, Book 1, p. 185; La Capra, 1994, p. 53).

This book examines the role of accounting as a fundamental, indeed essential, component of practices used in the implementation of the Holocaust, what the Nazis after the Wannsee conference referred to as the "Final Solution to the Jewish Question".[2] Unlike other instances of genocide in history, the Holocaust was the first time when the power of the technology of the modern world had been turned on a group of people, connected only through a religious heritage, systematically and methodically to murder them to the last person (Bauer, 1989a, pp. 83–84). According to Funnell (1998, p. 436), the enduring metaphor for the Holocaust is that of the operation of an efficient machine with the sole objective of processing millions of people as costless, quickly and effectively as possible to produce corpses. The outcome was to be a world, most notably the German Reich, without Jews; a world cleansed of what the Nazis saw as the Jewish pestilence, a world from which

DOI: 10.4324/9781032685328-1

they would remove the proclaimed polluting and degrading influence of Jewish capitalism. The "men, women and children who perished in the Holocaust died because an inexorable power had decreed that human beings with certain qualifications should, without exception ... be destroyed" (Zuccotti, 1987, p. 183). In Nazi Germany and Fascist Italy in 1944, Jews had become life without value and thus could be killed without legal consequences (Agamben, 1998, p. 138). After the racial condemnation of Jews, the killing of Jews, emphasises Agamben (1998, p. 114), constituted "simply the actualisation of a 'mere capacity to be killed' inherent in the condition of the Jew as such". Jews were "exterminated ... exactly as Hitler had announced, 'as lice ... as bare life'" (Agamben, 1998, p. 114).

By removing from an individual their political rights, that is, their right to be recognised as a citizen of a State because they do not meet specified qualifications, most notoriously those that are derived from legally enforceable racial requirements, they are no longer entitled to the legal protections and rights which citizenship, their political life, provides. This provides the means to allow the denial of their humanity, the right to life, and to be accorded only the bare life of any living organism, which could be destroyed at any time by anyone without any consequences for the killer (Foucault, 1990, p. 143; Agamben, 1998, pp. 138–139). This will be accomplished most efficaciously by pronouncing a crisis, which allows those in power to declare a "state of exception" when the normal law is suspended.

The most threatening consequence of the enactment of a state of exception is the way in which it can be used to erase "any legal status of the individual, thus producing a legally unnameable and unclassifiable being" who is now at the mercy of those who institute the state of exception (Agamben, 2005, p. 3). Accordingly, the declaration of a state of exception, as in Nazi Germany, gives those in power the right to decide on "the value or the non-value of life" (Agamben, 1998, p. 142). Those who are valued become the "included". All others are the "excluded". In their plans to destroy all Jews, the Nazis created a category of individuals who, according to edicts and enactments by the Nazis, did not meet required racial qualifications and, thus, they had no right to exist and could be exterminated. While on trial in 1961, Adolf Eichmann, who was mainly responsible for managing the deportation of Jews to the extermination camps, boasted that

> I did not take on the job as a senseless exercise. It gave me uncommon joy.... I found it fascinating to deal with these matters .... My job was to catch these enemies and transport them to their destination .... To be frank with you, had we killed all of them, the 10.3 million, I would be happy to say, Alright we managed to destroy an enemy ....
>
> (Bauer, 1982, p. 207)

Accounting practices helped to allow the Nazis to exercise power over life, which constituted what Foucault refers to as biopower, the ability to penetrate the very being of an individual to control all aspects of their life. This was most evident in the Nazi extermination camps where accounting practices were a significant means to condemn Jews to what Agamben refers to as "bare life", a mere existence which could be taken from them at any time. Those condemned to the concentration camp could be killed by anyone without consequence for the killer, for according to the law their killing was not murder.

Stokes and Gabriel (2010, p. 462) have shown that the way in which genocidal programs that can be permitted, even normalised, in a state of exception, are dependent upon "bureaucratic resources to initiate, sustain and, often cover it up" (see also Marti and Fernandez, 2013). This enabled the Holocaust to be "constructed industrially-with systems of rules, impersonally applied, which made it as technically efficient as genocide could be" (Grey, 2005, quoted in Stokes and Gabriel, 2010, p. 465). La Capra (1994, p. 90) describes the Holocaust as being "calculated coldly and with the maximum efficiency and economy". This would not have been possible, argue Hilberg (1985) and Browning (1980, p. 183), without the enthusiastic cooperation of the German civil bureaucracy. Destruction of human life on the scale of the Holocaust

> is not the work of a few mad minds. It cannot be accomplished by any handful of men. It is far too complex in its organisational build-up and far too pervasive in its administrative implementation to dispense with specialised bureaucrats in every segment of society.
>
> (Hilberg, 1980, p. 99; Dawidowicz, 1975, p. xv)

Enabling the Holocaust

Construing the extermination of Jews as an efficiency problem created the need to enlist accounting. Accounting was part of a structure of controls and practices designed to maximise the outcomes of Nazi policies contrived to deliver efficiency and effectiveness in the service of the State, most especially its attempt to achieve the Jewish Final Solution. Calculative rationalities provide the ability for political powers to extend their control well beyond their own institution. The seemingly unremarkable and benign role of accounting practices as the means to manage more efficiently the processes essential to the Nazi annihilation program allowed individuals who were taken to their deaths to become, effectively, invisible. Accounting numbers were substituted for qualitative attributes of individuals, thereby denying them their humanity and individuality (Funnell, 1998). Accounting provided the means to turn people into objects, allowing millions of Jews and others to be transported as inexpensively and quickly as possible to meet their executioners (Funnell, 1998; Annisette, 2009).

A conspicuous feature of accounting information that makes it so attractive is its ability to create new realities and visibilities (Miller, 1990, pp. 316–317). Miller (1990, p. 317) notes how, in the service of the State, "(t) echnologies of government materialize and visualize processes and activities to be regulated". Accounting as an instrument of the German civil and military bureaucracy provided new quantitative visibilities (Miller, 1990, p. 318), such as distinguishing the number of Jews from others, that were able to supplant the qualitative dimensions of the Jews as individuals by commodifying and dehumanising them and, thereby, for all intents make them invisible, non-existent as a person.

Accounting practices have the ability to privilege a limited set of interests and, thereby, deny a voice for the excluded or the "Other". In particular, accounting's aura of neutrality and objectivity (Gallhofer and Haslam, 1991), in part stemming from representations that emphasise accounting as a technology of inscription, has been the means to discount the subjective as something necessarily inferior to the products of the rational logic of accounting. It has also been a convenient means of isolating accounting from ethical questioning. However, as a significant, if mainly unheralded, participant of history, judgements about the use of accounting's calculative practices can no longer escape consideration of accounting's ethical dimensions and moral consequences (Pois, 1989, p. 1937; Lovell, 1995, p. 61). The scale and purpose of the Holocaust demand that accounting and accountants cannot be portrayed as socially and morally blameless and that accounting is not solely a rational technology geared to ends-means relationships that can escape moral reckonings.

Accounting as a moral practice

Accounting has an essential moral identity with consequences that do not fall within the quantifiable net of accounting. Accounting is an active moral agent in social processes and the implementation of political programs (Tinker, 1980; Tinker et al., 1991). Therefore, understanding what constitutes the moral nature of accounting can only be made sensible if its "wider social and political collectives" are recognised (Hopper and Powell, quoted in Humphrey and Scapens, 1996, p. 87; see also Miller, 1990). Accounting cannot be allowed to hide behind a disguise of neutrality and disinterested objectivity. Irrespective of the then-known ultimate fate of the Jews, the aggregation, reductionism, and anonymity of accounting numbers allowed the forced movement of millions of people great distances from their homes to be drained of any considerations that would imply that the numbers and costings on the pieces of paper that were passed from one bureaucrat to the next related to prescient human beings. They had become the "Other" without any right to life. Historically, tyrannised people have been condemned as the "Other", "primitive" and belonging to "unequal races and cultures" (Said, 1994, pp. 130–131). They could then be murdered without consequence for the perpetrator, the efficient, exhaustive achievement of which would be made possible with a penetrating reliance upon the information provided by accounting practices.

The Nazis recognised the moral potential of accounting practices in their efforts to *consecrate* the property that they forcefully expropriated from the Jews and, thereby, contribute to the *sanctification* of their policy of extermination, the Final Solution. Property taken included real estate, businesses, financial assets, and personal possessions. The latter had particular tragic significance when, immediately prior to their killing in the gas chambers, each person, including young children, had to remove all their clothing, which was then collected for later use or sale. Most appallingly, those killed would be further defiled when from their dead bodies gold fillings would be taken from their teeth and their hair cut off, each of which had to be recorded in great detail. The Nazis attempted to signify the purity of their actions and to sanctify their motives by insisting that all the property taken had to pass through rigorous, and in effect, morally unencumbered, accounting procedures to ensure that it would be available only for approved purposes.

Accounting provided the filter to transform "impure" Jewish property and the capitalist motives from which it was accused of having arisen into a hallowed and acceptable implement of State policy. In an analogous manner, in Old Testament times, offerings to God were not acceptable until they had first been given priestly approval, after which they were deemed cleansed of earthly imperfections and therefore worthy of God. In the extermination camps nothing was to be taken for individual or State use from those who were murdered without a rigorous accounting. The accounts would show that those at the killing centres and directly engaged in the annihilation of the Jews were not carrying out their actions for their own selfish benefit, of which Jews were constantly accused, but as good, devoted Aryans. Thus, the accounts were used as the symbolic means of spiritual cleansing.

If accounting is a moral practice, then those who use it are moral agents. According to Fleischman and Funnell (2007, p. 384), the separation between accounting and morality "was not only a means of expediting the annihilation of the Jews but was also one of the means by which people who had no direct involvement in the murder of millions of Jews were able to divorce themselves from the objectives and consequences of their work". This allowed civil and military bureaucrats working at a distance from the extermination camps to later claim ignorance and their innocence when accused of being active participants in the murder of more than 6 million Jews. In this travesty of facts and separation of responsibilities, the role of accounting practices and those who carried them out for immoral purposes in an amoral manner were decisive (Funnell, 1998; Fleischman and Funnell, 2007; Annisette, 2009).

Under the Nazi regime, those who used accounting practices to implement the Nazi's extermination program sought to prove their commitment to the Aryan Race and their loyalty to the Nazi regime by ensuring the success of its anti-Semitic programs. Members of the German accounting profession and other accounting practitioners who, either directly or indirectly, contributed to the scale and merciless nature of the Holocaust have been, like other

Nazi bureaucrats, identified as obedient, efficient, amoral, and cold in their treatment of Jews (Lovell, 1995; Lippman and Wilson, 2007). Nazi ideology appealed mainly to the middle classes, the primary source of the professions, without whose cooperation little would have been achieved (Carsten, 1967, pp. 232–233; Grunberger, 1971, p. 167; Muller-Hill, 1994, p. 68). Crucial to the success of Nazi policies directed against the Jews was the active participation of the legal and medical professions, amongst others.

The initiation of and participation by doctors in Nazi euthanasia programs before the war, whereby the mentally and physically feeble were selected by doctors for "mercy killings"[3] and later medical experimentation with inmates of the concentration camps, have been well documented and attested (Brieger, 1980; Noakes, 1989, pp. 458, 459). Also exposed has been the legal profession's eager assistance to the Nazis in a program of legal and social alienation of the Jews, their contributions as judges in German courts in ensuring that the Jews felt the full impact of Nazi laws, and their prostitution of the precepts of natural justice to persecute and condemn Jews and others who offended the Nazis (Taylor, 1980; Bauer, 1989b). Unlike the disciplines of law, medicine, education, and engineering, there has been much less attention to the roles played by accountants and the relevance of their accounting practices to making possible the Holocaust. This is despite Hilberg's (1985, p. 1011) assurance that all the professions, including those he refers to as "finance experts", were represented in the management of the Holocaust.

The enthusiastic support of accounting practitioners, whether in private practice or as part of the government bureaucracy, was not hidden but was evident in a regime whose racist foundations were transparent and where the call to the accounting profession changed to reflect Aryanization and State control (Matz, 1938; Walker, 2000). Lovell (1995) shows that accounting practitioners who wholly adhered to what the Third Reich expected, that is, to manage and organise the extermination of the Jews, operated at what Kohlberg (1984) refers to as the "conventional" level of morality. Practising accountants in, for example, Germany and Italy who were not condemned as Jewish made up an indoctrinated, loyal professional class, ready and easily driven to process and disclose the information they prepared in perpetrating the horrors experienced by the victims of the extermination camps during the Holocaust.[4] The most striking features of their day-to-day actions were a desire to please superiors and to adhere strictly to laws, conventions, and codes of practice, irrespective of the ultimate bestiality in which many would have been aware they were engaged (Lovell, 1995). Overwhelming evidence indicates that movement to Kohlberg's ultimate level of "universalistic" or "principled" moral reasoning, where individuals are prepared to stand against laws and orders that contravene natural justice, was not a feature of those who practised accounting in relation to the Jews throughout the Holocaust (Lovell, 1995, p. 61). They would also become the prime means to banish their colleagues classified as Jewish from the accounting profession under racist anti-Semitic laws.

Accounting practices

Consistent with the growing body of research that regards accounting as a social, political, and moral phenomenon, as opposed to a collection of sterile techniques or "an innocuous mapper of reality" (Broadbent and Laughlin, 1994, p. 4), a broad conception of accounting informs the chapters in this book. Accounting practices can be broadly defined as numerical "calculations and techniques which mediate the relations between individuals, groups, and institutions as well as the accountability relationships that result from these social relations" (Neu, 2000, p. 270). Therefore, this study of the Holocaust cannot be limited to only financial inscriptions. To do so would prevent giving visibility to the non-financial "Other" Jews and how their attempted extermination was enacted.

Accounting can be conceived as a technology of inscription that provides "information for decision making which leads to action" (Broadbent and Laughlin, 1994, p. 2). Action is a purposeful activity designed to bring about consequences (see Schweiker, 1993, p. 243). Sometimes, individual actions of themselves may be insignificant but, as with the Holocaust, their combined effects can be both far-reaching and penetrating. Achieving a final goal will result from many consistent actions carried out by numerous participants. As a significant input into many decision processes, accounting information may be seen as having the potential to have an impact not only on decisions but also on consequences. This was to be important and obvious in the management of the concentration camps, especially those that became the extermination camps created specifically for the murder of Jews.

Stages in the Final Solution

The book follows stages by which the contributions of accounting practices and those who carried these out led to, allowed and expedited the murder of more than 6 million Jews and others. As noted above, accounting numbers were ultimately substituted for qualitative attributes of individuals, thereby denying Jews their humanity and individuality, effectively making them invisible. This involved, firstly, Jews being removed from the German and Italian economies by having their assets seized and being precluded from most occupations. Becoming financially destitute effectively stigmatised them, leading to their segregation and isolation from the non-Jewish Aryan population. The "financial death" of Jews was proclaimed by the Nazis and the Italian Fascists to be a just consequence of the Jewish threat to the wellbeing of Aryans which, alleged the acclaimed historian and Nazi supporter Werner Sombart, was because of their ruthless pursuit of selfish profit. This was reinforced when they were banned from most public spaces and organisations, thereby socially isolating them.

The brutal, unrelenting pillorying and ostracisation of Jews from normal life as threats to the German people and the German State provided the means to justify their loss of all legal and political protections – their loss of political life. This meant that, ultimately, with only bare life, they lost their right to live when most were murdered in the extermination camps. Chapter 2 provides an overview of this process, the critical elements of which are developed in subsequent chapters. In particular, it focuses on the way in which, effectively, a state of exception was created with anti-Semitic legislation and policies commencing with the passing of the *Enabling Act* in 1933. This provided the unprecedented legal framework that constituted a state of exception from which emanated the permissions for the persecution of Jews.

Chapters 3 and 4 provide the context in which the anti-Semitic policies of the Nazis and the Fascists were developed that were used to justify their determination to punish and eventually eradicate all individuals who met the racial qualifications of being Jewish. Consistent with the key themes of the book, this is demonstrated in Chapter 3 with how the Nazis drew upon Werner Sombart's professional standing and his highly regarded, even to the present day, studies of the history of double-entry bookkeeping as another means to help justify their persecution and attempted destruction of Jews. Sombart condemned Jews for the way in which he believed that they personified the spirit of capitalism. He accused Jews of being exceptional exponents of double entry bookkeeping, the overriding purpose of which was to allow penetrating rational profit calculations and, thereby, the perpetuation of capitalism, the evils of which the Nazis condemned.

The way in which the arts and cultural pursuits were used to implement anti-Semitic policies and how accounting practices helped to justify and praise their use in the totalitarian Fascist State of Italy between 1934 and 1945 is examined in Chapter 4. Throughout history, both democratic and totalitarian States have sought to take advantage of the possible political contributions of art and culture. Accounting documents in the form of budgets and reports provided by the Fascist government, along with other accounts prepared by the Fascists, were used to justify their malignment of Jewish culture and beliefs and build a convincing narrative that identified how the Fascist regime sought to rally the Italian people around new values that excluded a Jewish presence.

Chapters 5, 6, 7, and 8 introduce the financial measures taken against Jews by the Nazis and the Fascists, which constituted the first stage in reducing Jews to a level where they would cease to have any rights or protections, thereby enabling the implementation of the Final Solution. Chapter 5 examines how the extensive measures taken to destroy a people were facilitated by a complex matrix of interrelated actors and practices of business and accounting that, with the forced seizure of their property, allowed the State-sanctioned financial death of Jews. As a means by which this was achieved, Chapter 6 provides the example of the race-based expulsion of Jews from the accounting profession in Fascist Italy as a further step in the isolation and ultimate elimination of Jews. It is shown that following their fascistisation, accountancy organisations in Italy functioned as agencies to purify the profession. The chapter draws upon Foucault's concepts of biopolitics and race to explore the apparatuses of biopower deployed to eliminate the Jews from the professional population. These included anti-Semitic legislation to define the offending part of the population, a census to identify and locate it, and bureaucratic mechanisms to secure its removal. When parts of Italy came under German control in 1943, "indirect murder" through expulsion was supplanted by the actual murder of many Jewish accountants.

Chapter 7 reveals how accounting practices were used in the destruction of Jewish financial life (*bios*) as part of the Nazis' Aryanisation policy, which prioritised the elimination of Jews from German business as a prelude to their annihilation. Accounting was part of the Nazi-Deutsch rhetoric used to disguise the expropriation of Jewish businesses and other assets and, thereby, facilitate the eradication of the financial *bios* of Jews who owned German banks. Unknown to the Nazi authorities, Deutsche Bank, a significant medium for Aryanisation, also sought to ameliorate the long-term effects on Jewish owners, recognising that not all those within Nazi Germany were fully committed disciples of Nazism. Chapter 8 identifies the significant role of accounting in expropriating Jewish real estate after the enforcement of race laws under Benito Mussolini's Fascist regime in Italy. Implementation of the program of expropriation was the responsibility of a government body, *Ente di Gestione e Liquidazione Immobiliare*[5] (EGELI), which was created specifically for this purpose. The language and practices of accounting provided the means to disguise the nature and brutality of the process and allow bureaucrats to be removed from the consequences of their actions.

Chapter 9 provides a tragic example of the use of concentration camps as an instrument of genocide when the Fossoli concentration camp was established in northern Italy, from which the Germans later transported Jews to the extermination camps. Accounting practices used in the management of the Fossoli concentration camp when under German control allowed Italian Jews in the camp to become known only with measurable attributes, not individuals with a right to life. Jewish prisoners sent to the extermination camps to be killed became mere numbers, bare life, data to be processed in a way that would expedite their murder.

Chapter 10 reveals the slave labour operations managed by German corporations and Nazi State-run entities and identifies accounting information and financial analyses used to assist management in the operation of these facilities. The chapter appraises the role of accountants and the information they prepared in perpetrating these injustices experienced by concentration camp victims during the Holocaust. The history of the German accounting profession and the changes to the profession during the war years are considered as a means to explain the behaviour of accountants. Finally, the culpability of accountants for the Holocaust is considered.

Chapter 11 provides details of the impact on Jewish accountants of their professional persecution and exclusion, examined in Chapter 6, with a collective biography of ten Jewish accountants and auditors under Fascism and

Nazism in Italy. Implementing racial laws and the expulsion and "discrimination" of Jewish professionals involved complex bureaucratic processes. Through the interactions of accountants and auditors with these processes, insights can be gained into the everyday experiences of Jewish professionals under Fascism. It is shown that the careers of Jewish accounting practitioners were seriously impacted by their exclusion, persecution, and stigmatisation. Their personal and family lives were also severely disrupted. With Nazi control of Northern Italy from 1943, Jewish accountants were deported to concentration camps where they were murdered. Five of the individuals examined in the chapter survived the Final Solution. Five did not. The chapter also throws light on survival strategies, such as the attempts by Jewish accountants to migrate or construct alternative identities.

Chapter 12 provides a conclusion to *Accounting for the Holocaust* by reflecting on the crucial contributions provided by accounting to the perpetration of the Holocaust. By giving visibility to selected aspects of the conditions to which Jews were condemned, accounting practices denied Jews their humanity. The apparently banal and even benign calculative practices of accounting gave legitimacy to racial justifications for the internment of Jews in concentration camps and ensured the smooth functioning of the Nazi murderous machine. The devastating eye-witness detail recorded in accounting reports gives even greater impact and authority to the evidence of those who became the victims of the Nazis. The chapter also calls for further investigations into the role of accounting in enabling the Holocaust both in Europe and in other locations that were occupied by the German Nazis and Italian Fascists.

It is hoped that this book will help uncover the accounting practices which when viewed through the events of the Holocaust demonstrate their salience in not only everyday life but also in perpetrating violence, suffering, and even death.

Notes

1 Adolf Eichmann during his interrogation after his capture agreed that 6 million was close to the number of Jews killed by all methods (Von Lang, 1983, p. 110). Eichmann admitted being responsible for the transportation of the Jews to the killing centres but denied involvement with their deaths (Von Lang 1983, pp. 103–104).

2 The Wannsee conference that was held in Berlin on 20 January 1942 was attended by Reinhard Heydrich, chief of the Reich Security Main Office who was responsible for the Einsatzgruppen. The Einsatzgruppen were members of the SS who were responsible for the actual killing of Jews and others in occupied territory. Also at the conference were Heinrich Muller, chief of the Gestapo, and Adolf Eichman. At his trial in 1961, Adolf Eichmann confirmed that he had suggested "these words 'Final Solution'. At the time I meant by this the elimination of the Jews .... Later ... these harmless words were used as a camouflage for the killing" (Bauer, 1982, p. 207).

3 On 1 September 1939, Hitler issued an order which widened "the authority of individual doctors with a view to enabling them ... to administer incurably sick persons to a mercy death" (Hitler quoted in Gilbert, 1986, p. 238).

4 Despite the racist, strident ideological beliefs of members of the accounting profession in Germany under the Nazis, they enjoyed an international status which allowed international accounting practitioners, mainly British, to organise one of their meetings in Nazi Germany just before the outbreak of World War II (Walker, 2000).

5 Literally: Organization for Management and Liquidation of Property.

References

Agamben, G. (1998). *Homo Sacer. Sovereign Power and Bare Life*. Stanford: Stanford University Press.

Agamben, G. (2005). *State of Exception*. Chicago: University of Chicago Press.

Annisette, M. (2009). Race and ethnicity. In: J.R. Edwards, and S.P. Walker (Eds.). *The Routledge Companion to Accounting History* (pp. 451–469). London: Routledge.

Bauer, Y. (1982). *A History of the Holocaust*. London: Franklin Watts.

Bauer, Y. (1989a). Genocide: Was It the Nazis' Original Plan. In: M. Marrus (Ed.). *The Nazi Holocaust: Historical Articles on the Destruction of the European Jews*, Book 3, Vol. 1. Westport: Meckler.

Bauer, Y. (1989b). *Remembering for the Future: The Impact of the Holocaust on the Contemporary World*. Oxford: Pergamon.

Brieger, G. (1980). The medical profession. In H. Friedlander, and S. Milton (Eds.). *The Holocaust: Ideology, Bureaucracy, and Genocide*. Millwood: Kraus International Publications.

Broadbent, J., and Laughlin, R. (1994). *Moving Towards an Accounting That Will Be Enabling: Accounting, Habermas and Issues of Gender*. Seminar paper, Department of Accounting and Finance, University of Wollongong.

Browning, C. (1980). The government experts. In: H. Friedlander, and S. Milton (Eds.). *The Holocaust: Ideology, Bureaucracy, and Genocide*. Millwood: Kraus International Publications.

Browning, C. (1988). Bureaucracy and mass murder: The German administrator's comprehension of the Final Solution. In: A. Cohen, J. Gelber, and C. Wardi (Eds.). *Comprehending the Holocaust*. Frankfurt am Main: Verlag Peter Lang.

Carsten, F.L. (1967). *The Rise of Fascism*. Berkeley: University of California Press.

Dawidowicz, L. (1975). *The War against the Jews 1933–1945*. London: Weidenfeld and Nicholson.

Fleischman, R.K., and Funnell, W.N. (2007). The relevance of the past. In T. Hopper, D. Northcott, and R.W. Scapens (Eds.). *Issues in Management Accounting* (pp. 377–398). Edinburgh: Pearson Education Ltd.

Foucault, M. (1990). *The History of Sexuality*. London: Penguin Books.

Funnell, W. (1998). Accounting in the service of the Holocaust. *Critical Perspectives on Accounting*, *9*(4), 435–464.

Gallhofer, S., and Haslam, J. (1991). The aura of accounting in the context of a crisis: Germany and the First World War. *Accounting, Organizations and Society*, *16*(5–6), 487–520.

Gilbert, M. (1986). *The Holocaust: The Jewish Tragedy*. London: Collins.

Grunberger, R. (1971). *The 12-Year Reich: A Social History of Nazi Germany 1933–1945*. Toronto: Hold, Rinehart and Winston.

Hilberg, R. (1980). The significance of the Holocaust. In: H. Friedlander, and S. Milton (Eds.). *The Holocaust: Ideology, Bureaucracy, and Genocide*. Millwood: Kraus International Publications.

Hilberg, R. (1985). *The Destruction of the European Jews*. New York: Holmes and Meir.

Humphrey, C., and Scapens, R. (1996). Theories and Case Studies of Organisational and Accounting Practices: Limitation or Liberation. *Accounting, Auditing and Accountability Journal*, *9*(4), 86–106.

Katz, F. (1989). Implementation of the Holocaust: The behavior of Nazi officials. In: M. Marrus (Ed.). *The Nazi Holocaust: Historical Articles on the Destruction of the European Jews*, Book 3, Vol. 2. Westport: Meckler.

Kohlberg, L. (1984). *The Psychology of Moral Development: The Nature and Validity of Moral Stages (Vol. 2)*. New York: HarperCollins College Div.

La Capra, D. (1994). *Representing the Holocaust*. Ithaca: Cornell University Press.

Lippman, E.J., and Wilson, P. (2007). The culpability of accounting in perpetuating the Holocaust. *Accounting History*, *12*(3), 283–303.

Lovell, A. (1995). Moral reasoning and moral atmosphere in the domain of accounting. *Accounting, Auditing & Accountability Journal*, *8*(3), 60–80.

Marti, I., and Fernandez, P. (2013). The institutional work of oppression and resistance: Learning from the Holocaust. *Organization Studies*, *34*(8), 1195–1223.

Matz, A. (1938). The position of the German accountant. *The Accounting Review*, *13*(4), 392–395.

Miller, P. (1990). On the interrelations between accounting and the State. *Accounting, Organizations and Society*, *15*(4), 315–338.

Muller-Hill, B. (1994). The Final Solution and the role of experts. In: D. Cesarani (Ed.). *The Final Solution: Origins and Implementation*. London: Routledge.

Neu, D. (2000). Accounting and accountability relations: colonization, genocide and Canada's first nations. *Accounting, Auditing and Accountability Journal*, *13*(3), 268–288.

Noakes, J. (1989). Social outcasts in the Third Reich. In: M. Marrus (Ed.). *The Nazi Holocaust: Historical Articles on the Destruction of the European Jews*. Book 2. Westport: Meckler.

Pois, R. (1989). The Holocaust and the ethical imperative of historicism. In: M. Marrus (Ed.). *The Nazi Holocaust: Historical Articles on the Destruction of the European Jews*. Book 3, Vol. 1. Westport: Meckler.

Rosenberg, A. (1983). The philosophical implications of the Holocaust. In: R. Braham (Ed.). *Perspectives on the Holocaust*. Boston: Kluwer-Nijhoff Publishing.

Said, E. (1994). *Culture and Imperialism*. London: Vintage Books.

Stokes, P., and Gabriel, Y. (2010). Engaging with genocide: The challenge for organization and management studies. *Organization*, *17*(4), 461–480.

Schweiker, W. (1993). Accounting for Ourselves: Accounting Practice and the Discourse of Ethics. *Accounting, Organisations and Society*, *18* (2/3), 231–252.

Talmon, J.L. (1989). European history – seedbed of the Holocaust. In: M. Marrus (Ed.). *The Nazi Holocaust: Historical Articles on the Destruction of the European Jews*. Westport: Meckler.

Taylor, T. (1980). The legal profession. In: H. Friedlander, and S. Milton (Eds.). *The Holocaust: Ideology, Bureaucracy, and Genocide*. Millwood: Kraus International Publications.

Tinker, A.M. (1980). Towards a political economy of accounting: An empirical illustration of the Cambridge controversies. *Accounting, Organisations and Society*, *5*(1), 147–160.

Tinker, T., Lehman, C., and Neimark, M. (1991). Falling down in the hole in the middle of the road: Political quietism in corporate social reporting. *Accounting, Auditing and Accountability Journal*, 4(2), 28–54.

Von Lang, J. (1983). *Eichman Interrogated.* London: The Bodley Head.

Walker, S.P. (2000). Encounters with Nazism: British accountants and the fifth international congress on accounting. *Critical Perspectives on Accounting*, *11*(2), 215–245.

Wellers, G. (1978). Reply to the neo-Nazi falsification of historical facts concerning the Holocaust. In: S. Klarsfeld (Ed.). *The Holocaust and the Neo-Nazi Mythomania.* New York: The Beate Klarsfeld Foundation.

Wiesel, E. (1988). Some questions that remain open. In: A. Cohen, J. Gelber, and C. Wardi (Eds.). *Comprehending the Holocaust.* Frankfurt am Main: Verlag Peter Lang.

Zuccotti, S. (1987). *The Italians and the Holocaust: Persecution, Rescue, and Survival.* New York: Basic Books.

2 Accounting for the "Final Solution"

Warwick Funnell

Introduction

Accounting as a profession and as a set of practices has been able to maintain a marked degree of anonymity and invisibility in relation to the Holocaust largely because of its highly specialised, arcane calculus that is designed to serve the interests of dominant economic elites and those of the State (Gallhoffer and Haslam, 1991, p. 492). Amongst criticisms of the participation in the Holocaust of the legal and medical professions, accountants as a professional group have almost entirely escaped scrutiny[1] (see, for example, Friedlander and Milton, 1980, pp. 133–218; Taylor, 1980). They barely receive a mention from Hilberg, either in his three-volume work *The Destruction of European Jewry* (1985) or in his other works. Consistent with the unchallenged view held until very recently that accounting was a neutral, technical practice, it was unlikely either during the Nazi era or after, when retribution was being sought against those who were responsible for crimes against humanity, that any culpability of accountants would have been obvious. Echoing the stand taken by bureaucrats in Nazi Germany, Francis (1990, p. 6) laments how "(a)ll too often the accountant may imagine they are just reporting the facts" when accounting "is also a moral practice" (p. 7). This description of accounting alludes to the consequences of its use, which have far more importance, deeper social penetration, and enduring residual effects than the events reported upon.

Morality, unlike the events that prompt moral judgements, is not circumscribed by time and place. In contrast to appraisals of the results of accounting routines, morality judgements contain the imperative that something is either right or wrong according to criteria that transcend individual social and political contexts. There is an expectation that irrespective of the context, there are invariable, trans-social, and ahistorical standards of conduct. For the accountant to behave morally, Schweiker (1993, p. 233) argues, is to "act on the principle of equal respect for others, to treat them as ends in themselves". Therefore, consideration of the moral nature of accounting demands more than a self-interested and short-sighted cry of approval for accomplishments that are in part attributable to accounting practices.

DOI: 10.4324/9781032685328-2

Accounting reports are not collections of impotent facts that implode upon themselves. Rather, the information they convey sets up waves of consequence that radiate from the reports in a manner similar to the effect produced when a stone is thrown into a still pond. Even those at a great distance from the initial impact of an accounting report may have cause to regret its effects. Directing his argument more at those who use accounting, Francis (1990, p. 7) proposes that

> (a)ccounting, to the extent that it is a choice about how to affect our lived experience - our ends – is a practice grounded in moral discernment. Accounting is important precisely to the extent the accountant can transform the world, can influence the lived experience of others in ways which cause the experience to differ from what it would be in the absence of accounting.

In contrast to the status of accounting, the consequences of laws in Nazi Germany that stripped people of their rights at law and confiscated their property were far more obvious. It was also not difficult to understand the effects of euthanasia or medical experiments on concentration camp inmates. Assignment of responsibility for the consequences of information made possible by accounting procedures and the industrious participation of those trained in their use requires recognition that accounting was a potent weapon of Nazi social policy and a force in its own right instead of an insignificant tool of the military and civil bureaucracies that were responsible for the implementation of the measures that constitute the Holocaust. Within the context of the civil bureaucracy

> (a)ll components of German organized life were drawn into this undertaking. Every agency was a contributor; every specialization was utilized; and every stratum of society was represented in the envelopment of the victims.
>
> (Hilberg, 1985, p. 20; Katz, 1989)

When it came time to enlist the bureaucracy in implementing the murderous policies of the Nazis, the use of anti-Semitic propaganda by the Nazis was proven to be successful in conditioning an already susceptible bureaucracy to regard as legitimate the government's treatment of German citizens who were Jewish. In order to understand Nazi attitudes towards the Jews, the first section that follows examines Nazi racial ideology to establish the justifications they promoted for their persecution and programmed annihilation of Jews. This is followed by a discussion of the main phases by which this was implemented during the Holocaust. The final sections of the chapter present the Holocaust as an example of the application of accounting's functional rationalist technology to create instrumental visibilities and to consecrate acts against Jews and others, which were later judged to be crimes against humanity at the Nuremberg trials after World War II.

The Jew in Nazi ideology

Anti-Semitism in Germany and the demonisation of Jews as the source of the evils of capitalism and the difficulties of Germany in the 1920s and early 1930s was not an invention of Hitler and the Nazis. In common with most other European countries, Germany had a long history of antipathy towards the Jews in its midst (Mosse, 1970, pp. 19, 34–60; Winston, 1980; Langmuir, 1980; Weber, 1980; Dawidowicz, 1975, p. 163, 1976, pp. 25, 28; Hilberg, 1985, pp. 8–9; Talmon, 1989, Book 2). Ostracisation of the Jews was sustained by emotive history stereotypes of the predatory Jewish financier teachings of the Christian church and spurious race theories riding on the prestige of 19th century science. In the 16th century, Martin Luther, for example, had warned against the Jews and the perils that association with them would bring to Christians. Jews were seen as perennial outsiders who owed no allegiance to any country, only to their religion, to the accumulation of more wealth and to their own well-being (Sombart, 1913, p. 5). In the process, they were accused of giving little thought to the consequences of their activities and selfishness for the non-Jewish Germans, their allegedly unsuspecting and defenceless victims.

German anti-Semitism was given new life at the beginning of the 20th century with mounting opposition amongst extremist polemicists to the social transformations accompanying capitalism. A rational economic glaze was given to anti-Semitism in the works of noted German economists, including Sombart,[2] who sought to take well-entrenched prejudices out of the realm of mythology and folklore by identifying the supposed economic perversity of Jews. Particular objection was taken with what was seen as the "mechanical", "abstract", and "artificial", and therefore to an Aryan, the alien, features of capitalism which, it was suggested, particularly suited Jews who had no empathy or understanding with the natural and the organic (Sombart, 1913, pp. 274–275, 277; Sombart, 1929; Mosse, 1970, p. 9; Herf, 1984, p. 134). Jews were condemned as the embodiment of capitalism and all its defects (Sombart, 1913, p. 50) and, therefore, epitomised everything that was foreign and not German (Sombart, 1913, p. 115; Fleming, 1985, p. 8; Herf, 1984, pp. 136–137; Mosse, 1970, p. 20). In contrast, the German at heart was projected as an idealist, aspiring to all that was great and pure (Mosse, 1970, p. 18). From this pure spirit came "the creative force which ... created the monuments of human culture" (Hitler, 1987, p. 271; Dawidowicz, 1975, p. 18). Set against, and the major threat to, this purity was said to be Jews. With the arrival of Jews came urbanisation, a contempt for manual work and the subservience of the German to the monied, industrial economy of Jews (Hitler, 1987, p. 288). It was "due specifically to the Jewish spirit that these characteristics of modern economic life came into being" (Sombart, 1913, pp. 61, 115).

At the centre of German romanticism was identification with the land and its embodiment of the greatness of the German nation, while to Jews it was said to be another thing to be exploited and defiled. The result was a debasement of rural life (Hitler, 1987, p. 281). Jews, it was purported, had created a form of modern capitalism in which everything was available for a Jew's own selfish gain. Capitalism exalted the individual. It encouraged the decoupling of the individual from their social context and trivialised all relationships by measuring them in terms of economic consequences. Accordingly, conceptions of community and self-sacrifice were accused of never being part of Jewish culture (Sombart, 1913, p. 263). Summarising what to him was an obvious feature of Jews, Sombart (1913, p. 264) proposed that the "Jews's whole being is opposed to all that is usually understood by chivalry, to all sentimentality ... Politically he is an individualist.... It comes to this, that they behold the world not with their 'soul' but with their intellect". As a result

> (t)he rationalization of life accustomed the Jew to a mode of living contrary to ... Nature and therefore also to an economic system like the capitalistic, which is likewise contrary to ... Nature. What in reality is the idea of making profit, what is economic rationalism, but the application to economic activities of the rules by which the Jewish religion shaped Jewish life? Before capitalism could develop the natural man had to be changed out of all recognition, and a rationalistically minded mechanism introduced in his stead.
>
> (Sombart, 1913, p. 238; see also Herf, 1984, pp. 136–137, 141)

Hitler believed that the Aryan was the source of all creativity and greatness (Hitler, 1987, pp. 262–263; see also Sombart, 1913, pp. 262, 271; Dawidowicz, 1975, p. 18). The claimed inability of Jews to create meant that they would have to feed off the endeavours of others. They would always be "a *parasite* in the body of other peoples ..., a sponger who like a noxious bacillus keeps spreading ..." (Hitler, 1987, pp. 276, 277). The only hope of protecting the Aryan race against the wiles of the Jew, according to Hitler (1987, pp. 195, 367), was for the State to take an active role in maintaining the purity of German blood (see also Wiesel, 1988, p. 11). In this program of eugenics, the State was to act "without regard to understanding or lack of understanding, approval or disapproval" (Hitler, 1987, p. 368). The purpose of the State

> lies in the preservation and advancement of a community of physically and psychically homogeneous creatures..... Thus, the highest purpose of the folkish State is concern for the preservation of those original

> racial elements which bestow culture and create the beauty and dignity of a higher mankind....
>
> (Hitler, 1987, pp. 357–358)

Less than a decade after Hitler expressed his vision for the German State in Mein Kampf, he set it in place in a period now referred to as the Holocaust.

The will of the State and the main phases of the Holocaust

Exclusion of the Jews in Germany 1933–1939

The powers governments have make them potentially supreme in all matters. In the case of elected governments, these powers are given for a defined period by citizens entitled to vote. To ensure that these powers will not be used to avoid electoral censure, most systems of government have controls built into them that can be activated to reinstate the sovereignty of the people. In circumstances where governments seek to thwart the will of the people, these controls can be suspended either by way of force, as in a military coup, or by stealth through the passing of laws to create a "state of exception" to entrench the existing powers and deny competing groups the opportunity to govern. Often, the latter approach is accompanied by a reign of terror directed towards dissidents or political groups and those who provide a convenient target to play on the fears of the Nation. This form of usurpation has been most common in the 20th century in the establishment of one-party States, whether socialist regimes of the far left or fascist governments of the far right, including the Nazis. In either case, the aim has been to establish systems of control that enable the sovereignty of the ruling group to be complete, entrenched, and undeniable. Such was the case in Germany between 1933 and 1945, the period which the Nazis designated as the Third Reich, when the full power of the State was malevolently brought to bear on, firstly, German Jews and then all European Jewry.

In Eastern Europe throughout the 19th century Jews had been the subject of numerous pogroms, especially in Russia. Unlike the policies of the Nazis, pogroms were limited, although still often deadly, harassments of Jews. They were not attempts to eliminate Jews or to force them to flee to other countries. Instead, they were responses by governments to the periodic venting of local hostilities towards a vulnerable minority that had become a convenient scapegoat for economic problems. The period of the Holocaust was something very different. From within the Warsaw Ghetto, Chaim Kaplan described German Jewish policies as a

> gigantic catastrophe, which ... has no parallel even in the darkest periods of Jewish history. Firstly – the depth of the hatred. This is not hatred whose source is simply in a party platform, invented for political purposes. It is a hatred of emotion, whose source is some psychopathic

disease, in its outward manifestation it appears as physiological hatred, which sees the object of its hatred as tainted in body, as lepers who have no place in society.

(*Extracts from the Warsaw Ghetto Diary of Chaim A. Kaplan, March 10, 1940*, in Arad et al., 1981, p. 201)

The Nazis had prepared their policy of exclusion towards the German Jews well before Hitler was appointed Chancellor and asked to form a government on 30 January 1933. In the presence of the enfeebled President, Field Marshall von Hindenburg, the passage through the Reichstag of the *Enabling Act* on 23 March 1933 gave Hitler almost dictatorial powers, which, when combined with the declaration of a state of emergency soon after being elected, enabled Hitler to harass, kill and imprison his political opposition and to mute any criticism. Much of the Nazi vitriol was directed at the Jews who, based on Nazi racial theories, were progressively driven out of public service occupations, the universities, and the professions (*The Law for the Restoration of the Professional Civil Service,* and *Law Regarding Admission to the Bar*, 7 April 1933). In 1935, under the Nuremberg Laws, Jews[3] were stripped of their German citizenship and deprived of the rights and benefits that all German citizens had previously enjoyed (see an example in Arad et al., 1981, pp. 199–200; Bullock, 1973, p. 339). Once Jews ceased to exist as legal entities who possessed rights at law and no longer enjoyed the benevolence of the State, they became easy targets for more extreme forms of Nazi attacks. After 1937 Jews were forbidden to attend most public places, including schools, libraries, and swimming pools and to use some forms of public transport. By the outbreak of World War II a comprehensive system of segregation or apartheid had been forced upon all German Jews.

Not content with excluding Jews from public life, the Nazis passed laws that excluded Jews from operating many types of businesses and gave the government the authority to seize Jewish businesses or to force their sacrificial sale (for an example, see *Regulation for the Elimination of the Jews from the Economic Life of Germany, November 12, 1938*, in Arad et al., 1981, pp. 115–116). At the same time, the level of economic persecution increased and the various military arms of the Nazis became more brazen in their attacks on Jews and Jewish property. This culminated on 10 November 1938 with the destruction of Jewish synagogues and property, known as Kristallnacht or the Night of Broken Glass. The opportunity was also taken to round up Jewish community members who had displeased the Nazis[4] (Klarsfeld, 1978, p. 29). With the rise in attacks sanctioned by the government and condoned by anti-Semitic legislation, those Jews who could see that while they remained in Germany they would be at risk attempted to settle in other countries (Klarsfeld, 1978, pp. 1–6). Almost two-thirds of Germany's 500,000 Jews managed to escape. Unfortunately, most of these settled in other European countries that were soon to be overrun by the German army.

The final descent 1939–1945

With the declaration of war against Poland on 1 September 1939, the fate was sealed for nearly two out of every three Jews in Europe. Between the outbreak of hostilities and the war's end two phases can be identified in the German treatment of Jews. From 1939 to the beginning of 1942, the laws already in place were enforced with ever-increasing fervour and ruthlessness. From October 1939 the Nazis commenced the transportation of all Jews under their control to the east, principally to Poland. Later, an order from the Reich Security Main Office was issued on 23 October 1941 that forbade any emigration of Jews (in Arad et al., 1981, pp. 153–154). From early 1942, the full effects of a policy of annihilation began to be felt.

The journey to death for most Jews began when they were loaded into, most often, railway cattle wagons and taken over large distances. A thousand miles was not uncommon in conditions of great brutality (*Instructions for the Deportation of the Jews from the Palatinate, October 1940*, in Arad et al., 1981, pp. 145–146). At first, most Jews were concentrated in sealed towns or ghettos, amongst which the Warsaw ghetto is possibly the best known, where the deprivations they were forced to endure caused the deaths of many thousands (Hilberg, 1972, pp. 40–41). Later, in 1942, the policy of containment was replaced in favour of the systematic killing of Jews in the death camps of Poland[5] (Von Lang, 1983, p. 94). Goebbels (1948), in his diary on 27 March 1942, makes very clear the intentions of the Nazis towards Jews, at the same time describing the treatment of Jews during this period of the Holocaust as

> pretty barbaric ... and not to be described here more definitely. Not much will remain of the Jews ... No other government and no other regime would have the strength for such a global solution of this question. Here too the Fuhrer is the undismayed champion of a radical solution necessitated by conditions and therefore inexorable. Fortunately a whole series of possibilities presents itself to us in wartime that would be denied us in peacetime.

Initially, the killings were accomplished by mass shootings. However, it was soon found that killing thousands of people with bullets was very slow and complicated. A more effective method of killing a large number of Jews required using gas in a similar manner to how it had been used extensively before the war to kill, it is estimated, over 75,000 Germans who suffered from incurable diseases, were mentally disabled or were persistent sexual offenders (Hilberg, 1985, p. 872). The first stage in the gassing of the European Jews was carried out by Einsatzgruppen using mobile vans modified for the purpose of using carbon monoxide from the exhaust to kill (Fleming, 1985, p. 63; Streim, 1989). These Einsatzgruppen, who were not under the control of the local army commanders, were given free rein in the early part of the campaign against Russia to carry out their work (Browning, 1985; *Special*

Duties for the SS in Operation Barbarossa, March 13, 1941, in Arad et al., 1981, p. 375). Mobile vans were later superseded by the establishment of the six main death camps in Poland. It was in one of these killing centres that most Jews were to die as the Nazis implemented their "Final Solution" (Mayer, 1990).

The German bureaucracy and the Final Solution

The ability of the Nazis to collect, transport, process, kill and dispose of the remains of at least six million Jews was due less to any extraordinary management abilities on their part and more to the presence of a very co-operative, enthusiastic and thorough German civil bureaucracy (Browning, 1980; Speer, 1981, p. 5; Rosenberg, 1983). Members of the Nazi party of themselves could not have given Hitler the strong economy and the efficiency he needed to conduct a war on several fronts. In one of his memoirs, Albert Speer (1981, p. 4) referred to the party members as people of low intellect who

> were so hidebound that they slowed down development... The economic upswings after 1933 were due chiefly to the cooperation of those echelons that derived from the days of the Kaiser and the Weimar Republic ... an excellent officialdom and outstanding technocrats in the widest sense of the word offered their services in 1933.
>
> (see also Fest, 1970, p. 135)

Rosenberg (1983, p. 13) called these anonymous technocrats the "desk-killers". The bureaucrat was

> a functionary in a vast bureaucratic organisation, who kill(ed) from behind a desk without wielding any weapons more lethal than a typewriter that issues reports dealing out death ... along deliberately anonymous channels or through a labyrinth of bureaucratic routines and apparatus.
>
> (Rosenberg, 1983, p. 13)

In part, as a consequence of the participation of the bureaucracy, La Capra (1994, p. 90) describes the Holocaust as being "calculated coldly and with the maximum efficiency and economy". The killing of a very large number of people in a relatively short space of time was nothing more than "an efficiency problem of the greatest dimensions ... With an unfailing sense of direction ... the German bureaucracy found the shortest road to the final goal" (Hilberg, 1985, p. 9; Hilberg, 1980, p. 101; see also Bauman quoted in La Capra, 1994, p. 91). Thus, it was in no small measure due to the professionalism of the civilian bureaucracy that the attempted extermination of Jews, most frequently referred to as the Final Solution, went close to achieving its goal of annihilation. The actions of faceless and industrious bureaucrats and their unexceptionable identities, when compared to the legacy left by the zealots who were their leaders, were, for Browning and Hilberg, the most alarming feature of the process of destruction (Browning, 1988, pp. 172–173). Hilberg noted that

> (a)lthough the destructive work was largely embedded in administrative routines, much more was required of a bureaucrat than automatic implementation of anti-Jewish measures. Without timely proposals and initiatives, the process would have been crippled, as various complicated steps against Jewry would inevitably have been postponed, dissipated, or aborted.
>
> (Hilberg, 1985, p. 25)

Civilian bureaucrats were able to carry out their duties associated with the Final Solution separated from the ultimate consequences of their actions by distance and their indirect participation. Their work to expedite the collection, accounting for and delivery of Jews to the death camps formed only part of their daily work. Thus, amongst the pressures of a busy day, especially when the country was at war, Jews assumed a commonplaceness. They became just another cargo to be marshalled, loaded, costed, and moved. In the departments responsible for the railways, for example, transportation of Jews involved essentially the same considerations as other scheduling.

Even accepting that civilian and military bureaucrats may not have known about the murders taking place due to devotion to their duties, they were aware that vast numbers of people were being uprooted in the most extreme and uncertain circumstances, never to be heard of again. Contrary to the protestations of the bureaucrats, Read argues that

> the moral duties of the person are greater than any of the duties which the individual possesses as a member of society. His [sic] moral responsibilities, both to himself and others, transcends the given social context, are conceived to be independent of the social ties which link him to his followers.
>
> (Quoted in Velayutham and Perera, 1996, p. 67; see also Rosenberg, 1983, p. 14; Lovell, 1995, p. 61)

By not actually observing and taking an active part in administering the cause of death, bureaucrats at all levels later attempted to relieve their consciences by arguing that, like their more notorious colleagues who supervised and ordered the killings, they were only following orders. In addition, they protested that they did not know the ultimate object of the orders or their work. They may have seen orders for railway wagons, railway timetables, costings, purchase requisitions and other pieces of paper giving effect to the

Final Solution, but they did not have contact with the subjects of these documents. Unlike the SS,

> most of the participants did not fire rifles at Jewish children or pour gas into gas chambers ... Most bureaucrats composed memoranda, drew up blueprints, signed correspondence ... They could destroy a whole people by sitting at their desks.
>
> (Hilberg, 1985, p. 1024)

While acknowledging the self-serving nature of the bureaucrats' objections, for most, there is some validity in their claims of ignorance of the monstrous enterprise in which they had become an essential part. Apart from unconfirmed and dangerous rumours, the great majority of the German people, for much of the war, had no direct knowledge of the annihilation process in which their leaders were engaged. Indeed, the top Nazi echelons went to extraordinary lengths after the Wannsee conference in January 1942[6] to keep secret both the existence of the death camps and the eventual destiny of Jews removed from Germany (Gilbert, 1986, p. 284; Hilberg, 1985, pp. 962, 1012; Klarsfeld, 1978, p. 62). To help accomplish this, the intentions of the Nazis towards the Jews were hidden behind seemingly innocuous euphemisms[7] sometimes referred to as "Nazi-Deutsch" (see Friedlander and Milton, 1980; Dawidowicz, 1976, pp. 14–16). Jews who were to be expelled from Germany were said to be "resettled" or "put to work" in the East (Eichmann in Von Lang, 1983, p. 93). In deference to the Nazi preference for numbers to describe their organisations, gassing was called Action 14f13 or *Sonderbehandlung* (special treatment) (Eichmann in Von Lang, 1983, p. 144). Most notoriously, the term "Final Solution of the Jewish Question" was successful in suppressing the true intent of the Nazi policy towards the Jews. Corruption of the German language by the Nazis, argues Dawidowicz (1976, p. 14), was designed to narrow the range of thinking and to provide "a language that concealed more than it communicated, its very nature and vocabulary buffering speaker and listener from reality".

Not only was the Nazi leadership uncertain as to the reaction of the German public if they knew that their former neighbours and associates were being systematically killed in their millions, but they also did not want to expose their plans to the Jewish community or foreign nationals. The Nazis may have wanted to give history the legacy of a world without Jews, but they did not want to publicise the process by which this was achieved. Possibly, most of all, the Germans needed to keep their terrible secret hidden away from each new batch of victims. Hence the cruel charade of the "bathhouses" at Auschwitz. Jews of all ages were forced to undress and fold their clothing neatly, to be collected by them after their shower, they were told, after which they were herded into the gas chambers.

Accounting was part of this network of euphemisms and disguises to mask the eradication of an entire group of people from the inmates, the German public, and the world. Accounting numbers also enabled the civil bureaucracy and their masters to control from a distance by capturing key dimensions of the extermination process without being in constant attendance (Humphrey and Scapens, 1996, p. 89; Miller, 1990, p. 318). In terms of Francis' (1990, p. 7) description of accounting, as with all sectors and resources within a ruthless totalitarian State, accounting in Nazi Germany was, above all else, a political practice that was not value-free, nor were the decisions of bureaucrats with expertise in accounting that was used to serve the Nazi State *diligently*. Rather,

> (t)he rationality of accounting – what we account for, how we account, to whom we account, about whom we account, when we account, and so on – are value choices made with respect to relations between members of the *polis*.
>
> (Francis, 1990, p. 7)

The theme of interdependency, when an account is given, is also emphasised by Schweiker (1993, pp. 234, 240), who describes accounting as

> a discursive act of saying or writing something about intentions, actions, relations and outcomes to someone – even if this is ourselves – ... in such a way that an identity is enacted as intrinsically interdependent with others.... As *moral* agents we give various accounts of those actions, relations and sufferings in a way that binds us to others....

Accounting as a moral practice, therefore, means that the accountant is never acting in isolation. Always there will be others affected by the accountant's actions.

In the following section the political nature of accounting is demonstrated with the way in which accounting practices effectively made Jews invisible as human beings. It also highlights the moral dimension of accounting referred to by Francis and how accounting was used to mediate between Jews and their oppressors. Accounting played an unobtrusive part in the efficient annihilation of most Jews in Europe.

Accounting for the invisible

The Holocaust involved the extension of functional reasoning from the factory, where it assists management in transforming inputs into desired outputs, to process human beings and their property (see Rubinoff in Rosenberg, 1983, p. 13). More particularly, according to Rosenberg (1983, p. 14), it resulted in the "corruption of rationality into ideological forms of functional reasoning". At the heart of functional reason is the use of technologies of calculation, most importantly accounting. A great advantage of these technologies is the perception that they are amoral, value-free, and that of themselves they cannot be made to be responsible or to have prescience. In the service of the Holocaust they were used to

> reduce human beings to quantified objects, thus eliminating their troublesome qualities of humaneness ... Functional reason must treat people as objects, as things, as mere numbers that can be easily manipulated and casually disposed of ... It allows individuals to manipulate fellow human beings as things until they were done away with when no longer perceived as useful or needed.
>
> (Rosenberg, 1983, p. 12)

Accounting information has the ability to create visibilities that had not previously existed, with the result that control is enhanced (Broadbent and Laughlin, 1994, p. 4). The visibilities created by accounting enhance control by making possible modes of control tailored to the smallest level of activity and resource within an organisation (see Hopwood, 1983; Humphrey and Scapens, 1996, p. 87). Velayutham and Perera (1996, p. 76) also refer to the ability of accounting to create organisational visibilities. These visibilities created by the persuasive logic of accounting help to entrench a discourse and, thus, the exclusion of other criteria to assess value (see also Andrew and Kaidonis, 1996). When specific aspects of reality are made visible, their presence makes a more penetrating control possible.

The creation of visibilities by accounting will be at the expense of other things moving into the shadow and becoming or remaining invisible (Easthope and McGowan, 1992). That which does not possess the dimensions captured by accounting records is excluded. Thus, accounting provides a partial rendition of reality whereby "visibilities created by accounting become reality and, thereby, those issues that have been stripped away in order to create the metaphor become invisible" (Broadbent, 1995, p. 71). To be invisible is to risk becoming valueless. Thus, the partial representation that accounting creates has the ability to constitute a serious threat. Unfortunately for those adversely affected by the bifurcation of reality by accounting into that which is visible and that which is invisible, by definition, that which is not captured by accounting must be without value and becomes the silenced "Other". In the present chapter, the invisible "Other" is the individuality and humanity of the victims who were put to death or suffered as a consequence of the Nazi determination to annihilate the Jews of Europe. In the place of these human qualities, the bureaucratic processes commodified Jews by reducing each person firstly to an anonymous unit in a group of condemned individuals and then at the killing centres to either a resource of some temporary value to the German war effort or expensive debris to be disposed of as costlessly as possible.

Broadbent and Laughlin (1994) have noted that the consequence of creating particular visibilities is that some things are allowed to be seen as tangible and, therefore, to exist. As a result, "they can more easily be decoupled from the social milieu in which they are embedded and discussion of these issues in the 'public' sphere is enabled" (Broadbent and Laughlin, 1994, p. 7). The conversion of Jews to a one-dimensional metric, an integer as a component of tabulations that could be arithmetically manipulated, stripped the identity and all other qualities from Jews and gave their tormentors the anonymity for the subjects of their work that enabled them to avoid divulging the human correspondence of their accounts. Jews were no longer recognised as social beings and, in the absence of this measure, they became invisible and ceased to exist. They could then be discussed in the public domain through their surrogates found in the calculations in accounting reports. Unlike other social participants, they no longer had a life history, the potential to make worthwhile contributions, responsibilities as family members, or the capacity to love and have feelings. Debased numbers are not able to experience emotions, nor do they have a past. Numbers are contrived for a purpose and then cease to have the same importance beyond that purpose.

As noted earlier, the steps in this destruction of the European Jews were obsessively documented by the German civil bureaucracy and the military (see comments by Dawidowicz, 1976, pp. 1–21). These documents of the Holocaust Hilberg (1985, p. x) reminds, are

> not merely a record of events, but artefacts of the administrative machinery itself. What we call a documentary source was once an order, letter, or report. Its date, signature, and dispatch invested it with immediate consequences.

As one who later had cause to regret the bureaucracy's pedantic ways, Eichmann derisively complained that "the various departments defended every inch of their competency tooth and nail ... The bureaucracy ... stuck to the regulations with an obstinacy, a punctiliousness" (quoted in Von Lang, 1983, p. 146; Arendt, 1964). In the records of the bureaucracy, as the next section illustrates, accounting as a technology of management is clearly implicated in all stages of the destruction of European Jews. From the creation of lists of victims used to plan railway rolling stock needs and the timetabling of transports to the disposal of Jewish property left outside the gas chambers or near the shooting pits, accounting can be seen to have fulfilled an essential part at each step. Thus, those who diligently used accounting precisely to track and account for the merciless killing of over 6 million people cannot escape their share of responsibility for the success of their undertaking. Fleming (1985, p. 46) notes that the "planned killing" of the Holocaust "required a procedure thought out with absolute precision down to the smallest detail". In a similar manner to production in a factory, the Holocaust was killing based on the detailed organisation and principles of the assembly line.

The creation of lists of deportees to the extermination camps was the final stage in a process that had grown from the Nuremberg Laws in 1935 to make Jews non-existent. They were not recognised as anything other than an input of varying degrees of value in a conversion process, which resulted in corpses. As a member of a class of objects, they were denoted as a number that formed the basis of a system whereby the Germans could account for the progress of their policy of extermination. Thus, in reports to Hitler and Himmler, for example, the emphasis is on reporting the *number* of people who had been killed and the number yet to be killed. As an example, in a report prepared by the head of the Statistics Department in Himmler's office in March 1943, detailed figures are given of the number of "moves" from the Sudetenland, Austria, and other areas under German control. It concludes that the total "evacuations" for *Special Treatment* were 1,786,356 (*SS Statistics of the Final Solution*, in Arad et al., 1981, pp. 333–334). This process of accounting and accountability was made possible by the detailed lists of Jews living in most areas that had been kept or created for the Germans by Jewish community organisations.

Well before preparations for the Final Solution were put in place, the Germans knew the extent of their task. They knew that in Poland, there were 2,284,000 Jews, 2,994,684 in the Ukraine and 742,800 in Hungary. With their lists of Jews, all that remained was for the Germans to count the number killed and deduct this from the number available to be killed. Wellers (1978, p. 139) calls this "macabre accounting". The lists of Jews were often so accurate that with the assistance of community leaders, the Germans knew precisely how many people lived in each house. If they did not collect the correct number of people from each house, Jewish community representatives would be arrested to make up the numbers. Thus, far from being innocuous, documents that specified numbers of Jews to be collected were effectively death warrants in the form of charge-discharge accounting. Jewish leaders would be charged with the number on requisition documents and held personally liable until the charge was discharged with a corresponding number of people transported.

Extermination accounting

Confiscation of property

As if they knew that the owners would never return, civilian government employees immediately confiscated and meticulously accounted for all property left by Jews, "including personal property, apartments, community assets, blocked accounts, ... sequestered securities, firms ... credits and debts, pensions, insurance. All these odds and ends ... were now dropped into the laps of the Finance Ministry's experts" (Hilberg, 1985, p. 471). The process, which was systematic, well organised and extremely thorough, was greatly enhanced by the existence of detailed lists of property and wealth required by the *Decree Regarding the Reporting of Jewish Property* (26 April 1938). The key provisions of this decree stated that

> s.1(1) Every Jew ... must report and assess his entire domestic and foreign property as of the effective date of this decree, in accordance with the regulations that follow....
> s.3(1) Each item of property is to be assessed, in reporting, at its common value on the effective date of this decree ...
> s.4(1) ... the property must be tentatively reported with an estimated value by 30 June 1938.

All property disclosed was liable to be used in the interests of the State (*Decree Regarding the Reporting of Jewish Property,* s.7) according to the wishes of the Reich Minister of the Interior, Herman Goering. In cases where property was not disclosed according to the Decree, the owner risked imprisonment for a period of up to ten years and immediate confiscation of all property, including that previously disclosed (*Decree Regarding the Reporting of Jewish Property,* s.8). Conforming to the Decree was, in essence, an accounting exercise whereby each Jew had to draw up a truncated balance sheet containing nothing but assets. In order to produce the list, the Decree made it clear that only values that could be substantiated were to be placed on the property. For Jews with extensive fixed property holdings, this and the final compilation of the lists would have entailed the assistance of professionals with accounting skills to arrive at valuations and create reports in conformity with the legislation. Accounting, therefore, was involved in the spread of State surveillance, both of domestic and foreign affairs, and in identifying resources in the possession of condemned Jews that could be made available to the State.

After the passage of the 11th Ordinance of Reich Citizenship Law in November 1941, the property of any Jew who left Germany was immediately lost to the State. Prior to this, confiscation of property could only occur after the courts pronounced, in each case, the Jew to be an enemy of the State (Hilberg, 1985, p. 471). With the prospect of the inevitable seizure of their property, many Jews were induced to sell their property and businesses in an attempt to gain at least something. At the forefront of this process

> (a)ccountants and bookkeepers ... could busy themselves with contracts that were products of pressure put on Jewish owners to sell their property ... The accountants could always say to themselves that acquisitions were acquisitions.
>
> (Hilberg, 1993, p. 65)

Accounting was the essential ingredient that allowed the sequestration of Jewish property by the Nazis to be comprehensive and exhaustive. In a State where terror was an institutionalised practice of the government, where infractions of onerous laws directed against the Jews were met with retribution that was severe and disproportionate to the offence, accounting provided another weapon of threat and intimidation to police easily decrees such as the *Decree Regarding the Reporting of Jewish Property.* Without the collaboration of accountants, laws, and decrees that firstly catalogued Jewish property and then denied Jews their rights to the property that had been identified would have been far less effective if not unenforceable (see Miller's (1990, p. 318) comments on the relationship between political programs and "technologies of government"). It was also accounting that provided the linkages and transitions that cohered the different phases of annihilation without the need to divulge to each the specifics of previous stages.

Transportation of the condemned

Crucial to the success of Nazi extermination policies was the ability to gain access to railway rolling stock to transport Jews to the extermination camps and to schedule these transports. Once a train had been allocated, it was up to the bureaucrats on the railways and the Gestapo to ensure that each train was fully utilised and that the time for each shipment was rigorously met (Hilberg, 1985, pp. 455–465, 1989). Prior to the trains being made available, it was the responsibility of the Traffic Division of the Reichsbahn and its accountants to set the rates to charge for the transports. The Gestapo, primarily responsible for providing the "cargo" for the death camp trains, was charged the third-class one-way fare of 4 pfenning per track kilometre for each adult carried. A fare of 2 pfenning was charged for children under 10 while children under 4 travelled free. A discount of half the normal third-class fare was offered for groups of 400 or more.

Sometimes transportation bills would be sent to the Gestapo through the official Nazi travel agency, the Mittelewopaische Reiseburo. As the scale of the deportations grew, however, the Gestapo found it more difficult to meet the costs of transportation out of their budget. To deal with this problem, a charge was levied on the Jewish community for each person deported (Hilberg, 1985, pp. 467–468). They, in turn, charged the deportees 25% of their liquid assets. Thus, in effect, Jews were paying for their own death. This money was to be deposited into a special SS account called Account W at the Reichsbank. At the conclusion of each transport, a detailed account was required of movements into and out of Account W associated with the transport (*Instruction of Reich Association of the Jews in Germany to Jewish Community Associations, December 3, 1941,* in Hilberg, 1972, pp. 115–116).

In occupied countries, the Germans paid for the use of the State railway infrastructure. If there were insufficient funds in accounts that contained proceeds from the sale of confiscated Jewish property, a charge might be made to the Reich Finance Ministry. Examination of correspondence between the

Ministry of Transport and the High Command of the Army in March 1944, which referred to difficulties being experienced by the Greek State Railways in being paid 1,938,488 Reichsmark for shipments of Jews to Auschwitz, provides details of payment arrangements and, possibly more importantly, gives a good idea of the business-like approach of those responsible for the transports. The Ministry of Transport officer writing the request for payment, presumably well after those who had been transported had been killed soon after arriving at Auschwitz, concludes by asking that

> this matter be cleared up with the Reichsfuhrer-SS and Chief of the German Police/Command Security Police and possibly the Reich Economy Minister and that care be taken to assure transmittal of the transport costs to the Directorate of the Greek State Railways. Kindly inform me about the progress of negotiations.
>
> (Quoted in Hilberg, 1972, pp. 164–165)

Directing the logistics of transportation, including the work of the RSHA, was Eichman's office, which referred to the trains as *Sonderzuge* or "special passenger trains" (Hilberg, 1985, pp. 410–415). Eichmann confirmed that organising the transports and ensuring they were all paid for was an extremely complicated process that became increasingly more difficult towards the end of the war. Consequently, the cooperation of a number of German agencies was required for

> no matter how large a German force was present, they couldn't just round up people, put them in freight cars, and ship them out.... We had to requisition the trains ... and contract Administration and Supply headquarters.
>
> (Eichmann in Von Lang, 1983, p. 99)

Moral accounting for murder

Upon arrival at the camps, the inmates came under the control of the SS Economic Administration Main Office under Obergruppenfuhrer Oswald Pohl. In Auschwitz, inmates allowed to live long enough to work in the camp were given numbers tattooed onto their forearms. They were called *figuren* or simply numbers (*Evidence Given at the Nuremberg Trials*, in Arad et al., 1981, pp. 358–360), with the numbers recorded in a *Totenbuch* or "death book". Other dimensions of their being as individuals were thereby displaced by their number, for "once they had been tattooed, the only thing that was important about them was their number. Whatever productive work that was to be had from them was as if from a machine" (Gilbert, 1986, p. 824).

As part of the efforts to delude Jews to their ultimate fate before deportations, everyone was permitted to take a small amount of money and some clothing. After each batch of killings the remaining belongings were carefully sorted, including gold extracted from teeth, and sent back to Germany. Great care was taken to account for everything. Hilberg (1985, p. 473) notes how everything was collected "to the last hairpin". Himmler insisted that there be "painstaking exactness" in all dealings with Jewish property, warning that "(w)e cannot be accurate enough" (quoted in Hilberg, 1985, p. 951). As an example, in a secret report in June 1943 from the Commander of the SS in Galicia a detailed inventory is provided of all property confiscated from Jews, including:

25.580 kg	Copper coins
97.190 kg	Gold coins
20.952 kg	Wedding rings
11.730 kg	Gold teeth
343.1 kg	Cigarette cases
6.166 kg	Pocket watches, various
3.425 kg	Pocket watches, silver
7.495 kg	Fountain pens and propelling pencils

Source: Final Report by Katzman, Commander of the SS in Galicia, in Arad et al. (1981, pp. 335–341).

Himmler's demand for meticulous accounting was mainly to ensure that all possible proceeds found their way into the accounts of the SS. He was also concerned that in the absence of clear accountability the way would be open for theft, which would be detrimental to the spiritual well-being of his troops (Hilberg, 1985, p. 951). By enforcing stringent standards of accountability, Himmler believed that "in carrying out this most difficult of tasks ... we have suffered no harm to our inner being, our soul, our character" (*Speech by Himmler to SS Officers, October 4, 1943*, in Arad et al., 1981, p. 345). Indicating the seriousness with which meticulous accounting was regarded, Himmler threatened that

> anyone who takes so much as a single Mark, of this money is a dead man.... There will be no mercy. We had the moral right, we had the duty towards our people, to destroy this people that wanted to destroy us. But we do not have the right to enrich ourselves by so much as a fur, as a watch, by one Mark or a cigarette or anything else.
>
> (*Speech by Himmler to SS Officers, October 4, 1943*, in Arad et al., 1981, p. 345)

Himmler's strident emphasis on accountability for Jewish property meant that the Nazis endeavoured to transform accounting into the means by which they could be purged of impure motives and avoid being contaminated by a difficult task that Jews had "forced" upon the Nazis. Himmler's insistence on punctilious accounting for property seized in the concentration camps and killing centres was the use of accounting for the purpose of *sanctification*.

The stolen wealth of the Jews had to pass through the accounts of the SS to transform its purported corrupt nature, which threatened the purity of those with whom it came in contact, into something wholesome and that could be a consecrated servant of the Aryan State. The seizure of Jewish property could be blessed by rigorous accounting to demonstrate that the acts that produced the property were motivated not by the material results but by the need to purify the German race. For members of the SS and others to benefit materially in an indiscriminate, avaricious manner allegedly similar to those who had previously owned the property and obtained it by methods injurious to the German people would be to become one of the fallen race and to put into question the right of the Nazis to conduct their crusade against Jews. Thus, in addition to ensuring that the State benefited from property seizures, accounting offered the means of redemption, a clear conscience, and the protection of the inner self. Accounting and the State were mutually dependent upon one another.

The rationales that the Nazi State accorded to accounting gave accounting a level of significance and power far beyond its obvious recording and reporting roles. Accounting provided the State with what appeared to be a neutral and, more importantly, disinterested technology of accountability, which allowed the State to characterise its actions to those who knew it as nothing more than a technical process. Accounting was one element of a repertoire of rhetoric used by the Nazis to establish that the Final Solution was not a program that had sprung from demented, irrational minds motivated by base selfish motives. Rather, the essentially calculative nature of accounting drained from the objects of its calculations features which were not amenable to measurement and reporting in a numerical format. As each summary of events became part of a higher level of summarisation, the underlying, original set of circumstances became ever more remote and inaccessible to those reading the reports.

The accounting reports made it difficult to see past the numbers and conclusions, to disaggregate the totals, to interrogate the reports, and to ask questions about the origins of the final numbers. When the bureaucracy's reports moved along and up the chain of authority, the geographical and empathetic distance increased between the fate of those who gave rise to the reports and those using or reading the reports. This increasing distance made it even more probable that there would be less questioning, less recognition of the enterprise that gave rise to the reports and the opportunity to deal in numbers that had become drained of everything other than their ability to facilitate calculation. Depiction of Jews passed the point where they were objectified to where they were *numerised*: they were numbers and little else.

All cash seized both before and after the death of Jews and others murdered was deposited in accounts at the Reichsbank, along with the safekeeping of precious metals and jewellery (Dawidowicz, 1975, p. 147). According to Eichmann, the Swiss assisted in the sale of jewellery and watches in Switzerland (Von Lang, 1983, p. 123) and in the safekeeping of the proceeds, for which there had to be a detailed accounting. In addition to benefiting financially from the disposal of property, the SS established an extensive business empire centred on the death camps. Inmates not immediately chosen for the gas chambers were employed, as shown in Chapter 10, in SS factories and hired out to private business firms. Of the latter, the most notorious was I.G. Farben, the chemical and dye manufacturer. Zyklon B, the trade name for hydrogen cyanide, which was used extensively in the gassing chambers of Auschwitz, was produced by a subsidiary of I.G. Farben, which also manufactured a stabilising agent for transportation of the gas but sold to the SS through another company in which Farben had a major share. I.G. Farben's association with the SS and the Final Solution provided them with an unbroken series of high profits throughout the last years of the war.[8] Other German companies benefited by constructing dormitory buildings, gas chambers, and crematoria (Klarsfeld, 1978, p. 111). These profits are found expression in company accounts but without any ethical qualifications.

Conclusion

The Nazis took advantage of a long history of German romanticism that portrayed the Aryan race as the source of creativity, spiritual strength, and purity and, therefore, a sure bulwark against the deprecations that Jews were said to have introduced into German life. What was, in reality, a campaign to bring about the political bondage of the German people to the National Socialists was masqueraded as a religious crusade against the Jews. Hitler was the saviour who would release the German people from the destructive influences of Jews. By definition, the defiler could not be tolerated if Aryan Germans were to be brought back to their simple roots and innocent happiness. The program to achieve this progressively coalesced around more extreme measures against Jews to eventually constitute the Holocaust, the Nazis "Final Solution".

Accounting has been shown to have been involved at all stages in the Holocaust to facilitate the efficient implementation of the Nazis' program of the exclusion of Jews and, later, their attempted annihilation. In particular, accounting provided an unassuming and uncontested means to objectify Jews and to hallow the motives of the Nazis. The use of accounting has consequences, most of which should be intended, otherwise, it has no value. Therefore, the use of accounting cannot be neutral or disinterested if it is to fulfil its mission. Accounting is not solely an instrument of calibration and description. Its operation is dynamic, and its effects are often far-reaching, affecting not only the operations of organisations that use accounting but also the individuals who constitute an organisation's stakeholders, upon whom the results of decisions made using accounting information are visited. Unfortunately, there is no evidence that the accounting profession during the Nazi reign provided any "principled" moral leadership for accounting practitioners or was any different to the other professions in its sycophantic homage to the will of the State.

This chapter is based on the paper by Warwick Funnell titled "Accounting in the service of the Holocaust", which originally appeared in *Critical Perspectives on Accounting*, vol. 8, no. 4, pp. 435–464. The author would like to thank the publisher, Elsevier, for permission to use this material.

Notes

1 In correspondence with the author, Hilberg and Browning, the two best known authorities on the role of the professions as part of the bureaucracy during the Holocaust, were unable to recall any discussion in the Holocaust literature which specifically concerned accounting and the accounting profession.

2 Landes described Sombart's *The Jews and Economic Life* as "a pseudo-scholarly hoax, a pedantic effort to confer by the lavish use of polyglot footnote references, an academic respectability to errant nonsense ..." (quoted in Herf, 1984, p. 135).

3 The *Reich Citizenship Law* and the *First Ordinance to the Reich Citizenship Law*, in November 1935, defined a Jew as someone who had three grandparents who were "fully Jewish by race" (Article 5). The second law decided upon in Nuremberg by the Nazi party was *The Law for the Protection of German Blood and Honor.* The law prohibited marriages between Jews and Aryan Germans, permitted annulment of existing marriages, prohibited sexual intercourse between Jews and pure blood Germans and limited the household employment of Jews.

4 This persecution was not limited to the Jews. Jehovah's Witnesses, homosexuals, gypsies, and most other minority religious groups suffered similar privations to those of the Jews.

5 The death camps were Belzec, Sobibor, Treblinka, Chelmno, Majdanek, and Auschwitz-Birkenau. The first train to the death camps left Germany on 18 October 1941 (Fleming, 1985, p. 67).

6 It was at the town of Wannsee on 20–21 January 1942 that the implementation of the Final Solution was discussed. This had been preceded by a conference on 10 October 1941 amongst members of the RSHA, the Reich Security Main Office created by Reinhard Heydrich.

7 Also, SS participating in extermination operations were required to sign an oath of silence (see Arad et al., 1981, pp. 274–275).

8 I.G. Farben was also an enthusiastic supporter of the elimination of Serbians by the Croatian Ustasha who were an ally of the Nazis (Aly and Heim, 1988, p. 13).

References

Andrew, J. and Kaidonis, M. (1996). *Accounting for the Environment in Order for It to Count: Possibilities for Accounting as an Enabling Voice.* Seminar paper, Department of Accounting and Finance, University of Wollongong.

Aly, G., and Heim, S. (1988). Economics of the Final Solution. *Simon Wiesenthal Centre Annual, 5*, 3–48.

Arad, Y., Gutman Y. and Margarliot A. (1981). *Documents on the Holocaust: Selected Sources on the Destruction of European Jewry.* Jerusalem: Yad Vashem.

Arendt, H. (1964). *Eichmann in Jerusalem: A Report on "The Banality of Evil".* New York: Viking.

Broadbent, J. (1995). The Values of Accounting and Education: Some Implications of the Creation of Visibilities and Invisibilities in Schools. *Advances in Public Interest Accounting*, 6, 69–98.

Broadbent, J., and Laughlin, R. (1994). *Moving towards an Accounting That Will Be Enabling: Accounting, Habermas and Issues of Gender*. Seminar paper, Department of Accounting and Finance, University of Wollongong.

Browning, C. (1980). The Government Experts. In: H. Friedlander, and S. Milton (Eds.). *The Holocaust: Ideology, Bureaucracy, and Genocide*. Millwood: Kraus International Publications.

Browning, C. (1985). *Fateful Months*. New York: Holmes & Meier.

Browning, C. (1988). Bureaucracy and Mass Murder: The German Administrator's Comprehension of the Final Solution. In: A. Cohen, J. Gelber, and C. Wardi (Eds.). *Comprehending the Holocaust*. Frankfurt am Main: Verlag Peter Lang.

Bullock, A. (1973). *Hitler: A Study in Tyranny*. London: Book Club Associates.

Cohen, A., Gelber, J., and Wardi, C. (Eds.) (1988). *Comprehending the Holocaust*. Frankfurt am Main: Verlag Peter Lang.

Dawidowicz, L. (1975). *The War against the Jews 1933–1945*. London: Weidenfeld and Nicholson.

Dawidowicz, L. (1976). *A Holocaust Reader*. New York: Behrman House Inc.

Easthope, A., and McGowan, K. (Eds.). (1992). *A Critical and Cultural Theory Reader*. Sydney: Allen and Unwin.

Fest, J. (1970). *The Face of the Third Reich*. Harmondsworth: Penguin Books.

Fleming, G. (1985). *Hitler and the Final Solution*. London: Hamish Hamilton.

Francis, J. (1990). After Virtue? Accounting as a Moral and Discursive Practice. *Accounting, Auditing and Accountability Journal*, *5*(5), 5–17.

Friedlander H. and Milton S. (Eds), (1980). *The Holocaust: Ideology, Bureaucracy, and Genocide*. Millwood: Kraus International Publications.

Gallhofer, S., and Haslam, J. (1991). The aura of accounting in the context of a crisis: Germany and the First World War. *Accounting, Organizations and Society, 12(5-6), 487–520.*

Gilbert, M. (1986). *The Holocaust: The Jewish Tragedy*. London: Collins.

Goebbels, J. (1948). *The Goebbels Diaries 1942–43*. New York: Doubleday.

Herf, J. (1984). *Reactionary Modernism: Technology, Culture and Politics in Weimar and the Third Reich*. Cambridge: Cambridge University Press.

Hilberg, R. (1972). *Documents of Destruction*. London: W.H. Allen.

Hilberg, R. (1980). The Significance of the Holocaust. In: H. Friedlander, and S. Milton (Eds.). *The Holocaust: Ideology, Bureaucracy, and Genocide*. Millwood: Kraus International Publications.

Hilberg, R. (1985). *The Destruction of the European Jews*. New York: Holmes and Meir.

Hilberg, R. (1989). German Railroads/Jewish Souls. In: M. Marrus (Ed.). *The Nazi Holocaust: Historical Articles on the Destruction of the European Jews*, Book 3, Vol. 2. Westport: Meckler.

Hilberg, R. (1993). *Perpetrators, Victims, Bystanders: The Jewish Catastrophe*. New York: Harper Collins.

Hitler, A. (1987). *Mein Kampf*. Boston, MA: Hutchinson.

Hopwood, A. (1983). On Trying to Study Accounting in the Contexts in Which It Operates. *Accounting, Auditing and Accountability Journal*, *8*(2/3), 287–305.

Humphrey, C., and Scapens, R. (1996). Theories and Case Studies of Organisational and Accounting Practices: Limitation or Liberation. *Accounting, Auditing and Accountability Journal*, *9*(4), 86–106.

Katz, F. (1989). Implementation of the Holocaust: The Behavior of Nazi Officials. In: M. Marrus (Ed.). *The Nazi Holocaust: Historical Articles on the Destruction of the European Jews*, Book 3, Vol. 2. Westport: Meckler.
Klarsfeld, S. (Ed.). (1978). *The Holocaust and the Neo-Nazi Mythomania*. New York: The Beate Klarsfeld Foundation.
La Capra, D. (1994). *Representing the Holocaust: History, Theory, Trauma*. New York: Cornell University Press.
Langmuir, G. (1980). Medieval Anti-Semitism. In: H. Friedlander, and S. Milton (Eds.). *The Holocaust: Ideology, Bureaucracy, and Genocide*. Millwood: Kraus International Publications.
Lovell, A. (1995). Moral Reasoning and Moral Atmosphere in the Domain of Accounting. *Accounting, Auditing and Accountability Journal*, *8*(3), 60–80.
Marrus, M. (Ed.) (1989). *The Nazi Holocaust: Historical Articles on the Destruction of the European Jews*, Book 3, Vol. 2. Westport: Meckler.
Mayer, A. (1990). *Why Did the Heavens Not Darken?: The "Final Solution" in History*. London: Verso.
Miller, P. (1990). On the Interrelationships between Accounting and the State. *Accounting, Organisations and Society*, *15*(4), 315–338.
Mosse, G. (1970). *Germans and Jews: the Right, the Left, and the Search for a "Third Force" in Pre-Nazi Germany*. New York: Howard Fertig.
Rosenberg, A. (1983). The Philosophical Implications of the Holocaust. In: R.L. Braham (Ed.). *Perspectives on the Holocaust*. Boston: Kluwer-Nijhoff Publishing.
Schweiker, W. (1993). Accounting for Ourselves: Accounting Practice and the Discourse of Ethics. *Accounting, Organisations and Society*, *18*(2/3), 231–252.
Sombart, W. (1913). *The Jews and Modern Capitalism*. London: T. Fisher Unwin.
Sombart, W. (1929). Economic Theory and Economic History. *The Economic History Review*, *2*(1), 1–19.
Speer, A. (1981). *The Slave State: Heinrich Himmler's Masterplan for SS Supremacy*. London: Weidenfeld and Nicolson.
Streim, A. (1989). The Tasks of the SS Einsatzgruppen. In: M. Marrus (Ed.). *The Nazi Holocaust: Historical Articles on the Destruction of the European Jews*, Book 3, Vol. 2. Westport: Meckler.
Talmon, J.L. (1989). European History – Seedbed of the Holocaust. In: M. Marrus (Ed.). *The Nazi Holocaust: Historical Articles on the Destruction of the European Jews*, Book 3, Vol. 2. Westport: Meckler.
Taylor, T. (1980). The Legal Profession. In: H. Friedlander, and S. Milton (Eds.). *The Holocaust: Ideology, Bureaucracy, and Genocide*. Millwood: Kraus International Publications.
Velayutham, S. and Perera, M.H.B. (1996). The Influence of Underlying Metaphysical Notions on Our Interpretation of Accounting. *Accounting, Auditing and Accountability Journal*, *9*(4), 65–85.
Von Lang, J. (1983). *Eichman Interrogated*. London: The Bodley Head.
Weber, E. (1980). Modern Anti-Semitism. In: H. Friedlander, and S. Milton (Eds.). *The Holocaust: Ideology, Bureaucracy, and Genocide*. Millwood: Kraus International Publications.
Wellers, G. (1978). Reply to the Neo-Nazi Falsification of Historical Facts Concerning the Holocaust. In: S. Klarsfeld (Ed.). *The Holocaust and the Neo-Nazi Mythomania*. New York: The Beate Klarsfeld Foundation.

Wiesel, E. (1988). Some Questions That Remain Open. In: A. Cohen, J. Gelber, and C. Wardi (Eds.). *Comprehending the Holocaust*. Frankfurt am Main: Verlag Peter Lang.

Winston, D. (1980). Pagan and Early Christian Anti-Semitism. In: H. Friedlander, and S. Milton (Eds.). *The Holocaust: Ideology, Bureaucracy, and Genocide*. Millwood: Kraus International Publications.

3 Accounting and the "Jewish Spirit"

Justifying Jewish persecution

Warwick Funnell

Introduction

The nexus between the practices and technologies of accounting and their social contexts gains special importance in times of major political crises. Accounting can no longer be naively and exclusively conceived as a neutral information-gathering and reporting tool. Research by Bryer (1991) has demonstrated how accounting can be used as a sinister instrument of social control in the hands of a cohesive, defensive social elite intent on preserving its privileged position, if necessary, by destroying competitors.

The potential for accounting to be an instrument of social engineering, used by one social cohort to the disadvantage of another, also attracted the attention of the German economic historian Werner Sombart (1863–1941) in the early decades of the 20th century. Sombart was an early advocate of the importance of accounting in shaping social relations and entrenching the position of some groups (for him, Jews) at the expense of others. However, accounting historians have remembered him mainly for his extravagant praise for double entry bookkeeping and not for his social commentary (Yamey, 1949, 1964; Most, 1972). He agreed with an earlier German writer, Goethe, that double entry bookkeeping was "one of the most beautiful discoveries of the human spirit" (Sombart, 1919, p. 272). Sombart saw double entry bookkeeping as the product of

> the same spirit which produced the systems of Galileo and Newton, and the subject matter of modern physics and chemistry.... By the same means it organises perceptions into a system, and one can characterize it as the first cosmos constructed on the basis of mechanistic thought. Double entry bookkeeping captures for us the cosmos of an economic, more precisely, a capitalist world by the same means that later the great naturalist scientists used to construct the solar system and the corpuscles of the blood ... Without too much difficulty, we can recognise in double entry bookkeeping the ideas of gravitation, of the circulation of the blood, of the conservation of energy and others which the physical sciences have discovered ...
>
> (Sombart, 1919, pp. 110–136)[1]

DOI: 10.4324/9781032685328-3

Contrary to the supportive appearance of his views about accounting, Sombart's praise of double entry bookkeeping instead was used as a means to denigrate the achievements of capitalism in its mature form and to support his belief that the rapid maturation, if not the origins, of modern capitalism benefited from the presence of a unique "Jewish spirit". According to Sombart, Jews[2] had taken the greatest advantage of accounting technologies' ability to shape economic and social relations in the modern era. Regrettably, he argued, double entry bookkeeping in the hands of Jews had also propelled Germany into the spiritual void of capitalism.

Sombart argued that double entry bookkeeping was used very successfully by Jews, who were conveniently dispersed throughout Europe, to transform the economic and social relations within traditional, agrarian, and handicraft economies to the point where they could sustain modern capitalism. The chapter will show how Sombart alleged that while other groups and individuals may have also used double entry bookkeeping to manage very profitable businesses, modern bookkeeping was used most effectively and ardently by Jewish businessmen who were part of a distinct, cohesive religious and racial grouping, which, despite centuries of persecution resulting in an often perilous and precipitous existence, had managed to retain a peculiar identity and character.

Sombart argued that, with the spread of the modern form of capitalism in the 18th century, unique racial and religious aspects of the Jewish character, forged over long periods of adversity, had made the Jews well suited to the consequences and opportunities of capitalism by becoming significant advantages in the pursuit of profits without limit and devoid of social conscience (Sombart, 1913, p. 159). Despite the persistence of this anti-Semitic theme throughout Sombart's writings on capitalism, historians have preferred to read him in a literal sense for the historical perspective his work casts on the history of accounting. This chapter moves behind the logical, scholarly façade constructed by Sombart to reveal the interested, prejudiced, anti-Semitic trajectory of his writings on accounting and the way in which the Nazis used them to justify their murderous anti-Semitic programs.

To the extent that Sombart argued that Jews were essentially a different species of individual and, therefore, fundamentally alien to Germany and upon whom should be placed responsibility as the bearers of the worst evils of capitalism (Sombart, 1913, p. 115; see Mitzman, 1973, p. 204), his views were certainly anti-Semitic. A good rendition of Sombart's position is provided by Sartre (1948, p. 5), who describes an anti-Semite as anyone who "attributes all or part of his country's misfortunes to the presence of Jewish elements in the community, and if he proposes to remedy this state of affairs … by depriving the Jews of certain of their rights …". This definition is sufficiently comprehensive to provide a clear statement of the essential elements of anti-Semitism which appear in Sombart's writings on Jewish capitalism and which identify him as an anti-Semite aligned with Nazi anti-Semitic priorities and programs.

Sombart's unique praise of double entry bookkeeping was not admiration but denunciation of the ability of this powerful technique of rationalisation to destroy, and not nurture, the soul of the German people. While few historians have agreed with the specifics of the relationship between capitalism and double entry bookkeeping as portrayed by Sombart, most do accept that more sophisticated accounting technologies contributed to the rapid maturation of modern capitalism. Sombart's maligning of Jews as the progenitors of capitalism's worst excesses and his antipathy towards capitalism as the unwelcome replacement of a fondly remembered simple, agrarian Germany are shown in this chapter to have been informed by romantic[3] notions of Germany's peasant past and the experiences of his own youth. German romantics saw a mystical connection between peasant society and the land, which brought with it a purity of thought and selfless consideration for others in the German community, attributes that Jews allegedly betrayed. The chapter emphasises how Sombart's views on capitalism and the role of Jews in establishing capitalism's hegemony over other economic systems are shown to have aligned him clearly with aspects of Nazi anti-Semitism.

Sombart and the distortion of history

Sombart's extravagant praise for double entry bookkeeping, which Yamey (1964, p. 118) refers to as "too elaborate and fanciful", and his belief that it was an essential ingredient in the appearance of modern capitalism[4] has held an understandable, although somewhat episodic, fascination for accounting historians ever since his conclusions were given prominence by Basil Yamey (1940, 1949, 1964). Yamey (1964, p. 136) suggested that Sombart's ideas, irrespective of their veracity, have been "intellectually attractive, aesthetically satisfying, or provocatively esoteric" for many scholars. Primarily, they have attracted the attention of both accounting and economic historians not for the persuasiveness of Sombart's arguments but for historical errors that result from his partial and selective reading of the history of double entry bookkeeping in the evolution of capitalism. Indeed, some have accused him of blatant and intentional intellectual dishonesty for manipulating the historical record for his own purposes. Many agree that Sombart argues from premises designed to ensure that they agree with his own previously settled position, which was anti-Semitic in intent. Throughout his study of capitalism, Sombart was so intent on promoting his accusations against Jews that he was apparently prepared to forsake historical veracity.

Pirenne argued that, contrary to Sombart's support for the appearance of capitalism in the late 18th century, the pursuit of profit from commercial transactions and speculation was present in at least the 12th century. Sombart had mistaken a "difference of intensity" for a "difference of nature" (Pirenne, 1914, pp. 495–497). Sée also disagreed with Sombart's proposition that commerce in the Middle Ages had not been capable of accumulating large amounts of capital (Sée, 1968, p. 27). de Roover (quoted in Yamey,

1940, p. 335) protested that "nothing could be further from the truth than to pretend as Werner Sombart does that the medieval merchant's accounts were in such a state of muddle that it was impossible for him to tell how he stood". Alleging that merchants of the 14th and 15th centuries were ignorant amateurs who had no idea of accumulating wealth, according to Pirenne, was both insulting to the sophistication of their businesses and was a violation of the historical record (Pirenne, 1961, pp. 162–163). Instead, the pursuit of profit "is to be met in all periods ... though in differing degrees of development because it corresponds with man's acquisitive instinct" (Pirenne, 1961, p. 164).

Winjum's (1972) work provides some very persuasive rebuttals of Sombart's conclusions. Winjum suggests that double entry bookkeeping was not essential to the development of capitalism, nor was double entry bookkeeping used in the 18th century to separate the affairs of the owner from those of the business. He and Yamey (1949) take particular exception to Sombart's conclusion that double entry bookkeeping was used extensively for calculating profit when the historical evidence indicates that it was primarily used as an accountability technique to allow agents to report to their principals and as the means to create greater order in the businessman's accounts (Yamey, 1949, pp. 110–111; Winjum, 1972, p. 240). Yamey (1949) and Most (1972) are especially critical of the significance Sombart gives to the contributions of double entry bookkeeping to capitalism (see Most, 1972, pp. 724–725).[5] Within these criticisms of Sombart's ideas about double entry bookkeeping, there is no reference to the linkage created by Sombart between Jews, double entry bookkeeping, and capitalism or any attempt to refute Sombart's anti-Semitic allegations, the motive behind his extreme, prejudiced views.

Although Sombart may have admired double entry bookkeeping as a system of logical business calculation, he scorned the economic and social consequences that its use allowed and, by association, condemned those who were the prime beneficiaries of the ability of accounting to rationalise and objectify business. Overwhelmingly, for Sombart, these were Jews.

The Good German

Sombart readily acknowledged how, despite the researcher's best efforts, the results of any scientific study would always be affected by the scientist's attitudes and predispositions. He believed that the impact of the author was even more marked for Germans, for "whoever is a good German, will paint German pictures, compose German poems, think German thoughts, even when he is least conscious of being German; in fact precisely when he is not conscious of it" (Sombart, 1939, p. 28, see also p. 25). As someone who saw himself as a "good German", Sombart accepted that the same forces were at work in his own writing. The importance of placing a particular work of an author into the broader context of their other work and views becomes particularly relevant when the works become an instrument of social oppression or when the author's views are masqueraded as scholarly contributions to legitimise essentially discriminatory and socially corrosive political ends. Nowhere is this more pertinent than the enlistment of the German intelligentsia in the 1930s by the Nazis in their scheme to isolate and then annihilate European Jewry.

The Nazis inherited spurious scientific racial theories, which were the product of a long period of evolution within German culture that benefited from many writers' contributions, especially throughout the 19th century. Accordingly, anyone who may have contributed to the success of the Nazi's program of murderous genocide, however innocuous it may seem in isolation from the ultimate consequences of Nazi policies, should not be allowed to remain anonymous. Thus, for far too long, Werner Sombart's anti-Semitism was allowed to remain hidden behind his passionate views on double entry bookkeeping. This separation of the work and the author has failed to recognise, in Sombart's case, that "anti-Semitism is not simply a 'matter of opinion' .... the anti-Semitic attitude involves the whole of the personality" (Sartre, 1948, p. 27). His work on capitalism and his views on double entry bookkeeping place Sombart firmly within the stream of German romantic thought, including its demonisation of Jews.

Sombart was excited by the National Socialist's vision to reinvigorate and restore the German nation, even to the extent of being prepared to contemplate war to resurrect German greatness in order to protect "our national body" (Sombart, 1937, p. xi). Both Sombart and the Nazis idealised life in the Middle Ages, exaggerated the rural basis of German society (see below) and held passionate nationalist views in which Jews were portrayed as the greatest threat to national cohesion and Germany's spiritual destiny. Most importantly, both Sombart and the Nazis opposed the effects of 19th-century liberalism and the individualism this allegedly had promoted at the expense of community interests.

The task confronting the new German socialism of the National Socialist government urged Sombart, was "nothing less than turning away from the economic age (i.e. modern capitalism) ... in its entirety" (Sombart, 1937, p. 41, also see p. 146). Accordingly, he was full of praise for the new national spirit of community and sacrifice embodied in the Nazi slogan "All for our country" (Sombart, 1937, p. xii). For Sombart, these hallmarks of true socialism characterised the "view held by leading members of the German National Socialist Party" (Sombart, 1937, p. 49). He quotes with approval Dr. Robert Ley, the head of the Nazi's National Labor Front, that "National Socialism ... has developed the personality of the individual to the highest point of its capacity for, and not against, the community. That which we have achieved is true socialism" (Sombart, 1937, p. 49).

Husbands (quoted in the introduction to Sombart, 1976, p. xvi) believed that some of Sombart's views were so similar to those of the Nazis that "it is only with considerable good nature that one can refrain from calling him a Nazi during the last years of his life". Harris (1942) has argued that Sombart's sympathy for the political program of the Nazis was not surprising. Indeed, it was a logical consequence of his long estrangement from capitalism and his strong attachment to an idealised, romantic notion of the German nation, which he shared with the Nazis. Plotnik (1937, p. 43), referring to the views expressed by Sombart in his 1934 treatise *Deutscher Sozialismus,* lamented how towards the end of his life "the 'old Sombart' has disappeared completely; nothing of the old scientist is left in it: in its stead- a Hitlerite Nazi!" Mitzman (1973, pp. 135–136) also condemns Sombart for his "flirtation with fascist ideology …" which moved him to "a position not far removed from Nazism". In the introduction to one of his last major works, which Sutton (1948, p. 329) sees as a "pledge of allegiance to the Third Reich", Sombart (1937, p. ix) reassured his audience that he was not "indifferent or unfriendly to the Hitler government; not in the least". Sombart's increasingly dogmatic and irrational views on German nationalism, his enduring antipathy towards the "Jewish spirit" and his refusal to speak out against the Nazis led Plotnik to describe him in his later years as "a genius gone wrong" (Plotnik, 1937, p. i).[6]

Although Sombart admired the National Socialist vision for a strong Germany and shared their contempt for what they conceived as Jewish capitalism, he differed significantly on how to achieve the ideal State for which they both yearned. Thus, the Nazis, while giving Sombart's writing considerable cultural and ideological importance, saw his singular romantic, bucolic prescriptions for Germany as inconsistent with their vision of an industrialised, modern Germany. Despite strong support for the rise of a nationalist government that promised to be the source of redemption after the failed experiment of the Weimar Republic and the imposed guilt from World War I, Sombart's preference was to allow Jews to co-exist, albeit with the proper controls, with their German neighbours. Apart from this, Jews should expect little else from the nation.

The following section highlights the influence of Sombart's earlier life and the German romantic movement on his ideas about capitalism and accounting and his opinions of Jews. It establishes the close connection between German romanticism, its denunciation of capitalism, and hostility towards Jews, which Sombart was to incorporate in his writings on the evolution of capitalism. Sombart's beliefs about the relationship between society and economic systems were the products of the German romantic movement, which reached its zenith in the years 1790–1830 (Abraham, 1982, pp. v–vii; von Engelhardt, 1988, p. 109) and which reappeared for a brief, but influential, period between 1893 and 1918, coinciding with the time of Sombart's greatest productivity.[7] Sombart's ideal German society had no room for either an economic system that resembled modern capitalism or for those who insisted on sustaining its worst vices. From his ideal prescriptions, Sombart fashioned an extreme form of socialism, which was offended by the consequences of the spread of the double entry bookkeeping calculus, which he alleged was mainly in the hands of Jewish businessmen.

The influence of German romanticism

The ideal society

Sombart's life encompassed the beginnings of the rise of Germany as a great industrial and imperial power and the start of its ignominious fall under the Nazis. His formative years were spent in privileged surroundings on large farm holdings owned by his father, who took an active role in German politics later in life. The years spent by Sombart on his father's manorial estates, surrounded by a system of deferential landless peasants who were the responsibility of a protective, paternalistic nobility, were to provide him with the foundations for his ideal economic system of National Socialism. His greatest works combined sociology and economic history in an attempt to understand the features that best characterised different economic epochs. However, his enduring interest was in the rise and evolution of capitalism.

In the late 19th century Sombart became an ardent follower of Marx, receiving the blessing of Friedrich Engels on some of his earlier socialist writing. Later, Sombart was able to use his intimate knowledge of Marxism to good effect to become one of Marx's more authoritative critics towards the end of his life, referring to Marxism and proletariat socialism as aberrations of "true" socialism. Marx's international, proletarian conception of socialism became, for Sombart, the antithesis of nationally based socialism which drew its main principles from 19th-century German romanticism which were to form the core of Nazi beliefs (Sombart, 1937, p. 77 and chapter XI, 1939, p. 7; Sutton, 1948, p. 317).[8] German national socialism sought "its realization in a national union … (A) real order can be established nationally only if it accords with the various external, spiritual and intellectual conditions of the particular nation which God has created" (Sombart, 1937, p. 113).

German romanticism's appeal to God, country, and nature as the foundation of Germany's spiritual greatness particularly appealed to Sombart, for whom "life acquires a meaning only through its relation to a value which is higher than life itself: to country and to God" (Sombart, 1937, p. 150). Prior to the appearance of modern capitalism, Sombart saw a symbiosis on the land between an idealised peasantry who worked the land and a benevolent land-owning class. Each knew their station in life and the importance of honouring the expectations of each calling within a hierarchical and unchanging society. As long as each class continued to be satisfied with their lot and did not strive for more than was necessary for a subsistence living, German society would maintain the balance God intended. However, this nostalgic yearning for a time of greater certainty explicitly excluded German Jews who were seen to have none of the characteristics which entitled them to be regarded as *volkish* (see, for example, Chamberlain, 1911, p. 329). According to Sombart, the ordained social balance was destroyed by the onset of high capitalism (*Hochkapitalismus*) in the 18th century, on the back of which rode the Jews who had never been part of the German *volk* or, as city dwellers, had any stake in traditional communal living (Sombart, 1913, chapters VII and X).

The ideal society and the ideal set of economic relations were epitomised for Sombart by the peasant society of the Middle Ages in Germany. He looked past the grim reality of the daily struggle for existence, which was the lot of the landless peasant and saw a society built upon consideration for the community and each other. It was a society where the spirit of cooperation (*Bedarfsdeckungsprinzip*) characterised relations both within and between classes. People engaged in economic relations to satisfy their basic needs without taking from others the same opportunity (see Commons and Perlman, 1929, p. 79; Dobb, 1947, p. 4). The medieval German theologian Johan Agricola (1496–1570) warned that "trying to be rich is avarice. Now it is not possible for one man to gain wealth without inflicting harm on another, unless he attempt it by means acceptable to God, namely, reticence, thrift, and moderation" (quoted in Strauss, 1971, p. 115). Medieval life revolved around the dictates of nature and the satisfaction of each individual's natural wants. Striving for an excess of goods or wealth was unnatural in God's sight and a dangerous social innovation. The pre-capitalist man was a

> natural man, man as God made him, man who did not stand on his head or run on all fours (as the case today in economic activities). The pre-capitalist man stood firmly on his two legs ... His economic outlook springs quite easily from human nature.
>
> (Sombart, 1967, p. 13)

In the handicraft industries, artisans were to provide for themselves according to their station in life and no more. Their needs were fixed and limited. What mattered most to the artisans in Sombart's extreme, romanticised vision of medieval society was a product they could feel proud of. Payment was almost incidental to their obligation to use their talents as if in the service of God. So committed were they and the peasant to their calling that it grieved them to be parted from the results of their handiwork: "when the dappled cow was led from the stables to the shambles, the old peasant woman's eyes were wet" (Sombart, 1967, p. 18). In a manner similar to their peasant brethren, the artisan's existence was governed by laws that were "thoroughly natural, comparable to the growth of a tree or the singing of a bird" (Sombart, 1967, p. 19).

Consistent with Sombart's misty-eyed longing for a time long past, reappearing throughout his work is his dichotomous division of societies into those that were "individualist" and those that were "universal". Individualist societies (*Gesellschaft*), of which capitalism was the archetype, were loose aggregations of separate, isolated individuals held together by explicit social contracts to guarantee their rights to pursue their selfish ends. In contrast, universalistic societies (*Gemeinschaft*), the ideal form of which was a peasant economy, were living organisms whose service individuals would work for the good of all (Plotnik, 1937, p. 54; Kohn, 1969, p. 16). Change in universalistic societies was infrequent and destructive of existing cooperative relations. Left to themselves, the community concerns of universalistic societies allowed them to maintain an enduring balance between different social levels. They epitomised the stability possible for societies based on an intimate association with, and understanding of, nature and preparedness by everyone to submit themselves to the interests of the community. Progress, argued Sombart (1937, p. 149), was fatal to this romantic conception of the "natural" German.

The origins of German romanticism

The romantic ideal of German society was a nationalistic response to the loss of identity and the humiliation the Germans felt as a consequence of the invasion of Napoleon in the first decade of the 19th century and the rapid spread of French culture (Butler, 1942, p. 30). In particular, they rejected the rationalism of the French Enlightenment that was seen as the means of destroying the organic order of German society. Therefore, adherents of German romanticism in the late 18th and early 19th centuries took upon themselves the responsibility for shaking the German people out of the stupor induced by the seductive changes and events of the late 18th century in France.

The wider effect of the questioning by the French philosophers and scientists of the 18th century contributed to the demise of the old order, the demystification of both nature and an individual's relationship with God. Intuition, faith, and feeling were replaced by reason and rational calculation. Where the Enlightenment project encouraged a logocentric and material approach to the world, the romantics reacted to this by emphasising the metaphysical aspects of existence (Harris, 1942, p. 820). They substituted the rationalist's mechanical conception of God's universe with one that drew close to the beauty of the natural environment. The common enemy for German romantics and nationalists was "Western and identified with beliefs in the rights of man, individualism and political rationalism" (Pulzer, 1994, p. 30; see also Chamberlain, 1916, p. 58). These were qualities that the German romantics were only too ready to attribute to Jews whom, according to Wolfgang Menzel in the 1830s, embodied "all the loathsomeness that lies in the boundless insolence, in the pandering to French fashion, in the malicious … hatred of all things German …" (quoted in Pulzer, 1994, p. 20).

Denied political unity by the Napoleonic wars, Germans turned instead to their past to seek refuge from the spiritual assault of the present and to discover a common cultural identity which they believed had been submerged by the events of history (Halsted, 1965, p. xvi; Mosse, 1970, pp. 8, 10). The call of a more glorious past was all the more appealing at a time when Germany was a loose association of economically backward regions that did not have France's advantage of the well-developed, unified culture which most of the civilised world sought to mimic. Thus, German poets and dramatists were encouraged to seek inspiration in their Teutonic past, from which medieval Germany's folk poetry and epic sagas best captured the mythical, idealistic intent of romanticism. Wilhelm Grimm, of the brothers Grimm, described folk poetry as written by God "as he did the ten commandments; it was not pieced together like the mere work of man" (quoted in Kohn, 1969, p. 56). The prominent romantic Friedrich Schlegel's *An die Deutschen (To the Germans)*, published in 1800, reminded the Germans that their destiny was spiritual (Kohn, 1969, p. 58). Accordingly, the romantic appeal to an idealised past both sought to reassure Germans who were not Jewish that there remained in all of them an unbreakable, incorruptible family bond and to use this past as a template for the future. Man, protested the romantics, was not a free agent whose actions were governed only by the application of objective, relentless reason and base selfish instincts. Thus, the French author Georg Sand observed that romanticism was an era of "emotion rather than reason; the heart opposed to the head" (Furst, 1969, p. 3).

From the writings of Goethe,[9] Klinger, Novalis,[10] and Schiller, romanticism in the late 18th and early 19th centuries spread to art, music, philosophy, politics, and the law. Indeed, the decades spanning either side of the first years of the 19th century constituted a period of great cultural richness in which the different arts shared a common vision of Germany's destiny. Novalis saw the essence of romantic writing and art as the ability to give "what is common place an exalted meaning, what is ordinary a mysterious aspect, what is familiar the impressiveness of the unfamiliar, to the finite an appearance of infinity" (quoted in von Engelhardt, 1988, p. 109). The rich mythology and imagery of the Teutonic sagas and folk tales found expression in the romantic music of Wagner (1813–1883), Beethoven (1770–1827), Weber[11] (1786–1826), Schubert (1797–1828), Schumann (1810–1856), and Liszt (1811–1886). Karl Philipp Emanuel Bach's (1714–1788) *Fantasien, Abschied von meinem Silbermannischen Claver* (1781), Weber's romantic operas and Beethoven's *Pastoral Symphony* and *Fifth Symphony* captured dramatically the passionate exultation of nature and homage to the peasants which were at the heart of romanticism. The folksong (*volkslied*) movement, best of all, was able to express the romantic nostalgia for Germany's medieval past, which had been swept away by the Enlightenment's relentless challenge to the existing order.

In the wake of the Enlightenment came industrialisation, cities, and, for the romantic, the alienation of individuals from each other. The peasants and the artisans, without any say on their part, were torn from the land and herded into large cities to feed the needs of capitalism. In the process, they lost their sense of community, their love of God, the dignity which came from living close to nature, and their spiritual purity was threatened. Indeed, a sense of community could only come from a belief in God. Thus, for Sombart, the worst thing that had happened to Germany and individuals in general was the loss of their faith in God (1937, p. 31). Love could only come from God, "nothing like love can ever come from community of labour, community of production and still much less from community of commerce" (Sombart quoted in Plotnik, 1937, p. 37).

Cities corrupted the *volkish* spirit by pitting individuals against each other and devaluing their contributions to the community. The natural organic order of the peasant economy, which had been the source of Germany's greatness, was destroyed, and in its place appeared an order of Godless artificiality and materialism (Sombart, 1937, p. 32). The peasant economy's folkish spirit (*volksgeist*) was submerged, although not entirely extinguished, by its antithesis and unnatural adversary, the capitalist spirit, which, for Sombart, was embodied in Jews. As the communal structure of medieval society receded, the *volk*, or the German racial community, assumed prominence as an ideal that had endured throughout Germany's past, binding together all "true" *volkish* German people in their common origins and eternal spirit (Mosse, 1970, p. 8; see Herder in Butler, 1942, p. 26). Some romantics believed that this *volkish* spirit was unique to Germany. It was "obvious ... that only the German ... has a folk and is entitled to count on one, and that he alone is capable of real and rational love for his nation" (Fichte quoted in Butler, 1942, p. 46). Their *volkish* nature, announced Schiller, made the Germans the sole repository and guardians of morality (Butler, 1942, p. 30). Therefore, Germans had a duty to live a folkish life, and the State had the obligation to ensure that social conditions were conducive to preserving the *volksgeist* (Sombart, 1937, p. 130).

The State above all

Preservation of the true German nature could only be assured if the State was supreme and each member of society subjugated their individuality to the needs of the State, thereby identifying themselves with the State. If necessary, to achieve this, Sombart advocated that Germany should "take as much land for ourselves as appears necessary" (quoted in Mitzman, 1973, p. 263). Hegel credited the German State with divine qualities, describing it as "the Divine Idea as it exists on Earth" (quoted in Harris, 1942, p. 823). According to the 19th-century romantic Fichte, true freedom is the desire to follow the standards of behaviour and morality inherent in the *volk* (Harris, 1942, p. 822). The pursuit of selfish individualism weakened the State to the detriment of all. Thus, in the interests of the greater good, the State should have the right to override individual wishes whenever these are seen to conflict. Totalitarianism, suggested by the early 19th-century romantic Rademacher, was an inescapable characteristic of German romanticism. Members of the folkish community had meaning in proportion to the extent to which they were prepared to surrender their individuality to the group. Society could then be described as *Gemeinschaft*, not *Gesellschaft* (Harris, 1942, pp. 818, 821). The authority of the State was to be supreme and, given that it emanated from the *volk* and worked in their interests, all laws were to be obeyed as the embodiment of the will and the spirit of the *volk*. The greater the spirituality of the State, promised the romantic writer Novalis, "the more it approaches the poetical, the more joyfully will every citizen ... limit his demand and be ready to make the necessary sacrifice" (quoted in Kohn, 1969, p. 53).

German romanticism and its conception of a special *volk* meant that the world was divided into those who carried within them the German *volksgeist* and those who were the excluded outsiders. In this way, romantics sought to awaken the German people to the threats outsiders posed to their essential German identity, as expressed in the *volksgeist*. It was necessary, therefore, to identify the outsider, especially those who lived in the midst of the German people and coveted the privileges of being accepted as part of the *volk*. The easiest exotics to recognise, reassured the romantics, were business-like Jews who had managed to maintain a strong, separate, and prominent social identity across the centuries. By honing the abilities best suited to capitalism, it was alleged that they had helped sustain capitalism throughout its history and were now reaping considerable benefits at the expense of the *volk*. In 1818, Garlieb Merkel warned his German readers that Jews "had increased their wealth at a terrifying rate. They knew how to gain equality with the Christians everywhere and they zealously set about developing this equality into further privileges" (quoted in Katz, 1980, p. 94). Jews were condemned at the height of the romantic period for being a "widespread band of merchants closely welded by faith ... and outlandish customs ... deliberately inhibiting any participation in any local national association" (quoted in Katz, 1980, p. 87). The German nation, therefore, had been "compelled by virtue of national character to close itself up against them" (quoted in Katz, 1980, p. 87).

Capitalism, accounting, and the Sombart thesis

Sombart's explanation for the disappearance of peasant and handicraft economies and the appearance of capitalism differed in important aspects from the work of Marx. Significantly, Sombart did not see the different economic systems as part of an onward, evolutionary process where material differences between antagonistic classes precipitated the move to another stage. Instead of Marx's dialectical materialism as the motive force of change, Sombart preferred a psychological approach. The impetus for change did not exist outside the participants but was a manifestation of deeper-seated social attitudes and beliefs, which combined to create identifiable psychological predispositions peculiar to each economic epoch. Parsons (1937, p. 498) refers to Sombart's work on capitalism as part of the "main line of German historicoideolistic methodological thought".

Unlike Marx, who was more concerned with the origins and destiny of capitalism, Sombart's mission was to distil the essence of capitalism and to contrast it with the previous handicraft stage. Marx's work, rather than looking backward, possesses a forward momentum leading to the final socialist stage emerging from the remains of capitalism after its inner, contradictory forces had shaken it to pieces. In Marx's conception of the onward march of economic change, the process was evolutionary and continuous. For Sombart, this view of history was too simple and deterministic. Instead of continuities, at "each change in economic organisation we find a break of continuity ... (H)istory does not present itself to the eye of the observer under the guise of an inclined plane; it resembles rather a staircase ..." (Sombart quoted in Pirenne, 1914, pp. 494–495).

The arrival of capitalism was said by Sombart to put an end to the natural harmony of the pre-capitalist society. In the place of the spirit of co-operation came a passion for *Erwerbsprinzip* (unlimited and unrestrained acquisition), a lust for unlimited profit and the habit of rational calculation (Parsons, 1928, p. 646; Sombart, 1937, p. 5, 1967, p. 154). According to Sombart (1937, p. 6), this amounted to the worship by capitalists of the "god of the underworld". Under capitalism, the only values that mattered were those that could be expressed in monetary terms. All other features of life were denied recognition, including "beauty, strength, goodness, wisdom, artistic ability, birth, race, family, traditions ..." (Sombart, 1913, pp. 131, 133, 274, 1937, p. 22). This metamorphosis in the nature of society and economic relations for Sombart resulted from a fundamental mental and spiritual transformation throughout society that Jews embodied and from which they benefited. Each member of society was no longer the centre of divinely ordained and immutable social relations but, instead, was the plaything of anonymous economic forces.

Whereas in pre-capitalist society, the peasant and artisan had no use for calculations of wealth and profitability, or even the need to have the capacity to hold numbers in their head, capitalism favoured a small elite who were able to refine these abilities to the point where they became distorted social and personal pathologies (Sombart, 1937, p. 23, 1967, p. 18). Sombart's simple, almost childlike, pre-capitalist peasant and craftsman had no use for calculation beyond "the knots in the kerchief made by the peasant going to market" (Sombart, 1967, p. 18). In the presence of the unnatural calculating man, the simple peasant or artisan, to whom the desirability of amassed wealth had "never once entered" their head (Sombart, 1967, p. 18), was at a considerable disadvantage. Although the avaricious, untrustworthy businessman with base morals may have been able to get the better of the trusting peasant, he could not take from the peasant their noble dignity. The innocence and lack of guile of the peasant and the artisan, which were the source of their unsophisticated attitude towards others, were the guarantees of their spiritual purity and moral superiority.

In his best known work, the massive *Der Moderne Kapitalismus,* which appeared in three volumes and many editions between 1902 and 1927, Sombart defined capitalism as

> a particular economic system, recognizable as an organisation of trade, consisting invariably of two collaborating sections of population, the owners of the means of production, who also manage them, and

> propertyless workers ..., which displays the two dominant principles of wealth creation and economic rationalism.
>
> (Sombart, 1976, p. 722)

He divided capitalism into three stages: *Frühkapitalismus* (pre-capitalism), which ended before the mid-18th century; *Hochkapitalismus* (high capitalism), 1760–1914, and *Spätkapitalismus* (late capitalism), the period in which Sombart wrote the final volume of *Der Moderne Kapitalismus* (see Usher, 1921–1922, p. 528). His abiding primary interest was the period of high capitalism. Business in the first stage was led by merchants, artisans, and adventurers, while the capitalist entrepreneur dominated the second stage.[12] The main feature of *Hochkapitalismus* and *Spätkapitalismus* is the unrestrained pursuit of profit.

Each economic system in Sombart's schema had three defining features: "a form of organisation, a technique, and a mental attitude or spirit", which was unique to each economic epoch (Sombart quoted in Parsons, 1928, p. 644; Parsons, 1937, p. 496). Most significant was the spirit that defined an age. This recognisable spirit or *geist*, the presence of which Weber, Hegel, and other German idealists also recognised (Parsons, 1928, p. 645; Harris, 1942, p. 824), was "the sum total of the purposes, motives, and principles that determine men's behaviour in economic life" and gives each economic system its singular form (Sombart, 1919, Vol. I, p. 25, 1929, p. 14, 1939, pp. 5, 7). The capitalist spirit, "the spirit that rules our life and directs the fate of the universe" (Sombart, 1967, p. 22), was a combination of a spirit of enterprise, which was associated with acquisitiveness and competition, and a bourgeois spirit, which for Sombart was epitomised by methods of exact rational calculation, careful business planning and efficiency (Sombart, 1913, p. 160). These two spirits created capitalism by transforming traditional society and placing the natural man of pre-capitalism in an alien environment governed by what had been previously alien motives. Competition was substituted for cooperation, and sufficiency was supplanted by excess in the relentless "institutionalisation of self interest" (Sutton, 1948, p. 327).

Sombart portrayed capitalism as knowing no bounds and unable to recognise the social consequences of its limitless striving. Capitalist economic activity became the end rather than a means as it carried all before it with its persuasive logic of calculation and accumulation, eventually to be transformed into "a compulsive institutionalised system" (Parsons, 1928, p. 650; Sombart, 1937, p. 498). Capitalist businessmen were "occupied day and night in an almost feverish restlessness in order to bring about the most practical and rational shaping of economic and technical processes" (Sombart, 1909, p. 5). Accordingly, capitalism reduced "human modes of thought from the refined, the abstract, and the qualitative to the debased, the concrete, and the quantitative ...; (the) reduction of all relations to cash terms ..." (Introduction to Sombart, 1976, p. xvi). Essential to the spirit of capitalism was "the tendency, the habit ... the capacity, to think of the universe in terms of figures, and to transform these figures into a well knit system of income and expenditure" (Sombart, 1967, p. 125). In particular, double entry bookkeeping was "of the greatest significance for the full development of the capitalistic enterprise" (Sombart, 1919, p. 266). It allowed the businessman to trace the circulation of his capital through the business, from the initial injection of the capital to where it eventually bore fruit as profits and then back to the capital account. Capitalism, argued Sombart, was inconceivable without double entry bookkeeping.

Double entry bookkeeping allowed the concept of capital, created organisations dedicated to adding to the owner's capital, gave visibility to profit and allowed the separation of business activities from the other affairs of the owners (Sombart, 1919, pp. 273–274; Yamey, 1949, p. 99; Winjum, 1972, p. 236). It was as a result of the spread of double entry bookkeeping that "conditions were created that permitted the essential ideas of the capitalistic economic system to be fully developed: the creation of wealth and the idea of economic rationality" (Sombart, 1919, p. 272). Economic rationalism depended upon a plan to order business activity, which centred upon the need for efficiency and the ability to calculate the rate of progress towards the goals (Sombart, 1913, pp. 160–161). Thus, double entry bookkeeping was a powerful means to unify business goals and, thereby, efficiently direct its energies. However attractive this may have appeared, Sombart warned that it did not come without a substantial cost to both individuals and the society that had to accommodate the excesses of capitalism. In the frantic rush for great wealth,

> the amount invested ... is separated from all natural objectives of human welfare.... He who buries himself in double entry bookkeeping forgets all quantities of goods and work, forgets all the organic limitations of the necessity to satisfy human wants, and satisfies himself solely with the idea of wealth ...
>
> (Sombart, 1919, p. 272)

Jewish businessmen were accused of being at the forefront of the cynical, self-serving use of double entry bookkeeping envisaged by Sombart.

The "Jewish Question" and capitalism

Sombart's seemingly innocuous observations about the contributions of Jews to modern capitalism reinforced well-entrenched German and European stereotypes of Jews, which portrayed them as aliens wherever they were to be found. Sustained attacks on, and caricatures of, Jews by the late 19th century had become part of the German cultural tradition. At no time in Germany between 1871 and 1933, observes Pulzer (1994, p. 23), were Jews seen as anything other than different from other German citizens. According to one 17th-century German writer, Jews were "a race faithless and pusillanimous, enemies to all the world and especially to all Christians, caring not whose house burns so long as they may warm themselves at the coals ..." (Sombart, 1913, p. 133). They were well known to derive

> their profits *from* war, murder and assassination; while other peoples seek to derive it *by means of* war, murder, or assassination. Without a navy, without an army, the Jews work their way up to the position of being the mighty ones of the earth, using as their weapons those of the Florentines - money, treaties ... and knowledge.
>
> (Sombart, 1967, p. 101)

As a result, cultural stereotyping by Sombart was able to provide sustenance to the fledgling Nazi party in the 1920s as it sought firstly to gain recognition and then vindication for its policies of exclusion and victimisation in the 1930s. As the frequency and severity of attacks on Jews mounted after the Nazi rise to power in January 1933, Sombart took the opportunity to give further exposure to his views that pointed out the culpability of Jews for the social and economic problems Germany was facing. While he did not publicly advocate the extreme treatment favoured by the National Socialists, Sombart found himself in general agreement with their mistrust and condemnation of German Jews. As contributions to the substantial body of anti-Semitic writings of the interwar years, his condemnation of Jews was neither innocuous nor inconsequential in the contributory legitimacy this accorded anti-Semitic propaganda.

Jews were condemned in Sombart's eyes because they personified the spirit of capitalism. According to Sombart, there was a unique Jewish spirit that was effectively the same thing as the spirit of capitalism. Judaism, argued Sombart (1913, p. 205) in *Jews and Modern Capitalism,* provided the moral basis for capitalism; the same spirit was in each. Judaism, unlike any other religion,

> perfected and carried to their logical conclusions all those teachings that were beneficial to the capitalist spirit.... (A)ll those ethical regulations that were favourable to the development of the capitalist spirit were influential in Judaism a thousand years longer than in Christianity.
>
> (Sombart, 1967, pp. 264–265)

Sombart proclaimed Jews to be masters of the rationalisation of the world and, as history had shown, were best able to use modern accounting to get their own way. Double entry bookkeeping, as a means of rationalising business, for Sombart epitomised the unpalatable essential nature of Jews, which starkly contrasted with the virtuous German *volkish* spirit. Double entry bookkeeping allowed Jews, as a recognisable social grouping in Germany, to give full vent to their lust for money and wealth. Sombart agreed with the Nazis that those who most benefited from capitalism's encouragement of the selfish, lustful pursuit of profit had done so at the expense of their fellow German citizens. It was the responsibility of the State, therefore, to retrieve the advantage Jews had created so that it benefited the Jews' defenceless gentile neighbours. It was Jews who set out to "impregnate economic life with a modern spirit because it is they who first bring the innermost idea of capitalism to its full development ..." (Sombart quoted in Pulzer, 1994, p. 9; Sombart, 1913, p. 5, 50). Jewish felicity with rational calculation accustomed them

> to a mode of living contrary to ... Nature and therefore also to an economic system like the capitalist, which is likewise contrary to ... Nature. What in reality is the idea of making profit, what is economic rationalism, but the application to economic activities of the rules by which the Jewish religion shaped Jewish life. Before capitalism could develop the natural man had to be changed out of all recognition, and a rationalistically minded mechanism introduced in his stead.
>
> (Sombart, 1913, p. 238)

Recognising his romantic heritage, Sombart portrayed Jews as material, urban[13] and driven by money in all matters. These characteristics distinguished them from the genuine German *volk* and defined them as its antithesis. Their physical appearance also marked them as different. According to Chamberlain and Sombart, Jews had a "scientifically proven" characteristic physiognomy which marked them as a different species to the natural German (Chamberlain, 1911, p. xciii; Sombart, 1913, pp. 289–291; see also Mosse, 1970, p. 64). Their unscrupulous behaviour in business, whereby they "were never conscious of doing wrong, of being guilty of commercial immorality" (Sombart, 1913, p. 129), also made them distinctive. Jews were referred to pejoratively as the "commercial jackals" of the world, arriving in a timely fashion to take advantage of the misfortunes of others. They never initiated or created anything of lasting spiritual value, preferring instead to lie in wait for opportunities to use their finely honed skills. Consequently, "the Jew" lacked

> the quality of instinctive understanding; he responds less to feeling than to intellect. ... Akin to this characteristic is that of a certain lack of impressionability, a certain lack of receptive and creative genius. ... He does not think of his environment as something alive, and that is why he has lost his true conception of life ... of its being an organism ...
>
> (Sombart, 1913, pp. 261–263)

Being perceived as pariahs in Germany for centuries, indeed in all European societies, it was usual for many occupations to be closed to Jews.

Therefore, they were given little choice but to turn to those occupations overwhelmingly associated with business and finance, which their gentile neighbours had shunned (see Weber's comments in Pulzer, 1994, p. 10). Most facets of the business world, especially usury, were rejected as not worthy of good Christians and dangerous to their souls (Exodus 22:25; Leviticus 25:36, 37; Deuteronomy 23:19; Pacioli, 1974, Chapter 2). Governments were only too eager in the Middle Ages and later centuries to encourage Jews to take a dominant role in business. Monarchs needed capital to fight their wars and to sustain their lavish lifestyles. Jewish financiers proved to be reliable sources of funds and compliant victims should rulers not be able to repay the loans. Jews rarely enjoyed the same rights at law as other citizens and could be induced to accept greater social recognition for their families in exchange for the forgiveness of debts owed to them. These pacts of convenience were important in the rise of powerful Jewish family businesses by providing a measure of protection for their assets and an uncertain means of gaining some social legitimacy.

Sombart believed that the persecution suffered by the Jews and their resulting dispersion throughout the world had eventually been turned by them to their great advantage. Business networks established based on a common religious affiliation and a shared sense of alienation provided a strong basis for building trust (Sombart, 1913, pp. 169–170; Sée, 1968, p. 22). In an era when trading across national boundaries and over long and perilous distances was fraught with great uncertainty, long-established commercial and blood relationships between families protected Jewish businesses from many of the uncertainties facing their gentile competitors. These advantages, decreed Sombart, gave the Jews a pernicious influence, which sapped the spiritual strength of Germany. It has been claimed, therefore, that it was the responsibility of German socialism to free the country of the Jewish spirit, which sustained selfish capitalism, thereby bringing with it a "decomposing Jewish influence on our popular life" (German Conservative Party, 1892, as quoted in Pulzer, 1994, p. 2).

The spirit of capitalism was not a feature of "Heroic People",[14] that is, Germans, but of the trading peoples, of which the Jews were the leading example (Sombart, 1967, p. 217; Lebovics, 1969, p. 63). Heroic People had a strong attachment to the soil and valued beauty, loyalty, and honesty above all else. Capitalism was anti-heroic, unnatural, and injurious to the soul of the nation. Jews were accused of and condemned for a preference for the things of the world and not those of the spirit, which arose from within their unchanging base nature. Therefore, it was something over which they had little control. It was a predisposition, an inbuilt bias that they could do little to change as individuals and as a community. The State needed to recognise this, claimed Sombart, not for the purposes of eradicating entirely the Jewish influence from Germany, for Sombart believed that this might be politically impossible and potentially injurious to the German nation, but rather to contain it in the interests of the German

State and the German *volk* (Sombart, 1937, p. 180). If the essential Jewish nature could not be changed, the State had to recognise that Jews were different and would always remain outside the German *volk*. They were strangers and foreigners. As strangers, they had the suspect morals of strangers (Sombart, 1913, p. 177; Sombart referred to in Mitzman, 1973, p. 252). Thus, in all their business dealings they were wily, cunning, and indefatigable in their pursuit of profits. Even as "the natives are still in their warm beds the new-comers stand without in the sharp morning air of dawn ... They must of necessity determine ... what is the shortest cut to their goal" (Sombart, 1913, p. 176). As a result, they should be treated differently for their own benefit and that of the State. Indeed, according to Sombart, Jews could not expect to have the same rights as other German citizens (Sombart, 1937, p. 176).

To support his contention that Jews should not be treated as equals with their fellow Germans, Sombart pointed out that in pre-Wilhelmian German society, which had enjoyed a long period of relative social calm, Jews had been excluded from positions of judicial administration and the military. He lamented that "had this practice been retained and had the Jews been assigned to other important fields ... the German fatherland and ... the Jews themselves, would have been spared heavy afflictions" (Sombart, 1937, p. 177). It was the responsibility of the State to identify the different spirits of each group within its population and then to take advantage of these differences: "the state must endeavour to select individuals, in accordance with their nature, from the different races and with them build up its populations" (Sombart, 1937, p. 176). A form of eugenics was called for, which would be limited to economic segregation, not expulsion. History, concluded Sombart, had shown that expelling Jews had led to the financial ruin of the host country (Sombart, 1913, pp. 21, 171). Thus, Sombart did not believe that having a racially pure population was possible, however attractive "overcoming and removing" the Jewish capitalist spirit might be for Germany. To do so ultimately would be to harm Germany.

Conclusion

Although Sombart's nationalist prescriptions to combat the ills of 20th-century capitalism were decisively discredited by the events of World War II, his passionate belief in a unique "spirit", which is the hallmark and driving force of capitalism, continues to influence debate. His belief in the benefits that German socialism could bring to his country determined his opposition to capitalism and his judgement of the Jews whom he saw were best able, through the circumstances of their history, race, and nature, to selfishly take advantage of the worst aspects of capitalism.

While some of Sombart's beliefs may have changed direction during his life, he did not deviate from his conviction that the attributes that best equipped an individual to live successfully in a capitalist society appeared to a remarkable degree in Jews. Thus, his praise of double entry bookkeeping was used as a means to damn Jewish businessmen and Jews in general, not because he was an advocate of the virtues of double entry bookkeeping. While historians have suggested that he may have seen in double entry bookkeeping an appealing system of almost faultless logical financial calculation, he primarily used it to demonstrate the compatibility between what he condemned as the calculating, rational nature of Jews and the skills best suited to take advantage of the worst excesses of modern capitalism. The Jews could not have been as successful without double entry bookkeeping, and double entry bookkeeping would not have been so pervasive without Jews.

This chapter is based on the paper by Warwick Funnell titled "Distortions in History, accounting and the paradox of Werner Sombart", which originally appeared in Abacus in 2001, *37*(1), 55–78. The author would like to thank the publisher, Blackwell, for permission to use this material.

Notes

1 In a similar vein, Spengler describes double entry bookkeeping in metaphysical terms as "a pure Analysis of the space of values, referred to a co-ordinate system, of which the origin is the 'Firm'" (quoted in Yamey, 1964, footnote 7, p. 119).

2 Sombart (1913, p. 7) defined a Jew as someone who professed the Jewish faith. Sombart consistently used the stronger, pejoratively laden term "the Jew" in preference to simply "Jews". The effect and intent of the two descriptions are different and were knowingly so when used by Sombart.

3 The term "romantic" is used in a historical rather than a colloquial sense in this chapter. It originally referred to narrative prose and verse, which arose in the Middle Ages in Europe. It represented a break from the formal structures and limitations of classical literature, which until the 18th century had been the dominant paradigm. Romantic aspirations became synonymous with attempts to break from classical formality with its tight rein on emotions. Instead, intuition and imagination were allowed greater freedom.

4 Double entry bookkeeping was only one factor amongst several which Sombart believed contributed to the emergence of capitalism. Most importantly, capitalism had to wait for the establishment of the modern State and the discovery of immense deposits of precious metals in the New World. Greater national and individual wealth, along with technological advances, eventually led to the establishment of new forms of business enterprise, which had as its guiding aim the unlimited accumulation of profits. The technology of the late Middle Ages and Renaissance substituted scientific, rational discovery for the accumulated knowledge that came from experience. Further, the Renaissance presaged an emphasis on measuring and quantification (Crosby, 1997).

5 Pirenne (1914) accused Sombart and his supporters in their single-minded pursuit of their favoured theories of dishonestly excluding examples of towns in the 14th and 15th centuries, notably in Italy, which were far more advanced than German medieval towns upon which Sombart developed his theories. So obvious were the differences that Pirenne (1914, p. 496) accuses Sombart of doing "violence to reality". Later critics supported Pirenne's denunciation of Sombart's approach to scholarship, describing Sombart as led by preconceived ideas instead of historical fact (Carosso, 1952, p. 28; for other criticisms, see Dobb, 1947).

6 His pro-Nazi sympathies were expressed further in the publication *Vom Menschen* (1938), also referred to as *Versuch einer geistwissenschaftlichen Anthropologie.*
7 During its second phase in Germany, the music of Richard Strauss epitomised the longing for Germany's simpler, spiritual past. The mood was captured in Strauss' *Till Eulenspiegels lustige Streiche* (1895), *sprach Zarathustra* (1896), and *Ein Heldenleben* (1898) (Abraham, 1979, p. 794).
8 For additional biographical material on Sombart, see Lebovics (1969, pp. 51–53) and Mitzman (1973, pp. 140–141).
9 Goethe has been described as the intellectual centre of German romanticism and the "last and the greatest of the eighteenth century literary figures who made German culture the equal of the older civilisations of the West" (Kohn, 1969, p. 22).
10 Novalis was the pseudonym for the wealthy aristocrat Friedrich Freiher von Hardenberg.
11 Karl Maria von Weber is generally recognised as the leading exponent of romantic music. According to Einstein (1985, p. 2429), he was the first national German musician for which the *volk* was given a strong voice.
12 Soon after the first two volumes of *Der moderne Kapitalismus* were published in 1902, Sombart continued his examination of capitalism with *The Jews and Modern Capitalism* (1911) and *The Quintessence of Capitalism* (1913).
13 Pulzer (1994, pp. 2, 4–5) confirms that German Jews in the 19th century came to be increasingly concentrated in the cities and by 1910, over a quarter of Germany's Jews lived in Berlin.
14 Mosse (1970, pp. 63–65) suggested that a good example of the portrayal of the heroic nature of Germans and the stereotyping of the Jews as the opposite was Felix Dahn's very popular book, *Fight for Rome*, published in 1867. The heroes are the Germanic Goths, who are honest, courageous, and pure. Their enemies, the Italians, are betrayed by Jochem the Jew.

References

Abraham, G. (1979). *The Concise Oxford History of Music.* Oxford: Oxford University Press.

Abraham, G. (1982). *The Age of Beethoven 1790–1830.* Oxford: Oxford University Press.

Bryer, R. (1991). Accounting for the "Railway Mania" of 1845 – a Great Railway Swindle? *Accounting, Organisations and Society*, *16*(5/6), 439–486.

Butler, R. (1942). *The Roots of National Socialism.* Boston, MA: E.P. Dutton & Co.

Carosso, V. (1952). Werner Sombart's Contribution to Business History. *Bulletin of the Business Historical Society*, *26*, 27–49.

Chamberlain, H. (1911). *The Foundations of the Nineteenth Century.* London: John Lane.

Chamberlain, H. (1916). *The Ravings of a Renegade.* Peterborough: Jarrold and Sons.

Commons, J., and Perlman, S. (1929, March). Review of Der Moderne Kapitalismus. *The American Economic Review*, *XIX*, 78–88.

Crosby, A. (1997). *The Measure of Reality: Quantification and Western Society, 1250–1600.* Cambridge: Cambridge University Press.

Dobb, M. (1947). *Studies in the Development of Capitalism.* London: Routledge and Kegan Paul.

Einstein, A. (1985). Carl Maria von Weber. In: O. Thompson (Ed.). *The International Cyclopedia of Music and Musicians*, 11th Edition. New York: Dodd, Mead & Co.

Furst, L. (1969). *Romanticism.* North Yorkshire: Methuen.

Halsted, J. (1965). *Romanticism: Problems of Definition Explanation and Evaluation*. Lexington: D.C. Heath & Co.

Harris, A. (1942, December). Sombart and German National Socialism. *The Journal of Political Economy*, *L*(6), 805–835.

Katz, J. (1980). *From Prejudice to Destruction: Anti-Semitis, 1700–1933*. Cambridge, MA: Harvard University Press.

Kohn, H. (1969). *The Mind of Germany*. New York: Macmillan.

Lebovics, H. (1969). *Social Conservatism and the Middle Classes in Germany 1914–33*. Princeton, NJ: Princeton University Press.

Mitzman, A. (1973). *Sociology and Estrangement: Three Sociologists of Imperial Germany*. New York: Alfred A. Knopf.

Mosse, G. (1970). *Germans and Jews*. New York: Howard Fertig.

Most, K. (1972, October). Sombart's Propositions Revisited. *Accounting Review*, *4*, 722–34.

Pacioli, L. (1974). *An Original Translation of the Treatise on Double Entry Bookkeeping*. Tokyo: Shoseki.

Parsons, T. (1928). "Capitalism" in Recent German Literature: Sombart and Weber. *The Journal of Political Economy*, *36*(6), 641–661.

Parsons, T. (1937). *The Structure of Social Action*. New York: McGraw Hill.

Pirenne, H. (1914). The Stages in the Social History of Capitalism. *The American Historical Review*, *XIX* (October 1913–July 1914), 494–515.

Pirenne, H. (1961). *Economic and Social History of Medieval Europe*. London: Penguin.

Plotnik, M. (1937). *Werner Sombart and His Type of Economics*. Berlin: Eco Press.

Pulzer, P. (1994). *Jews and the German State: The Political History of a Minority, 1848–1933*. London: Blackwell.

Sartre, J-P. (1948). *Portrait of the Anti-Semite*. London: Secker and Warburg.

Sée, H. (1968). *Modern Capitalism: Its Origin and Evolution*. New York: Burt Franklin.

Sombart, W. (1909). *Socialism and the Social Movement*. London: J.M. Dent and Co.

Sombart, W. (1913). *The Jews and Modern Capitalism*. London: T. Fisher Unwin.

Sombart, W. (1919). *Der Moderne Kapitalismus. Vol. II*, 3rd Edition. Berlin: Dunker and Humblot.

Sombart, W. (1929). Economic Theory and Economic History. *The Economic History Review*, *II*(1), 1–19.

Sombart, W. (1937). *A New Social Philosophy*. Princeton, NJ: Princeton University Press.

Sombart, W. (1939). *Weltanschaung, Science and Economy*. Lancaster, PA: Veritas Press.

Sombart, W. (1967). *The Quintessence of Capitalism*. New York: Howard Fertig.

Sombart, W. (1976). *Why Is There No Socialism in the United States*? New York: Macmillan.

Strauss, G. (Ed.). (1971). *Manifestations of Discontent in Germany on the Eve of Reformation*. Bloomington, IN: Indiana University Press.

Sutton, F. (1948). The Social and Economic Philosophy of Werner Sombart. In: H. Barnes (Ed.). *An Introduction to the History of Sociology*. Chicago: University of Chicago Press.

Usher, A. (1921–1922). The Genesis of Modern Capitalism. *Quarterly Journal of Economics*, *36*, 525–535.

von Engelhardt, D. (1988). Romanticism in Germany. In: R. Porter, and M. Teich (Eds.). *Romanticism in National Context.* Cambridge: Cambridge University Press.

Winjum, J. (1972). *The Role of Accounting in the Economic Development of England 1500–1750.* Urbana, IL: Centre for International Education and Research in Accounting.

Yamey, B. (1940, November). The Functional Development of Double Entry Bookkeeping. *The Accountant*, *2*, 333–342.

Yamey, B. (1949). Scientific Bookkeeping and the Rise of Capitalism. *The Economic History Review*, 2nd series, *1*(2&3), 99–113.

Yamey, B. (1964). Accounting and the Rise of Capitalism: Further Notes on a Theme by Sombart. *Journal of Accounting Research*, *2*(2), 117–136.

4 Popular culture and totalitarianism

Accounting for propaganda in Italy under the Fascist regime (1934–1945)

Valerio Antonelli, Michele Bigoni, Warwick Funnell, Emanuela Mattia Cafaro, and Enrico Deidda Gagliardo

Introduction

Totalitarian regimes depend upon a unique combination of power structures, creation of a unique identity, the use of terror to intimidate and destroy opposition and propaganda (Gentile, 2013). Propaganda constitutes practices which allow a totalitarian regime to build a new "fictitious realm" based on values, beliefs, images, standards of life that are quite different from the previous political and social systems (Zamponi, 2003). Totalitarian propaganda is meant to become an element of people's lives which allows "the organization of the entire texture of life according to an ideology …" (Arendt, 1962, p. 363). In *Mein Kampf* Hitler reminded his followers that:

> Propaganda tries to force a doctrine upon an entire people […] *The first task of propaganda is the winning of people for the future organization*; the first task of the organization is the winning of people for the continuation of propaganda. *The second task of propaganda is the destruction of the existing condition and the permeation of this condition with the new doctrine*, while the second task of the organization must be the fight for power, so that by it, it will achieve the final success of the doctrine.
>
> (Hitler, 1941, pp. 850–851, emphasis added)

The essential characteristic of totalitarian propaganda is the prejudice created by confusing reality with truth, most tragically manifested with the Holocaust (Arendt, 1994). The "truth-reality" dichotomy created by a totalitarian regime requires the strict control of all modes of disseminating the lies and a rigid control of all sources of information, with the arts and cultural activities and symbols expected to take a leading role. As the main means to engage imagination, totalitarian governments should control artists and intellectuals, thereby organising and controlling "the regimentation of all intellectual and artistic life" (Arendt, 1962, p. 429).

DOI: 10.4324/9781032685328-4

Intervention in the artistic and cultural domain by States and powerful elites has served multiple purposes throughout history, ranging from revealing the power, splendour, and might of a sovereign to promoting the educational development of the citizenry around common values (McGuigan, 1996; Bigoni et al., 2018). States have long sought to intervene in the production of cultural artefacts for, in the exercise of governmental power, art and culture have been recognised as showing "significant governance potential" (Jeacle, 2012, p. 587). Art and culture can be "rendered useful by being harnessed to governmental programmes aimed at transforming the attributes – mental and behavioural – of extended populations" (Bennet, 2003, p. 70). Cultural institutions have the potential to strengthen the bonds of a community around common values (Berezin, 1991) and allow individuals to form "imagined solidarities not based on family structures, religion or other traditional social bonds" (Jones, 2011, p. 51). This political importance of art and culture has been especially obvious throughout history with totalitarian regimes. These regimes seek to influence and control all aspects of an individual's cultural and social life and, ultimately, to manage the population of a State, understood as an organic body, within a broader, far-reaching domination plan (Gurian, 1978; Žižek, 2002).

The present chapter examines the way in which "accounting can significantly impact the cultural context of a nation" (Jeacle and Miller, 2016, p. 3) in a totalitarian State, thereby influencing people's perception of the State and, therefore, the power that it can exercise. Despite the importance given to the arts as a political device and the human and material devastation resulting from totalitarian oppression throughout history, the contributions of accounting practices as a political artefact within the cultural domain in the achievement of the goals of totalitarian regimes have yet to receive a commensurate presence in the critical accounting literature. Studies have been mainly focused on democratic, liberal States where the need to exert power and influence in less obvious ways has meant that deceptively neutral, and even benign, practices such as accounting have become important tools of government (Ellwood and Greenwood, 2016; Antonelli et al., 2020; Abdullah and Khadaroo, 2022; Ferry and Slack, 2022).

This chapter reveals the ways in which arts and culture as the means to exercise power to persecute Jews were enlisted by the Italian Fascists to construct a reality that was consistent with their values and beliefs and how accounting practices were essential to this process. Very early, the Fascists were acutely aware of the potential of art and other cultural artefacts as weapons of propaganda to create a Fascist "popular culture" in the implementation of their idea of a Fascist totalitarian State. The chapter is structured as follows. The next section reviews the political scenario in which the Ministry of Popular Culture was established, that is, the construction of a Fascist totalitarian State and the contributions of popular culture to this endeavour, will then be presented. This is followed by a detailed analysis of accounting, funding, and reporting practices in the efforts by the Fascists to intervene in the artistic and cultural domain. The results are then discussed, and conclusions are provided.

Accounting in totalitarian States

Accounting practices have been enlisted to exercise extreme forms of power, notably through the beliefs that these regimes sought to spread. In Nazi Germany, most notoriously and tragically, accounting numbers were instrumental in the attempted extermination of European Jews, the implementation of the "Final Solution". Accounting numbers were the means by which Jews when captured were denied their humanity and, thus, their right to exist. Jewish prisoners sent to the extermination camps to be killed became mere numbers, data to be processed, thereby facilitating the efficiency with which the Nazis sought the extermination of Jews and helping bureaucrats to feel detached from and not responsible for the consequences of their actions (Funnell, 1998; Lippman and Wilson, 2007; Twyford, 2021; Twyford and Funnell, 2023). Walker (2000) identified the way in which the accounting profession was ultimately complicit in this process as part of the Nazi's Aryanisation of Germany. Research has shown also how academics were expected to account for their adherence to the beliefs of the Nazis rather than professional values or scientific achievements (Detzen and Hoffmann, 2020; see also Fülbier, 2021).

Among those organisations that play an important role in ensuring the spread and acceptance of an extreme partisan message in a totalitarian State, cultural institutions and the high regard with which they are held by the population are particularly important (Berezin, 1991). In Fascist Italy, a prominent example was the internationally renowned Alla Scala Opera House in Milan which changed significantly as the Fascists tightened their grip on a cultural organisation that was deemed essential to spread Fascist beliefs to all social classes (Bigoni, 2021; Bigoni et al., 2021). If, in the pre-Fascist period, the Opera House had been a privilege of the wealthy, during their rule the Fascists sought to open it to the working class. This priority was especially evident in the prominence given to the information contained in accounting reports that was needed by both the Municipality in which the Opera House was located and the central government in Rome to appreciate whether the Opera House had been able to attract a wider, more diverse audience. Reporting on attendance at performances was much more important than accounting for financial returns, whilst the presence of values that resonated Fascist ideology took precedence over financial considerations when deciding which shows were to be staged. Accounting became the means to construct the Opera House as a truly Fascist organisation.

Accounting practices and their rhetoric were also mobilised by the Fascists to control another important cultural organisation, the University of Ferrara (Papi et al., 2019). The University was one of the few in the country to have been set up as a "Free University", one which did not depend on State funding and could organise teaching and research activities without referring to government priorities. The State sought to weaken the institution by questioning its financial sustainability, which the University resisted by re-appropriating accounting discourses and turning them against the government. Unexpected and initially successful resistance meant that the State had to change its strategy by "starving" the organisation of funds. This included limitations to the fees that the University could charge and the imposition of new, debilitating investments. Local funders soon became unable to bear the pressure generated by State interventions, which ultimately caused the University to adhere to government demands in order to receive the resources it needed to survive.

Fascist popular culture was a "manifestation of an individual's social, spiritual and historical action" (Partito Nazionale Fascista, 1936, p. 4). This meant that although the Fascists did not obviously dictate the content of cultural artefacts, they expected products to be inspired by the new "spiritual ethos" promoted by the regime. Reporting that was mandated by the Fascists for the use of resources in the achievement of Fascist goals in the field of popular culture used accounting "numbers" to document the government's actions. These reporting practices involved both financial and non-financial information that was mainly documented by means of the parliamentary debates concerning matters of propaganda and popular culture in the Kingdom of Italy and the minutes of the cabinet of the Republic of Salò. Parliamentary debates were informed by accounting information, which was the main means to demonstrate the thorough nature of government action and the results it achieved.

Accounting records have the potential to offer insights into epochs and events that are not limited to traditional means used in historiographical analyses, most especially laws, policy documents, speeches, or diaries of eminent political figures. These records provide evidence of which political objectives actors sought to achieve and how they were pursued. Accounting data can provide a more reliable understanding of the real intentions behind political plans, as the allocation of resources or the issues on which accounting reports focus can even contradict the ostensible goals proclaimed by political leaders, thereby exposing the true nature of a government. Accounting records have the potential also to provide quantifiable evidence of the results of political plans and identify whether the original goals had been achieved and to what extent. Consistently, with the development of a narrative of the events surrounding Fascist propaganda as they emerged from the accounting documents, this study recognises the role of accounting records as a crucial tool for developing social history through less obvious sources (Jeacle, 2009; McWatters and Lemarchand, 2010; Pinto and West, 2017; Stacchezzini et al., 2023).

The totalitarian project of Fascism in Italy and the "new Fascist man"

The Fascists' rise to power following the March on Rome in 1922 marks a critical point in the transformation of Italy; first into an illiberal, dictatorial State, most especially through the so-called "very Fascist laws" in 1925–1926, and then into a totalitarian political system which aimed at identifying society, and hence individuals, with the Fascist State (De Felice,

1996a, 1996b). The Fascist totalitarian space was meant to occupy all aspects of an individual's social and moral life for, according to Mussolini (1935, p. 3), "everything is in the State, nothing human or spiritual exists, and even less has any value, outside the State. In this sense Fascism is totalitarian and the Fascist State … interprets, develops and boosts the life of the people". The Fascist totalitarian project therefore aimed at fulfilling an "anthropological revolution"; the construction of the "new Fascist man" (Bernhard and Klinkhammer, 2017). Initially this was not used to denigrate and exclude Jews.

The "perfect" Fascist man was exulted as a brave dominator and source of civilisation (Gentile, 2013) who displayed distinctive characteristics, including a civic and collective consciousness inherited from the tradition of imperial Rome, which was based on values encompassing modesty and a willingness to sacrifice oneself. It also required a fighting spirit, toughness, and ruthlessness in stark contrast to the stereotype of "Italians, the good people" and to the beliefs of the "decadent" liberal society that Fascism had replaced (Bernhard and Klinkhammer, 2017).

Arts and culture were deemed to be essential to the creation of the "new Fascist man" (Gentile, 2014). Conversion of the "chaotic masses" into a new people fully committed to Fascist values required a strong intervention by the State in the artistic and cultural sphere (Zamponi, 2003; Adinolfi, 2012). To the Fascists, the ultimate goal of cultural production was the "elevation of the human spirit", which could only be achieved when an individual's "improvement in knowledge and self-education" led to action that was consistent with the cultural humus generated by the Fascists (Partito Nazionale Fascista, 1936, p. 4). The essential role of culture as a part of the propaganda machinery was very evident when, in 1934, the Government Press Bureau, established in 1922, became the Under-Secretariat of State for Press and Propaganda. The Under-Secretariat was divided into three divisions: Italian Press, Foreign Press, and Propaganda. In the same year, another division was established, the Division of Cinematography, which was responsible for supervising the production of movies on behalf of the government (Cole, 1938). Soon after, in 1935, the Under-Secretariat was transformed into the Ministry of Press and Propaganda, which was composed of six divisions: Italian Press, Foreign Press, Propaganda, Cinematography, Tourism, and Theatre, through which the Fascist conception of what constituted popular culture was shaped (Regno d'Italia, 1936a).

On 27 May 1937, Mussolini changed the name of the Ministry of Press and Propaganda to the Ministry of Popular Culture, which did not lead to any significant modification in its organisation. The Ministry was to play a crucial role in constructing the "new Fascist man" by promoting, implementing, financing, and controlling campaigns acting on the cultural and anthropological beliefs of Italians. The new name given to the Ministry confirmed the crucial role that it had to perform as part of the Fascist indoctrination of Italians (Anonymous, 1937b). The official reason for the

Ministry's name change was the meaning that the regime associated with "popular culture". However, the reality was that the new name for the Ministry indicated its now broader goals. Indeed, the former Minister of Press and Propaganda, Dino Alfieri, who was appointed by Mussolini as the first Minister of Popular Culture, pointed out that the change was due to the State's need to exert control not only over propaganda but also over the generation and transmission of popular culture as a means to "educate" the masses. This would be instrumental in controlling the population and ensuring their allegiance to the regime. The Ministry of Popular Culture was also later part of the government structure of the Republic of Salò. The Ministry was reorganised into six Directorates to reflect the new propaganda priorities in times of conflict: Internal Radio and Press, Foreign Radio and Press, Cultural Exchanges, Performing Arts, Sport and Tourism, and Personnel and General Services[1] (Scardaccione, 2002, pp. 143–144).

During Alfieri's time as Minister of Popular Culture and that of his successor, Alessandro Pavolini (31 October 1939–25 July 1943), staff numbers quickly grew from 183 to more than 800. At the same time, as shown in Table 4.1, the Ministry and the government exercised their control, influence, or direct management of many public institutions and organisations involved in managing propaganda activities. Crucial among these was the *Istituto Nazionale Luce*, which produced movies and newsreels and had been set up as a stock company in 1924. It was turned into a non-profit entity with Royal Decree n. 1985 of 5 November 1925, but firmly placed under the control of the government. Mussolini himself had the power to supervise its activities and even to overrule any decision made by the Board

Table 4.1 Institutions and organisations under the influence of the Ministry

Institution/organisation	*Activities*
Istituto Nazionale Luce	Production of films for mass indoctrination
Automobile Club d'Italia	Promoting and regulating the car sector
SIAE	Copyright protection
Teatro San Carlo	Theatre
Teatro alla Scala	Theatre
EIAR	National Radio Station
Sindacato autori e scrittori	Authors and Writers Trade Union
Società Dante Alighieri	Promotion of the Italian language
Reale Accademia d'Italia	Protection and promotion of Italian science, literature, and arts
Istituto Nazionale di Cultura Fascista	Protection, dissemination, and development of the ideals and doctrine of Fascism
ENIT	Promotion and organisation of tourism in Italy
Ente Stampa del PNF	Press agent of the National Fascist Party
Ente Radio Rurale	Radio broadcasting in the countryside for the moral and cultural elevation of agricultural population

of Directors. Control of the two main Opera Houses in the country, the *Alla Scala* in Milan and the *San Carlo* in Naples, was achieved by issuing Decree-Law n. 438 of 3rd February 1936, which took control of these institutions from local notables and municipalities and placed them in the hands of the Ministry, which also appointed their top manager, the Superintendent. Other bodies were directly set up by the Fascists, such as the *Istituto Nazionale di Cultura Fascista*, whose goal was specifically to spread Fascist doctrine. Set up in 1925 and reformed with Royal Decree n. 1482 of 14 September 1939, it was subject to control by Mussolini, who appointed its President. Following reform in 1939, it played an important role in spreading racist anti-Semitic theories after the issuing in 1938 of the infamous racial laws.

The Ministry was responsible for "the generation of a popular spirit understood not simply as public opinion but as the development of the attitudes, feelings and taste of the masses", and also for "the promotion of Italian culture abroad to ensure its diffusion" (Anonymous, 1942, p. 3). The actions of the Ministry were seen at the time as successful in "detoxifying" Italian souls from the poison of a "decrepit materialistic and individualistic culture" of the previous liberal capitalist State and promoting new values and a national spirit (Anonymous, 1942, p. 3). The main task of the Ministry was "raising spiritually the Italians" (Anonymous, 1937c, p. 3) by "reaching out to the popular soul lifting it to pure ideals" (Anonymous, 1942, p. 2) through its activity in the fields of press, radio, cinema, theatre and tourism. A key, overreaching task of the Ministry was "to reduce the distance between the State and its people, being a useful and essential means for the diffusion of the ideology of the regime" (Camera dei Fasci e delle Corporazioni, 1939a, p. 185).

Implementation of the Ministry's many new propaganda programmes and achievement of other related Fascist plans depended upon the efficient, targeted allocation of resources. Achieving this would need a highly articulated, well-managed organisation that would require a vast array of information provided especially by accounting practices. Accounting was a technology needed for planning and controlling resources for propaganda, which involved every form of artificial construction or representation of reality. The extensive, penetrating calculative practices that were adopted to achieve the Ministry's goals and as a technology of propaganda to verify if, and to what extent, the desired results had been achieved testified to the importance given by the Fascists to the creation of Fascist art and culture.

Calculative practices in the field of popular culture

The official budget of popular culture

The way in which financial resources were allocated to propaganda activities evolved during the Fascist era and became more accurate over time, thereby enabling the creation of accounting objects which would give visibility to what the Fascists considered as popular culture and the most important means to construct it. Moreover, resources dedicated to popular culture as a means of propaganda that included the condemnation and persecution of Jews increased almost constantly during the latter years of the Fascist regime and remained high also when the Fascists were pushed north to Salò. When in 1934 the Under-Secretariat for Press and Propaganda was entrusted with the task to manage propaganda and cultural activities, it could not count on a significant amount of resources nor did it enjoy any freedom in their use. At that time, all the resources to be invested for propaganda purposes were allocated through the Budget of the Ministry of Finance (Regno d'Italia, 1935), which was under the control of the Minister of Finance rather than propaganda specialists.

The Under-Secretariat did not represent a clearly identifiable accounting object in all the accounting systems of the State. Instead, it was just a small section of the much more comprehensive Budget of the Ministry of Finance, which covered wide-ranging activities among which propaganda was rather unremarkable. This section of the Budget contained only a few items and the amount the State allocated to fund these activities during this period was very low. Propaganda expenses amounted to only 500,000 lire,[2] most of which was related to cinematography, whilst there was no mention of expenses for tourism or press services (Regno d'Italia, 1935, p. 55). Although propaganda was starting to become a "thinkable" object, its content had not yet been clearly identified in the accounts and funding was still insufficient.

In 1936, when the Under-Secretariat evolved into the Ministry of Press and Propaganda, it proclaimed a momentous change, for now, for the first time, propaganda activities were given a clear presence in the accounts of the State and their content was identified by means of dedicated items of expenditure. The increasing importance of propaganda to the Fascists was clear as the investments in these activities were strengthened. Table 4.2 shows the investment specifically in propaganda activities for the accounting year 1936–1937, when the Ministry of Press and Propaganda became responsible for intervening in the country's cultural life.[3] Therefore, starting from 1936

Table 4.2 The budget of the Ministry of Press and Propaganda for the year 1936–1937

Items	*1 July 1936–30 June 1937*
Expenses for tourism services	28,680,000
Expenses for theatre	5,150,000
Expenses for press services	410,000
Expenses for cinematography	3,100,000
Expenses for other propaganda services	3,100,000
Overheads	14,470,000
Total	**54,910,000**

Source: Authors' own elaboration based on Regno d'Italia (1936b). Amounts are in lire.

with the Ministry of Press and Propaganda, propaganda became visible as an "accounting object". The Ministry was seen as "one of the most important creations of the regime, which shapes State intervention in a key aspect of social life" by overseeing cultural production (Partito Nazionale Fascista, 1936, p. 25). To allow the Ministry to do so, the Budget was set up in a manner that mirrored the Fascist definition of popular culture. Ordinary and extraordinary expenses were identified for theatre, cinema, and press services, which included control of books, magazines, and newspapers, along with miscellaneous propaganda activities and tourism. Expenses were then detailed into 33 items of expenditure (Regno d'Italia, 1937). The evolution of the Ministry of Press and Propaganda into the Ministry for Popular Culture in 1937 showed the tight link that was now expected between propaganda and the creation of a new national culture informed by Fascist values.

The labels used for the Ministry's accounts, the reports of which were available to a wide audience, clearly identify the priorities of the Fascists in using popular culture as a propaganda weapon. An important innovation in the Ministry's accounts was the identification of "radio" with a separate heading. Although in the Fascist conception of popular culture the radio was under the broad umbrella of the press (Partito Nazionale Fascista, 1936), with the creation of the Ministry of Popular Culture it became a separate accounting object, which recognised the importance and potential of this new tool. For each heading, detailed line items were listed in the Budget of the Ministry of Popular Culture which were ultimately linked to the funding of strategic actions. In the detailed Budget accounts of the Ministry, expenses were divided into two categories. Firstly were the ordinary expenses that included all the costs for employees, rent, and contributions to increase theatrical, cultural, cinematographic activities and propaganda, and overheads (Regno d'Italia, 1937–1943c). Any extraordinary expenses were represented by resources allocated to each cultural activity under State control to achieve the specific ends of its programmes. These extraordinary expenses were divided into categories for each cultural activity: resources allocated to tourism, theatre, press at home and abroad, propaganda, cinematography, and radio broadcasting (Regno d'Italia, 1937–1943c). The importance of detailed appropriations, which enabled a clearer understanding of the purpose for which funding had to be used, is further testified by the fact that the number of line items grew to 57 in the last year of the life of the Ministry of Popular Culture (Regno d'Italia, 1943b).

A new accounting innovation for the Ministry, as seen in Table 4.3, was the use of "secret accounts" to encompass more politically sensitive government actions specifically for propaganda purposes. Importantly, as discussed below, this was just a fraction of the much higher resources managed through the Ministry of the Interior, which escaped parliamentary scrutiny and were used to silence or ensure the support of intellectuals. Fascist discipline extended to resource allocation and accounting as well. Budgetary appropriations were not to be changed and transfers between different accounts were

Table 4.3 The budget of the Ministry of Popular Culture for the year 1937–1943

Items	*1 July 1937–30 June 1938*	*1 July 1938–30 June 1939*	*1 July 1939–30 June 1940*	*1 July 1940–30 June 1941*	*1 July 1941–30 June 1942*	*1 July 1942–30 June 1943*
Expenses for tourism services	29,100,000	53,600,000	57,100,000	55,100,000	55,100,000	37,300,000
Expenses for theatre	7,550,000	7,600,000	12,200,000	12,250,000	12,250,000	20,540,000
Expenses for press officer abroad	780,000	2,423,000	2,423,000	3,500,000	3,630,000	4,070,000
Expenses for press services		780,000	800,000	930,000	1,580,000	5,080,000
Expenses for cinematography	13,100,000	13,100,000	20,100,000	10,200,000	31,230,292	36,900,000
Expenses for radio and TV broadcasting	100,000	500,000	1,600,000	3,030,000	3,030,000	3,030,000
Expenses for other propaganda services	3,600,000	3,600,000	4,500,000	4,500,000	5,600,000	5,600,000
Secret expenses				23,300,000	20,000,000	20,000,000
Overheads	15,295,000	19,565,000	19,675,000	44,175,000	66,130,000	43,835,000
Total	**69,525,000**	**101,168,000**	**118,398,000**	**156,985,000**	**198,550,292**	**176,355,000**

Source: Authors' own elaboration based on Regno d'Italia (1937, 1938, 1939, 1940, 1941, 1942a, 1942b, 1943a, 1943b, 1943c). Amounts are in lire.

not frequent. Nevertheless, the allocation of funding could change when deemed essential. This happened with theatre in 1937 when, following a parliamentary debate, it was decided to increase funding for the production of new operas (Camera dei Deputati, 1937a, p. 3739). Later, the funding for press officers abroad was increased during the war (Commissione Bilancio, 1943, p. 1247; Regno d'Italia, 1943c).

As shown in Table 4.3, although its propaganda function may not look obvious, among the activities carried out by the Ministry tourism was particularly important. Tourism was deemed essential to promote the regime's image, as testified by the remarkable amount of funds it was allocated; until 1941, nearly 50% of expenditures. The funds allocated in the Budget to tourism were "to convert each foreigner who visited Italy into a propagandist of what the Regime achieved in each field" (Camera dei Fasci e delle Corporazioni, 1939b, p. 207). In the field of cinema, the importance of which escalated between 1937 and 1943 as Italy became more embroiled in war, funds were allocated to activities related to controlling and supervising the production of national movies and to the creation of a large establishment for the production of movies in Rome.

The analysis of the Budgets of the ministries overseeing cultural production offers insights into the shifting approaches adopted by the Fascist government in the cultural domain. If in 1937 prizes for movies and producers amounted to 2 million lire this was increased to 55.3 million in 1943. At the same time, funding for the control of movies and censorship remained quite low, ranging from 100,000 lire to 400,000 lire (Regno d'Italia, 1937, p. 30, 1943b, p. 2084). The Fascists believed that because "art, as a direct function of politics, is the opposite of itself" (Partito Nazionale Fascista, 1936, p. 6), they needed to refrain from a penetrating *ex ante* control of production of movies, with *ex post* rewards for products which truly embodied Fascist values believed to be a much more effective means for the creation of "quality" cultural artefacts.

Despite their approach to movie production, Fascist intervention in theatrical production belied their apparently benign stance on culture. Expenses for censorship soared from 5.5 million lire to 13.5 million lire from 1937 to 1943 (Regno d'Italia, 1937, p. 30, 1943b, p. 2084). Unlike modern cinema, which was in the hands of a few major companies, theatre had a long-established tradition in Italy and was characterised by the presence of different types of performances and a myriad of small companies. The totalitarian regime was therefore not afraid to exercise strict control of theatrical production in the creation of a "State theatre", one which would avoid productions concerned only with "narrating the unremarkable vicissitudes … of a mediocre society or analysing the tortuous mental evolutions of some madman" (Partito Nazionale Fascista, 1936, p. 31). Budgeted expenses for theatre between 1937 and 1943 also included implementing "Saturday at the theatre", a programme which sought to open theatres to the working class to improve their cultural level and sense of belonging to a powerful community (Regno d'Italia, 1938, p. 2633).

Radio occupied a central role in the dissemination of Fascist ideas by emphasising any news reports in a way that was favourable to the regime. For this reason, funds were used to buy equipment for radio broadcasting to be placed in public places such as schools, barracks or the local offices of the Party (Regno d'Italia, 1943b, p. 2085). Such was the importance of the radio that it was expected to be both a "source of knowledge, education and propaganda" and, as a means of entertainment, "achieve a creativity which is not less artistic than that of cinema" (Partito Nazionale Fascista, 1936, pp. 26, 34). Consistent with one of the main programs of government for which the Ministry was responsible, attempts to influence the press abroad were considered strategically important by the Fascist regime in the dissemination of its ideology outside Italy. Costs associated with the development of international propaganda were mainly related to the salaries of the employees abroad, rent, and travel expenses (Regno d'Italia, 1937–1943c).

The final act of Fascist propaganda in the Italian territory occurred when the Fascists fled north and established the Republic of Salò. Table 4.4 shows the Budget of the Ministry of Popular Culture during the two years of the ephemeral Republic. The structure of the Budget remained unchanged and, despite the unstoppable advance of Allied troops from the south, supported by Italian partisans, significant resources were invested in propaganda

Table 4.4 The budget of the Ministry of Popular Culture for the year 1944–1945

Items	*1 July 1943–30 June 1944*	*1 July 1944–30 June 1945*
Expenses for tourism services	39,100,000	21,500,000
Expenses for theatre	16,490,000	26,089,379
Expenses for press officer abroad	5,110,000	2,750,000
Expenses for press services	7,580,000	6,450,000
Expenses for other propaganda services	5,600,000	5,600,000
Expenses for cinematography	55,700,000	56,321,152
Expenses for radio broadcasting	3,400,000	6,200,000
Overheads	33,077,500	88,123,335
Total	**166,057,500**	**213,033,866**

Source: Authors' own elaboration based on Repubblica Sociale Italiana (1944, 1945). Amounts are in lire.

activities as a last, desperate attempt at winning the trust of the population still under the heel of the Fascists. Resources allocated to tourism decreased significantly and were almost 50% of what they had been at the height of the Fascist rule, consistent with the much-changed international scenario, with expenses mainly needed to repair facilities or transform them into accommodation for refugees. Performing arts remained very important, with theatre and cinema seen as means to try to boost the morale of the populations affected by the war. Nevertheless, State control became even stronger. The resources devoted to awarding prizes for the production of movies fell to 6.1 million lire, whilst money was invested mainly in newsreels by the *Istituto Nazionale Luce* which sought to provide the citizens of the Republic of Salò with partisan information on war events (Repubblica Sociale Italiana, 1944, p. 3036). A new fund for movie production was set up, access to which was strictly controlled. As far as theatre was concerned, almost all resources were invested in censorship activities (Repubblica Sociale Italiana, 1944, p. 3038).

The secret funding of intellectuals and artists

Beyond the use of resources from its own Budget, the Ministry also sought to influence cultural production in other more discreet ways. This took the form of individual grants awarded to intellectuals, artists, or journalists to ensure their committed allegiance to the regime and their use as a weapon for propaganda. The Ministry funded numerous intellectuals, even if many of them had limited impact on cultural life in the country. In return, they were expected to ensure that their actions were in line with the expectations of the regime or at least that their work did not openly criticise or contradict the priorities of the Fascists. Any act of insubordination was swiftly punished. The Fascists were particularly aware of the potentially significant impact on their fascistic indoctrination of Italians if well-known artists and writers publicly opposed the increasing anti-Semitic emphasis being given in all propaganda media. When renowned poet and war hero Giuseppe Ungaretti took part in a rally against racist laws in 1939, the Ministry immediately suspended his monthly subsidy of 1,500 lire (Archivio Centrale dello Stato (ACS) (1942d), Ministero della Cultura Popolare, Gabinetto, b. 1491, f. Giuseppe Ungaretti). This action, and the significant resources invested in achieving its goals, showed how the Fascists did much more than just expect cultural products to be "inspired" by their values.

The resources used to fund intellectuals were not part of the normal appropriations made in the Budget of the Ministry but were allocated through a secret procedure using money coming from the General Directorate for Public Security (Sedita, 2010, p. 18). This activity is identified in the secret accounts of the Ministry of the Interior, from which it is possible to appreciate the way in which the Fascist government sought to fund the press and individual intellectuals between 1934 and 1943. So important was winning the allegiance of apparently neutral intellectuals that this was deemed a matter of national security. Consequently, the most important feature of the funding activities of intellectuals organised by the Ministry was its secrecy. The "kindness" of the Regime towards intellectuals could not be made public (Sedita, 2010, p. 40). The secrecy of the practice was confirmed when in 1940 the Prefect of Verona suggested that the Minister of Popular Culture, Alessandro Pavolini, publicise through a press release the kindness of the regime to intellectuals, the answer of the Ministry was simply: "No! The measure is confidential" (ACS (1942c), Ministero della Cultura Popolare, Gabinetto, b. 246, f. Barbarani Tiberio).

The amount managed by the Ministry of Popular Culture to finance intellectuals, journalists, and newspapers was recorded in "shadow" accounting registers, called "general accounts", which hid the real purpose of these resources (Sedita, 2010, p. 18). The Head of the Police and the Minister of Popular Culture managed jointly and secretly these extra resources, but the transfer of resources from the General Directorate for the Public Security to the Ministry had ultimately to be approved by Mussolini himself. The Ministry recorded this amount through generic clearing entries during the year. In this way, money was not recorded in the Budget of the Ministry, thereby escaping parliamentary scrutiny and was not visible to whoever checked the official Budget, which was publicly available. Table 4.5 shows how the most important intellectuals of the time, among whom were important poets such as Giuseppe Ungaretti and future Nobel Prize winner Salvatore Quasimodo (ACS (1942a), Ministero della Cultura Popolare, Resoconti, b. 5, f. A), were regularly funded as part of the secret accounts and, thus, the importance with which their contributions were regarded by the regime. In particular, the Ministry secretly managed for this purpose over 634 million lire, four times the average annual amount allocated through the Budget of the Ministry during its life. These funds were used to finance the work of 906 intellectuals and 387 newspapers, magazines, and news agencies, hence making them "indebted" to the government (Sedita, 2010, pp. 17, 22, 232).[4]

Those who received funding entered into a "tacit agreement" with the government, whereby they agreed to perform propaganda activities on behalf of

Table 4.5 Funds for intellectuals from the Ministry (in lire)

Name	*Regular funds*	*Occasional payments*	*Activity*
Aleramo, Sibilla	168,000		Writer and poet
Antonelli, Luigi	120,000	23,500	Playwright and journalist
Archidiacono Nicola	150,000		Journalist
Barilli, Bruno	84,000	16,600	Actor and music composer
Barbani, Tiberio Roberto	96,000		Poet
Bonciani, Carlo	52,200		Journalist
Cabella, Giorgio	72,000	3,200	Writer and journalist
Caporilli, Pietro	72,000	56,100	Writer and journalist
Cardarelli, Vincenzo	114,000	18,000	Poet and journalist
Civinini, Guelfo	126,000	28,000	Poet and journalist
Corra, Bruno	96,000	7,000	Writer and screenwriter
De Begnac, Ivon	120,000	4,000	Writer and journalist
Evola, Giulio	48,000		Philisopher
Filippini, Anton Francesco	84,000	20,500	Poet and writer
Giorda, Marcello		235,000	Actor
Govoni, Corrado	216,000	46,000	Poet
Orazi, Vittorio	72,000		Writer
Patti, Gino	72,000		Painter
Quasimodo, Salvatore		4,000	Poet. Nobel Prize winner in 1959
Ungaretti, Giuseppe	144,000		Poet and journalist

the State by means of articles, books, or other artistic products which were consistent with the values promoted by the regime now embedded as the popular culture (Sedita, 2010, p. 35). This was obvious from the ministerial responses to intellectuals who had requested funding. Minister Alfieri made very clear how the funded intellectual was expected to collaborate with the regime when he exclaimed: "I decided to meet you halfway and offer you a temporary form of collaboration with the Ministry, which from time to time will be sending requests to you. The Ministry will pay you a cheque of 2,000 lire starting from 1 September and will expect … a collaboration that will involve [contributions to] newspapers and magazines or several additional tasks" (ACS (1942a), Ministero della Cultura Popolare, Resoconti, b. 5, f. A). The discreet way in which funding was used meant that the claims made by intellectuals and artists looked credible, spontaneous, disinterested, and not influenced by the regime. In this way, there appeared to be consensus in public opinion in Italy whilst to those abroad it seemed even deeper and wider.

Reporting the results of propaganda activities

Theatre

Theatre has been traditionally one of the most obvious manifestations of Italian cultural production, most especially opera. Theatre was seen by the Fascists as a form of art that is "eminently social and, hence, necessarily political" and a weapon more powerful than direct propaganda (Camera dei Deputati, 1937a, p. 3749). Quality theatrical production was expected to "stage noble and virile passions which can profoundly shake the souls of the masses, awakening their best selves. Faith, patriotism, the conquests of the workers, the theme of self-sacrifice and the other qualities and ideals that Fascism praises in its doctrine" (Partito Nazionale Fascista, 1936, p. 31). Parliamentary debates on the Budget of the Ministry show how this goal was pursued by means of promoting quality productions and avoiding the spread of small theatre companies that did not have the means to stage the spectacular shows demanded by the Fascists and ensure a wider audience for the performances (Camera dei Deputati, 1937a, p. 3749; Commissione Bilancio, 1942, p. 1013).

New initiatives to open theatres to the working class by means of low-price shows, such as the "Saturdays at the theatre", were to expose as many people as possible to a Fascist message whilst showing the regime's benevolence towards lower classes. This policy meant that the State had to support theatres that saw their income significantly curtailed by the imposition of expensive shows at reduced prices (Bigoni et al., 2021). State subsidies for theatres grew almost every year as the use of low-price shows became widespread, with extra taxes imposed on movie theatre tickets as a form of cross-subsidisation between different forms of Fascist culture (Camera dei Deputati, 1937a, p. 3739). The Fascists sought to draw the working class to the theatre by promoting grassroots theatre in the form of performances organised by workers' associations and travelling companies known as "Carro di Tespi" that performed from the back of their wagons. Funding was also used to create new State-owned companies which would permanently perform in three Italian theatres (Partito Nazionale Fascista, 1936, p. 31) and commission new shows (Camera dei Fasci e delle Corporazioni, 1940b, p. 555). These were the first steps towards the creation of the much sought-after "State theatre" which would liberate the Fascists from "unreliable" private companies, a process that the outbreak of World War II abruptly halted.

The development of Italian theatre was further supported when the Ministry imposed limitations on the number of foreign plays and operas that could be performed in Italian theatres, which from the late 1930s had to be those by Italian writers and composers (Commissione Bilancio, 1942, p. 1013). Minister Pavolini proudly exclaimed that 55% of all plays and operas staged in the country in 1939 were by living Italians (Camera dei Fasci e delle Corporazioni, 1940b, p. 555). At the same time, theatre was used as a means of propaganda abroad, one which could show the greatness and might of the Italian nation reformed by the Fascist revolution.

Detailed financial and non-financial information was often used in parliament to demonstrate the results achieved by the Ministry and to incentivise further action. For example, it was noted how in the 1935–1936 season, there had been 80 new Italian plays and 933 shows, which generated receipts of 3,540,347 lire, a significant improvement on the previous season, and 33 new foreign plays and 424 shows, with receipts of 1,707,641 lire (Camera dei Deputati, 1936a, p. 2698). Even the number of amateur and travelling companies were accounted for, thereby testifying to the pervasiveness of Fascist control and the importance placed by the government on theatre as a propaganda tool. This was made very clear with the level of detail reported to parliament such as in 1937 when the travelling "Carro di Trespi" was reported to have performed 264 shows that attracted 264,512 spectators between 1929 and 1934 (Camera dei Deputati, 1937a, p. 3770).

Theatre was supported by the Fascists even during the war as a desperate attempt to show the commitment of the regime to its people and to boost troop morale. Mussolini himself granted an extra subsidy for operas amounting to 300,000 lire in 1943 to cover part of the cost of new shows, which were attended by 160,000 spectators, of which 50,000 were military personnel (Commissione Bilancio, 1943, p. 1255). Given the difficulties in organising professional performances during the war, more was expected of workers' associations, which in 1942 organised 20,668 performances attended by over 16 million people (Commissione Bilancio, 1943, p. 1254). The payment of subsidies continued even when the Fascists set up the Republic of Salò (Scardaccione, 2002, p. 698).

The press

Crucial to the control of the press and publishing generally was the very strong censorship activities carried out by the Ministry, which contradicted the image that the Fascists sought to spread as a regime which did not dictate the content of artistic production (Partito Nazionale Fascista, 1936). These activities consisted of approving published materials and examining books and other publications before they could be printed. All publications were subjected to increasing scrutiny, including those targeting younger generations, for youth "need to grow following the cult of the great ideas and great figures of the Motherland and worshipping heroism, struggle and sacrifice" (Camera dei Fasci e delle Corporazioni, 1939b, p. 214). Control of the press by the Ministry became particularly obvious following the creation of the Italian empire in 1937 and the ever-stronger opposition encountered by the country from Western powers, which led Italy into the deadly embrace of Nazi Germany.

The Ministry provided financial support for the Italian newspapers, all of which were expected to be strongly aligned with the regime, and also kept a register of Italian journalists; only those approved to be included in the register could work for the Italian press whilst each newspaper's editor was made legally responsible for anything that was published (Partito Nazionale Fascista, 1936, p. 23). Control by the Ministry meant that the content of Italian newspapers was to give prominence to political events and the achievements of the regime at home and abroad, whilst crime news was to be kept to a minimum to avoid exciting people's "lowest instincts" (Camera dei Deputati,

1936a, p. 2653). Negative reporting also threatened the idea of the perfectly safe and ordered Fascist society.

Production of books was invigilated by the Ministry and used as a propaganda tool. Special publications were produced and disseminated to promote specific events, such as the war in Ethiopia. When Fascist Italy attacked Ethiopia between 1935 and 1936, over 2.5 million books and pamphlets were distributed in Italy and abroad to explain the reasons for the war and its benefits, with another 500,000 publications on the Italian empire and the "salvific" interventions by the Fascists in the local economy and the health of indigenous populations (Camera dei Deputati, 1937a, p. 3776). Books and other publications on Fascist doctrine and the State's interventions in the economy and society were distributed at international conferences and were also a means to strengthen the bonds with Italy's allies, most especially Germany. Moreover, the Ministry made all approved Italian magazines accessible abroad, especially in America and Japan (Anonymous, 1939; Camera dei Fasci e delle Corporazioni, 1939a, pp. 185–186). Libraries abroad were inundated with books that were dense with Fascist rhetoric (Camera dei Fasci e delle Corporazioni, 1940b, p. 558). These actions by the Ministry were carefully documented with accounting numbers as a means to demonstrate the Ministry's all-pervasive action and its achievements. In 1938 alone, the regime had funded the printing and delivery of 250,000 new books in 14 languages and 850,000 reprints in 16 languages (Camera dei Fasci e delle Corporazioni, 1939b, p. 203).

The Ministry could seize any publication if they were deemed incompatible with the government's moral or political vision (Anonymous, 1937a). Budgets and parliamentary debates show how significant resources were devoted to the "book reclamation campaign", which sought to purge authors and books that were not consistent with the Fascist creed, which included reducing imports and translations of foreign works and, following the issuing of racial laws in 1938, books by Jewish authors. As a result, in 1939, 1,472 books came to the attention of the Ministerial censorship committee, and 913 were withdrawn by the publishers, whilst another 425 were seized. In the same year, 40 books were withdrawn from circulation, another 45 were prevented from being re-printed, and four were approved following revisions (Camera dei Fasci e delle Corporazioni, 1940b, p. 558). Similar control and supporting statistics can be found for newspaper articles (Commissione Bilancio, 1941, p. 748). So detailed was the measurement system supporting censorship activities that members of parliament were even made aware that if in the past 67% of the space in children's magazines was dedicated to adventures of "pirates and outlaws", by 1942, these had completely disappeared (Commissione Bilancio, 1943, p. 1251).

The use of newspapers and books as means of propaganda continued when the Fascists moved to Salò. The far-reaching control on all publications appearing in the territory was no longer possible given the lack of resources.

Nevertheless, the Fascists were prepared to commit 38 million lire to support newspapers that incurred losses during the war to ensure they could survive and serve the dying regime (Scardaccione, 2002, p. 858).

Radio

The Fascists invested significantly in the development of radio broadcasting, the "most powerful and substantial means of divulgation available to the Ministry", made possible by "the great genius of a great Italian", Guglielmo Marconi (Partito Nazionale Fascista, 1936, pp. 34–35). The first Fascist radio station was inaugurated at the end of 1924. It was soon followed by many others as the regime sought to reach every part of the Italian territory, not only with entertainment programmes but also daily news. Radio programmes had to be compliant with the needs of the regime and broadcast immediately all the news that the government approved to be broadcast (Camera dei Fasci e delle Corporazioni, 1939a, p. 186).

Generous resources were allocated in the Budget to support the construction of new radio stations and more powerful infrastructure, to the point that by 1938 radio signals in Italy were stronger than in Germany and France and almost equal to those of Great Britain (Camera dei Fasci e delle Corporazioni, 1939b, p. 209). These investments sought to ensure that even those with limited financial means, who could afford just a low-quality radio, had access to the Fascist offerings. The propaganda intentions of the regime went even further by launching their own budget radio, the so-called "Radio Balilla", to give even wider access to radio programmes, especially in the countryside (Camera dei Deputati, 1937a, p. 3778). By 1938, the regime had distributed for free 26,143 radios to schools, which could reach over 4 million students (Camera dei Fasci e delle Corporazioni, 1939a, p. 187).

Investments in the development of infrastructure were mirrored by a careful monitoring of the number of subscriptions to radio broadcasts. There were approximately 700,000 subscribers in 1936, 840,000 in 1937, 1 million in 1938, and 2 million in 1941 (Camera dei Deputati, 1937a, p. 3777; Camera dei Deputati, 1938b, p. 4891; Camera dei Fasci e delle Corporazioni, 1939b, p. 209; Commissione Bilancio, 1942, p. 1013). Also monitored was the number of subscribers per 100 inhabitants in the main Italian cities, which enabled the government to see where intervention was most needed (Camera dei Fasci e delle Corporazioni, 1939b, p. 209). The offering was measured by recording the number of broadcasting hours, which in 1939 reached 75,000 hours, twice as many as three years before (Camera dei Fasci e delle Corporazioni, 1939b, p. 209). Given its ample reach, radio was not limited to propaganda activities at home but also to reach an audience abroad. Italian broadcasts in 27 different languages that sought to counter the "lies" on Fascist Italy spread by its enemies (Camera dei Fasci e delle Corporazioni, 1940b, p. 559) reached Europe, Asia, Australia, the Americas, and the Italian colonies in Africa. To ensure further links with potential supporters of the regime abroad, Italian language classes broadcasted by radio were offered. In 1936 they already reached 23,000 students (Camera dei Deputati, 1937a, p. 3778). During the war, radio infrastructure was used to capture and remove foreign broadcasts. Again, the results were carefully measured and reported to parliament as shown in 1942 when an average of 260,000 words were intercepted per day (Commissione Bilancio, 1943, p. 1254).

Cinema

As an obvious symbol of modernity, cinema soon attracted the attention of the Fascists. Italy had been at the forefront of silent movie production, but with the advent of sound it had lagged behind in a market dominated by the USA, a trend that the government sought to tackle with significant investments. Cinema was seen by the government and its supporters as "a true product of our time ... (C)inema is to us what cathedrals were at their time" (Camera dei Deputati, 1936a, p. 2659). Cinema had the potential to significantly influence the thoughts and feelings of the masses, thereby representing a "tool for leisure, education, moral growth and a very effective means of propaganda" (Camera dei Deputati, 1936b, p. 2678).

Soon after the establishment of the Ministry of Press and Propaganda, a fund of 10 million lire per year was created to support the development of new movies. It was understood that access to these resources required ministerial approval of the screenplay and a check on the financial situation of the production house (Partito Nazionale Fascista, 1936, p. 32). Further support was provided in the form of facilitated access to credit by a State-owned bank for a total of 20 million lire, along with monetary prizes for those high-quality productions that "have best embodied the spirit of our time" (Camera dei Deputati, 1938b, p. 4893; Partito Nazionale Fascista, 1936, p. 33). Support, and control, of productions was not limited to movies but extended to cartoons for children (Camera dei Deputati, 1937a, p. 3736).

Beyond direct financial support, the State also sponsored the development of an "Experimental Centre for Cinematography", which offered specialist training for those working in the movie industry, with courses ranging from acting and direction to make-up and sound technologies. The largest film studio in Europe modelled on Hollywood, the *Cinecittà*, was built in Rome (Partito Nazionale Fascista, 1936, p. 34; Camera dei Deputati, 1936b, p. 2679). Specific agreements were also made for exporting Italian movies as part of the regular offering of movie theatres abroad, most especially in Germany, whilst new movie theatres were opened in the Italian colonies in Africa (Camera dei Deputati, 1938b, p. 4887). Protectionist interventions for Italian production meant that movie theatres were expected to show at least one Italian film for every three foreign works, whilst over time, stricter limits were introduced on the import of foreign movies until those from America were banned outright during the war (Camera dei Deputati, 1937a, p. 3785; Commissione Bilancio, 1941, p. 750).

Support by the State resulted in a slow but steady growth of the film industry in Italy, which was regularly inspected and reported to the parliament. When the Ministry of Press and Propaganda was created in 1935 Italy produced only 30 movies per year. This increased to 48 in 1938, to 80 in 1939, and to 112 in 1940, when the export of movies became higher than movie imports. In the same period private investment in movies rose from 39 million lire to 170 million (Camera dei Deputati, 1936a, p. 2660; Camera dei Fasci e delle Corporazioni, 1939a, p. 186; Camera dei Fasci e delle Corporazioni, 1939b, p. 205; Camera dei Fasci e delle Corporazioni, 1940a, p. 553; Commissione Bilancio, 1941, p. 744). Productions that attracted significant interest from the audience were often reported, as was the case of the *Casta Diva,* which was projected "1,007 times, as opposed to an average of 670 for foreign movies" (Camera dei Deputati, 1937a, p. 3737). Every opportunity was taken to provide in reports details such as these that were meant to create a very convincing rendition of the success of the Fascists in the creation of their vision of popular culture.

The development of the cinema industry was also monitored through comparisons with other countries. It was documented how the average spending per person in movie theatres in Italy was half of that of France and one-fourth of that of the USA, with ticket prices abroad significantly higher. Also monitored was the number of movie theatres and box office receipts as Italy sought to close the gap with market leaders (Camera dei Deputati, 1936b, p. 2680; Camera dei Fasci e delle Corporazioni, 1939b, p. 205). Nevertheless, the development of local production and the interest in cinema was such that the Fascists estimated that by 1941 annual average attendance was around 700 million spectators (Commissione Bilancio, 1942, p. 1013). The investment of significant amounts of public money meant that the Ministry was also able to show that these investments were not simply bearing fruit in terms of propaganda but also from a financial standpoint with increasing revenue generated by duties on tickets (Camera dei Deputati, 1937b, p. 3770). To show that investment in cinema was desirable even during the war, a report was presented to the parliament in 1943 showing that from 1935 to 1942 the net contribution to the State offered by cinema had been always positive and doubled in the period considered, reaching 110 million lire even if in 1942 the State had paid an unprecedented 80 million lire in contributions to producers and movie theatres (Commissione Bilancio, 1943, p. 1258).

Control of cinema did not end with the fall of the regime, for shortly after the creation of the Republic of Salò the Fascists decided to "normalise and moralise" movie production. All production houses operating in the Republic had to re-apply for a new licence to carry out their activities. This licence would only be granted to those businesses which "based on their past activity, financial stability, technical ability and, most especially, political behaviour, are deemed able to properly develop and improve national movie production" (Scardaccione, 2002, pp. 699–700). At the same time, the ministerial commission for checking new screenplays was re-established. A State-owned entity was established to oversee the import and export of movies, with the power to acquire stakes in production houses and even take over their management (Scardaccione, 2002, p. 696). Despite the worsening war effort that was absorbing most of the Republic's resources, financial support for movies by the State was continuously confirmed and a new fund of 52 million lire for movie production was created (Scardaccione, 2002, p. 702).

Tourism

A less obvious propaganda weapon was tourism. Members of parliament clearly stated that tourism was "an activity with indirect political importance ... which is of great value to all nations, and in particular to Italy" (Camera dei Deputati, 1936b, p. 2690). Tourism from abroad was seen as particularly important for improving the image of the regime in other countries, as those who came to Italy to enjoy its architectural and natural beauties could not fail to notice, according to the government, the great works inaugurated by the regime, such as reclaimed lands, modern roads and facilities, and the safety and order brought by the Fascists (Camera dei Deputati, 1936a, p. 2655). Tourists were, therefore, believed to be important propaganda agents once back in their home countries.

The State supported the improvement of tourist activities by providing financial resources to pay interest on loans taken out for the construction of new hotels or the improvement and expansion of existing ones, which stimulated private investments of one billion lire (Camera dei Deputati, 1937b, p. 3789; Camera dei Deputati, 1938a, p. 4867). The impact of interventions in the tourism industry was carefully monitored and reported. This meant identifying not only the number of tourists from abroad who spent their holidays in Italy but also the number of cars entering the borders of the country and the average stay (Camera dei Deputati, 1936a, p. 2663). The Ministry engaged with other government departments to ensure that the infrastructure needed to facilitate tourist flows could be well maintained and improved, therefore reporting on the number of kilometres of primary and secondary roads constructed or repaired (Camera dei Deputati, 1936a, p. 2665). The outbreak of war, with its obvious consequences for tourism, did not stop the Fascists. The years between 1939 and 1942 saw the highest amount of resources invested in tourist activities, including preparation for the 1942 World Expo, which was meant to be held in Italy (Camera dei Fasci e delle Corporazioni, 1939b, p. 207).

Reporting to parliament about achievements in tourism continued even during the war. For example, in 1940, the State paid 6 million lire to 1,200 tourist enterprises, whilst another 2,000 private concerns accessed funding for the construction of new hotels worth 3 billion lire, which would have generated 29,700 new beds in hotels, including those for the 1944 Winter Olympics, which the Fascists still thought would have been held (Camera dei Fasci e delle Corporazioni, 1940b, p. 553). Details of controls on the quality of hotels were also provided, including the number of facilities inspected and those of hotels that were temporarily shut down for not meeting the quality requirements set by the government (Commissione Bilancio, 1941, p. 749; Commissione Bilancio, 1943, p. 1262). Just ten days before the fall of the regime, the Fascists were still proudly reporting in detail their investments in advertising to attract tourists, which involved "48 newspapers and 60 reviews for 559 pages and 147,500 millimetres [total length of text] in Italy … and 40 articles for 126 pages and 7,000 millimetres abroad" (Commissione Bilancio, 1943, p. 1263).

Conclusion

This chapter has provided evidence of the importance of accounting documents as a means to develop social history. Accounting records providing financial and non-financial information are not simply "dusty piles of numbers" but rather "they can provide vivid information on the everyday lives of real people in important historical epochs" (Pinto and West, 2017, p. 158). Accounting data has helped to uncover how the Fascists sought to mobilise popular culture as a less obvious means to win the committed allegiance of the Italian population and instil habits and forms of behaviour that were consistent with the regime's values and beliefs. Moreover, also identified have been the ways in which accounting numbers in the form of Budgets, reports to the parliament, and secret payments to notable intellectuals were part of the Fascist machinery of power and helped to enact Fascists plans in the field of popular culture. State intervention took the form of direct repression but also of funding and incentives promoting a spontaneous adhesion to Fascist values.

In Fascist Italy, arts and culture were not simply promoted and funded but closely controlled as a fundamental part of the totalitarian project developed by the Fascists for which the information and discipline generated by accounting practices were an essential component. In particular, the study documents the role of accounting as a technology in the State's endeavour to control intellectuals and also to hide that this had happened. The study, therefore, offers a new perspective on the functioning of accounting in totalitarian regimes (Funnell, 1998; Ezzamel et al., 2007; Lippman and Wilson, 2007; Detzen and Hoffmann, 2018, 2020; Twyford, 2021; Funnell et al., 2022).

The Fascists weaponised the use of culture to dismantle any form of opposition and to construct a totalitarian State (De Felice, 1996a, 1996b; Forgacs and Gundle, 2007; Gentile, 2013, 2014; Bernhard and Klinkhammer, 2017). Accounting records in the form of the Budgets of the Ministry and financial and non-financial reports as a source of social history enable a clearer, stronger understanding that is not as accessible with other sources of how Fascist ideas, such as their understanding of popular culture, were acted upon and turned into actions aimed at spreading Fascist beliefs. The accounts of the Ministry identify the content of popular culture permitted by the Fascists and the main ways in which it was enlisted as a propaganda weapon. Accounting records also enable finer grained analyses of the shifting priorities of the Fascists over time as reflected in the appropriations in the Budget, and in the detail and emphasis placed on documenting the activities in the different fields of cultural production in the accounting reports provided to parliament. The Budgets of the Ministry show very convincingly the increasing importance of investments in popular culture as a means of propaganda.

The use of accounting records as a means to develop social history is also useful to expose the partisan philosophical and political assertions made by those in power. As shown by the case of Fascist intervention in the artistic domain, budgetary appropriations belied the apparent "light touch" approach to culture the Fascists sought to popularise. The Fascists, allegedly, simply wished that all cultural artefacts be imbued with the values promoted by them, such as force, ruthlessness, and self-sacrifice: "the artist works and creates, and cannot truly see themselves if not in in the spiritual activities promoted by the political system" (Partito Nazionale Fascista, 1936, p. 7). Far from limiting their action to ensuring that cultural artefacts would be inspired by the "spiritual ethos" promoted by the regime, Budgets show how significant resources were invested in censorship activities in a field such as theatre which had been traditionally difficult to control given the myriad of small companies, writers and producers revolving around theatrical productions. Moreover, data presented to parliament further indicated how effective Fascist censorship was, with many books or other publications withdrawn from the market or reinstated only after significant changes were made.

Accounting records also demonstrate how a significant amount of resources invested in the creation of Fascist culture was not managed through traditional means and, thereby, escaped parliamentary scrutiny. This was all the more obvious with the funding of the activity of famous artists, the propaganda activity which attracted most resources. The reputation that these artists enjoyed boosted their propaganda function, for their allegiance with the regime may not have been known to those who enjoyed the artistic creations of militant artists, hence leading the audience into believing that Fascist ideals were inherently good for they were endorsed by even such eminent and "independent" intellectuals. At the same time, reliance upon terror to persecute well-known intellectuals could have been very counterproductive, for their reputation would have provided them with an audience that would be ready to condemn the totalitarian actions of the State. Accounting records related to artists show how Fascist intervention in the cultural domain was much stronger and more direct than their official publications and speeches would lead an audience to believe.

Accounting "numbers" that were not kept secret were employed to make immediately visible and easily understandable to the members of parliament, and whoever consulted the accounting reports, the results achieved by the Fascist government in the cultural domain. Financial and non-financial data were used to demonstrate the progress made in certain fields, such as the evolution of Italian cinema, or raise awareness about the work that needed to be done in others, as in the case of insufficient attendance at theatrical performances.

So important were accounting numbers in giving substance and prestige to government action that a very developed system of data recording was set up, one which could measure even the number of daily words intercepted by Italian radio operators, the space occupied by different types of stories in children's magazines and the length of touristic advertisements. This information provides further evidence of the Fascist effort in building ideologies, images, messages, beliefs, and everyday life standards and homologating and controlling the population by mobilising a large portfolio of tools and measures which were to become increasingly anti-Semitic in their intent. Financial and non-financial information enabled the regime to appreciate if, and to what extent, the resources in the Budget had been put to good use and had informed policy (Camera dei Deputati, 1937a, p. 3739; Commissione Bilancio, 1943, p. 1247). This information was also a propaganda tool itself as it was then used in specialised reports and magazines to proclaim the achievements of the regime in the development of a truly Fascist culture. Despite their disdain for everything that was liberal and capitalist, the Fascist did not refrain from using accounting tools in their attempt to "Fascistise" Italy.

This chapter is based on the paper by Valerio Antonelli, Michele Bigoni, Warwick Funnell, Emanuela Mattia Cafaro, and Enrico Deidda Gagliardo titled "Popular culture and totalitarianism: Accounting for propaganda in Italy under the Fascist regime (1934–1945)" which originally appeared in Critical Perspectives on Accounting in 2023, article number 102524. The authors would like to thank the publisher, Elsevier, for permission to use this material.

Notes

1 The Directorate for Foreign Radio and Press was expected to engage with foreign press and try to influence the perception of the Republic and the war abroad. The Directorate of Sport and Tourism absorbed the Olympic Committee, which in Italy had overseen professional and amateur sport, thereby widening the mandate of the Ministry.

2 By contrast, resources invested in propaganda activities peaked to over 198 million lire in 1942, a 396% increase. Total propaganda expenses in 1935 were just little more than amount spent by the Ministry of Popular Culture on purchasing newspapers alone in 1942.

3 Tables 4.2–4.4 do not depict the entire Budget for each year but consist of an elaboration of original data by the authors indicating the aggregated amount for each heading.

4 Intellectuals wishing to apply for funding needed to send a letter to the Ministry with their request. Once the Ministry had evaluated the request, it was then sent directly to the attention of Mussolini with a note providing the main elements of the intellectual's application (ACS (1942), Ministero della Cultura Popolare, Resoconti, b. 15). Mussolini himself decided whether to approve the subsidy. Funding could have been recurrent, with monthly payments, or take the form of a lump sum, with the amount and duration of the subsidy decided on a case-by-case basis (ACS (1942), Ministero della Cultura Popolare, Resoconti, b. 5, f. A). A personal dossier was then kept by the Police on each funded intellectual, with notes on their loyalty (Sedita, 2010, p. 38).

References

Primary Sources

Archivio storico della Camera dei Deputati

Camera dei Deputati (1936a). Session of Thursday 7 May 1936.
Camera dei Deputati (1936b). Session of Friday 8 May 1936.
Camera dei Deputati (1937a). Session of Thursday 13 May 1937.
Camera dei Deputati (1937b). Session of Friday 14 May 1937.
Camera dei Deputati (1938a). Session of Friday 18 March 1938.
Camera dei Deputati (1938b). Session of Monday 21 March 1938.
Camera dei Fasci e delle Corporazioni (1939a). Session of Thursday 11 May 1939.
Camera dei Fasci e delle Corporazioni (1939b). Session of Friday 12 May 1939.
Camera dei Fasci e delle Corporazioni (1940a). Session of Wednesday 24 April 1940.
Camera dei Fasci e delle Corporazioni (1940b). Session of Thursday 25 April 1940.
Commissione Bilancio (1941). Commissioni Legislative Riunite del Bilancio, della Cultura Popolare e delle Professioni ed Arti. Session of Thursday 3 April 1941.
Commissione Bilancio (1942). Commissioni Legislative Riunite del Bilancio e della Cultura Popolare. Session of Friday 8 May 1942.
Commissione Bilancio (1943). Commissioni Legislative Riunite del Bilancio, della Cultura Popolare e delle Professioni ed Arti. Session of Wednesday 14 April 1943.

Gazzetta Ufficiale del Regno d'Italia

Regno d'Italia (1935). Budget of the Ministry of Finance for the financial year from 1 July 1935 to 30 June 1936. Gazzetta Ufficiale del Regno d'Italia (SO).
Regno d'Italia (1936a). Creation of the Ministry of Press and Propaganda Royal decree-law 24 September 1936-XIV, n. 1834. Gazzetta Ufficiale del Regno d'Italia.
Regno d'Italia (1936b). Budget of the Ministry of Press and Propaganda for the financial year from 1 July 1936-XIV to 30 June 1937-XV. Gazzetta Ufficiale del Regno d'Italia (SO).
Regno d'Italia (1937). Budget of the Ministry of Press and Propaganda for the financial year from 1 July 1937-XV to 30 June 1938-XVI. Gazzetta Ufficiale del Regno d'Italia (SO).
Regno d'Italia (1938). Budget of the Ministry of Popular Culture for the financial year from 1 July 1938-XVI al 30 June 1939-XVII. Gazzetta Ufficiale del Regno d'Italia (SO).
Regno d'Italia (1939). Budget of the Ministry of Popular Culture for the financial year from 1 July 1939-XVII al 30 June 1940-XVIII. Gazzetta Ufficiale del Regno d'Italia (SO).
Regno d'Italia (1940). Budget of the Ministry of Popular Culture for the financial year from 1 July 1940-XVIII al 30 June 1941-XIX. Gazzetta Ufficiale del Regno d'Italia (SO).
Regno d'Italia (1941). Budget of the Ministry of Popular Culture for the financial year from 1 July 1941-XIX al 30 June 1942-XX. Gazzetta Ufficiale del Regno d'Italia.
Regno d'Italia (1942a). Budget of the Ministry of Popular Culture for the financial year from 1 July 1942.XX al 30 June 1943.XXI. Gazzetta Ufficiale del Regno d'Italia.
Regno d'Italia (1942b). Variations to the budget of different Ministries and to that of other autonomous entities for the financial year 1941–1942 and other financial decisions. Gazzetta Ufficiale del Regno d'Italia.

Regno d'Italia (1943a). Allocation of funds for the expenses reserved to the Ministry of Popular Culture for the financial year 1942–1943. Gazzetta Ufficiale del Regno d'Italia.

Regno d'Italia (1943b). Budget of the Ministry of Popular Culture for the financial year from 1 July 1943-XXI al 30 June 1944. XXII. Gazzetta Ufficiale del Regno d'Italia.

Regno d'Italia (1943c). Increase in funds available within the budget of the Ministry of Popular Culture for the financial year 1942–1943. Gazzetta Ufficiale del Regno d'Italia.

Repubblica Sociale Italiana (1944). Budget of the Ministry of Popular Culture for the financial year from 1 July 1943 to 30 June 1944. XXII. Gazzetta Ufficiale d'Italia.

Repubblica Sociale Italiana (1945). Budget of the Ministry of Popular Culture for the financial year from 1 July 1944 to 30 June 1945. XXII. Gazzetta Ufficiale d'Italia.

Newspapers

Anonymous (1937a). Popular culture in the speech by His Excellency Alfieri to the Senate. *La Stampa*, 22 May 1937.

Anonymous (1937b). The Ministry of Press and Propaganda will change its name to Ministry of Popular Culture from 1 June. *La Stampa*, 27 May 1937.

Anonymous (1937c). Theatre and radio. The challenge of popular culture. *La Stampa*, 30 May 1937.

Anonymous (1939). The commentary to the budget of the Ministry of Popular Culture. *La Stampa*, 7 May 1939.

Anonymous (1942). The speech by Minister Pavolini on the budget of the Ministry of Popular Culture. *La Stampa*, 23 May 1942.

Archivio Centrale dello Stato

ACS (1942a). Ministero della Cultura Popolare, Resoconti, b. 5, f. A. Complete list of all the subsidies paid to Italian journalists, artists, and writers.

ACS (1942b). Ministero della Cultura Popolare, Resoconti, b. 15, notes to the duce relating to applicants for propaganda funds.

ACS (1942c). Ministero della Cultura Popolare, Gabinetto, b. 246, f. Barbarani Tiberio.

ACS (1942d). Ministero della Cultura Popolare, Gabinetto, b. 1491, f. Giuseppe Ungaretti.

Secondary Sources

Abdullah, A., and Khadaroo, I. (2022). Controlling UK national museums and galleries: The pursuit of conflicting politico-economic and socio-cultural objectives. *Accounting and Business Research*, *52*(2), 201–220.

Adinolfi, G. (2012). The Institutionalization of propaganda in the Fascist era: The cases of Germany, Portugal, and Italy. *The European Legacy: Toward New Paradigms*, *17*(5), 607–621.

Antonelli, V., Bigoni, M., Cafaro, E.M., and D'Alessio, R. (2020). Railway systems and the "universal good of the state": Technologies of government in the nineteenth-century Papal State. *Accounting History*, *25*(3), 375–402.

Arendt, H. (1962). *The Origins of Totalitarianism*. Cleveland and New York: The World Publishing Company.

Arendt, H. (1994). *Essays in Understanding (1930–1954). Formation, Exile, and Totalitarianism* (Edited with an introduction by Jerome Kohn). New York: Schocken Books.

Bennet, T. (2003). Useful culture. In: V. Blundell, J. Shepherd, and I. Taylor (Eds.). *Relocating Cultural Studies. Developments in Theory and Research* (pp. 67–85). New York: Routledge.

Berezin, M. (1991). The organization of political ideology: Culture, state, and theater in Fascist Italy. *American Sociological Review*, *56*(5), 639–651.

Bernhard, P., and Klinkhammer, L. (2017). *L'uomo nuovo del fascismo: La costruzione di un progetto totalitario*. Roma: Viella.

Bigoni, M. (2021). Accounting for hegemony. Fascist ideology and the shifting roles of accounting at the University of Ferrara and the Alla Scala Opera House (1922–1943). *Accounting History*, *26*(4), 640–664.

Bigoni, M., Funnell, W.N., Deidda Gagliardo, E., and Pierotti, M. (2021). Accounting for control of Italian culture in the Fascist ethical state: the Alla Scala Opera House. *Accounting, Auditing & Accountability Journal*, *34*(1), 194–222.

Bigoni, M., Funnell, W.N., Verona, R., and Deidda Gagliardo, E. (2018). Accounting and *raison d'État* in the Grand Duchy of Tuscany: Reopening the University of Pisa (1543–1609). *Critical Perspectives on Accounting*, *56*, 1–19.

Cole, T. (1938). The Italian Ministry of Popular Culture. *Public Opinion Quarterly*, *2*(3), 425–434.

De Felice, R. (1996a). *Mussolini il Duce. Gli anni del consenso, 1929–1936*. Torino: Einaudi.

De Felice, R. (1996b). *Mussolini il Duce. Lo stato totalitario, 1936–1940*. Torino: Einaudi.

Detzen, D., and Hoffmann, S. (2018). Stigma management and justifications of the self in denazification accounts. *Accounting, Auditing & Accountability Journal*, *31*(1), 141–165.

Detzen, D., and Hoffmann, S. (2020). Accountability and ideology: The case of a German university under the Nazi regime. *Accounting History*, *25*(2), 174–192.

Ellwood, S., and Greenwood, M. (2016). Accounting for heritage assets: Does measuring economic value "kill the cat"? *Critical Perspectives on Accounting*, *38*, 1–13.

Ezzamel, M., Xiao, J.Z., and Pan, A. (2007). Political ideology and accounting regulation in China. *Accounting, Organizations and Society*, *32*(7–8), 669–700.

Ferry, L., and Slack, R. (2022). (Counter) accounting for hybrid organising: A case of the Great Exhibition of the North. *Accounting, Auditing & Accountability Journal*, *35*(3), 681–705.

Forgacs, D., and Gundle, S. (2007). *Mass Culture and Italian Society from Fascism to the Cold War*. Bloomington: Indiana University Press.

Fülbier, R.U. (2021). Digging deeper: German academics and universities under Nazi tyranny – a comment. *Accounting History*, *26*(3), 375–385.

Funnell, W. (1998). Accounting in the service of the Holocaust. *Critical Perspectives on Accounting*, *9*(4), 435–464.

Funnell, W., Antonelli, V., Bigoni, M., Cafaro, E.M., and D'Alessio, R. (2022). Accounting for Jewish "bare life" in the Fossoli concentration camp, 1943–44. *Critical Perspectives on Accounting*, *88*, 102323.

Gentile, E. (2013). *Fascismo: Storia e interpretazione*. Bari. Editore Laterza.

Gentile, E. (2014). *E fu subito regime: Il fascismo e la marcia su Roma*. Bari. Laterza & Figli.

Gurian, W. (1978). The totalitarian state. *The Review of Politics*, *40*(4), 514–527.

Hitler, A. (1941). *Mein Kampf*. New York: Reynal & Hitchcock.

Jeacle, I. (2009). "Going to the movies": Accounting and twentieth century cinema. *Accounting, Auditing & Accountability Journal*, *22*(5), 677–708.

Jeacle, I. (2012). Accounting and popular culture: Framing a research agenda. *Accounting, Auditing & Accountability Journal*, *25*(4), 580–601.

Jeacle, I., and Miller, P. (2016). Accounting, culture, and the state. *Critical Perspectives on Accounting 37*, 1–4.

Jones, P. (2011). *The Sociology of Architecture*. Liverpool: Liverpool University Press.

Lippman, E.J., and Wilson, P.A. (2007). The culpability of accounting in perpetuating the Holocaust. *Accounting History*, *12*(3), 283–303.

McGuigan, J. (1996). *Culture and the Public Sphere*. London and New York: Routledge.

McWatters, C., and Lemarchand, Y. (2010). Accounting as story telling: merchant activities and commercial relations in eighteenth century France. *Accounting, Auditing & Accountability Journal*, *23*(1), 14–54.

Mussolini, B. (1935). *La dottrina del Fascismo. Idee fondamentali*. Roma: Istituto della Enciclopedia Italiana.

Papi, L., Bigoni, M., Deidda Gagliardo, E., and Funnell, W.N. (2019). Accounting for power and resistance: The University of Ferrara under the Fascist regime in Italy. *Critical Perspectives on Accounting*, *62*, 59–76.

Partito Nazionale Fascista (1936). *La cultura Fascista. Testi per i corsi di preparazione politica*. Roma: La Libreria dello Stato.

Pinto, O., and West, B. (2017). Accounting, slavery and social history: The legacy of an eighteenth-century Portuguese chartered company. *Accounting History*, *22*(2) 141–166.

Scardaccione, F.R. (2002). *Verbali del Consiglio dei ministri della Repubblica Sociale Italiana. Settembre 1943–Aprile 1945*. Roma: Ministero per i beni e le attività culturali.

Sedita, G. (2010). *Gli intellettuali di Mussolini. La cultura finanziata dal fascismo*. Firenze: Le Lettere.

Stacchezzini, R., Masiero, E., and Lai, A. (2023). Histories as counter-accounting. *Critical Perspectives on Accounting*, *91*, 102397.

Twyford, E.J. (2021). A thanatopolitical visualisation of accounting history: Giorgio Agamben and Nazi Germany. *Accounting History*, *26*(3), 352–374.

Twyford, E.J., and Funnell, W. (2023). Accounting for the Nazi Aryanisation of German banks. *Accounting, Auditing & Accountability Journal*, *36*(1), 1–23.

Walker, S.P. (2000). Encounters with Nazism: British accountants and the fifth international congress on accounting. *Critical Perspectives on Accounting*, *11*(2), 215–245.

Zamponi, S.F. (2003). *Lo spettacolo del fascismo*. Soveria Mannelli: Rubbettino Editore.

Žižek, S. (2002). *Did Somebody Say Totalitarianism? Five Interventions in the (Mis) Use of a Notion*. London and New York: Verso.

5 Accounting for Jewish financial death

Erin Twyford

Introduction

Explaining the destruction of people "is a daunting task empirically and even more so theoretically, so much so that some have argued … that it is 'inexplicable'" (Goldhagen, 1996, p. 5). This is due, in part, to the extensive measures that are taken to destroy a people, as facilitated by a complex matrix of organisations, institutions, ideologies, policies, and practices. Examples of historical genocide, such as the Holocaust, can, therefore, be studied from a variety of perspectives that contribute to new ways of knowing or understanding. From a business and accounting perspective, there are still underdeveloped, or unacknowledged, impacts of the wider moral and political implications of calculative practices.

In the attempt to explain the "inexplicable", this chapter situates the historical events of the Holocaust within a framework that draws upon the work of Giorgio Agamben to deepen our understanding of the way in which politics that is fixated on the physical death of a section of the population, now referred to as thanatopolitics, will be made possible by first seeking their financial death which justifies their political death. Agamben focuses on the political systems that enable the persecution and internment of citizens within a state of exception, a place of legalised lawlessness on the fringes of civil society justified by the declaration of an alleged state of emergency. Those who become the persecuted targets of the state of exception are reduced to having only *zoē*, a "bare" life, while those who retain their legitimacy in the State have *zoē* with the addition of *bios,* a "political" life. A third form of life can be added to those identified by Agamben: financial *bios.* By drawing attention to financial *bios*, the oft-neglected financial persecution of citizens and its consequences are emphasised. Thus, the Holocaust tragedy can be told through three stages: loss of financial life, loss of political life, and loss of actual life.

To include financial *bios* within Agamben's thanatopolitics, the framework used here is presented as a triptych, or a "story" told in three panels in a manner often used in religious iconography (see Figure 5.1). The triptych provides a tripartite understanding of State/citizen relations to appreciate how State ideology is mediated through business and calculative practices.

DOI: 10.4324/9781032685328-5

Figure 5.1 Triptych example. Digital reconstruction of Taddeo Gaddi's triptych. Left to right: "Annunciation and Nativity", "Madonna and Child Enthroned with Ten Saints: Maestà", and "Crucifixion" Image courtesy of the New York Historical Society, licensed under the Creative Commons Attribution-Share Alike 4.0 International license

To consider the issues relevant to accounting within the triptych, a broad interpretation of what constitutes accounting has been applied, namely, the giving and receiving of financial accounts, which have moral, ethical, and hermeneutical implications (Arrington and Francis, 1993, p. 108). The framework presented in this chapter seeks deeper knowledge of accounting in its social and political contexts (Vollmer, 2007). Accounting, as a translation device, ensures that the lives of citizens are writ in accounting discourse and goes beyond "practices and institutions of a professionalised elite" (Arrington and Francis, 1993, p. 107) to include a range of calculative practices such as measuring, counting and enumerations. In these representations, the human element is negated by accounting, devaluing and rendering invisible lived experiences. What was *un*accounted for, either through silences or integers that masked the human element of transactions and events, requires alternative forms of accounts and accounting that re-situate the human experience as worthy of inclusion and value.

The application of the triptych to understand the stages that made the Holocaust possible is informed by the ideas of Agamben, most especially the concept of biopower developed initially by Foucault. Biopower relates to actions of the State that support some citizens (that is, make live) and reject others (let die). Foucault (2003) conceives that with the logic of biopower, "undesirable" elements of the population are allowed to die, and the "superior" group is made to proliferate. Given the role that accounting plays within society and in deployments of power (Miller, 1990; Miller and Rose, 1990), Agamben's conceptualisations have the potential to enrich our understanding of the role of accounting in the management of (financial) lives, more specifically the role of accounting in the State's pursuit of thanatopolitics. It reveals how a loss of financial life is one of three major ways the State can subject citizens ultimately to death. Agamben pays attention to the power apparatuses that enable the loss of life and the inextricable links between law, politics, and economics. Genocide, thereby, can be deconstructed as the last horror of a systematic process of eradicating citizen wealth, stripping away political identity, and only then killing people. Agamben's ideas offer a means of gaining greater insight into the thanatopolitical agenda of especially totalitarian regimes by examining the interrelationships between businesses, the State, and the citizenry.

Forms of life and State power

Forms of life

Agamben emphasises how the delineation of life forms serves to separate humans from all living things and partition humans into two jurisdictions, with potentially devastating consequences. He notes that

> the Greeks had no single term to express what we mean by the word 'life.' They used two terms that ... are semantically and morphologically distinct: *zoē*, which expressed the simple fact of living common to all living beings (animals, men or gods), and *bios*, which indicated the form or way of *living proper* to an individual or group.
>
> (Agamben 1995, p. 1, emphasis added)

Zoē is the most basic form of life common to both humans and animals, a bare life concerned with survival and reproduction. The rapid development of technology and associated biological imperatives of the 20th century politicised bare life, and *zoē* "entered into the sphere of the polis" (Agamben, 1995, p. 4). *Zoē*, which was conceptually non-political, the life of "fungible anonymous bodies" (Bazzicalupo, 2006, p. 115), became an object of State interest. Caught within the realm of the polis, *zoē* does not participate politically, yet ironically, "no life, as exiles and bandits know well, is more 'political' than [this]" (Agamben, 1995, p. 184).

With only *zoē,* whole populations when a state of exception is declared may become subject to the will of the State as a potentially legally sanctioned object of exile, violence, or death. When existence is reduced to a bare life, every right bestowed that differentiates humans from other living organisms is stripped by the State, effectively "killing" without committing homicide (Agamben, 1995). Opportunities for genocide then emerge, reflected as a loss of *zoē*. The ability to kill whole populations, coupled with technologies capable of mass murder and action at a distance, yielded Arendt's (2013, p. 91) horrific and yet plausible conjecture that

> one fine day a highly organised and mechanised humanity will conclude quite democratically – namely by majority decision – that for humanity as a whole it would be better to liquidate certain parts thereof.

Bios refers to the uniquely human ability to participate politically, be present in the political arena, and have a right to political existence and the benefits this provides. *Bios* refers to the right to have rights (Arendt, 2013, p. 91). This does not mean that *bios* protects the citizen from violence by the State, as rights are also "the instruments that the sovereign uses for imposing [its] own domination" (Esposito, 2013, p. 363), and once revoked, the *zoē* is exposed to State-derived impediments to survival and reproduction.

Lost *bios* results in lost liberty and personal freedoms, exemplified through the practice of forced labour where during World War II labour carried out by foreigners was generally in exchange for payment, and slave labour carried out by Jews and other non-Aryan Germans was paid not to the labourers but to the State in a "lease" agreement and internment within concentration camps in Nazi Germany. The active encouragement of forced and slave labour in German corporations, perceived as cheap and good for business, disregarded the violence, degrading treatment, and starvation to which the workers were exposed. The human side of forced and slave labour was largely discounted by not only the guards at the camps but also the managers and executives of businesses who employed "unpaid workers earmarked for destruction" (Ferencz, 1979, p. xxv). The loss of *bios* removed the personal freedom and liberty of non-Aryans and forced workers by infringing on previously held rights. Accounting condensed the cost of labour and associated costs of labour, for example rations and clothing, into one-dimensional metrics, but survivor testimony discloses the conditions of the camp, the violence endured, and the lasting trauma of lost *bios*.

The singularity of *bios* neglects the financial self, which is central to State/citizen relations. Accordingly, the notion of financial life (financial *bios)* is given prominence in this study to recognise a more nuanced understanding of Agamben's *bios*, which in subsequent discussion will be distinguished as political *bios*. Financial *bios* requires differentiation from political *bios*, as each refers to distinctly different modes of "living proper" (Agamben, 1995). Citizen identity is often couched in terms of their labour or possession of capital and property. Situating our place in the world, we do not usually refer to our intrinsic values or political action. This is essentially beyond societal expectations. For example, when most citizens ask "What do you do?" they seek an answer in economic terms, that is, what job/labour do you partake in or "Where do you live?" which gives socio-economic connotations. Instead, our sense of identity is shaped by a series of transactions that cheapen our identity to "economic men [sic]" (Arendt, 1964; Miller and O'Leary, 1987; Bhimani, 1994). To bring the notion of political *bios* back to its Aristotelian origins, being the first to denote the *zoē* and *bios* ("active" life), an aspirational life which was purely political, without economic connotations, financial life should be seen as a means to a political life rather than modernity's reversal of this process (Arendt, 1964). To achieve this, the financial aspect is highlighted, rather than immersed into the political, so the impact of financial persecution on citizens and the role(s) of accounting can be acknowledged.

Citizens have financial lives (Martins, 2002; Bay, 2018), and accounting is the dominant mode of understanding people's financial lives. As a translation device, accounting ensures that citizens' lives are writ in accounting discourse. Financial accounts are given between people daily in the form of budgets for the household, the value of commodities, or the cost of utilities. This often mundane expression of an individual's life is frequently discounted in other social, political, and legal theories. It is, therefore, unsurprising that major theorists such as Agamben have been disinterested in the veiled power of accounting. Accounting operates surreptitiously but nonetheless imparts human (re)presentation in accounting terms as the "indispensable" and unifying language of economics (Lavoie, 1987, p. 602). Accounting can then become a tool (weapon) apt for use by a State, mediated through business, in implementing its policies. Accounting is intimately linked to the exercise of State power (Miller, 1986, 1990) in that it is used as a technique by the State to operationalise its abstract political objectives (Hopwood, 1984, 1986; Miller, 1990). Thus, accounting, as part of the private sphere of citizens, delivers and enforces State directives, which can make live, or make die, financial *bios*.

The addition of financial *bios* recognises the pervasive and concealed role of accounting in facilitating State/citizen relations. Understood as "a process of attributing financial values and rationales to a wide range of social practices" (Miller, 1990, p. 316), accounting can confer specific visibilities, calculability, and operational utility (Burchell et al., 1985; Miller and O'Leary, 1987; Miller, 1990). Broadbent (1995, p. 4) argues that "making certain aspects of reality 'visible' [accounting] creates the possibility of controlling these elements. It is this partiality in representation and its control potential which constitutes its real social influence, as well as its social danger". Accordingly, accounting can make (in)visible by creating enumerated "silences" which can obscure the social, moral, ethical and ultimately human elements. The perpetuation of such silences requires exposure, such as examining financial *bios,* which gives extra dimension to "numbers" through the integration of context and participants (Vollmer, 2007).

The role that financial death plays in political and physical death provides scope to explore the power of accounting in initiating and concealing that death. The distinction between the *zoē*, political *bios*, and financial *bios* becomes vital during the operation of thanatopower, as those without financial *bios* are placed within a separate space, the state of exception, where they are then subjected to further losses, including a loss of political *bios* and a loss of *zoē* (actual life).

State of exception

The state of exception is "the extension of the military authority's wartime powers into the civil sphere, and ... a suspension of the constitution (or of those constitutional norms that protect individual liberties)" (Agamben, 2005, p. 5). It is "an ambiguous, uncertain, borderline fringe, at the intersection of the legal and the political" (Fontana, 1999, p. 16), or, in other words, a "legal form of what cannot have legal form" (Agamben, 2005, p. 1). The state of exception becomes activated when a crisis or emergency occurs that is alleged to threaten the life of the nation and, as a concept, is historically endorsed by constitutions and international human rights treaties (Humphreys, 2006, pp. 679–680). The state of exception has been mobilised historically and globally by a number of States in varying instances of emergency. For example, a state of exception was effectively declared during the financial crises in Germany in 1923 and France in 1925, 1935, and 1937, during union strikes and social upheaval in Britain in 1920, earthquakes in Italy in 1908, and by President Lincoln, to provide a basis for the abolition of slavery in 1862, and President Roosevelt to ensure passage of the New Deal in 1933 (Humphreys, 2006, pp. 679–680). Agamben (2005, pp. 86–87) argues that a state of exception obliterates the normative quality of law and condones "with impunity ... a governmental violence that – while ignoring international law externally and producing a permanent state of exception internally – nevertheless still claims to be applying the law".

Over the last century, "legal civil war" increasingly entered the political sphere, enabling the state of exception to be an accepted mode of operation in a crisis. As Erlenbusch (2013, pp. 49–50) explains, "the exception is not so much an exception as the becoming obvious of a usually hidden mechanism of politics". The state of exception inevitably becomes the rule (Benjamin, 1942; Agamben, 2005; Huber and Scheytt, 2013), transforming from that exceptional measure to a technique of government that exercises a perpetual exercise of (realised or potential) violence over citizens (Agamben, 2005, pp. 6–7). This places citizens in the form of purgatory, with rights suspended and without the possibility of leaving the state of exception unless the State permits, leaving the potential for a citizen to be reclassified as *zoē*.

The demarcation between who will be designated *bare life* within the state of exception and stripped of financial and political *bios* is predicated on Foucault's concept of modern racism, operationalised through State ideology. Modern racism, distinguished as racism directed internally toward the

State's own citizens, created enemies who became the impetus for a power mechanism that maintained the State's power while endorsing the policies of the State, such that the State could "scarcely function without becoming involved with racism at some point" (Foucault, 2003, p. 74). Modern racism was exemplified in the Nazi State, where race became pseudo-scientifically extended to groups such as Jews and Roma. Foucault (2003, p. 77) conceded that "the word 'race' itself is not pinned to a stable biological meaning", instead offering that

> we can say that two races exist when there are two groups which, although they coexist, have not become mixed because of the differences, dissymmetries, and barriers created by privileges, customs and rights, the distribution of wealth, or the way in which power is exercised.

Modern racism sanctions the actions of the State, which by any other name would be persecution, war, murder, or massacre. Given these conditions, Foucault (2003, p. 77) outlines, "the most murderous of States are also, of necessity, the most racist". Nazism demonstrates the tight, insistent biological regulation that underpins a racist State and allows for the division of a citizenry into *zoē* and *bios,* the civil sphere, and the state of exception. The declaration of a state of emergency in Nazi Germany came swiftly after Hitler was appointed Chancellor in January 1933. An arson attack on the *Reichstag*, allegedly by political enemies, provided Hitler and the Nazis with the state of emergency that justified enacting a series of laws and policies that would fundamentally reshape the German political, social, and historical landscape (Goldhagen, 1996). The first of these laws was the *Reichstag Fire Decree* (1933), which suspended the German constitution and "swept away precious civil liberties at a stroke" (Newton, 1990, p. 191). The Decree set out in Article 1 that:

> Sections 114, 115, 117, 118, 123, 124, and 153 of the Constitution of the German Reich are suspended until further notice. Therefore, restrictions on personal liberty, on the right of free expression of opinion, including freedom of the press, on the right of assembly and the right of association, and violations of the privacy of postal, telegraphic, and telephonic communications, warrants for house searches, orders for confiscations, as well as restrictions on property, are also permissible beyond the legal limits otherwise prescribed (Decree of the Reich President for the Protection of the People and the State, 28 February 1933).

Following this, the *Enabling Act* (1933) authorised Hitler's supreme executive power, sanctioning the democratic enaction of what would become a 12-year state of exception (Newton, 1990, p. 194). What underlined the ideology and political strategy of the Nazis was anti-Semitism, as a form of modern racism, where "without anti-Semitism, Nazism would have been inconceivable, both as an ideology and as a catalyst of the emotions" (Grunberger, 1971, p. 466). The Nazi State sought to re-establish the Aryan ideal, where citizens would conform to the State's notion of Germanic heritage based mainly on physical attributes and religion. The State particularly separated the Jewish population, adopting an active and aggressive campaign of racist propaganda and legislation in an attempt to remove Jewish influence from Nazi Germany. This policy, predicated on thanatopower, had the corollary of promoting and advancing the Aryan ideal and endorsing the citizens who possessed the "correct" biological heritage. The result was internal biological warfare and indiscriminate killings of Jews, justified and carried out by the State for the good of the State and certain citizens.

The Nazi regime called for the total transformation of society and the economic system, resulting in an inverted capitalist model where private companies became complicit actors in anti-Semitic policies directed by the State. This economic inversion saw the State implement autarky, a specific policy aimed to ensure that Nazi Germany became completely self-sufficient economically while transforming private initiatives, business goals, and property into ideological directives sought by the State through the implementation of *Gleichschaltung*. Bullock (1952, p. 245) describes *Gleichschaltung* as a process by which "the whole of the organised life of the nation was to be brought under the single control of the Nazi party". The far-reaching influence of the new government was articulated by the Minister of Economy Walther Funk, who stated that industrial groups and businesses "should accomplish, in addition to their own affairs, all those tasks which the national government imposes upon them" (cited in Matz, 1940, p. 178). What followed during the next six years, leading up to the outbreak of World War II, was a total change in German life. The National Socialist regime "brought an abrupt about-face in political, cultural, social, economic and professional thinking in Germany. No phase of national life has remained untouched" (Matz, 1938, p. 392). Under *Gleichschaltung*, "the firm was then seen not only as an instrument for attaining private ends but also as part of a broader context of collective goals" (Cinquini, 2007, p. 220). In carrying out the thanatopolitical imperatives, the regime worked closely with businesses such as the Deutsche Bank (James, 2001), Ford Werke (Billstein et al., 2000), Degussa (Hayes, 2004), Krupp (Newton, 1990; James, 2012), Siemens (Newton, 1990), Volkswagen (Mommsen, 1996), Daimler-Benz (Hamburg Foundation for Social History, 1987), and IG Farben (Hayes, 1987). Businesses became strategic centres that operationalised the loss of financial and political *bios*, impacting the lives of non-Aryan citizens even to the point of death.

Thanatopolitical triptych

Concealing the invisible

The role of accounting in thanatopolitical imperatives remains invisible, and despite its position on the periphery of the wider matrix that operationalises thanatopower, accounting still holds powerful effects that we do not recognise or see because we have not had the theoretical tools to do so. Agamben gives us such tools, and the triptych mobilises his work into an empirical device to enable the interrogation of texts and artefacts as a means to make visible that which was concealed, as assisted by accounting (see Figure 5.2). This chapter focuses primarily on the first two panels of the theoretical triptych.

The origins of thanatopolitical thinking stem from Foucault's biopolitics and modern racism and Agamben's forms of life and state of

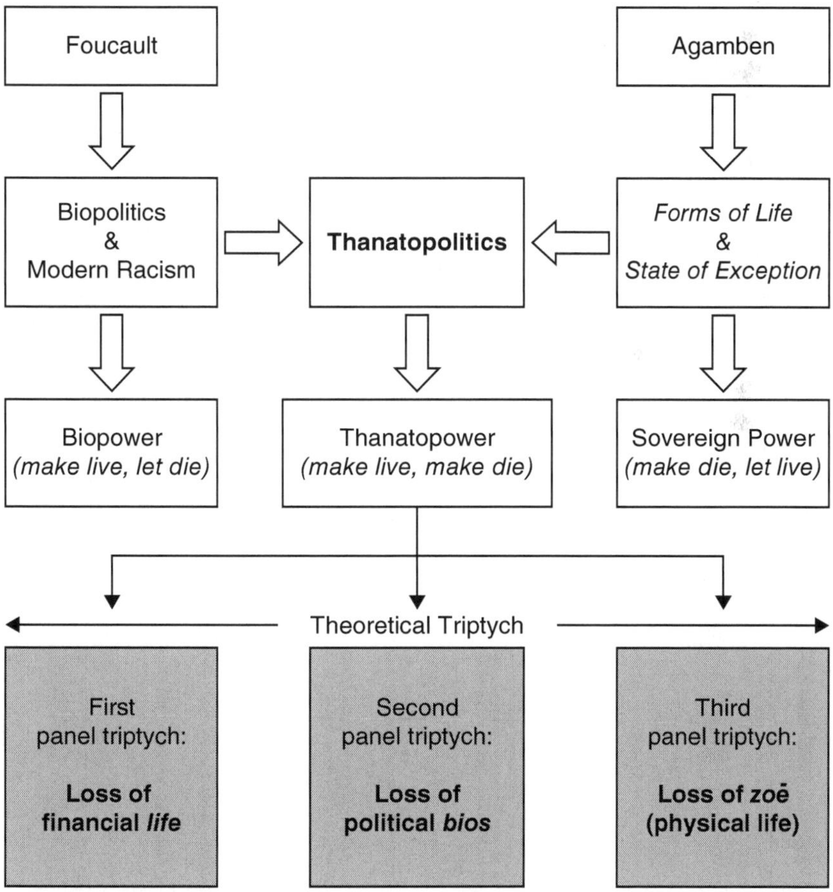

Figure 5.2 Thanatopolitical framework

exception, as depicted in the top section of the diagram. This is further elucidated by the triptych, in which each panel is explored in turn using various forms of accounts. Accounting has to "represent complex multidimensional constructs that are always limited and incomplete ... encouraging a numerical view of reality" (Morgan, 1988, p. 480), and this serves to deny a voice for the excluded or the "Other" (Broadbent, 1995; Funnell, 1998). Therefore, the numbers produced by accounting at times require alternate renderings, with other forms of accounts (re)presenting reality (Bay, 2018, p. 50).

Alternative accounts are a way of talking back to the limited and sterile practice of accounting by giving marginalised and suppressed "Others" the opportunity to account for themselves (Shearer, 2002; Tregidga, 2017). These accounts form alternate renderings of accounting information, which produce new visibilities or ways of knowing and understanding events (Dey et al., 2010, p. 64). This account can take many forms, including oral histories in the form of testimonies. Testimony, as an alternative account, is for Campbell (2011, p. 41) "the privileged mode of a new genre to be called thanatopolitical writing". Hammond and Sikka (1996, p. 10) argue that it "offers the opportunity to change the focus towards accounting's effects on people". Holocaust testimonies are unique in that the victims of lost political *bios*, at least those who survived, were able to speak to their own experiences as slave and forced labourers to give depth and understanding to what a loss of political *bios* meant, felt like, looked like and what living with that legacy is like. This unique dedication to (re)telling the business history through the testimony of victims of that company enabled a movement beyond the traditional confines of business documentation to create space for "Others" to give account and narrate their loss of political *bios* on their own terms.

The first panel explores the loss of financial *bios,* which has significant scope for examination through an accounting lens. The business history of Deutsche Bank, in conjunction with their publicly available annual reports (Deutsche Bank Annual Reports, 1933–1944), was examined to unveil how what was *un*accounted for, namely transactions, people, and figures related to Aryanisation, allowed the company to hide its connections to this process. As a result, the extent of the human ramifications of the financial persecution was largely hidden by euphemisms and special accounts that absorbed Aryanisation-related activities.

The second panel, which focuses on the German subsidiary Ford Werke (of American parent Ford Company), brings richness to the accounting literature by re-centring people as the primary focus of accounting, recognising it as a social practice. Testimony from former labourers at Ford Werke is used in examining the second panel of the triptych.

The triptych approach and the inclusion of financial *bios* pay attention to calculative practices and the insidious nature of hiding, or masking, the loss of financial, political, and eventually physical life. Focusing on the business sphere, which throughout the Holocaust was motivated primarily by profit, the infiltration of the private sphere reveals the consequences for people when accounting creates invisibilities.

The first panel of the triptych: Loss of financial bios

Banks in Germany formed the epicentre of the economy. "Banks owned the majority of corporate stock, served on corporate boards, were involved with stock market speculation and had little concern with the interests of individual minority shareholders" (Harston, 1993, p. 5). Deutsche Bank, as one of the largest banks in Germany, administered accounts of other businesses and citizens by being "involved in shifts of assets and transfers of property", which inevitably led to complicity "in what amounted in practice to a large-scale purge of German economic life" (James, 2001, p. 5).

Deutsche Bank became an instrument for facilitating the loss of financial *bios* while adopting sinister means of redirecting the wealth of exterminated Jews back to the Reich. The "administration" of bank accounts was major business for the Deutsche Bank, where "most of the true owners of this property were the murdered victims of the National Socialist genocide" (James, 2001, p. 171). Its role in fulfilling the State policy of Aryanisation was no doubt "a vital element in a chain of exploitation and theft" (James, 2001, p. 208), which deprived non-Aryans of their financial *bios*. Once depleted of economic resources and the social privileges those resources once provided, most non-Aryans who had not escaped Nazi Germany were exposed to further exploitation and degradation. This triptych panel emphasises that confiscation of wealth and "seizure of property acts as an important catalyst in accelerating the downward spiral across the threshold to genocide" (Dean, 2008, p. 15), leaving non-Aryans vulnerable to further exercises of thanatopower. With reference to the Holocaust and in terms of the history of accounting, the loss of financial *bios* is played out in two ways: first, through the Aryanisation policies of the Nazis and the concomitant role of businesses, and second, erasure of financial *bios* exemplified by the silences in Deutsche Bank's annual report.

The first action to remove Jewish influence from Nazi Germany was to exclude the Jews from the German economy, a policy known as "Aryanisation". James (2001, p. 212) outlines the rollout of Aryanisations by dividing the process into several phases:

> In the first, from 1933 to 1937, there were no [explicit] State initiatives … to expropriate or eliminate Jewish-owned business [this stage was termed 'voluntary']. In the second, from 1937 to 1939, in Germany, the state aimed at the elimination of Jewish business life … In the third, from 1938 onward, the expropriation of Jewish property outside the former German territories took place in the context of a radical mobilisation of anti-Semitic resentment, and then of a racial war. The seizure of property in Austria and the Czech lands, and the immediate and brutal persecution of Jews, provided a precedent for later occupation strategy.

On 12 June 1933, the *Law Against Betraying the German National Economy* (1933) was introduced (Bajohr, 2002, p. 154). This left the Jewish population particularly vulnerable, giving power to the banks to freeze assets, investments, and income, confiscate accounts receivable and seize passports to ensure Jews could not escape without paying an emigration levy – the *Reich Flight Tax* (1931) (Bajohr, 2002, p. 157). Restrictions were imposed on the use of Jewish assets, which prevented Jews from owning businesses and "the right to earn a living … the program effectively demanded the exclusion of Jews from economic life and their progressive expulsion from Germany" (Dean, 2008, p. 19).

After mass boycotts of Jewish businesses, called for by the State and its agencies, other laws were passed to curtail the economic life of the Jews. This included the *Law for the Restoration of the Professional Civil Service* (1933), which dismissed thousands of Jews from work when "race" became a qualification for employment (Goldhagen, 1996, p. 91). Other sanctioned racist and discriminatory practices towards Jews included the *Law on the Admission to the Legal Profession* (1933), *The Law Against Overcrowding in Schools and Universities* (1933), *The Denaturalization Law* (1933), *The Law on Exchange Control* (1935), *The Army Law* (1935), and the *Nuremberg Laws* (1935) (United States Holocaust Memorial Museum, 2018). These laws were designed to physically remove Jews from the legal profession, from attending school or university, from receiving marriage loans, to revoke German citizenship, and to block bank accounts. In sum, they were implemented to narrow the space Jews could occupy in Nazi Germany progressively.

By 1938 Aryanisation was in full effect through constricting legislation, including The Decree against the Camouflage of Jewish Firms (1938), the *Order for the Disclosure of Jewish Assets* (1938), the *Jewish Capital Levy* (1938), *the Decree on the Confiscation of Jewish Property* (1938), which culminated in the *Decree on the Exclusion of Jews from German Economic Life* (1938) (United States Holocaust Memorial Museum (USHMM), 2018). The Nazis had effectively reduced the Jewish people to poverty, casting them aside with no financial means to live or to survive. Goldhagen (1996, p. 137) explains that "the Germans' exclusion of Jews from the economy proceeded throughout the first years of the regime as the economic health of the country permitted, and then with increased vigour in 1938" with the first stages of death enabled through the policies of Aryanisation instrumentalised through businesses such as Deutsche Bank which explicitly targeted financial *bios*.

In fulfilling the State policy of Aryanisation, Deutsche Bank used "Nazi-Deutsch" rhetoric which the Nazis used to euphemistically disguise the true meaning of words or phrases to make Jewish economic extermination less visible. Accounting was altered to a form of Nazi-Deutsch, obscuring the human element of events and transactions. Transactions related to Aryanisations were subsumed under a Nazi-Deutsch account titled "Special Items or One-off Transactions" (Annual Report, 1936, p. 11; James, 2001). Supplemental material for Deutsche Bank's 1938 Annual Report includes a "breakdown of profits from transactions not regularly recurring", described by James (2001, p. 208) as pertaining to "special profits and brokerage fees in connection with Aryanisations, sales of securities and real estate, fees for listing on the stock exchange, trustees, mortgage brokerage etc.". Apart from rare instances of particularly important or unusual cases, money procured from the devastation of Jewish financial *bios* was placed into the "Special Items or One-off Transactions" account, which obscured the details of the transaction, silencing

> the core element of the whole process of Aryanisation. Jews were pressed or forced to sell businesses that they would not otherwise, in the absence of a viciously persecuting regime, have sold. They did not want money that could be transferred out of Germany only with great difficulties, and further losses (by 1938–1939 an emigrant owning financial assets would be required to leave ninety-eight to ninety-nine percent of these behind in Germany).
>
> (James, 2001, pp. 208–209)

The human account of those impacted by the Aryanisations was silenced as it fell outside the predominant discourse of accounting. Nazi-Deutsch was further utilised in the bank's annual reports to disguise the removal of Jewish financial *bios* through an Aryanisation of the workforce, bolstered by the *Law for the Restoration of the Professional Civil Service* (1933); *Law for the Protection of German Blood and German Honour* (1935), and *Reich Citizenship Law* (1935). Deutsche Bank stated that "we were able to make considerable new hires in the reporting year and fully replace the number of our employees who retired or *who left our services for other reasons*" (Annual Report, 1935, p. 18, emphasis added). Given the contextual and political pressures of the time, it is speculated as including the dismissal of workers on racial grounds that occurred in the same year.

In the absence of Nazi-Deutsch, Deutsche Bank simply remained silent on their role within Aryanisations. In examining Deutsche Bank's Annual Reports from 1933 to 1944, only one specifically mentions details surrounding an Aryanisation: "In Berlin we have taken over customers of the bank Mendelssohn & Co. for our newly acquired business associates ..." (Annual Report, 1938, p. 8). The silence on any further details obscures several important things. First, this "take over" was, in effect, a forced Aryanisation of a Jewish-owned banking firm (James, 2001). Second, Deutsche Bank had an active role in this Aryanisation and was therefore complicit in denuding the Jewish owners of their financial *bios*. Third, if the accounting had been made visible, it would likely have shown an acquisition far below its market value (Hayman, 2009). These predatory Aryanisations gave little or no goodwill consideration for such purchases, and the ensuing financial distress of the Jews was compounded by extortionate taxes on their wealth. Ultimately, this left Jews with few options: to emigrate in poverty or remain in an increasingly hostile German Reich.

Further investigations into Aryanisations carried out by Deutsche Bank revealed that while some of the non-Aryans who had been stripped of financial *bios* managed to emigrate, albeit in a destitute state, others were placed into concentration camps, and few survived (James, 2001; Hayman, 2009). Deutsche Bank, in close collaboration with the Nazis, identified Jewish businesses to Aryanise, took them over, and discarded the financial livelihoods of the former owners. Increasingly, Deutsche Bank became wedded to the Nazi party, employing party members and displaying the swastika on official company documents (Annual Report, 1939). Deutsche Bank's accounting for Aryanisations, particularly the "Special Items or One-off Transactions" account, mystified the actual nature of the events as they impacted humans, further silencing "the intrinsic value of the people's lives that [were] being destroyed" (Chwastiak and Lehman, 2008, p. 321) and its role in the instrumentalisation of Nazi thanatopolitical ideology. This rendered the human ramifications invisible, as lost financial *bios* provided the catalyst for further losses of life, both political and existential.

The second panel of the triptych: Loss of political bios

Many of the distinctive legislative instruments designed to rid the Jews of their financial *bios* similarly facilitated the removal of their political *bios*. The series of laws designed to remove Jews from the economy and from Nazi Germany itself also served to alienate and inhibit liberty. The revocation of political *bios* facilitated by the *Nuremberg Laws* (1935) ensured "life and death [were] not properly scientific concepts but rather political concepts" (Agamben, 1995, p. 164). Without financial means and civil rights, Jews and other "undesirables" either emigrated under duress or were forcibly placed into camps and used as slave or forced labour (Newton, 1990, pp. 366–367). Minister Goebbels recorded in his diary in 1942 that "the procedure is a pretty barbaric one … not much will remain of the Jews … it can be said that about 60% of them will have to be liquidated whereas only about 40% can be used for forced labour" (cited in Ferencz, 1979, p. 18). It was evident that at the outset, Jews were only allowed a stay of execution based on their productive capacity; instructions from Auschwitz's Commander Höss directed that

> the whole Jewish question will be solved in general for all of Europe after the war at the latest … Jewish manpower is to be used for heavy manual labour … Care is to be taken that Jewish labour is used only in productions which will suffer no noticeable interruption in case of a rapid withdrawal of these labour forces … It is to be avoided in every case that Jewish workers become indispensable in essential production….
>
> (cited in Ferencz, 1979, p. 13)

The outbreak of war precipitated constant and severe labour shortages in Nazi Germany. This shortage was met by involuntary labour, such as that of Yvon Thibaut from Belgium, who was compelled to perform forced labour at Ford Werke at 18 years old. He testifies:

> I was drafted to go to Germany as a forced labourer. They told me there that if I didn't go, my father or my brother would have to go in my place. Because I didn't want that, I went to Germany, to work there ... On 28 October 1942 I was transported from the train station in Charleroi. There I had to sign papers that I was going voluntarily. Of course!
>
> (Billstein et al., 2000, pp. 182–184)

Depicted only partially through accounting representations, the loss of financial *bios* of Jews established the conditions for complete exploitation by profit-driven companies such as Ford Werke, leading to a loss of political *bios*. Ford Werke was one of many companies that used 7.6 million foreign labourers and prisoner of war (POW) labour in contravention of the 1929 Geneva Convention. Ford Werke became indispensable to the Nazi war effort. For example, the Blitzkrieg that nearly secured the European continent for Nazi Germany between September 1939 and December 1941 was made possible by Ford Werke military vehicles (Billstein et al., 2000). Despite maintaining close ties to its American parent, Billstein et al. (2000, p. 158) note, "during the twelve years of the 'Thousand Year Reich', [it] took every effort to look and act like a loyal German company".

Ford Werke also made use of slave labour from the Buchenwald concentration camp, where the program of extermination-through-labour was practised within the state of exception (Billstein et al., 2000). Workers were differentiated into racial categories as mandated by the State, which dictated the wage rate, conditions, food supplied, and work to be performed. The wage rate was between 6.5 and 8 RM for German workers, 4 RM for foreign workers, and 3 RM for Jewish workers per day (Bureau of Labor Statistics, 2002; Hayes, 2004, p. 256), acknowledging that Jewish labour "could not be as productive as a free, normal, well-fed German worker. Thus, it was estimated ... that a seventy-five percent efficiency was all that could be expected" (Hayes, 1987, p. 117). These wages paid for transportation, food, and clothing costs, where Ford Werke could make "use of a large leeway to deduct for food and lodging. The payroll accountant at Ford Werke testified, soon after the war, that after withdrawals for taxes, insurance, lodging and food the [POWs] received less than half the wages due them under the regulations" (Billstein et al., 2000, p. 154). Beyond wages, accounting for slave and forced labourers is restricted to mere enumerations of employees, listed by gender and work performed.

The profit-seeking of Ford Werke enabled through the alteration of accounts, prevailed over the care of its workers while concurrently supporting thanatopolitical imperatives towards the death of the Jews and other prisoners. Funnell (1998, p. 452) explains that the value of Jewish labour was converted to a "one-dimensional metric, an integer as a component of tabulations that could be arithmetically manipulated, [that] stripped the identity and all other qualities from the Jews ... [and avoided] divulging the human correspondence of their accounts. The Jew was recognised no longer as a social being".

Inhumane treatment of forced labourers was encouraged by the Nazis, in accordance with State-directed thanatopolitical racial hierarchies, to separate the racial pedigree between foreigners. Thus, the financial racism predicated on the Nazi iteration of modern racism and legislated as part of Aryanisation policies played out into a political divide between foreign, Jewish, POW, and other labourers. Kamila Felinska, a Polish national mistaken firstly for a Russian forced labourer and then for a French woman, recollected the differences between the Ford Werke camps that housed Russians and those that housed the French as

> like heaven and earth, that was a completely different life, we even got to dance in the evenings, there was coffee ... It was that way because the French were getting Red Cross packages. The food was better there ... We had one-hour lunch break ... We got fifty marks a month at Ford ... In the Russian camp we got nothing.
>
> (Billstein et al., 2000, p. 193)

Of all the degrading and horrific experiences of the forced labourers at Ford Werke, the most common survivor memory relates to the de-individualisation and dehumanisation accorded through identification by number. Stripping people of their individuality and sense of self through legal instruments and Nazi thanatopolitical actions designed to make the humanness of the "Other" invisible through numerical representation brutalised the human experience. When not viewed as humans, they were not treated as such, leading to acts of violence and exposure to death(s). Accounting contributed to the removal of political *bios* on an individual naming level by reducing all problems (people) to numbers, where the intrinsic worth of the victims was lost. The calculative nature of accounting drained "from the objects of its calculations features which were not amendable to measurement and reporting in a numerical format" (Funnell, 1998, pp. 458–459). The numbers suppressed the people, their uniqueness and their worth, exemplified in the alternative accounts of the survivors of Ford Werke's factories:

> We got numbers. We had a sign with a card, they hung that around our necks, where we were all naked, and that was your entry number as a prisoner in Buchenwald. I had number 481756. You had to be able to

> read that in German and remember it, because constantly, when you were in the camp, later, you might be called for any reason, they called us by number, never by name …
>
> (Yvon Thibaut, in Billstein et al., 2000, pp. 209–210)

> When we first arrived with the transport, during the roll call my number was called: 465, and I didn't understand. No family, nothing, I had only had the number. Prisoner numbers, ah I took many blows for that …
>
> (Kazimierz Tarnawski, in Billstein et al., 2000, pp. 186–187)

> [What number did you have? – Interviewer] 456. They had all the numbers listed at the guardhouse. The policeman came, he would call a number, never the first or last name. As though he was calling your name. Maybe it was on a list somewhere, the name, where I come from and so on. But in the camp no names were used … I had begun to piss in my pants, I was completely neglecting myself (cries).
>
> (Stepan Saiko, in Billstein et al., 2000, p. 171)

> After fifty years everything is smoothed out, and hunger, beatings and injuries are forgotten, but it will always remain in memory that I was not Kulagina Inna, but No. 987 – Inna Kulagina, forced labourer for Ford Werke
>
> (Inna Kulagina. in Billstein et al., 2000, p. 228)

It is clear from the testimonial accounts that the workers felt, in the local, time-specific context of slave labour and at the time of their interview, that one of the most enduring violations of the war was dehumanisation and the assignation of numbers as identification to conceal personal identity.

Ford Werke profited from both the war and the competitive advantage stemming from the forced labour used from 1940 to 1944, so much so that when a high-level tax inspector was sent in September 1943 to audit Ford Werke:

> he observed an impressive growth in assets at all of the companies. He found that [Ford Werke] assets had grown from 14.8 million RM in 1938 to 36.7 million RM in 1942, and that net liquid assets had in the same period risen from 10 million RM to 28 million RM. [He] attributed this phenomenal growth [to] the use of cheap labour, such as prisoners of war and 'Ostarbeiter' [Eastern European forced labourers].
>
> (Billstein et al., 2000, p. 154)

It is interesting to note that despite profiting significantly from the Nazi war effort and maintaining a "Nazi German" face throughout the war, "as soon as the US troops arrived, [Ford Werke] turned into the courageous protectors of American property" (Billstein et al., 2000, p. 158). This shielded

Ford Company and Ford Werke from the fate of other Nazi companies criminally tried at Nuremberg. It was not until the 1990s, when survivors of the Holocaust sought restitution for forced and slave labour, that Ford Werke was questioned about its role during the war.

The example of the actions of Ford Werke allows an appreciation of how the precarious nature of personal freedom and political life can be formed when States implement a state of exception. The ideal of human rights "always simultaneously prepare[s] a tacit but increasing inscription of individuals' lives within the [S]tate order, thus offering a new and more dreadful foundation for the very power from which they [want] to liberate themselves" (Agamben, 1995, p. 121). Lost political *bios* facilitated dehumanisation which enabled inhumane treatment, for which Lippmann (2009, p. 76) blames accountants, as "their reports hid the human dimension of what occurred". Accounting practices were, therefore, intermediaries in the loss of financial and political *bios* but also the ensuing genocide, "as the accounting information disregarded basic human rights of the laborers" (Lippman and Wilson, 2007, p. 298), experiences which have been reinstated through alternative accounts. Once liberty, freedom, and rights were stripped away, either by law or by the threat of violence, the possibilities for inhumanity became endless. The next goal of the thanatopolitical State was the extermination of Jewish and non-Aryan *zoē*.

The third panel in the triptych: Loss of zoē

The final panel in the triptych relates to the loss of life experienced by over 6 million people during the Holocaust. This loss was enacted in a number of ways: poisoning in the gas chambers, execution through firing squads, starvation, death as a result of harsh conditions in the extermination camps, death through labour and violence meted out as punishment or even amusement by guards. Those who were killed at the death centres of the Nazi apparatus were not exterminated "in a mad and giant holocaust but exactly as Hitler had announced, 'as lice,' which is to say, as bare life" (Agamben, 1995, p. 114), made possible by the prior removal of their financial and political *bios*. The sacrosanct parts of humanity (encapsulated by *zoē*) became politicised and exposed to State control. Once conferred rights are revoked through legislation and the state of exception legalised, *zoē* enters the political and legal sphere in ways that were not possible before the dehumanisation took place.

As was the case with Aryanisation and slave/forced labour practices, business decisions became life and death decisions. Accountants, for example, "used a cost-benefit analysis to compare the cost of killing children with gas and then burning their bodies, to the alternative of burning the children to death" (Lippman and Wilson, 2007, pp. 288–289). The State could save ten cents per child by not gassing the children first (Fleischner, 1977). Mass gassings were devised as efficiency measures implemented to deal with the genocide "in a manner similar to production in a factory, [that is] ... killing based on the detailed organisation and principle of the assembly line" (Funnell, 1998, p. 453). German pharmaceutical companies, such as Degussa and IG Farben, through their joint venture Degesch, produced the gas Zyklon B used directly in this assembly line of death (Hayes, 2004; Twyford, 2018). Despite this fact, corporate officials denied knowledge of the use of the gas, noting that their job was to supply the Nazis "as far as output and the allocations of the Working Committee allowed, and what the Black Corps did with the substance was none of their business" (Hayes, 2004, p. 294).

The extermination of Jews was borne from the lawlessness in the state of exception, which exposed non-Aryans and other "undesirables" to unfettered violence, culminating in death. German Reich law passed over into thanatopower, which provided legal means to remove the financial and political *bios* of those previously legitimate members of the citizenry. As *zoē*, the physical death of these non-citizens was just a matter of time.

Conclusion

Thanatopolitical State imperatives facilitated by a complex matrix of interrelated actors and practices have had horrific consequences for individuals. The defining condition that allowed for the operation of thanatopower and the pursuit of death in various forms was the suspension of civil rights in conjunction with supreme executive power, the enactment of the state of exception. Within the broader socio-political and legal context, accounting has largely escaped implication for its peripheral, yet integral, role in suppressing citizen loss of life. Agamben's concept of thanatopolitics provides new understandings and renders visible that which was previously concealed by practices such as accounting by examining the silences in accounts and utilising subjects' testimonies as alternative accounts.

Extending Agamben's conceptualisations to include the notion of financial *bios* and demarcate the difference between a political and financial life have helped demonstrate how calculative practices are implicated in the violent machinations of State/citizen relations. The triptych has revealed how the Aryanisation policy stripped non-Aryans of financial *bios* as a necessary first step in the eventual genocide. The loss of financial *bios* illustrated how a mere record can have devastating effects, as it ignores the ways in which lives were (re)presented within it. Deutsche Bank became a conduit for State policy, which stripped citizens of their wealth and exposed them to destitution, violence, and death. From this vulnerable position, the stage was set for people to experience further losses, political and existential.

The second panel of the triptych reinstated the lived human experience through testimony as a form of thanatopolitical writing. It illustrated how non-Aryans were exploited by companies such as Ford Werke, who were willing conspirators in the destruction of political *bios*. This destruction is masked through quantification, and a range of alternative accounts have revealed this loss. The third and final panel in the theoretical triptych saw corporate complicity enable the mass murder of over six million Jews, with Zyklon B production helping to fulfil the thanatopolitical imperative to *make die* the *zoē* with impunity.

The power apparatuses that enabled the Holocaust, including accounting and business, were instrumental in implementing and disguising the losses initiated by the state of exception, made apparent through the theoretical triptych. Accounting as a social practice primes organisational systems, human behaviour, and political action, directly impacting people's lives. The mobilisation of accounting during totalitarian regimes or in the pursuit of thanatopolitics can mystify death in its financial, political, and actual forms by using one-dimensional integers to mask the amorality and immorality of such action. This thanatopolitical visualisation, or reinterpretation of history, can enhance our understanding of not only the Holocaust but also the impact of accounting as a practice that can silence, disguise or hide the lived human experience.

This chapter is based on the paper by Erin Twyford titled "A Thanatopolitical visualisation of accounting history: Giorgio Agamben and Nazi Germany", which originally appeared in *Accounting History* in 2021, vol. 26, no. 3, pp. 352–374. The author would like to thank the publisher, Sage, for permission to use this material.

References

Primary Sources

Deutsche Bank, *Annual Reports 1933–1944*.

Secondary Sources

Agamben, G. (1995). *Homo Sacer: Sovereign Power and Bare Life*. Stanford, CA: Stanford University Press.
Agamben, G. (2005). *State of Exception*. Chicago: The University of Chicago Press.
Arendt, H. (1964). Labor, Work, Action. *Christianity and Economic Man: Moral Decisions in an Affluent Society Conference*, November 10, University of Chicago.
Arendt, H. (2013). The perplexities of the rights of man. In: T. Campbell, and A. Sitze (Eds.). *Biopolitics: A Reader*. Durham: Duke University Press.
Arrington, C., and Francis, J. (1993). Giving economic accounts: Accounting as cultural practice. *Accounting, Organizations and Society*, *18*(2/3), 107–124.
Bajohr, F. (2002). *"Aryanisation" in Hamburg: The Economic Exclusion of Jews and the Confiscation of Their Property in Nazi Germany*. New York: Berghahn Books.
Bay, C. (2018). Makeover accounting: Investigating the meaning-making practices of financial accounts. *Accounting, Organizations and Society*, *64*, 44–54.
Bazzicalupo, L. (2006). The ambivalences of biopolitics. *Diacritics*, *36*(2), 109–116.
Benjamin, W. (1942). On the concept of history. In: H. Eilan, and M. Jennings (Eds.). *Selected Writings 1938–1940*. Cambridge: Harvard University Press.
Bhimani, A. (1994). Accounting and the emergence of "economic man". *Accounting, Organizations and Society*, *19*(8), 637–674.

Billstein, R., Fings, K., Kugler, A., and Levis, N. (2000). *Working for the Enemy: Ford, General Motors, and Forced Labour in Germany during the Second World War*. New York: Berghahn Books.

Broadbent, J. (1995). The values of accounting and education: Some implications of the creation of visibilities and invisibilities in schools. *Advances in Public Interest Accounting*, 6, 69–98.

Bullock, A. (1952). *Hitler: A Study in Tyranny*. New York: Harper Perennial.

Burchell, S., Clubb, C., and Hopwood, A. (1985). Accounting in its social context: Towards a history of value added in the United Kingdom. *Accounting, Organizations and Society*, *10*(4), 381–413.

Bureau of Labor Statistics (2002). *Prices and Wages by Decade: 1940–1949*, accessed 23/11/2020, https://libraryguides.missouri.edu/pricesandwages/1940-1949

Campbell, T. (2011). *Improper Life: Technology and Biopolitics from Heidegger to Agamben*. Minneapolis, MN: University of Minnesota Press.

Chwastiak, M., and Lehman, G. (2008). Accounting for war. *Accounting Forum*, *32*(4), 313–326.

Cinquini, L. (2007). Fascist corporative economy and accounting in Italy during the thirties: Exploring the relations between a totalitarian ideology and business studies. *Accounting, Business & Financial History*, *17*(2), 209–240.

Dean, M. (2008). *Robbing the Jews*. New York: Cambridge University Press.

Dey, C., Russell, S., and Thomson, I. (2010). Exploring the potential of shadow accounts in problematizing institutional conduct. In: A. Ball, and S. Osborne (Eds.). *Social Accounting and Public Management: Accountability for the Common Good* (pp. 64–75). New York: Routledge.

Erlenbusch, V. (2013). The place of sovereignty: Mapping power with Agamben, Butler and Foucault. *Critical Horizons*, *14*(1), 44–69.

Esposito, R. (2013). Biopolitics. In: T. Campbell, and A. Sitze (Eds.). *Biopolitics: A Reader*. Durham: Duke University Press.

Ferencz, B. (1979) Less Than Slaves: Jewish Forced Labour and the Quest for Compensation. Bloomington: Indiana University Press.

Fleischner, E. (Ed.). (1977). *Auschwitz: Beginning of a New Era*. New York: Cathedral Church of St John the Divine.

Fontana, A. (1999). Du droit de résistance au devoir d'insurrection. In: J. Zancarini (Ed.). *Lé droit de résistance*. Paris: EN.

Foucault, M. (2003). *Society Must Be Defended: Lectures at the Collège de France 1975–1976*. New York: Picador.

Funnell, W. (1998). Accounting in the service of the Holocaust. *Critical Perspectives on Accounting*, *8*(4), 435–464.

Goldhagen, D. (1996). *Hitler's Willing Executioners: Ordinary Germans and the Holocaust*. London: Abacus.

Grunberger, R. (1971). *The 12-Year Reich: A Social History of Nazi Germany 1933–1945*. Canada: Hold, Rinehart and Winston.

Hamburg Foundation for Social History (Ed.). (1987). *Das Daimler-Benz-Buch: Ein Rustungskonzern im Tausendjahrigen Reich*. Hamburg: Delphi Politik published by GRENO.

Hammond, T., and Sikka, P. (1996). Radicalizing accounting history: The potential of oral history. *Accounting, Auditing & Accountability Journal*, *9*(3), 79–97.

Harston, M. (1993). The German accounting profession – 1931 and before: A reflection of national ideologies. *The Accounting Historians Journal*, *20*(2), 139–162.

Hayes, P. (1987). *Industry and Ideology: IG Farben in the Nazi Era*. New York: Cambridge University Press.

Hayes, P. (2004). *From Cooperation to Complicity: Degussa in the Third Reich*. New York: Cambridge University Press.

Hayman, S. (Director). (2009). *Mendelssohn, the Nazis, and Me*. Motion picture, Renegade Pictures.

Hopwood, A. (1984). Accounting and the pursuit of efficiency. In: A Hopwood, and C. Tomkins (Eds.). *Issues in Public Sector Accounting*. Oxford: Philip Allan.

Hopwood, A. (1986). Management accounting and organizational action: An introduction. In: M. Bromwich, and A. Hopwood (Eds.). *Research and Current Issues in Management Accounting*. London: Pitman.

Huber, C., and Scheytt, T. (2013). The dispositif of risk management: Reconstructing risk management after the financial crisis. *Management Accounting Research*, *24*(2), 88–99.

Humphreys, S. (2006). Legalizing lawlessness: On Giorgio Agamben's state of exception. *The European Journal of International Law*, *17*(3), 677–687.

James, H. (2001). *The Deutsche Bank and the Nazi Economic War against the Jews*. Cambridge: Cambridge University Press.

James, H. (2012). *Krupp: A History of the Legendary German Firm*. Princeton, NJ: Princeton University Press.

Lavoie, D. (1987). The accounting of interpretations and the interpretation of accounts: The communicative function of "the language of business". *Accounting, Organizations and Society*, *12*(6), 579–604.

Lippman, E. (2009). Accountant's responsibility for the information they report: An historical case study of financial information. *Accounting Historians Journal*, *26*(1), 61–79.

Lippman, E., and Wilson, P. (2007). The culpability of accounting in perpetuating the Holocaust. *Accounting History*, *12*(3), 283–303.

Martins, R. (2002). *The Financialization of Daily Life*. Philadelphia, PA: Temple University Press.

Matz, A. (1938). The position of the German accountant. *Accounting Review*, *13*(4), 392–395.

Matz, A. (1940). Accounting as a tool for economy in German business. *Accounting Review*, *15*(2), 177–185.

Miller, P. (1986). Accounting for progress – national accounting and planning in France: A review essay. *Accounting, Organizations and Society*, *11*(1), 83–104.

Miller, P. (1990). On the interrelations between accounting and the State. *Accounting, Organizations and Society*, 15(4), 315–338.

Miller, P., and O'Leary, T. (1987). Accounting and the construction of the governable person. *Accounting, Organizations and Society*, *12*(3), 235–265.

Miller, P., and Rose, N. (1990). Governing economic life. *Economy and Society* 19(1), 1–31.

Mommsen, H. (1996). *Das Volkswagenwerk und seine Arbeiter im Dritten Reich*. Düsseldorf: Econ.

Morgan, G. (1988). Accounting as reality construction: Towards a new epistemology for accounting practice. *Accounting, Organizations and Society*, *13*(5), 477–485.

Newton, D. (1990). *Germany 1918–1945: From Days of Hope to Years of Horror*. Melbourne: Collins Dove.

Shearer, T. (2002). Ethics and accountability: From the for-itself to the for-the-other. *Accounting, Organizations and Society*, *27*(6), 541–573.

Tregidga H. (2017), "Speaking truth to power": Analysing shadow reporting as a form of shadow accounting. *Accounting, Auditing and Accountability Journal*, *30*(3), 510–533.

Twyford, E. (2018). The State in pursuit of thanatopolitics: Accounting and the citizenry. Doctor of Philosophy thesis, School of Accounting, Economics and Finance, University of Wollongong. https://ro.uow.edu.au/theses1/569

United States Holocaust Memorial Museum (2018). *Anti-Semitic Legislation 1933–1939*, retrieved 31/05/2018, <https://www.ushmm.org/wlc/en/article.php?ModuleId=10007901 2018>

Vollmer, H. (2007). How to do more with numbers. Elementary stakes, framing, keying, and the three-dimensional character of numerical signs. *Accounting, Organizations and Society*, *32*(6), 577–600.

Appendix – List of Persecutory Legislation

Reich Flight Tax (1931).
Reichstag Fire Decree (1933).
Enabling Act (1933).
Law Against Malicious Gossip (1933).
Law Against Betraying the German National Economy (1933).
Law for the Restoration of the Professional Civil Service (1933).
Law on the Admission to the Legal Profession (1933).
Law Against Overcrowding in Schools and Universities (1933).
Law for the Prevention of Progeny of the Genetically Unhealthy (1933).
The Denaturalization Law (1933).
Law for the Prevention of Hereditarily Diseased Offspring (1933).
The Law on Exchange Control (1935).
The Army Law (1935).
Law for the Protection of German Blood and German Honour (1935) (Nuremberg Law).
Reich Citizenship Law (1935) (Nuremberg Law).
Hitler Youth Law (1936).
Executive Order on the Reich Tax Law (1936).
Executive Order on the Law on the Alteration of Family and Personal Names (1938).
The Decree Against the Camouflage of Jewish Firms (1938).
Order for the Disclosure of Jewish Assets (1938).
Jewish Capital Levy (1938).
Decree on the Confiscation of Jewish Property (1938).
Decree on the Exclusion of Jews from German Economic Life (1938).
Ordinance on the Restoration of Street Scenery at Jewish Commercial Centres (1938).
Ordinance on the Registration of the Property of Jews (1938).
Ordinance on an Expiation Payments by Jews of German Citizenship (1938).

The Decree Concerning the Surrender of Precious Metals and Stones in Jewish Possession (1939).
Excess Profits Act (1939).
Decree of the Führer and Reich Chancellor on the Utilisation of the Requisitioned Property of Enemies of the Reich (1941).
Eleventh Ordinance of the Reich Citizen's Law (1942).
Audit of Dejewification Transactions (1942).

6 The expulsion of Jews from the accountancy profession in Fascist Italy

Valerio Antonelli, Raffaele D'Alessio, and Stephen P. Walker

Introduction

Numerous historical studies of the accounting profession have demonstrated how practitioner élites appropriate socio-economic privileges by restricting access to the vocation (Poullaos and Ramirez, 2020). Among the bases of exclusion are credentials, nature of work, religion, gender, class, and race. Exclusion relates to persons who meet the qualifications of a profession but are denied access by those who control it (Witz, 1992, pp. 45–46). In contrast to studies of *exclusion,* this chapter explores a project of race-based *expulsion* from the accountancy profession. As a concept, expulsion focuses on those who have been admitted and established residency in a domain, but their right to remain has been denied or terminated. In the world of professionalism, expulsion is primarily understood as a punitive measure meted out to insiders found guilty of an act of gross misconduct or a serious violation of an ethical code. The expulsion of a member for such reasons is a testament to a professional organisation's willingness to take the corrective action necessary to earn public trust (Freidson, 2001, pp. 213–216). However, the expulsion of an individual or group from a State can also be founded on their classification as undesirable or as a threat. Mass expulsions, such as ethnic cleansing, may be predicated on the basis of race, language, or religion. Such removals may be ordered not internally, by a profession itself, but by an external agency such as the State (Henckaerts, 1995). This chapter focuses on the expulsion of Jewish accountants from their profession as part of an overt programme of State racism.

To help navigate analysis of the collective expulsion of accountancy practitioners based on race the chapter draws upon Foucault's notion of biopolitics, "the attempt, starting from the eighteenth century, to rationalise the problems posed to governmental practice by phenomena characteristic of a set of living beings forming a population: health, hygiene, birthrate, life expectancy, race" (Foucault, 2008, p. 317). Biopolitics is actualised through the exercise of biopower, which Foucault (2007, p. 1) defined as "the set of mechanisms through which the basic biological features of the human species became the object of a political strategy". This is examined with

DOI: 10.4324/9781032685328-6

the deployment of apparatuses by the Fascist State to expel Jews from the Italian accountancy profession on the basis of race. In this project, fascistised professional organisations were themselves engaged as agents of racial purification.

To date, studies of the treatment of Jews in the accounting profession have focussed on National Socialist Germany. Markus (1997, pp. 63–93) documented the Nazification of the profession following Hitler's assumption of power in 1933 and the consequences for Jewish practitioners. While the scale of the genocide perpetrated by the Hitlerian State has inevitably resulted in a focus on Nazi Germany, and much attention has been devoted to the role of accountants within that regime (Funnell, 1998; Walker, 2000; Lippman and Wilson, 2011, 2013; Detzen and Hoffmann, 2018), Fascist Italy is also worthy of attention. Here, from 1938 to 1943, "a debilitating campaign" was pursued against the Jewish population in the name of racial purity (Zimmerman, 2005, p. 3). Indeed, it is increasingly recognised that the differences between anti-Jewish laws in Germany and Italy primarily relate to chronology and the degrees of violence associated with their implementation (Sarfatti, 2005).

One historian has observed that anti-Semitism was a common feature of Nazism and Italian Fascism, the principal difference being in the version of the authoritarian State that practiced it (Livingston, 2014, p. 117). Another commentator has ventured further, arguing that "Fascist Italy was the model and origin for Hitler's totalitarian racial state and adopted many of the latter's racist laws from the late 1930s onwards" (Gordon, 2012, p. 5). Not surprisingly, given such assertions, the limited attention traditionally devoted to the historiography of Italian race law is now being addressed (Zimmerman, 2005, p. 1; Livingston, 2014, pp. 2–7). Scrutiny, however, has yet to extend to the expulsion of Jewish accountants, who, along with entrepreneurs, bankers, managers, and property owners, were constructed as money-hoarding pollutants of a pure Italian race (Marro, 1940, p. 265; De Felice, 1993, p. 258; Avagliano and Palmieri, 2013, p. 41).

The chapter is structured as follows. The theoretical framing of the study, Foucault's concepts of biopower, biopolitics and race, are discussed in the next section. Sources and methods are then described after which the chapter describes the structure of the accountancy profession immediately prior to the adoption of the racial laws in Italy in 1938. Thereafter, the theoretical framework is used to explore the Fascist regime's attempt to gain knowledge of the Jewish population through mechanisms of identification and calculation and explain the bureaucratic apparatuses implemented to expel Jews from the accountancy profession. Later sections analyse the "taking" of the lives of Jewish practitioners through expulsion, and in some cases, their extermination, as well as the "let live" provisions that enabled some Jewish accountants to continue to practice, albeit with an inferior status. The chapter closes with a concluding discussion that offers a synthesis of the main findings.

The biopolitics of the racist State

Foucault's (1978, pp. 139–145) notion of biopolitics, which he initially articulated in Volume 1 of the *History of Sexuality*, concerns the manner in which modern States manage populations. In his formative contribution, Foucault (2003, p. 241) emphasised how the management of populations shifted from exercising (sovereign) power over death to exercising power over life. In the era of biopower, life, and its mechanisms became subjects of calculation, intervention, and transformation. Whereas sovereign power "took life and let live", biopower was concerned with "making live and letting die" (Foucault, 2003, p. 247). Foucault (1978, p. 139) asserted that from the 19th century, the pursuit of biopolitics was activated "through an entire series of interventions and regulatory controls". The complex bureaucracies of States used numerous apparatuses to observe, construct, and control their populations. Biopolitics involved the identification by the State of threats to life, the delineation of fields of intervention and the deployment of agencies, institutions, and procedures to address such threats (Lemke, 2001).

Governments could also attempt to manage populations on the basis of racism. For Foucault (2003, p. 255), race is "a way of separating out the groups that exist within the population". As a mode of biopolitical government, racism is focused on the differentiation of worthy and unworthy life, of those who must live and those who must die, between the biologically fit and the unfit (Foucault, 2003, p. 255; Mbembe, 2003; Dean, 2010, p. 165; Lemke, 2011, pp. 40–42; Rasmussen, 2011; Taylor, 2011). Foucault (2003, p. 82) argued that society needs to be defended from the contagion of those deemed biologically inferior. This requires that States take control of the biological field, gain knowledge about it, and subdivide the population into a hierarchy of races wherein some are deemed superior and worthy, and others are considered inferior and unworthy. Indeed, the racist State assumes the role of "protector of social purifications" (Stoler, 1995, p. 81). It activates projects of racial hygiene and the elimination of those deemed threatening.

When race intervenes, the biopolitical objective of maximising life can be conjoined by the exercise of sovereign power over death: "the death of the other, the death of the bad race, of the inferior race" (Foucault, 2003, p. 255; Erlenbusch, 2017, p. 139). When racist States operate in "biopower mode" racism provides the ideological justification for measures to cleanse the population, including killing (Foucault, 2003, pp. 256, 258). For Foucault (2003, p. 256), "racism is the precondition for exercising the right to kill". Nazi Germany represents the most extreme example (Foucault, 1978, pp. 149–150; 2003, pp. 82–83, pp. 258–260; Stoler, 1995, p. 28). Here, absolute State racism was manifested not only in intensive biopolitical control of the social body through apparatuses of regulation but also in the employment of the sovereign power to kill (Foucault, 2003, p. 260; Dean, 2010, p. 164).

Beyond the case of the Hitlerian State, and importantly for the purposes of this study, Foucault elaborated further on his meaning of "killing" when discussing the application of sovereign power by racist States operating in biopower mode: "When I say 'killing,' I obviously do not mean simply murder as such, but also every form of indirect murder: the fact of exposing someone to death, increasing the risk of death for some people, or, quite simply, political death, *expulsion*, rejection, and so on" (Foucault, 2003, p. 256, *emphasis added*). In the current study, while cases are identified after 1943 of the actual killing of Jewish accountants when parts of Italy fell under the control of Nazi Germany, the focus is on such "indirect murder" through expulsion.

To explore the biopolitical operation of a racial programme of the expulsion of Jews from the accountancy profession in Fascist Italy the study employs Foucault's thinking on the relationship between biopolitics and race. Institutions engaged in controlling the focal population exercised biopower through mechanisms such as enumeration, monitoring, and expelling.

The focal site of the study, Italy, has been a location from which key theoretical advances and empirical investigations of biopolitics have emerged (Welch, 2016, pp. 21–22; Vatter, 2017). The "biopolitical logics of racialization" and the institution of the apparatuses necessary for their actualising were especially evident in the discursive creation of the "nationalization" of the Italian population following unification (Welch, 2016, p. 10). This emphasised the removal of unworthy forms of life. In the case reported in this chapter, the State pursued biological anti-Semitism through the regulatory biopolitics of identifying and *expelling* an inferior race (Sarfatti, 2005). The aim was "to eliminate all Jews, whether Italian or foreign from Italian soil and from Italian society" (Sarfatti, 2005, p. 75). The chapter, therefore, examines the specific assemblage of biopower operated under Fascism that was directed at the expulsion of Jews from a profession. It shows how the accountancy organisations that represented practitioners featured as regulatory agencies in a biopolitical project of State racism. Also revealed are the complexities of attempting to "kill" through expulsion in a context where provision was also made to "let live" on grounds unrelated to biological race. Consistent with the call to penetrate the centrality of racism in the biopolitical management of life by examining it from a number of perspectives, the study also relates the experiences of some of the individual Jewish accountants who suffered its consequences (Mills, 2018, p. 166). Chapter 11 provides more accounts of such experiences.

Biopolitical empirics

Although Foucault's early articulation emphasised the "epochal and totalizing" surfacing of biopower, he later suggested inquiries into its particularities (Critical Genealogies Collaboratory, 2018). Indeed, while biopolitics is often analysed in general and abstract ways, it is also recognised that studies "need to be grounded in a situated analysis that accounts for how biopolitics operate in particular sites" (Scheel, 2020,

p. 573). Such an approach invites contextualised and empirical analyses of the archive. To that end, in the current investigation, numerous primary and secondary sources were consulted to gain insights into the macro population and micro biopolitics of expulsion from the accountancy profession in Fascist Italy.

At the macro level of the State the main primary sources used were the laws and supplementary regulations issued by the Fascist regime, which are available in the online archive of the Official Gazette of the Kingdom of Italy. Other documents utilised included the reports of the President of the National Centre of Statistics on the Jewish census of 1938 and national lists of Jewish auditors issued by the Ministry of Justice. Insights were also gained from articles published in contemporary newspapers (including *Il Popolo d'Italia*, *La Stampa*, *La Nazione*, *Corriere della Sera*, *Il Piccolo*, *Il Corriere Adriatico*), magazines (such as *La Difesa della Razza*, which was dedicated to anti-Semitic propaganda), and the official journal of Fascist professional accountants (*Il Commercialista*).

At the regional and local level, data relating to Jewish professional accountants who were expelled and/or separately categorised under the racial laws were gathered from the surviving records of local Fascist associations of professional accountants. Thirty-seven sets of minutes of the board meetings of these associations were examined. These related to the branches in Milan (for the Lombardy region), Bologna (Emilia Romagna), Venice (Veneto), Rome (Lazio), Turin (Piedmont), Trieste (Venezia Giulia and Zara), Trento (Trentino), Florence (Tuscany) and Genoa (Liguria). From these sources, information was collected about Jewish professional accountants in regions that, according to census data, contained 96.7% of the Jewish population in Italy (Mancinelli, 1938; De Felice, 1993, p. 263). No board minutes could be found in the relevant State archives for the six regions in which the remaining 3.3% of the Jewish population resided. The official lists of accountants who were labelled as Jewish practitioners in the Veneto and Piedmont regions were located and analysed.

At the micro level, the minute books of local Fascist associations of accountants offered detailed insights to individual encounters with the apparatus deployed to implement policies of expulsion. Experiences of expulsion were also revealed. For certain Jewish accountants, additional material was available from files in the State archives of Verona and Turin. These contained correspondence with the Department of Demography and Race at the Ministry of Interior as well as with the local judiciary, civil registration personnel (to establish Jewish status), Fascist Party officials, municipal officers, and accountancy organisations. The files also contained reports of police investigations into accountants. A number of cases that best illustrated the impacts of encounters with the apparatuses of biopower were selected for discussion in this chapter. Others feature in Chapter 11.

The next section introduces the structure of the accountancy profession in Italy during the years immediately preceding the focal period of the study.

The accounting profession prior to State racism

Before the enactment of anti-Semitic legislation, the accountancy profession in Italy was divided into three categories: accountants (*ragionieri collegiati*), doctors of commerce (*dottori commercialisti*), and official auditors (*revisori ufficiali dei conti*) (Cantagalli, 1996; Barone, 2000; Colecchia et al., 2013). Each of these categories was separately regulated. Accountants were the oldest legally recognised professional category. In 1906 it was legislated that the names of accountants should be entered on a register maintained by a local college (Article 2, Royal Decree 715/1906). Colleges were established in every province of the kingdom (Coronella, Sargiacomo and Walker, 2015). In order to be enrolled on the register a prospective accountant had to satisfy a number of conditions. These concerned Italian citizenship, absence of criminal convictions, possession of a diploma in accountancy, completion of a 2-year internship, and passing a practical examination (Article 2, Law 327/1906). The main responsibilities entrusted to accountants, as stipulated by a Royal Decree in March 1929, were to: provide services relating to the formation, merger, and liquidation of entities; sit on boards of statutory auditors; act as trustees in bankruptcy and related proceedings; act as judicial commissioners responsible for inspecting the books of joint-stock companies; draw up accounting plans for private and public companies; and, act as consultants in accounting and auditing. In addition, accountants were empowered to accept roles conferred on them by judicial authorities (Article 1, Royal Decree 552/1929).

The second category, doctors of commerce, was recognised by a Royal Decree of 28 March 1929. Doctors of commerce were required to be Italian citizens, have no previous convictions, hold a degree in economics, and pass a qualifying examination (Article 5, Royal Decree 588/1929). The names of doctors of commerce were enrolled on the local professional register, subject to scrutiny by a committee chaired by a judge (Article 9, Royal Decree 588/1929). Although they could perform a number of the duties assigned to accountants, doctors of commerce were also involved in the administration of public and private companies and the management of trading, banking, and insurance concerns. They could act as statutory auditors of joint-stock companies and be remitted to perform appraisals and arbitrations in relation to economic, commercial, financial, and administrative matters (Article 2, RD 588/1929).

The profession of official auditor, the third category, was regulated by a Royal Decree of 24 July 1936. This established that joint-stock companies with a capital of not less than one million lire should choose a number of members of their board of statutory auditors from the register of official auditors (RD 1548/1936, Article 1). The board of statutory auditors, which was appointed by the shareholders, was remitted to monitor the board of directors, audit annual reports, and review a company's legality (Articles 4–6). The national register of auditors, maintained by the Ministry of Justice (Article 11), was open to Italian citizens who had competently performed the functions of auditor, trustee, administrative officer, or accountant for at least fifteen years (Article 12). Candidates for admission to the register were also required to be of sound morals (Article 2, Royal Decree No. 228 of 10 February 1937). Accountants and doctors of commerce might also appear on the register of auditors (Article 14, RD 1548/1936).

A Law passed on 25 April 1938 (897/1938, Article 1) established the general principle that the professions in Italy could only be practiced by those whose name appeared on a register. Responsibility for keeping the registers of accountants and doctors of commerce was entrusted to the Fascist Local Branches of Doctors of Commerce (Article 3). The local associations of accountants, which had replaced the colleges of accountants, were abolished (Revere, 1936). A Royal Decree in May 1938 also required that auditors be registered with the National Fascist Party (Article 1, Royal Decree n 743 of 2 May 1938). A total of 3,206 professional accountants were thereafter enrolled in the Fascist local branches (Barone, 2000, p. 327). Of these, 1,149 were doctors of commerce, 993 of whom were registered members of the National Fascist Party (Cantagalli, 1996, p. 246). With each of these institutions, the racist Fascist State established apparatuses to expel the Jews as a biological category, an inferior race, from the institutions of the Italian accountancy profession.

Quantifying the inferior race

Although there was little evidence of racial anti-Semitism in the Fascist government that assumed power in Italy in 1922, this changed with the invasion of Ethiopia in 1935–1936 (Bernardini, 1977) and the regime's subsequent closer alignment with Nazi Germany (Duggan, 2008, pp. 511–512). A programme of racial biopolitics was inaugurated that found form with the introduction of a range of policies, statutes, and bureaucratic apparatuses.

An anti-Jewish policy was declared by the Fascist government in summer 1938. The race laws that followed were founded on biological concepts of racial difference (Bernardini, 1977; Sarfatti, 2005). Given limited adherence to anti-Semitism in the Italian population, the Fascist regime undertook a vociferous propaganda campaign against the Jewish minority. This began in spring 1938 and was directed at Jewish presence in all aspects of political, economic, and social life (Martelli, 2005, p. 31 ff.). A *Manifesto of Race* was published in July that offered a pseudo-scientific explanation for the construction of the "Italian race" as Nordic-Aryan and as unique and pure (Cuomo, 2005, pp. 128–130; Dell'Era, 2011, p. 11). It was asserted that the Italian race should not be contaminated by Jews, who were identified as belonging to lesser "non-European" races (Bernardini, 1977; Gillette, 2001). The *Manifesto* was followed by the appearance of the magazine *In Defence of Race*, which employed racial theories to distinguish and deride Jews

(Cassata, 2008, pp. 161–162). Newspapers also began to regularly publish articles with anti-Jewish content (Sarfatti and Tedeschi, 2006, pp. 105–112).

Biopower works by regulating populations, invariably territorialised as nation-States (Fiaccadori, 2015). In order to manage populations and groups therein they first need to be identified and constructed as "objects of government" (Scheel, 2020, p. 585). In Fascist Italy, the State sought to quantify and locate the "bad" race through statistical methods. Foremost among these was the census of population. On 22 August 1938, a census of Jews showed that there were 57,425 residents in Italy among a population of 43 million (Archivio Centrale dello Stato (ACS), 1938–1943c). The census of the Jews was an exceptional event (Edallo, 2023). It helped to establish clear boundaries between Jews and non-Jews. The enumeration was separate from the decennial census of the Italian population (Savorgnan, 1939, p. 1). It sought to enumerate all residents, whether temporary or permanent, who were recognised as "Israelites". Each Jewish citizen was to provide information about birth, gender, marriage, family, domicile, profession, war merits, race, religion and National Fascist Party registration (Sabatello, 1976). The data gathered by the census facilitated the management and control of the "contagion" represented by the presence of a race identified as inferior within the Italian population (Sarfatti, 1993).

It was propagandised that the number of Jews in spheres of Italian economic and social life should equal their demographic representation in the population, that is, one per thousand. Where the proportion of Jews in a sphere exceeded 0.1%, laws would be passed to constrain the rights of the Jewish minority (De Felice, 1993, p. 379). The 1938 census revealed that 9.4% of the Jewish population were professionals (accountants, lawyers, notaries, doctors, engineers, architects, surveyors, and pharmacists). The proportion of professionals, of all races, in the Italian population was 0.8% (Calimani, 2015, p. 463). Therefore, Jews were almost ten times more likely to be professionals than Italians in general. This was deemed a breach of the principle of "race and percentage" (Interlandi, 1938, p. 5). As a result, the pursuit of professions by Jews was to be addressed (ACS, 1938–1943b; De Felice, 1993, p. 381).

The State-censored press also embarked on local enumerations of Jewish accountants. On 30 August 1938, an article was published in *Il Popolo d'Italia*, the mouthpiece of the national Fascist Party, titled "Too many Jews among Doctors of Commerce". Consistent with the "race and percentage" policy, it was argued that Jews should constitute around one per thousand doctors of commerce. It was noted that in Milan, 8% of doctors of commerce and 3% of accountants were Jews (Anonymous, 1938a). In September 1938 other newspapers presented increasingly detailed analyses of the number of Jews in the accountancy profession (Anonymous, 1938b, 1938c, 1938d, 1938f, 1938g). For example, on 13 September 1938 *La Stampa*, commenting on Turin, printed an article titled "The Jewish Octopus. Accountants: 16.17 per cent". The author calculated, on the basis of

Jewish-sounding surnames contained in the Piedmont register of doctors of commerce, that 22 of the 136 registered practitioners in the province (that is, 16.17%) were Jewish.

These initial attempts to locate and enumerate Jews in the accountancy profession tended towards overestimation and exaggeration. However, they underpinned anti-Semitic propaganda intended to construct a racially defined group of professionals as biologically inferior and dangerous (De Felice, 1993, p. 381; Martelli, 2005, p. 43). The results derived from the application of these mechanisms were also used to legitimate biopolitical intervention. In accountancy, an opportunity to consider the purification of the profession came in October 1938 when the members of the National Fascist Association of Doctors of Commerce (SNFDC) gathered for their conference in Genoa (SNFDC, 1938). The Minister of Justice represented the government at this event (Anonymous, 1938e; Cantagalli, 1996).

At the opening session of the conference, the Director General of the Fascist Confederation of Professionals and Artists urged the association to deal with the problem of race. He asserted that Jews, rather than Italians, filled too many positions in the accounting profession. It was time for the Fascist regime to "replace these hoarders" (SNFDC, 1938, p. 385). On the final day of the conference, a motion was debated to expel Jews from the profession. It read as follows:

> The doctors of commerce, meeting at their National Conference ... on the issue of race declare the need that at this particular historical moment, each occupational category must place its specific competence and expertise at the service of the corporate state for the achievement of the purposes indicated by the Party and the Fascist Government. To this end, the doctors of commerce consider themselves to be mobilized to the orders and to the service of the Regime. *They also affirm the urgency of proceeding in accordance with the higher directives of the regime to the full revision of the professional registers and the expulsion of all the Jewish elements therefrom.*
>
> (SNFDC, 1938, p. 467 [*emphasis added*])

The conference participants, dressed in the black shirts and military uniforms of the Fascist Party, approved the motion by acclamation (SNFDC, 1938, p. 445).

Apparatuses of expulsion

As established earlier, for Foucault (2003, pp. 255–256), cleansing the population of the unfit may take the form of exposing the "contaminating" population to the possibility of death. However, killing may also take more "indirect" forms such as expulsion. During autumn 1938, the Fascist regime in Italy shifted towards such a policy. Drawing on the anti-Semitic

Nuremberg Laws enacted in Nazi Germany in 1935 as an "ideological starting point", race laws were drafted (Sarfatti, 1994, pp. 40–42; Livingston, 2014, p. 66). On 17 November 1938, a Royal Decree (No. 1728) was issued titled "Laws in Defence of the Race". This provided biological definitions of Jews and set out the principles for their treatment (Coen, 1988, p. 116; Acerbi, 2011, pp. VII–XI). Soon thereafter, a series of laws and decrees were introduced to expel Jews from schools, universities, public administration, the army, politics, and companies and to expropriate their real estate (Finzi, 1997; Yael-Franzone, 2004; Gentile, 2013).

Bureaucratic apparatuses were established to implement State-sponsored expulsion. On 5 September 1938, the Ministerial Council for Demography and Race was established to support the racial policies of the regime (Royal Decree 1938/1539). A ministerial office, the *Demorazza* (Race and Demography Office) (Garofalo, 2013), and an administrative-judicial body, the *Tribunale della Razza* (Race Court) (Speciale, 2007), were created and tasked with managing the registration of Jews. Of particular importance was the *Demorazza*, which was established by Royal Decree (No. 1531) as a department of the Ministry of Interior. The *Demorazza* was conferred with power on all matters relating to race and was headed by individuals "chosen for their ideological commitment to the anti-Semitic cause" (Livingston, 2014, p. 118). The *Demorazza* acted as a biopolitical centre of calculation – storing all lists and data collected during the 1938 Jewish census (Sarfatti, 1993, pp. 390–392). According to one of its reports, there were 39,000 Jews in Italy in August 1940 of which 5,200 were professionals (lawyers, engineers, accountants, doctors, etc.). The *Demorazza* was also engaged in the bureaucratic process of determining whether an individual was a member of the Jewish race (Garofalo, 2013).

As part of the ambitious project to expel Jews from Italian economic and social life, a "Law on the exercise of professions by Jewish citizens" was passed on 29 June 1939 (Law N° 1054). The statute had "the fundamental purpose of inhibiting or restricting the professional employment of Jewish citizens" (Camera dei Fasci e delle Corporazioni, 1939, pp. 37–38). Law N° 1054 affected 1,599 professionals, including the occupations of accountant, doctor of commerce, and auditor (Zimmerman, 2005, p. 4). The press reported that the legislation offered an effective means of reducing the "excessive and disproportionate number of Jews who had flocked to certain professions" (Anonymous, 1939a; also: Anonymous, 1939b, 1939c, 1939d, 1939e, 1939f).

In achieving the race law's objectives, the existence of registers of qualified practitioners that identified the occupational population was considered key. The President of the Fascist Confederation of Professionals and Artists declared that "rigorous monitoring of the transition of Jewish professionals from the professional register to lists ... would be opportune" (Camera dei Fasci e delle Corporazioni, 1939, p. 39). After the aforementioned laws regulating the work of accountants, doctors of commerce, and auditors stipulated that the exercise of the profession was restricted to those appearing on official registers, the expulsion of Jews was focused on registration and lists of practitioners. Thus, these bureaucratic mechanisms, previously employed to ensure the competency of professionals, were now to be utilised to operationalise race-based "killing" through expulsion. Indeed, in Fascist Italy, professional associations, controlled by the State (Cipriani, 1939; Gherri, 1940; UT, 1940), were enlisted as sub-State agencies in the biopolitical project to protect the population from the internal threat posed by the Jews (Foucault, 2003, pp. 250–251).

In the accountancy field, local branches of doctors of commerce were placed under the control of the Fascist National Association of Doctors of Commerce, which was a constituent of the Fascist Confederation of Professionals and Artists. The latter formed the principal link between the profession and the regime. The Fascist National Association of Doctors of Commerce played an important role in ensuring that the bureaucratic processes of State racism operated effectively in the profession. As mentioned above, key mechanisms for operationalising the purification of the profession were the official registers of accounting and auditing practitioners that were controlled by the State. The fascist local branches of doctors of commerce administered the registers of accountants and doctors of commerce, while the Ministry of Justice maintained the register of auditors (Law 897/1938, Article 3). The institutions involved in the "cleansing" of the accountancy profession of Jews following the enactment of the race laws are shown in Figure 6.1.

Although activation of the biopolitical project to "take" the lives of Jewish members of the accounting profession through expulsion commenced as a form of "indirect murder", from 1943, when northern and central Italy came under Nazi control, the biopolitical project progressed to actual killing (Foucault, 2003, p. 256). Both forms of "taking life" are explored in the next section.

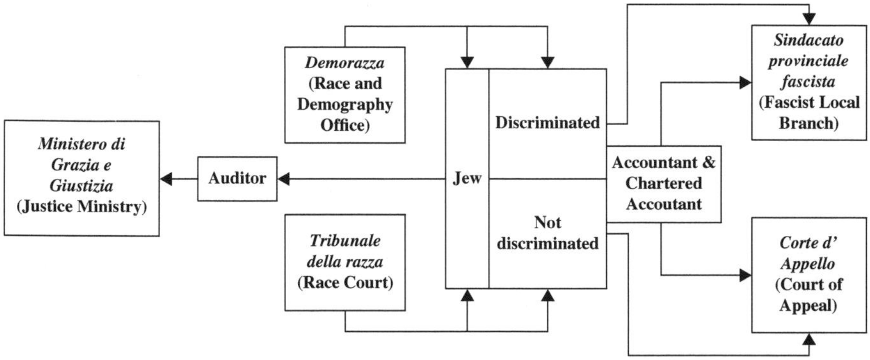

Figure 6.1 The application of race laws to professional accountants. Royal Decree 5th September (1938, n. 1531, n. 1539); Royal Decree 17th November (1938, n. 1728); Law, 29th June (1939, n. 105).

"Taking life"

Data on the expulsion of Jews from the accounting profession in Fascist Italy is most reliable in relation to auditors. Here, the State enacted a total prohibition of Jews and thereby took their professional lives. On 3 February 1940, a Ministerial Decree was issued naming 44 Jews who were to be removed from the register of auditors (Ministero della Giustizia, 1940b). A further individual was removed by a subsequent decree on 27 February (Ministero della Giustizia, 1940c). At the time, there were 1,143 "Italian" auditors (Carena, 1942). In 1942, one practitioner was restored to the official list of auditors because he was no longer considered a Jew (Ministero della Giustizia, 1942, p. 158). Seventeen of the 45 Jewish auditors removed from the list in 1940 also appeared on registers of accountants and doctors of commerce.

Although a precise quantification of the expulsion of Jewish accountants and doctors of commerce is frustrated by the destruction of relevant documents, the minutes of most of the boards of the local Fascist branches of doctors of commerce have survived and, as shown in Table 6.1 below, these offer insights to expulsions in regions where there existed a significant Jewish presence. The minutes report the names of those who were expelled.

In the ten regions of Italy with the highest concentration of Jews, a total of 151 Jewish professional accountants were expelled. In Lombardy, the names of two Jewish trainee accountants were also removed from the register of trainees (DISFDEC, 1940f). In cases where occupational status was

Table 6.1 Jewish professional accountants in Italy

Region	*Jewish accountants and doctors of commerce*			*Number of professional accountants (at 31 December 1938)*	*Number of Italian Jews (at census date, 22 August 1938)*
	Expelled	*Trainees expelled*	*"Discriminated"*		
Emilia – Romagna	9		2	206	2,771
Lazio	11		4	319	11,789
Liguria	6		2	212	2,039
Lombardy	35	2	9	746	6,814
Marche	2			28	1,218
Piedmont	44		4	310	4,807
Trentino	1		0	56	193
Tuscany	9		1	166	5,620
Veneto	8		6	182	3,460
Venezia Giulia and Zara	26		15	198	5,612
Other regions	–		–	783	1,238
Total	***151***	*2*	*43*	***3,206***	***45,561***

Sources: Albo Piemonte (1938, 1942); Anonymous (1940); Sindacato Fascista del Dottori in Economia e Commercio (DISFDEC) (1939a–1939f, 1940a–1940u, 1941a–1941d, 1942a–1942c); ACS (1938–1943c); Bon (2000, p. 148).

disclosed in the minutes of the boards of the local fascist branches of doctors of commerce (141 of the 151 cases), it appears that 69.5% of the practitioners expelled were doctors of commerce and 30.5% were accountants. Of the 151 initially expelled, 43 were successful in obtaining "discriminated" status (see below) and were enabled to continue to practice the profession, albeit in a restricted manner. The analysis thus reveals that the careers of 106 Jewish practitioners were negated in Fascist Italy following the erasure of their names from the registers of accountants and doctors of commerce.

Individual cases demonstrate how the mechanisms of biopower activated by the racist State resulted in the "indirect murder" of professional accountants through expulsion. In Emilia Romagna, Vittorio Formiggini, who had been a successful forensic accountant and judicial administrator, was removed from the register of doctors of commerce at a meeting of the Board of the Fascist Branch of Doctors of Commerce of Bologna in September 1939 (DISFDEC, 1939b). The law on the exercise of professions by Jewish citizens (Law 1054/1939) specifically prevented Jews from appearing in court. Although Formiggini had practiced in Modena in partnership with a non-Jew, his appeal against the decision to expel him was rejected in March 1940 (Formiggini, 1997).

In Rome, Amedeo Revere was an accountant who had contributed numerous articles to *Rivista Italiana di Ragioneria* during the 1920s and 30s on issues relating to professional practice. He also performed functions for the ministries of justice and education and was appointed as a bankruptcy trustee by the Court of Rome in 1930. Revere was removed from the registers of auditors and doctors of commerce in 1940 (DISFDEC, 1940g).

In Tuscany, Umberto Cava held positions as a judicial administrator at the Court of Florence and was a member of the governing body of the College of Accountants in that city. He married a Roman Catholic in 1911, claimed to have converted to Catholicism in 1934 and was baptized in 1937 (Maryks, 2012, pp. 58–59). Nevertheless, he was expelled as an accountant at a board meeting of the Fascist Branch of Doctors of Commerce of Florence in February 1940 (DISFDEC, 1940e). He was also expelled from the national register of auditors in the same month (Ministero della Giustizia, 1940b). He appealed both expulsions without success (RRC, n° 335, 18 October 1941; DISFDEC, 1941d).

In Lombardy, Arturo Milla was a highly respected accountant who served on the Council of the *Collegio dei Ragionieri* in Milan. He held numerous auditor appointments and was a judicial administrator and a bankruptcy trustee. He had been a member of the National Fascist Party since 1926 (Ministero della Giustizia, 1932, p. 1101). Milla was expelled from the local branch of accountants in Milan in 1940 and from the official list of auditors (DISFDEC, 1940f). In consequence, he was forced to abandon most of his lucrative professional appointments.

Following the German occupation of northern and central Italy from September 1943, the "indirect murder" of Jewish professional accountants through expulsion was supplanted by their actual murder. Whereas in Fascist Italy, "killing" Jews was initially pursued by expelling them from national life, in National Socialist Germany it was also manifest in their mass murder. Following the fall of Mussolini's government in July 1943, Hitler ordered the occupation of Italy and established a puppet State – the Italian Social Republic, or Republic of Salò (Oliva, 1997). From October 1943, the Government of the Italian Social Republic facilitated the extermination of Jews resident in the territory under its control (Di Sante, 2001, p. 200). A total of 6,806 Italian Jews were deported to Nazi camps by the end of World War II (Mayda, 2002, p. 243).

According to the site dedicated to Italian victims of the Shoah,[1] 11 Jewish accountants and doctors of commerce, and one auditor were deported to Auschwitz where they were murdered. Among those killed were Ugo Fano, who appeared on the register of auditors and was arrested in Turin on 3 December 1943 and later transported to Auschwitz.[2] Giorgio Fano was deleted from the register of doctors of commerce in Rome on 26 February 1940 (DISFDEC, 1940c), arrested in 1944, and shot in the Fosse Ardeatine massacre.[3] The experiences of Giorgio Ottolenghi, Giuseppe Parenzo, Riccardo Sezzi, and Enrico Dalla Volta are narrated in chapter 11. A number of other Jewish accountants, such as the aforementioned Vittorio Formiggini, escaped to Switzerland or went into hiding in Italy. The fate of many other accountants and auditors located in the Italian Social Republic remains unknown.[4]

"Letting live"

Foucault contended that when biopower functions through racism the State may invoke the sovereign power to "take life". This also implies its capacity to "let live". While the professional lives of 151 Jewish accountants in Fascist Italy were initially "taken" through expulsion, for some, there was also the possibility of "letting live", either by contesting assumptions about their racial status as Jews or by taking advantage of concessionary provisions in racial legislation. In relation to the first of these possibilities, if the *Demorazza* decided that the professional accountant did not fall within the biological definition of a Jew contained in Article 8 of RD 1728/1938, they were "Aryanised" and could continue to practice the profession. Individual cases illustrate how an accountant's racial classification could be challenged. In Lombardy, Alessandro Finzi was initially expelled from the list of doctors of commerce in 1940 having been declared as belonging to the Jewish race. His appeal was rejected in March 1940 due to a failure to adhere to prescribed procedures (DISFDEC, 1940j). Finzi's status was, however, later changed. On presenting a "certificate of non-belonging to the Jewish race", the Board of the Fascist Branch of Doctors of Commerce of Milan reinstated his name to the register (DISFDEC, 1941b).

Also in Lombardy, Sandro Dondi, an accountant in Cremona, received a letter from the Fascist Branch of Doctors of Commerce of Milan stating that he had declared in 1938 that his mother was Jewish. Consequently, he was likely to be expelled. Dondi responded in October 1940 by producing a birth certificate that suggested otherwise. His Aryan parentage established, in November, the Board of the Fascist Branch of Doctors of Commerce of Milan confirmed Dondi's presence on the register of doctors of commerce (ASCr, 1940).

In relation to the second potential route to "letting live", the race laws contained provisions for "discrimination" whereby exemptions from total expulsion were given for certain meritorious Jews. At this juncture, it is important to establish that while the biological foundations of racism in Fascist Italy established caesuras in the population between Jews and Aryans, political pragmatism also informed the implementation of measures to protect the Italian race (Duggan, 2008, pp. 511–518; Livingston, 2014, pp. 21–22). The biological project was tempered by nationalist and cultural considerations. Indeed, in drafting the race laws, while there was a determination to demonstrate connectedness to the Nazi equivalent, it was also intended to produce regulations that were distinctively Italian (Livingston, 2014, p. 23). Hence, a Jew who had fought for Italy in specified military conflicts, had contributed significantly to the fascist movement, or could demonstrate extraordinary service to the nation, might apply for "discriminated" status (Nidam-Orvieto, 2005).[5] One of the consequences of "discrimination" was that the proportion of Jews in the accountancy profession in Italy remained in excess of the one per thousand originally envisaged by the State under its "race and percentage" policy.

"Discriminated" accountants were "let live" in that they could continue to practice, albeit in a constrained and stigmatised way. Their names were entered on an "additional list", which appeared as an appendix to the official register of practitioners. Those accorded *Discriminato* status were clearly identified as Jews and as separate from their Aryan brethren. Their activities fell under the auspices of the local fascist branch of doctors of commerce. Discriminated accountants were prohibited from performing tasks that implied the function of a public official (such as an insolvency administrator), from acting as judicial trustee, or as an expert or consultant to the courts. Collaboration with non-Jewish professionals was also prohibited.

Jewish accountants who did not apply for, or did not satisfy, the conditions necessary for "discriminated" status were deemed "non-discriminated". They were expelled from their professional organisations and were ineligible for membership of Fascist associations. However, they were permitted to pursue a lesser form of professional life. "Non-discriminated" accountants could apply to appear on "special lists" of practitioners who could exercise their profession exclusively for those belonging to the Jewish race. Applicants for admission to "special lists" were required to be Italian citizens, of indisputable moral conduct, and to have acted in the interests of the fascist regime. Such attributes were attested to by certificates of good moral, civil, and political conduct issued by the judiciary and police authorities. Applications for

Table 6.2 The status of Jewish professional accountants under Law 1054/1939

Status / *Permissible practice*	*"Discriminated" admitted to "additional list"*	*"Not discriminated" admitted to "special list"*	*Expelled*
Judicial administrator	No	No	No
Bankruptcy trustee	No	No	No
Other judicial offices	No	No	No
Collaboration with non-Jewish professionals	No	No	No
Membership of the Fascist Union	Yes	No	No
Accountant	Yes	Jewish clients only	No

Source: Law 1054/1939.

admission to "special lists" were heard by Courts of Appeal and were subject to scrutiny by a special district committee that also maintained the "special lists" and carried out the disciplinary functions of the local fascist association (Law 1054/1939, Articles 5, 8, 9). A summary of the various statuses of Jewish professional accountants under State racism in Italy is provided in Table 6.2.

Identifying and classifying individual Jews as "discriminated" or "not discriminated" required the establishment of a complex bureaucratic apparatus. A professional accountant seeking to be discriminated would supply evidence relating to race, citizenship, profession, and residence. The veracity of the information was assessed and investigated by the local Prefect and the Fascist Police before submission to the *Demorazza* in Rome for a final decision (Royal Decree No. 1539 of 5 September 1938). If successful, the practitioner was presented with a "certificate of discrimination" (ACS, 1938–1943a).

Individual cases, a number of which are discussed in chapter 11, involving disputes and appeals over applications for discrimination, demonstrate that there could be fluidity and ambiguity in the operation of the mechanisms of biopower. They suggest states of transience in the binary distinction between "killing" (through expulsion) and "letting live" (through discrimination). These ambiguities often arose because the *Demorazza* might reject a request for discriminated status on various grounds in addition to race. These could include the existence of a criminal record, evidence of anti-fascist sympathies, criticisms of the regime, masonic affiliations, and/or bad moral or political conduct (ACS, 1938–1943d).

Although "discriminated" status was preferable to the severe economic, social, and psychological consequences of "killing" by expulsion (Nidam-Orvieto, 2005), it did represent a racially defined diminishment of status and also ascribed a stigmatising label that constrained the scope for professional practice. Further, like other members of the Jewish community, discriminated practitioners were also subject to surveillance, investigation, rejection, and intimidation by a range of agencies (Sarfatti, 2005). "Additional lists" disclosed the discriminated Jew's name and address, his mother and father's name (information confirmative of Jewish heritage), and other identifying information that could facilitate harassment. Further, discrimination was intended as a transitional measure. As the racial laws became more entrenched, it became increasingly difficult for Jews to secure that status (Livingston, 2014, pp. 64–65). This was especially the case following Italy's entry to World War II when Jews were identified as enemies within the State (Archivo di Stato di Verona (ASVr), 1938–1945). Further, all Jews, including those previously discriminated, were unconditionally expelled from the professions when the Italian Social Republic came to power in northern and central Italy in 1943 (Italian Social Republic Decree N°2, 4 January 1944, Article 1). With the intrusion of Nazism in Italian territory the prospect of "letting live" disappeared.

Conclusion

Drawing on Foucault's concept of biopolitics and race it has been shown how, in Fascist Italy, legal and bureaucratic apparatuses were deployed by government and State-captured accountancy bodies to purify the professional populace by expelling its Jewish members. The findings of this chapter confirm the observation of other commentators that the processes of expulsion were implemented by a racist State in ways that indicated a cold disdain for "the systematic pauperization of an entire people" (Livingston, 2014, p. 62). Indeed, among the community of Jewish accountants, the apparatuses of biopower had substantial implications for the economic and social status of the individual practitioners who were subjected to them (Nidam-Orvieto, 2005, p. 175). When, in 1943, northern and central Italy came under Nazi control, the "indirect murder" of Jewish accountants could be supplanted by actual murder.

The apparatuses of biopower in the Fascist State comprised a Jewish census and local enumerations to locate and quantify the inferior race to be expelled, the passing of race laws, and the establishment of new bureaucratic structures for their implementation – a venture in which extant institutions such as professional organisations were also deployed. These mechanisms of biopower were not simply activated at the macro level. While the Fascist State functioned as a central authority for managing the purity of the population, the implementation of its policies in regions and localities demonstrate the importance of also analysing the operation of biopolitics at the meso and micro levels (Mills, 2018, p. 25). Professional communities and their organisations were enlisted as agents in the project of racial expulsion by the fascist regime, along with the police, public administrators, and the judiciary. This presents a historical instance of the complicity of accountants in the implementation of racist legislation, in this case to the considerable detriment of many of their fellow professionals.

The study suggests that, in practice, constructing a race-defined binary division of the focal population is complex. Separating groups according to race can be complicated by political and other contingencies, and these have implications for the determination of who is "killed" and who is "let live". As Foucault (2003, p. 77) reminds us, "race is not pinned to a stable biological meaning". In consequence it is "easily exploitable and amendable" (Fiaccadori, 2015, p. 164). Hence, in Fascist Italy, Jewish accountants might take advantage of the "discrimination" provisions of the race laws that effectively "let live" those members of the inferiorised population who were politically, as opposed to biologically, constructed as "meritorious". Also indicative of the intrusion of non-biological factors was the fact that such concessions were not available to Jewish auditors who were all expelled, not only on grounds of their race but also because their duties were akin to "public officials for all legal purposes" (Article 13, RD 1548/1936). The relevance of nationalist and cultural factors in the Fascist programme of racial purification reflected compromises made in the construction of racist legislation (Livingston, 2014, p. 72).

This chapter is based on the paper by Valerio Antonelli, Raffaele D'Alessio, and Stephen P. Walker titled "Operationalizing Expulsion. Jewish Accountants in Fascist Italy, 1938–1943", which originally appeared in Critical Perspectives on Accounting in 2023, article number 102462. The authors would like to thank the publisher, Elsevier, for permission to use this material.

Notes

1 https://www.cdec.it/i-nomi-della-shoah/
2 http://digital-library.cdec.it
3 http://digital-library.cdec.it. The massacre on 24 March 1944 concerned the shooting of 335 Italian hostages (Jews, political prisoners, and convicts) ordered by Hitler as retaliation for a partisan attack on a platoon of German soldiers in Via Rasella, Rome.
4 https://www.ushmm.org
5 It should be noted that discriminated status was not available to Jewish auditors. It was explicitly stated that Italian Jews could not be included on the official list of auditors (Ministero della Giustizia, 1939, 1940a, 1940d, 1941a, 1941b, 1942a, 1942).

References

Primary Sources

Laws, decrees, parliamentary debates, and other regulations

Camera dei Fasci e delle Corporazioni (1939). Debate about the Racial Law on Jewish Professional Discrimination. 26th May 1939. Minutes. Laws Commissions – Interior, Justice, Professions, Minute of the Meeting, XXX, pp. 37–48.

Law 15th July (1906). n. 327. Gazzetta Ufficiale del Regno d'Italia, n. 167, 18th July 1906, 3474.
Law 25 April (1938). n. 897. Gazzetta Ufficiale del Regno d'Italia, n. 152, 7th July 1938, 2808–2809.
Law 29th June (1939). n. 1054. Gazzetta Ufficiale del Regno d'Italia, n. 179, 2nd August 1939, 3578–3582.
Royal Decree 28th March (1929). n. 552. Gazzetta Ufficiale del Regno d'Italia, n. 101, 30th April 1929, 1923.
Royal Decree 28th March (1929). n. 588. Gazzetta Ufficiale del Regno d'Italia, n. 101, 30th April 1929, 1918–1921.
Royal Decree 24th July (1936). n. 1548. Gazzetta Ufficiale del Regno d'Italia, n. 197, 26th August 1936, 2681–2683.
Royal Decree 10th February (1937). n. 228. Gazzetta Ufficiale del Regno d'Italia, n. 62, 15th Mars 1937, 949–952.
Royal Decree 2nd May (1938). n. 743. Gazzetta Ufficiale del Regno d'Italia, n. 135, 15th June 1938, 2449.
Royal Decree 5th September (1938). n. 1531. Gazzetta Ufficiale del Regno d'Italia n. 230, 7th October 1938, 4214.
Royal Decree 5th September (1938). n. 1539. Gazzetta Ufficiale del Regno d'Italia n. 231, 8th October 1938, 4236.
Royal Decree 17th November (1938). n. 1728. Gazzetta Ufficiale del Regno d'Italia, n. 264, 19th November 1938, 4794–4796.

Auditors' Official Lists and Calls for Applications

Ministero della Giustizia (1932). Bollettino ufficiale del Ministero della Giustizia e degli Affari di Culto. Roma: Istituto Poligrafico e Zecca dello Stato.
Ministero della Giustizia (1939). Ministerial Decree 22nd August 1939. Sessione di novembre per la nomina a revisore dei conti. Gazzetta Ufficiale del Regno d'Italia, n. 205, 2nd September 1939, 4212.
Ministero della Giustizia (1940a). Ministerial Decree 27th January 1940. Sessione di aprile 1940 per la nomina a revisore dei conti Gazzetta Ufficiale del Regno d'Italia n. 29, 5th February 1940, 498.
Ministero della Giustizia (1940b). Ministerial Decree, 3rd February 1940. Gazzetta Ufficiale del Regno d'Italia, n. 32, 8th February 1940, 563–564.
Ministero della Giustizia (1940c). Ministerial Decree, 27th February 1940. Gazzetta Ufficiale del Regno d'Italia, n. 49, 27th February 1940, 847.
Ministero della Giustizia (1940d). Ministerial Decree 6th August 1940. Sessione di novembre per la nomina a revisore dei conti. Gazzetta Ufficiale del Regno d'Italia, n. 194, 20th August 1940, 3111.
Ministero della Giustizia (1941a). Ministerial Decree 11th January 1941. Sessione di aprile per la nomina a revisore dei conti. Gazzetta Ufficiale del Regno d'Italia, n. 39, 14th February 1941, 762.
Ministero della Giustizia (1941b). Ministerial Decree 1st August 1941. Sessione di novembre per la nomina a revisore dei conti. Gazzetta Ufficiale del Regno d'Italia, n. 189, 12th August 1941, 3188.
Ministero della Giustizia (1942). Ministerial Decree 12th March 1942. In Bollettino Ufficiale del Ministero di Grazia e Giustizia, 13, 158.

Sindacato Nazionale Fascista dei Dottori Commercialisti (SNFDC) and Direttorio Interprovinciale Sindacato Fascista dei Dottori in Economia e Commercio (DISFDEC)

DISFDEC (1939a). Trieste. Verbale di direttorio. 13 February 1939. *Il Commercialista, 12*, 108–109.

DISFDEC (1939b). Bologna. Verbale di direttorio. 23 September 1939. *Il Commercialista, 12*, 397–398.

DISFDEC (1939c). Milano. Verbale di direttorio. 14 November 1939. *Il Commercialista, 12*, 457.

DISFDEC (1939d). Bologna. Verbale di direttorio. 18 November 1939. *Il Commercialista, 12*, 453.

DISFDEC (1939e). Milano. Verbale di direttorio. 20 July 1939. *Il Commercialista, 12*, 359.

DISFDEC (1939f). Iscritti al Sindacato Nazionale Fascista dei Dottori Commercialisti. *Il Commercialista, 12*, 376–377.

DISFDEC (1940a). Trieste. Verbale di direttorio. 22 September 1939. *Il Commercialista, 13*, 86–87.

DISFDEC (1940b). Genova. Verbale di direttorio. 25 October 1939. *Il Commercialista, 13*, 36–37.

DISFDEC (1940c). Milano. Verbale di direttorio. 22 December 1939. *Il Commercialista, 13*, 125.

DISFDEC (1940d). Genova. Verbale di direttorio. 8 January 1940. *Il Commercialista, 13*, 37–38.

DISFDEC (1940e). Firenze. Verbale di direttorio. 7 February 1940. *Il Commercialista, 13*, 122.

DISFDEC (1940f). Milano. Verbale di direttorio. 24 February 1940. *Il Commercialista, 13*, 126–128.

DISFDEC (1940g). Roma. Verbale di direttorio. 26 February 1940. *Il Commercialista, 13*, 130.

DISFDEC (1940h). Venezia. Verbale di direttorio. 28 February 1940. *Il Commercialista, 13*, 133.

DISFDEC (1940i). Bologna. Verbale di direttorio. 2 March 1940. *Il Commercialista, 13*, 170.

DISFDEC (1940j). Milano. Verbale di direttorio. 5 March 1940. *Il Commercialista, 13*, 129.

DISFDEC (1940k). Milano. Verbale di direttorio. 8 April 1940. *Il Commercialista, 13*, 239–240.

DISFDEC (1940l). Venezia. Verbale di direttorio. 4 June 1940. *Il Commercialista, 13*, 338.

DISFDEC (1940m). Milano. Verbale di direttorio. 18 July 1940. *Il Commercialista, 13*, 336.

DISFDEC (1940n). Milano. Verbale di direttorio. 20 July 1940. *Il Commercialista, 13*, 359.

DISFDEC (1940o). Trieste. Verbale di direttorio. 27 July 1940. *Il Commercialista, 13*, 338.

DISFDEC (1940p). Bologna. Verbale di direttorio. 23 September 1940. *Il Commercialista, 13*, 397–398.

DISFDEC (1940q). Bologna. Verbale di direttorio. 28 September 1940. *Il Commercialista, 13*, 427.

DISFDEC (1940r). Venezia. Verbale di direttorio. 16 October 1940. *Il Commercialista, 13*, 431–432.
DISFDEC (1940s). Milano. Verbale di direttorio. 23 November 1940. *Il Commercialista, 13*, 430.
DISFDEC (1940t). Trento. Verbale di direttorio. 19 February 1940. *Il Commercialista, 13*, 131.
DISFDEC (1940u). Milano. Verbale di direttorio. 21 May 1940. *Il Commercialista, 13*, 276.
DISFDEC (1941a). Torino. Verbale di direttorio. 15 April 1941. *Il Commercialista, 14*, 268–269.
DISFDEC (1941b). Milano. Verbale di direttorio. 7 June 1941. *Il Commercialista, 14*, 268–269.
DISFDEC (1941c). Milano. Verbale di direttorio. 11 October 1941. *Il Commercialista, 14*, 365–366.
DISFDEC (1941d). Firenze. Verbale di direttorio. 8 November 1941. *Il Commercialista, 14*, 365–366.
DISFDEC (1942a). Roma. Verbale di direttorio. 13 April 1942. *Il Commercialista, 15*, 101.
DISFDEC (1942b). Roma. Verbale di direttorio. 15 September 1942. *Il Commercialista, 15*, 160–162.
DISFDEC (1942c). Milano. Verbale di direttorio. 21 November 1942. *Il Commercialista, 15*, 199.
SNFDC (1938). Atti ufficiali del Congresso Nazionale dei Dottori in Economia e Commercio, tenutosi in Genova nei giorni 19 – 20 – 21 ottobre 1938-XVI. *Il Commercialista, 11*, 377–486.

Newspapers and journals

Anonymous (1938a). Too many Jews among the Doctors of Commerce. *Il Popolo d'Italia*, 30th August 1938, 7.
Anonymous (1938b). Jewish Doctors of Commerce in Milan. *La Stampa*, 30th August 1938, front page.
Anonymous (1938c). The Jewish Octopus. Doctors of Commerce 16.17%. *La Stampa*, 13th September 1938, 6.
Anonymous (1938d). The Jewish Octopus. Degree Doctors of Commerce 13.23%. *La Stampa*, 15th September 1938, 6.
Anonymous (1938e). Congresso dei dottori in economia e commercio. *Bollettino della Associazione Primo Lanzoni, fra gli Antichi Studenti del Regio Istituto Superiore di Economia e Commercio di Venezia, 39*, 15.
Anonymous (1938f). New evidence on Jewish presence. *Corriere della Sera,* 7th September 1938, 5.
Anonymous (1938g). High percentage in Trieste of Jewish professionals. *Il Popolo d'Italia*, 6th September 1938, 2.
Anonymous (1939a). The Jews and the Professions. *La Stampa*, 1st May 1939, front page.
Anonymous (1939b). The Racial Laws issued by the Cabinet. How many Jewish professionals are there in Trieste? *Il Piccolo*, 2nd May 1939, 2.
Anonymous (1939c). The Jews and the Professions. *La Stampa*, 6th June 1939, 2.
Anonymous (1939d). The Senate Commission approves the modifications to the laws on professionals. *La Nazione*, 2nd June 1939, 2.

Anonymous (1939e). On the professions and Jews. *La Nazione*, 16th August 1939, 3.
Anonymous (1939f). On the obligation to be registered in the official lists of members. *La Nazione*, 26th August 1939, 34.
Interlandi, T. (1938). Race and percentage. *La Difesa della Razza*, *1*, 5.
Mancinelli, E. (1938). The problem of the race. Jews in Italy. *La Nazione*, 14th–16th August 1938, 5.

Regional Branches of Doctors of Commerce – Official Lists

Albo Piemonte (1938). Albo degli esercenti in materia di economia e commercio per le provincie del Piemonte, aggiornato a tutto agosto 1938.
Albo Piemonte (1942). Albo professionale esercenti di economia e commercio, aggiornato al 30 giugno 1942.

State Archive Records

ACS (1938). Ministero dell'interno, Direzione generale della pubblica sicurezza, Affari generali e riservati [DGPS, AGR], cat. G 1, b. 14, fase. 1 72, s.fasc. 1/2.
ACS (1938–1943a). Ministero dell'Interno – Direzione Generale per la Demografia e la razza. B. 4, f. 17.
ACS (1938–1943b). Ministero dell'Interno – Direzione Generale per la Demografia e la razza. B. 5, f. 19.
ACS (1938–1943c). Ministero dell'Interno – Direzione Generale per la Demografia e la razza. B. 22, f. Dati riassuntivi sul censimento degli ebrei.
ACS (1938–1943d). Ministero dell'Interno – Direzione Generale per la Demografia e la razza. B. 183, f. 8. Procedimenti penali e provvedimenti di polizia a carico di ebrei.
ASCr (1940). Archivio di Stato di Cremona. Collegio dei ragionieri, busta 1.4.
ASVr (1938–1945). Archivio di Stato di Verona, Prefettura, Gabinetto, Ebrei. "Reichenbach Attilio fu Leopoldo. A-1 40".

Secondary Sources

Acerbi, G. (2011). *Le leggi antiebraiche e razziali italiane ed il ceto dei giuristi*. Milano: Giuffrè.
Avagliano, M., and Palmieri, M. (2013). *Di pura razza italiana. L'Italia «ariana» di fronte alle leggi razziali*. Milano: Baldini Castoldi.
Barone, E. (2000). L'evoluzione della professione del ragioniere e del dottore commercialista. In *Atti del V Convegno Nazionale della Società Italiana di Storia della Ragioneria. La Ragioneria verso il terzo Millennio tra continuità e rinnovamento. Bergamo, 8–9 ottobre 1999* (pp. 315–333). Padova: Cedam.
Bernardini, G. (1977). The origins and development of racial anti-semitism in Fascist Italy. *Journal of Modern History*, *49*(3), 431–453.
Bon, S. (2000). *Gli ebrei a Trieste 1930–1945: identità, persecuzione, risposte*. Trieste: Libreria Goriziana.
Calimani, R. (2015). *Storia degli ebrei italiani nel XIX e nel XX secolo*. Milano: Mondadori.
Cantagalli, A. (1996). La professione del dottore commercialista. In M. Malatesta (Ed.). *Storia d'Italia. Annali 10: I professionisti* (pp. 225–258). Torino: Einaudi.
Carena, A.A. (1942). Revisori ufficiali dei conti. *Rivista Italiana di Ragioneria*, *42*(1), 45–48.

Cassata, F. (2008). *La "Difesa della razza". Politica, ideologia e immagine del razzismo fascista*. Torino: Einaudi.

Cipriani, P. (1939). La funzione del sindaco nelle società per azioni. *Rivista Italiana di Ragioneria, 39*(2), 171–172.

Coen, F. (1988). *Italiani ed ebrei, come eravamo. Le leggi razziali del 1938*. Genova: Marietti.

Colecchia, L., Manetti, G., and Pozzoli, M. (2013). L'evoluzione e il ruolo delle professioni economico-contabili nel periodo 1906–1934. *Contabilità e cultura aziendale, 13*(1), 9–33.

Coronella, S., Sargiacomo, M., and Walker, S. P. (2015). Unification and dual closure in the Italian accountancy profession, 1861–1906. *European Accounting Review, 24*(1), 167–197.

Critical Genealogies Collaboratory. (2018). Standard forms of power: Biopower and sovereign power in the technology of the US birth certificate, 1903–1935. *Constellations, 25*, 641–656.

Cuomo, F. (2005). *I dieci: chi erano gli scienziati italiani che firmarono il Manifesto della razza*. Milano: Baldini & Castoldi.

De Felice, R. (1993). *Storia degli ebrei italiani sotto il fascismo*. Torino: Einaudi.

Dean, M. (2010). *Governmentality. Power and Rule in Modern Society*. London: Sage.

Dell'Era, T. (2011). *Il manifesto della razza. Luglio 1938: il decalogo del razzismo italiano*. Torino: UTET.

Di Sante, C. (2001). I campi di concentramento in Italia: dall'internamento alla deportazione, 1940–1945. Milano: Franco Angeli.

Detzen, D. and Hoffmann, S. (2018). Stigma management and justifications of the self in denazification accounts. *Accounting, Auditing & Accountability Journal, 31*(1), 141–165.

Duggan, C. (2008). *The Force of Destiny. A History of Italy since 1796*. London: Penguin Books.

Edallo, E. (2023). The racial census of 22 August 1938: The first political persecutory act of anti-Semitic fascist policy in Italy. An overview and the Milan case study. *Journal of Modern Jewish Studies, 22*(1), 1–28.

Erlenbusch, V. (2017). From race war to Socialist racism: Foucault's second transcription. *Foucault Studies, 22*, 134–152.

Fiaccadori, E. (2015). State racism and the paradox of biopower. *Foucault Studies, 19*, 151–171.

Finzi, R. (1997). *L'università italiana e le leggi antiebraiche*. Roma: Editori Riuniti.

Formiggini, S. (1997). Testimonianza orale. In A.M. Ori (Ed.). *Le leggi razziali. Materiali per le scuole* (pp. 12–14). Modena: Istituto Storico di Modena.

Foucault, M. (1978). *The History of Sexuality. Volume 1: An Introduction*. New York: Pantheon Books.

Foucault, M. (2003). *Society Must Be Defended. Lectures at the Collège de France, 1975–76*. New York: Picador.

Foucault, M. (2007). *Security, Territory, Population. Lectures at the Collège de France, 1977–78*. Houndmills: Palgrave Macmillan.

Foucault, M. (2008). *The Birth of Biopolitics. Lectures at the Collège de France, 1978–79*. Houndmills: Palgrave Macmillan.

Freidson, E. (2001). *Professionalism. The Third Logic*. Chicago, IL: University of Chicago Press.

Funnell, W.N. (1998). Accounting in the service of the Holocaust. *Critical Perspectives on Accounting*, *9*(4), 435–464.
Garofalo, L. (2013). La Demorazza: storia di un archivio. *Italia Contemporanea*, *272*, 374–401.
Gentile, S. (2013). *La legalità del male. L'offensiva mussoliniana contro gli ebrei nella prospettiva storico-giuridica (1938–1945)*. Torino: Giappichelli.
Gherri, A. (1940). Collegi sindacali e sindaci revisori. *Rivista Italiana di Ragioneria*, *40*(1), 53–56.
Gillette, A. (2001). The origins of the "manifesto of racial scientists". *Journal of Modern Italian Studies*, *6*(3), 305–323.
Gordon, R. (2012). *The Holocaust in Italian Culture, 1944–2010*. Stanford, CA: Stanford University Press.
Henckaerts, J.M. (1995). *Mass Expulsion in Modern International Law and Practice*. The Hague: Kluwer Law International.
Lemke, T. (2001). The birth of biopolitics – Michel Foucault's lecture at the Collège de France on neo-liberal governmentality. *Economy and Society*, *30*, 190–207.
Lemke, T. (2011). *Biopolitics: An Advanced Introduction*. New York: New York University Press.
Lippman, E.J., and Wilson, P.A. (2011). Accountants and what they may wish to forget (but do so at their profession's peril). In M.M. Hogan and J. Lies (Eds.). *History (1933–1948). What We Choose to Remember* (pp. 303–314). Portland: Garaventa Center.
Lippman, E.J., and Wilson, P.A. (2013). Accountants and Holocaust. In R.K. Fleischman, W.N. Funnell, and S.P. Walker (Eds.). *Critical Histories of Accounting: Sinister Inscriptions in the Modern Era* (pp. 69–81). New York: Routledge.
Livingston, M.A. (2014). *The Fascists and the Jews of Italy. Mussolini's Race Laws, 1938–1943*. Cambridge: Cambridge University Press.
Markus, H.B. (1997). *The History of the German Public Accounting Profession*. New York: Garland Publishing Inc.
Marro, G. (1940). *Primato della razza italiana*. Milano and Messina: Principato.
Martelli M. (2005). *La propaganda razziale in Italia, 1938–1943*. Rimini: Il Cerchio.
Maryks, R.A. (2012). *Pouring Jewish Water into Fascist Wine. Untold Stories of (Catholic) Jews from the Archive of Mussolini's Jesuit Pietro Tacchi Venturi*. LeidenBoston, MA: Brill.
Mayda, G. (2002). Storia della deportazione dall'Italia: 1943–1945: militari, ebrei e politici nei lager del Terzo Reich. Torino: Bollati Boringhieri.
Mbembe, A. (2003). Necropolitics. *Public Culture*, *15*(1), 11–40.
Mills, C. (2018). *Biopolitics*. Abingdon: Routledge.
Nidam-Orvieto, I. (2005). The impact of anti-Jewish legislation on everyday life and the response of Italian Jews, 1938–1943. In J.D. Zimmerman, (Ed.). *Jews in Italy under Fascist and Nazi Rule, 1922–1945* (pp. 158–181). Cambridge: Cambridge University Press.
Oliva, G. (1997). *La Repubblica di Salò*. Firenze: Giunti.
Poullaos, C. and Ramirez, C. (2020). Professionalization. In J.R. Edwards, and S.P. Walker (Eds.). *The Routledge Companion to Accounting History* (pp. 279–306). London: Routledge.
Rasmussen, K.S. (2011). Foucault's genealogy of racism. *Theory, Culture & Society*, *28*, 34–51.

Revere, A. (1936). La soppressione dei collegi dei ragionieri. *Rivista Italiana di Ragioneria*, *36*(1), 11.

Sabatello, F. (1976). Il censimento degli ebrei del 1938 (note metodologiche sulla sua preparazione, la sua realizzazione ed i suoi risultati). *La rassegna mensile di Israel*, *42*, 25–55.

Sarfatti, M. (1993). Il censimento degli ebrei del 22 agosto 1938 nel quadro dell'avvio della politica antiebraica di Mussolini. In *Italia judaica. Gli ebrei nell'Italia unita 1870–1945. Atti del IV convegno internazionale (Siena, 12–16 giugno 1989)* (pp. 358–413). Roma: MIBACT.

Sarfatti, M. (1994). *Mussolini contro gli ebrei: cronaca dell'elaborazione delle leggi del 1938*. Torino: Einaudi.

Sarfatti, M. (2005). Characteristics and objectives of the ant-Jewish radical laws in Fascist Italy, 1938–1943. In J.D. Zimmerman (Ed.). *Jews in Italy under Fascist and Nazi Rule, 1922–1945* (pp. 71–80). Cambridge: Cambridge University Press.

Sarfatti, M., and Tedeschi, A.C. (2006). *The Jews in Mussolini's Italy: From Equality to Persecution*. Madison, WI: University of Wisconsin Press.

Savorgnan, F. (1939). Relazione del presidente. In *Annali di statistica. Serie VII. Vol. IV. Sessione ordinaria 22 dicembre 1938-XVI* (pp. 1–6). Roma: Failli.

Scheel, S. (2020). Biopolitical bordering: Enacting populations as intelligible objects of government. *European Journal of Social Theory*, *23*(4), 571–590.

Speciale, G. (2007). *Giudici e razza nell'Italia fascista*. Torino: Giappichelli.

Stoler, A.L. (1995). *Race and the Education of Desire. Foucault's History of Sexuality and the Colonial Order of Things*. Durham: Duke University Press.

Taylor, C. (2011). Race and racism in Foucault's Collège de France lectures. *Philosophy Compass*, *6*, 746–756.

UT (1940). Sui criteri di scelta per l'iscrizione nel ruolo dei revisori dei conti. *Rivista Italiana di Ragioneria*, *40*(1), 21–23.

Vatter, M. (2017). Community, life, and subjectivity in Italian biopolitics. In S. Prozorov and S. Rentea (Eds.). *The Routledge Handbook of Biopolitics* (pp. 123–137). Abingdon: Routledge.

Walker, S.P. (2000). Encounters with Nazism: British accountants and the fifth international congress on accounting. *Critical Perspectives on Accounting*, *11*(2), 215–245.

Welch, R.N. (2016). *Vital Subjects. Race and Biopolitics in Italy, 1860–1920*. Liverpool: Liverpool University Press.

Witz, A. (1992). *Professions and Patriarchy*. London: Routledge.

Yael-Franzone, G. (2004). La normazione antiebraica in Italia tra il 1938 e il 1943. Alcune annotazioni di natura giuridica ed economica. In *Gli effetti delle leggi razziali sulle attività economiche degli ebrei nella città di Roma (1938–1943)* (pp. 23–47). Roma: CCIAA.

Zimmerman, J.D. (2005). Introduction. In J.D. Zimmerman (Ed.) (2005). *Jews in Italy under Fascist and Nazi Rule, 1922–1945* (pp. 1–15). Cambridge: Cambridge University Press.

7 Accounting for the Nazi Aryanisation of German banks

Erin Twyford and Warwick Funnell

Introduction

All attempts to understand the perpetration of the Holocaust are confronted with "the incredibility of the horrors" (Arendt, 2000, p. 126) that defies explanation. The Nazis operated a murderous, State-centric, corporative, and anti-Semitic fascist regime (Goldhagen, 1996; Cinquini, 2007), achieved by first eradicating Jews from the economy. Through the financially persecutory policy of Aryanisation, which comprised the important first stage of the genocide of European Jewry, the Nazi State destroyed Jewish financial life (*bios*) (Twyford, 2021). Legislation that denied Jews the right to employment and to conduct business eradicated their financial *bios,* while the forced Aryan[1] takeovers of Jewish businesses, without adequate compensation, simultaneously excluded Jewish influence from the economic sphere and concentrated Aryan ownership.[2] The impact of Aryanisation for many Jews resulted in the degradation and ultimate devastation of their *zoē* (existential/physical life) in the extermination camps, engendered through the loss of their financial *bios*.

The plundering of the Jewish economy and robbing Jews of their economic livelihood was especially pronounced with banks, conducted most importantly by the largest German bank, Deutsche Bank. In their accounts, Deutsche Bank appeared as a cooperative participant, intent on increasing their power in the banking sphere and influence with the Nazi regime. This chapter exposes how Deutsche Bank used these same accounts to seek avenues to prolong or even save Jewish financial *bios* and *zoē* while attaining profits, despite Nazi policy, by concealing or masking efforts to prevent the destruction of Jewish *bios*. The Nazis may have used Deutsche Bank as an important tool in Aryanisation and the dismantling of Jewish presence in the German economy, but the actions of Deutsche Bank reveal that the company was not a fully committed disciple of Nazism. Although it is hardly disputed that "politics and terror under the National Socialist regime were mixed together in a seamless web" (Bajohr, 2002, p. 17), the use of economic measures to curtail the influence of Jews and the role played by accounting in achieving this remains an under-researched aspect of the Holocaust.

DOI: 10.4324/9781032685328-7

Accountants were "actively engaged in the formation and implementation of the laws that discriminated against Jews" (Lippman and Wilson, 2007, p. 294) and, as a means of institutionalising the racial discrimination within Germany, accounting altered to a form of "Nazi-Deutsch". Nazi-Deutsch was a rhetoric of euphemism to disguise the true meaning of words or phrases, most notoriously the "Final Solution" that was used as a mask for genocide and "selection" for the transfer of Jews and others to the death camps (see Dawidowicz, 1976; Friedlander, 1980). Accounting practices were intrinsically enmeshed in the process of Aryanisation and the destruction of financial *bios* by identifying, representing, and valuing property and wealth expropriated from Jews, then using Nazi-Deutsch to hide such exploitative acts in financial reports. Deutsche Bank's financial accounts of the Aryanisation of banks masked the human impact of the process, highlighting the inability of accounting to move beyond an economic discourse. This obfuscated how the financially racist policies of the Nazis enabled the loss of Jewish financial *bios*, laying the foundation for the genocide of Jewish people during the Holocaust. Aryanisation depended upon the complicit role of business and the practices of accounting, specifically in the concealment of Aryanisation processes and the resultant destruction of Jewish financial *bios*. This destruction and degradation was a vital foundation for the later enslavement and the attempted extermination of Jewish people during the Holocaust (James, 2001; Twyford, 2021).

The accounting practices of businesses and related financial reports during the Nazi period were rudimentary forms of accounting, with regulated "bookkeeping" principles introduced in 1937 as part of State centralised control over the economy (Standish, 1990, p. 337, see also *Grundsätze für Buchhaltungsrichtlinien*, or the Göring Plan (1937)). This was evident, for example, when Deutsche Bank reminded interested parties using its financial reports that "when evaluating these statistics it should not be forgotten that the boundaries between the individual economic trends are very often fluid and that the digits therefore only have a limited actual value" (Deutsche Bank Annual Report, 1936, p. 12), and "the *counting* has been done according to the long-established method …" (Deutsche Bank Annual Report, 1941, p. 12, emphasis added). Thus, they were silent on the actual processes that led to financial events enacted by State-imposed anti-Semitic, racist policies. Accordingly, to ensure that these silences are exposed and their consequences for the persecuted Jews revealed, the study has adopted a broad understanding of possible forms of accounting. Accounting includes "documents which typically use text and numbers to report upon or provide an account of an entity" (Preston, 2006, p. 560), which is extended in this study by attending to what was *un*accounted for by basic calculative practices: the persecution and ultimate destruction of Jews (Arrington and Francis, 1993; Gray et al., 1997; Funnell, 1998; Preston, 2006; Broadbent and Laughlin, 2013; Lehman et al., 2016).

This chapter examines Aryanisations by Deutsche Bank using Giorgio Agamben's work on the "state of exception" and *bios* to highlight the consequences of policies that enabled the elimination of Jewish influence from the German economy. Emphasis is given to the importance of the enactment of a state of exception by the German government *(Ausnahmezustand)* as a response to an alleged emergency when the normal rule of law was suspended, forming a dynamic boundary between the *exception* and the norm that exposed every citizen, or business, to the possibility of a financial death. This is achieved by their exclusion from the economic and political life and rights of the citizenry through inclusion in the new oppressive space of the state of exception where now, as the *exception*, the loss of their political rights denies them the protection of the State. Thus, as informed by Agamben, this study focuses on the complicity and actions of Deutsche Bank in the Nazi Aryanisation policy as it was applied to Jewish-owned banks that were the designated *exception*.

The chapter proceeds first with a discussion of Agamben's notion of *bios* in a state of exception. This is followed by an outline of the financially racist policy of Aryanisation. The discussion then focuses on how Aryanisations were accounted for within the Nazi corporative and State-centric economy. Particular emphasis is given to the accounting carried out by Deutsche Bank during Aryanisations that enabled the destruction of Jewish economic life to be concealed, consistent with anti-Semitic ideology. The chapter then moves to specific Aryanisations of other banks carried out by Deutsche Bank and the consequences for Jews and the Aryan businesses.

Nazi Germany and the 'state of exception'

On 27 February 1933, less than a month after Hitler was appointed Chancellor, the *Reichstag* was set on fire. Within hours, the Dutch communist Marinus van der Lubbe was identified as the arsonist. Hitler proclaimed that van der Lubbe was acting on behalf of an organised group seeking a communist revolution (Newton, 1990, p. 191). On February 28, neither President Hindenburg of the Weimar Republic nor any of the conservative ministers resisted when Hitler declared an emergency decree to meet the alleged communist threat. The *Reichstag Fire Decree* (1933) "swept away precious civil liberties at a stroke" (Newton, 1990, p. 191), with the decree setting out in Article 1 that:

> Sections 114, 115, 117, 118, 123, 124, and 153 of the Constitution of the German Reich are suspended until further notice. Therefore, restrictions on personal liberty, on the right of free expression of opinion, including freedom of the press, on the right of assembly and the right of association, and violations of the privacy of postal, telegraphic, and telephonic communications, warrants for house searches, orders for confiscations, as well as restrictions on property, are also *permissible beyond the legal limits otherwise prescribed.*
>
> (*Reichstag Fire Decree*, 1933, emphasis added)

The declaration of a "state of emergency" that remained in place throughout the 12-year reign of the Nazis, even when the so-called "communist threat" crisis passed, effectively suspended normal law and rights. On 23 March 1933, the weak remnants of the Weimar Republic allowed the escalation of Nazi power when "Hitler put forward a proposal for a drastic new law that would enable his cabinet to govern by decree" (Newton, 1990, p. 194) – the *Enabling Act* (1933). Hitler now had extraordinary and legitimate powers, which subsumed the legislative and judicial branches of government (Agamben, 2005). Thus, the separation of powers that defined liberal democracy, ostensibly the foundation upon which the Weimar Republic was built, entered into a zone of indistinction as a state of exception was created (Agamben, 1995). This provided Hitler with consent for what Peukert (1982, p. 198) calls "the use of terror as an emergency measure in order to restore 'order', and approval of its use as a means of excluding those who were alien to the 'national community'". The power inferred by the *Enabling Act* (1933) de-democratised the Nazi State, leaving open a space for fascism and its exclusionary anti-Semitic racial programmes.

Totalitarian State power is sustained by political imperatives favouring individuals who satisfy specified criteria, mostly notoriously based on racial characteristics. Those regarded as the "included" will have political rights that protect their liberty and property. All others, the "excluded", could be deprived of all economic and political rights at any time, thereby giving them only a "bare life", a condition of great vulnerability. The ancient Greeks distinguished between the *zoē*, "the simple fact of living common to all living beings" – a bare life – and the *bios*, the "form or way of living proper to an individual or group" that constituted a political life imbued with rights (Agamben, 1995, pp. 1, 66). The modern State, argues Agamben (2005), has the power to segregate the *bios* and the *zoē* and, thereby, to declare some races as sub-races and deny them *bios*, leaving them as bare life at the mercy of the State. Agamben (1995, p. 142) emphasises that this is most effectively achieved by declaring a "state of exception". Anyone with both *zoē* and *bios* is not susceptible to being interned within the state of exception. In contrast, those with *zoē* only are included in the state of exception and, therefore, as *exceptions,* excluded from the protection of the State. Ultimately, the declaration of a state of exception gives those in power the ability to decide on "the value or the nonvalue of life ..." (Agamben, 1995, p. 142).

Declaration of a state of exception in response to an alleged crisis portrayed as a significant threat to the State justifies suspension of the juridical order to permit actions by the State that would ordinarily be outside the law (Agamben, 2005, p. 39). The result is that the state of exception is not a "state of law" but a space without law where an "exception is an element in law that transcends positive law in the form of its suspension" (Agamben, 1995, p. 17). The *Reichstag Fire Decree* (1933) and the *Enabling Act* (1933) authorised Hitler to handle his political opponents in completely undemocratic and unlawful ways within the state of exception that was created.

By July 1933, "the Ministry of the Interior recorded that 26,789 persons were being held in 'protective custody,' the Nazi-Deutsch term for the internment of political opponents" (Dean, 2008, p. 21). For the next four months, any political opposition either disappeared or was forcibly suppressed (Newton, 1990, p. 195). By the following May, all assets belonging to the former Communist Party had been seized by the State.

An important feature of the state of exception created by Hitler was that its demarcation from the civil sphere was indistinct and constantly in motion (Agamben, 2005). What one day constituted the *nomos* of social and political space, where the authority of the State was derived from laws enacted according to prescribed constitutional procedures, could the next day form part of a state of exception. In the state of exception, what was once the exception instead becomes the rule (Benjamin, 1942; Agamben, 1995, p. 8; Humphreys, 2006; Huber and Scheytt, 2013). Thus, the entire German population was vulnerable to the suspension of rights. This was evident very quickly after the ascension of the Nazis to power when the various legislative instruments and the promotion of Nazi racial ideology saw the boundaries of the state of exception widen from political opponents such as communists to include additional "Others", most especially those categorised according to Nazi racial criteria as Jewish. Jews became the "new" crisis and threat.

The dynamic space of the state of exception throughout the 12-year Reich used Aryanisation to place people within the *exception*, overwhelmingly Jews but also homosexuals, gypsies, people with mental and physical disabilities, Jehovah's Witnesses, Catholics, and Freemasons, making their lives invisible and of no value. Those regarded as "valueless" were encompassed by fascist racism and lost their financial *bios* through the Nazi process of Aryanisation, facilitated by compliant Aryan businesses.

Aryanisation and the advent of the Nazi corporative economy

Aryanisation comprised the implementation of Nazi policies founded on deeply held beliefs of anti-Semitism. Aryanisation cannot be condensed into one single action but rather "a multiplicity of measures aimed at the extinction of [Jewish] business life" (James, 2001, p. 211), as demonstrated by the progressively inhibiting ordinances and decrees issued by the Nazi government (see Appendix). For Agamben (1995, p. 119), Aryanisation was primarily about thanatopolitics, the politics of death, where the political goals of a State are to *make die,* that is, destroy, certain citizens who are condemned according to a set of criteria while *making live* others by promoting their interests. In Nazi Germany, the thanatopolitical goals were to *make live* Aryan citizens and businesses and *make die* Jews and other non-Aryans (Twyford, 2021). This would be achieved by "the growing *inclusion* of man's [sic] natural life in the mechanisms and calculations of power" (Agamben (1995, p. 119). Fundamental to the success of Aryanisation was ensuring increased assets and revenues for the State while centralising power over German industry and the economy, especially that belonging to Jews, to create the "corporative state". Aryanisation required that accounting procedures be enacted so Jewish property could be "measured, compulsorily recorded and finally appropriated" (Funnell, 1998, p. 450), ensuring the exclusion of Jews from the German economy as a prelude to their ultimate elimination as a condemned race (Adler, 1939).

There were primarily two contributing elements of Aryanisation that led to the exclusion, and therefore *inclusion* within the state of exception, of the Jewish population (Agamben, 2005). The first was the numerous laws that prevented Jewish employment and wealth creation, which left Jews in a difficult and vulnerable position where they were unable to sustain their financial life to fund even their daily basic needs. The Reich

> still clothed their anti-Jewish initiatives in the garb of legality and suggested to the public...that they were implemented according to the principles of law, order and fairness – according to the principles of 'merit and decency', as the National Socialist press put it.
>
> (Bajohr, 2002, p. 193)

The centrepiece of anti-Jewish legislation was the well-known *Nuremberg Laws* (1935). The *Nuremberg Laws*, consisting of *The Reich Citizenship Act* and *Blood Protection Act*, ensured that Jews and *Mischling* (part-Jews) were stripped of their German citizenship and associated rights, of their financial and political lives, thereby exposing them to the genocidal intentions of the Nazis. The Minister of People's Enlightenment and Propaganda, Joseph Goebbels, proclaimed that:

> the Jews have no right to pretend to have rights equal to ours. Wherever they want to open their mouths, in the streets, in lines in front of the stores, or on public transportation, *they are to be silenced*, not only because they are wrong on principle, but because they are Jews and have no voice in the community.
>
> (cited in Hochstadt, 2004, p. 130, emphasis added)

The racial discrimination inflicted by Aryanisation grew steadily with various State and industry-led boycotts, increasing anti-Semitic action (most notably during *Kristallnacht*), and anti-Jewish legislation, which moved Aryanisations from being "voluntary" in 1933 to "compulsory" in 1938. Ordinances such as *The Reich Flight Tax* sought to prevent wealth from leaving Germany, making emigration, possibly the only realistic alternative to the German Jews, "so unattractive through taxes and compulsory levies that many Jews preferred to remain in Germany rather than to leave, that in many cases could only be done at the cost of confiscation of their property" (Bajohr, 2002, p. 121). A 1 billion Reich mark (RM) mandatory contribution was also demanded through the *Ordinance on Expiation Payments by Jews of German Citizenship* (1938), further crippling the Jewish community.

A prominent feature of Aryanisation was the transfer of businesses and property from Jewish to Aryan and State possession (Feldman and Seibel, 2005), purging Jewish ownership as an economic aspect of racial discrimination, thus removing the financial *bios* of Jews and beginning the demarcation of Agamben's *exception*. After 1938, Jewish owners were forced to sell their businesses with little consideration for market value, leaving them destitute and unable to flee. Male Jews were rounded up and "herded into the German Labour Front [DAF] Offices, where notaries were on tap, and coerced into signing powers of attorney … [transferring] their property … at 10 per cent of the value assessed for tax purposes" (Grunberger, 1971, p. 102). The combination of financial penalties stripped Jews of their wealth, property, and ability to earn a living, leading to destitution, which later enabled the operation of the labour and death camps:

> The insane mass manufacture of corpses is preceded by the historically and politically intelligible preparation of living corpses. The impetus and what is more important, the silent consent to such unprecedented conditions are the products of those events which during a period of political disintegration suddenly and unexpectedly made hundreds of thousands of human beings homeless, stateless, outlawed and unwanted, while millions of human beings were made economically superfluous and socially burdensome by unemployment.
>
> (Arendt, 2000, p. 128)

The steady introduction of legal instruments and crippling imposition of debt decimated the financial *bios* of Jews, curtailing the space Jews could occupy in Nazi Germany and rendering them particularly vulnerable to the actions and policies of the State. Jews were now the *exception*, where the suspension of law exposed them to unfettered State violence (Agamben, 1995).

Aryanisation also completely changed the structure of economic life in Germany, forming an "inverted imperialist capitalism" (Schweitzer, 1964, p. 532) that was entirely State-centric and devoid of Jewish influence. This form of economy, known as corporative, sought to transform property and private initiatives in the ideological direction pursued by the Nazi State (Spirito, 1932) while simultaneously implementing the autarky policy.[3] Corporatism involves State intervention in the economic sphere to align business goals with State imperatives and monitor larger businesses that might threaten State supremacy. Cinquini (2007, p. 220) notes that "the firm was then seen not only as an instrument for attaining private ends but also as part of a broader context of collective goals". In a corporative economy, businesses implemented State economic policy, instrumentalising action designed to meet the overarching Nazi ideological commitment to racism. Businesses became an integral part of corporatism, such that they implemented State policy while navigating difficult economic terrain where State interests diverged from those of businesses. Aryan businesses like Deutsche Bank acted as conduits for the State, instrumentalising Jewish loss of financial *bios*, complying with financially and socially racist legislation within the specious economy created by the Nazis while seeking (unsuccessfully) to profit from it at the expense of human lives (Hayes, 1987, 2004; Billstein et al., 2000; James, 2001).

The Nazi corporative State was concerned that the Aryan companies profiting from Aryanisation may be deriving excessive benefits, making these businesses *examples* by capping their profits under the *Excess Profits Act* (1939) and imposing a special "Aryanisation levy" (James, 2001, p. 38), along with elaborate audit systems bolstered by the *Audit of Dejewification Transactions* decree (Nuremberg Source 5138). The State's disregard for the dominant economic model at the time, that is, capitalism, emphasised that their racist ideology superseded profit and market growth. The Nazis, therefore, ensured all Aryanisations directed no excess profits for either Aryan businesses or Jewish owners. When these corporative controls proved ineffective at redirecting profits back to the State, a special ruling of the Ministry of Finance instituted "retroactive taxation" (Grunberger, 1971, p. 174), increasing company tax expenses exponentially. These controls were complemented by a Nazi-appointed Regional Economic Advisor (*Gauleiter*) who was to ensure that the key aspect of an Aryanisation project was to "drive down the sale price of the Jewish company as far as was possible. In principle, therefore, the *Gauleiter* did not authorise any payments for the 'goodwill' of the enterprise" (Bajohr, 2002, p. 150). This was in service to their thanatopolitical ideology, which also demanded a new emphasis, intent and, therefore, form of accounting by devoted Aryan businesses. This form of accounting became secretive, using Nazi-Deutsch or special accounts to hide transactions that deprived Jews of their financial *bios*, allowing the accounting statements to show minimal profits and adherence to Nazi policy. This political distortion of accounting practices was to become especially important for the Aryanisation of German banks conducted by Deutsche Bank.

Deutsche Bank: Accounting for Aryanisations

Deutsche Bank was founded in 1870 and had nearly 200 branches across Germany, many of them in areas of thriving trade and commerce with higher concentrations of Jewish-owned businesses. Consequently, Deutsche Bank had strong business and personal ties with many Jewish people and businesses in the years before the Nazi takeover. At the time of the Great Depression, the bank faced tremendous backlash with accusations of being the cause of the financial crisis, while the emergent and dynamic market economy post-Industrial Revolution saw finance capitalism and banking perceived as primarily a Jewish enterprise. Following the Banking Crisis of 1931, the industry was viewed as harmful to society and the economy, which made

> the banks – including Deutsche Bank – vulnerable to attacks and ... accused of being 'plutocratic' or 'Jewish.' One defence mechanism was to purge Jewish directors ... Part of the price of State reconstruction was a purging of the bank officials who were thought to have been responsible for the mistakes of the 1920s. The two purges – anti-Semitic and banking – came together.
>
> (James, 2001, p. 24)

Thus, Deutsche Bank, unlike other Aryan businesses, found itself in a similarly vulnerable position to Jewish firms, forcing them to adopt practices that would communicate more obvious allegiance to Nazi economic programmes. The environment particularly alarmed the spokesman for Deutsche Bank's managing board:

> I fear we are only at the beginning of a development that is deliberately aimed, in accordance with a well-thought-out-plan, at the economic and moral extermination of all members of the Jewish race living in Germany – quite indiscriminately.
>
> (cited in James, 2001, p. 34)

Nazi influence was evident as early as 1933 when Deutsche Bank's annual report asserted adherence to the new regime: "we consider it our special task to promote the ideas of the business community in the sense of the National Socialist movement among all members of our institute" (Deutsche Bank Annual Report, 1933, p. 17). Although Deutsche Bank used its annual report to demonstrate to a wider audience their alignment with the Nazis from the outset, this apparent adherence to Nazi policy did not reflect all the actions of Deutsche Bank. The accounting records continued to reinforce Deutsche Bank's apparent strong commitment to the goals of Nazi policies when the 1934 annual report detailed a new "District Advisory Board" implemented by the State, involving a "reorganisation" of management. Dispatching board members to these district advisory boards freed up the bank's executive space to populate with NSDAP[4] members while simultaneously "decentralising" management in line with corporative principles. After Aryanisation was decreed, Deutsche Bank primarily operated as brokers, which gave the company an appealing new profit line:

> on the one hand, they looked for business opportunities that would strengthen their individual competitive position; on the other hand, they looked to business solidarity as a way of establishing a united front against those aspects of the new policy that they felt to be threatening or unacceptable to their interests.
>
> (James, 2001, p. 53)

In response to the Nazis' determination to prevent businesses from benefiting financially from Aryanisations, by 1935 Nazi-Deutsch was being utilised by Deutsche Bank in its accounting statements to disguise the benefits that the bank obtained from its Aryanisation contributions. In 1936, the annual report noted that the expansion of activities in all its business sectors increased commissions from "special items or one-off transactions" (Annual Report, 1936, p. 11). James (2001, p. 206) explains that "special items and one-off transactions" were forms of Nazi-Deutsch accounting, referring specifically to Aryanisation-related activities, including "special profits and brokerage fees in connection with Aryanisations, sales of securities and real estate, fees for listing on the stock exchange, trustees, mortgage brokerage etc.". Nazi-Deutsch was also used to shroud the suspected dismissal of workers racially categorised as Jewish: "as in previous years, we were able to make considerable new hires in the reporting year and fully replace the number of our employees who retired or *who left our services for other reasons*" (Deutsche Bank Annual Report, 1935, p. 18, emphasis added).

In 1937, Deutsche Bank was operating under the new *German Stock Corporation Act* (1937), which stipulated changing the authority of the supervisory board, electing an entirely new supervisory board, and forcing members into early resignation on racial grounds (Deutsche Bank Annual Report, 1937, p. 3). The report also announced the appointment of Mr Hermann Abs to the board, a man who was to oversee almost every compulsory Aryanisation, including those discussed in this chapter. The *German Stock Corporation Act* (1937) also required a restructuring of the profit and loss account, most significantly transforming operating expenses into personnel expenses (Annual Report, 1937, p. 15) and increasing tax expenses for State revenue raising, which went from RM 12 million in 1936 to RM 79 million by 1942 (Annual Report, 1936, p. 15; 1942, p. 3). The exponential increase in taxation lasted until the "special and one-off transactions" income ceased (Deutsche Bank Annual Report, 1943, 1944). The annual reports in 1936 and 1937 illustrate the careful manipulation of "naming" accounts to put forward a curated narrative devoid of explicit Aryanisation activity, instead reframing as part of "special and one-off transactions". This perpetuated the silence of the Aryanisations and the impact on Jewish financial *bios* that was replicated by the silences in wider society.

The accounting statements of Deutsche Bank adopted the nationalistic tone set by the Nazis, further displaying outward allegiance to the party. In 1939 the annual report for the first time contained the Nazi insignia of the swastika and a memorial for members who had fallen "in the field of honour" (Deutsche Bank Annual Report, 1939, p. 3). The Bank stated that despite the outbreak of war, "the effects of this change are barely visible on our balance sheet" (Annual Report, 1939, p. 9). The Bank reported cryptically that all income from one-off and special transactions had been placed in an internal reserve, where such income was assigned until 1944. The bank also announced increased social engineering style payments to their members: "we are now paying our younger male followers a one-off marriage allowance ... we also grant a surcharge to the third and each additional child allowance" (Annual Report, 1939, p. 10). This text from the annual report indicates the use of financial incentives to motivate Aryan employees to proliferate in line with the broader social engineering at play within Nazi policy. Jews placed within the state of exception were treated somewhat differently, listed instead as "unstable creditors" in the financial statements (James, 2001, p. 171), which amounted to RM 94 million by 1943, including emigration monies and resettlement accounts of "expelled" and "resettled" Jews – Nazi-Deutsch for imprisoned or murdered Jews (James, 2001, p. 171).

The bank proceeded with similar annual reports until the tide of war started turning, and the annual reports went from 30-page documents to a mere 3–4 pages. The bank continued to pay tribute to its workers, stating, "we thank our followers for their unconditional and understanding attitude to the requirements of the time. At the end of the financial year, almost half of our male followers were in the service of the Wehrmacht. Many of our ranks gave their lives in the fulfilment of their patriotic duty, others suffered serious injuries" (Deutsche Bank Annual Report, 1942, p. 3). The bank used its annual reports to list the number of employees who had died in service to Nazism, with 195 deaths in 1942 (Annual Report, 1942, p. 3), rising to 225 in 1943 (Annual Report, 1943, p. 1) and 360 in 1944 (Deutsche Bank Annual Report, 1944, p. 1). This extraordinary aspect of what was primarily a report on the finances and accounting of the bank showed both reverence for the dead and alignment with the Nazi war effort by highlighting the bank's vicarious support through their employees who perished for the "cause". The bank also took special accounting measures by expanding reserves, placing RM 3 million from the profits in 1942 into a newly established foundation called "War Victim Aid" and RM 5 million for economic "recovery" post-war (Annual Report, 1942, p. 3). While an examination of the financial statements of Deutsche Bank confirms that the company was strongly aligned with the Nazis, the accounting by Deutsche Bank during that time uncovers only part of the story of the Aryanisations in which it was engaged. Close-reading of the reports reveals that they do not faithfully represent the bank's activities as a medium through which State-directed transactions occurred.

The Nazi's inherent distrust of banks, considering the banking industry to be speculative and "Jewish" in nature (James, 2001, p. 67), meant greater supervision and control was exerted over Aryanisations carried out by banks. The banking sector and Deutsche Bank thus found themselves during the forced Aryanisations part of the Aryan ideal yet outside of Nazism. Conforming to their indifference to capitalism, the Nazis exhibited little concern for the continued existence of German banks. They were explicit in their intentions to limit the growth of the great banks, most especially Deutsche Bank. Thus, the State would often curtail opportunities for Deutsche Bank to make a profit and instead redirect excess funds to the government. The result was that

> Deutsche Bank did not take over any major banks in Germany in the 1930s (by contrast with the experience of the 1920s, when it had been massively acquisitive). This was not because of self-restraint, moral scruples or doubts about the process of 'Aryanisation,' or an unwillingness to expand. Rather, the absence of takeovers was a consequence of government policy and of the unwillingness of the Reich Economics Ministry and the bank commissar ... to see an extension of the economic power of Deutsche Bank.
>
> (James, 2001, p. 81)

Neoclassical economic rationales were subordinated to Statist-political rationales as Aryan businesses were operationalised to destroy Jewish financial *bios*. This was very evident in the Aryanisation of banks carried out by Deutsche Bank, among which were Bankhaus Mendelssohn & Co. Berlin ("Mendelssohn"); Simon Hirschland, Essen ("Hirschland") and Adler & Oppenheimer (Norddeutsche Lederwerke Aktiengesellschaft Berlin) ("A&O"). These examples of Deutsche Bank Aryanisations highlight how the State's efforts to destroy Jewish financial *bios* inevitably involved the cooperation and complicity of businesses such as Deutsche Bank, their managers, and accounting practices to expedite and disguise the process and its consequences for Jews. Under Aryanisation, the Nazi party was trying to achieve two aims: to eradicate Jewish influence in the economy and to prevent the banking industry, notably Deutsche Bank, from centralising and gaining influence and profit from State ideological aims. However, rather than strengthening the German economy, the corporative economy created by Aryanisation crippled it through racist policy by removing Jewish expertise, experience, and influence.

The Aryanisation of German banks

Bankhaus Mendelssohn & Co. Berlin

Mendelssohn was one of the oldest firms within the German banking sector, founded by Joseph and Abraham Mendelssohn, who belonged to a distinguished lineage of contributors to German culture and economy.[5] Mendelssohn operated until 1938 without Nazi intervention. It then became subject to various anti-Jewish legislation that forced its Aryanisation, including the *Reich Flight Tax* (1931), the *Law against Betraying the German National Economy* (1933), and the *Order for the Disclosure of Jewish Assets* (1938).[6]

Throughout 1938, the ownership of Mendelssohn was exclusively Jewish, with 75% ownership held by the Mendelssohn family. When the demise of their bank became apparent (James, 2001), a long-established business relationship saw the owners choose to negotiate a takeover by Deutsche Bank. However, the Nazi suspicion of banks meant they were uncomfortable with increasing the concentration of power in the banking industry should Deutsche Bank absorb Mendelssohn (James, 2001, p. 72). The state of exception border had become blurred; the *exception* and the norm had become indistinct. Deutsche Bank should have been immune from the law that excluded Jews, but Agamben (1995, 2005) concludes that once the state of exception is declared, all become exposed to the meted violence of the sovereign, even if it is just a *potentiality*.

After protracted negotiations involving the Reichsbank Vice President, Deutsche Bank Aryanised Mendelssohn in October 1938, assuming on behalf of other Aryan businesses control of all assets and liabilities with no proceeds left for the Jewish owners (Köhler, 2005, p. 11). The extent of the catastrophic nature of what happened to the Mendelssohns was hidden by the related accounting entries, which conferred specific visibilities, calculability, and operational utility of the Aryanisation (Burchell et al., 1985; Miller and O'Leary, 1987; Miller, 1990) to the point of rendering the Jewish account of the Aryanisation to a single line: "In Berlin we have taken over customers of the bank Mendelssohn & Co. For our newly acquired business associates ..." (Deutsche Bank Annual Report, 1938, p. 8). "Taken over" forming the Nazi-Deutsch for a compulsory acquisition outside the usual realms of business.

To reduce this influential German family and their business to a single line in the annual report highlights both the significance of this Aryanisation and the ability of accounting practices to attempt to conceal the complicity of Deutsche Bank in facilitating the Nazi's destruction of the financial *bios* of the Mendelssohns. The fact that it was alluded to at all within the annual report illustrates the value Deutsche Bank placed on being "seen" to conduct such an Aryanisation, using accounting to "make visible" their cooperation with Nazi policy (Hopwood, 1986; Miller, 1990, p. 317) to a certain extent. By using the guise of accounting representations to demonstrate political allegiance, the malleability of accounting to present and represent "situations in limited and one-sided ways" (Morgan, 1988, p. 477) is made apparent. The silence on the financially racist policy that drove and justified this "take over" saw Deutsche Bank obscuring its active role in the Aryanisation, as well as masking the accounting that would show an acquisition well below its true value by subsuming it within the catch-all account of "Special Items and One-off Transactions". However, in the accounting, this apparent selfless allegiance to the Nazi's Aryanisation programme also hid the real, more dangerous intent of Deutsche Bank to secretively defy the objective of Aryanisation, namely the complete destruction of Jewish financial *bios*.

Investigations undertaken after the war by the Office of Military Government for Germany, United States (OMGUS), concluded that "the participants in the negotiations always agreed that Mendelssohn & Co should be re-established as an independent banking house as soon as the economic and political conditions permitted" (Feldman and Seibel, 2005, p. 53). Thus, Deutsche Bank was flouting the *Decree Against the Camouflage of Jewish Firms* (1938) by holding Bankhaus Mendelssohn & Co. in what was effectively an informal trust for the Jewish owners so they could reclaim it. Deutsche Bank, therefore, saw the Aryanisation as only a temporary loss of financial *bios* for the owners. Deutsche Bank Aryanised the private-banking industry according to the law but secretly sought to rectify the abuses they perceived once the Nazis were out of power. However, they had not understood the ultimate Nazi goal to exterminate the Jews. Accordingly, despite the brutal manner in which the Mendelssohn family and others were dispossessed of their equity in their bank, the takeover was viewed as "friendly" by Abs and the Mendelssohn family (Lothar and Underwood, 1999; Feldman and Seibel, 2005).

Several Mendelssohn descendants were saved through emigration, others were placed into concentration camps, and few survived, their *zoē* eradicated (Hayman, 2009). Germany had tried to crush the lineage of one of its most culturally important family dynasties by removing their *bios* and rendering them "the bearer of the link between violence and law" to become *zoē* (Agamben, 1995, p. 65). The impact of the Aryanisation extended beyond the Mendelssohn family to the Jewish employees, for a condition of takeover was that "Deutsche Bank would also take over the employees and, for a period of three years pay them at the higher rates customary in Mendelssohn" (James, 2001, pp. 74–75). In Nazi Germany, however, such a stipulation could not be permitted. Thus, contract law was sacrificed to the executive *ban,* as Jewish employees were dismissed within days of the agreement. The financial statements make little mention of this beyond allusions to the racially derived transactions conducted by the bank, including Aryanisations and terminations of Jewish workers. The Mendelssohn Aryanisation was a prominent case of how, in a state of exception, "he [sic] who has been *banned* is not, in fact, simply set outside the law and made indifferent to it but rather *abandoned* by it, that is, exposed and threatened on the threshold in which life and law, outside and inside become indistinguishable" (Agamben, 1995, p. 28).

Hirschland Bank, Essen

Similar to the Aryanisation of Mendelssohn, reliance upon long-established relationships between senior members of the banks saw Hirschland seek Deutsche Bank as a potential ally. Over 20% of Hirschland's employees were Jewish, which James (2001, p. 77) states made the bank "a focal point of Jewish financial dominance in the Ruhr district" and the object of Nazi party intervention. Original negotiations for the Aryanisation of Hirschland Bank aimed to sustain the financial *bios* of Jewish owners and directors. They proposed an arrangement whereby Deutsche Bank would purchase the Hirschland shares through a managed consortium, with the capital provided by Ruhr industrialists and standstill credits (*Stillhaltekredite*) held by the bank assumed by Deutsche Bank (James, 2001, pp. 77–78). Hirschland Bank was in a unique situation in that it held standstill credits of RM 38 million in 1937 (James, 2001). *Stillhaltekredite* represented foreign credit lines frozen during the 1931 banking crisis, subject to annually negotiated German Credit Agreements. These credits represented a liability

> with the proprietors personally, in fact, through their private assets, and, under the provisions of the Standstill agreement, the part amounts concerned when a proprietor withdraws would fall due immediately, payable in foreign currency … it follows that Jewish assets located abroad would be jeopardized.
>
> (James, 2001, p. 73)

Consequently, the transfer of *Stillhaltekredite* to another bank or the German government would require the consent of the foreign creditors. This made emigration particularly difficult for the Jewish owners. The owners would prefer another German bank to take over the credits to appease the creditors. Thus, the ability of Jews associated with the Hirschland bank to maintain their financial *bios* and survive the state of exception depended on the cooperation of Aryan banks. The deal negotiated by Deutsch Bank for the purchase of Hirschland Bank shares was strongly opposed by the Essen NSDAP, with the *Gauleiter* writing to the Reich Economics Minister Walther Funk that the plan was

> completely out of the question, since the political leadership *does not wish this business to survive*, because if it did the result would be to usher in a fresh version of the Essen banking industry.... This preliminary agreement gives such unilateral preference to Deutsche Bank and further provides for such powerful dependence on the part of Deutsche Bank that there could be no more talk of a 'private bank' in the strict meaning of the word.
>
> (cited in James, 2001, p. 78, emphasis added)

Fearful of a centralised and powerful banking industry, the government preferred liquidating Hirschland instead of allowing Deutsche Bank to increase its market share. The words used by the *Gauleiter* echo the thanatopolitical ideology of the Nazis, linking notions of life and death to the application of economic policies in the form of "survive". In eliminating Hirschland Bank, the *Gauleiter* sought the loss of Jewish influence and participation in the Essen economy. Eventually, the problematic *Stillhaltekredite* proved to be propitious for Deutsche Bank. Out of the available acquirers, only Deutsche Bank could pay the credits, with Germany in no position to repay in foreign currency without industry capital. Deutsch Bank recorded the

Aryanisation as a "one-off transaction" valued at a token RM 213,310.16 for the bank (Annual Report, 1938).

During negotiations, the Essen *Gauleiter* continued to admonish the deal due to "the possibility of Deutsche Bank's achieving a unilateral advantage through a profitable 'Aryanisation' [and] it was also quite out of the question that Deutsche Bank should come into Hirschland's entire inheritance" (James, 2001, p. 79). James (2001, p. 79) asserts that it was suggested by the Nazi Party that unless "some of the *Gauleiter's* industrial friends become personal and financial partners in the new firm" Deutsche Bank's plans were unworkable. This mirrors the case of Mendelssohn, in that the State included Deutsche Bank as part of the *ban* that was only supposed to extend to Jews.

Deutsche Bank's accounts were generally silent on the bank's participation in this Aryanisation, brief insinuations hidden through the veneer of Nazi-Deutsch in which accounting terminology transformed into techniques to conceal the reality of "special and one-off transactions": namely the destruction of Jewish financial *bios*. Nazi-Deutsch allowed the accounts to display an unproblematic figure under the guise of business as usual, a figure which was silent on so many other aspects of the Aryanisation of Hirschland Bank (Morgan, 1988; Chwastiak and Young, 2003), most especially the gravity of the events and the exploitative nature of the transaction, relegating the lived experiences of the humans involved "outside" of accounting (Miller, 1998). These included Hirschland Bank's employees, all of whom would have to be dismissed and "remain hidden from the eyes of justice" (Agamben, 1995, p. 37). Accounting techniques utilised by Deutsche Bank to record the acquisition of Hirschland Bank mystified and masked "the intrinsic value of the people's lives that [were] being destroyed" (Chwastiak and Lehman, 2008, p. 321), as well as the true actions of businesses and government. This reinforces the notion that when accounting creates visibilities, a value choice is made, and information is depicted and rendered important through a visible presence (Rose and Miller, 1992, p. 184). The absorption of the Aryanisation of Hirschland Bank into a Nazi-Deutsch account with no further information given, not even the single line that had been afforded to Mendelssohn, ascribes this Aryanisation little "value" and, "by definition, that which is not captured by accounting must be without value" (Funnell, 1998, p. 452). This is echoed by Schmitt (1922, p. 80, cited in Agamben, 1995, p. 137), who emphasised that "he[sic] who determines a value [thereby] always fixes a nonvalue. The sense of this determination of a nonvalue is the annihilation of the nonvalue". This annihilation of the nonvalue would later be radicalised during the Nazi regime in a literal sense.

Progressively, Jews were written out of the business accounts and records, their financial *bios* erased, and the exploitative acts of Aryanisation concealed by the accounting reports of the Aryan firms. This reinforces Funnell's (1998, pp. 458–459) idea that the "essentially calculative nature of accounting drained from the objects of its calculations features which were not amenable to measurement and reporting in a numerical format". Once financial *bios* were removed, the accounting records, at best, used Nazi-Deutsch to euphemise and, at worst, completely exclude the true nature of the transactions. The consequences of Aryanisation for the Hirschland family reveal that which was *un*accounted for in the "silences [that] allow us to ignore more easily the distasteful and objectionable aspects of the systems in which we live[d]" (Chwastiak and Young, 2003, p. 535).

The Hirschland family, with the meagre proceeds from the sale of their bank, were still expected to pay the debts owed under the *Order for the Disclosure of Jewish Assets* (1938) and *Kristallnacht*. Financially distressed from the sale of the bank, the Hirschland family tried explaining to the tax office that during *Kristallnacht,* they had buildings, a children's home, and a synagogue destroyed, as well as silver, jewellery, and paintings (including some by van Gogh), confiscated (James, 2001, p. 80). The reparations demanded, as well as the exorbitant costs of emigration, bankrupted the family, forcing them to pay nearly RM 5 million to the State, resulting in the cataclysmic loss of their financial *bios*. The cumulative forces of racist ideology, restrictive legislation, forced confiscations, and exorbitant taxes ensured the Hirschland family was unable to maintain the dual *bios* and *zoē* to sustain life. The Hirschland family escaped to North America, eventually building a new life despite losing financial *bios*. Future generations would later seek compensation for the financial theft of their ancestor's wealth, resulting in the paltry award of 162,500 Swiss francs (Claims Restitution Tribunal, 2012).

After the Mendelssohn and Hirschland acquisitions, Deutsche Bank continued facilitating Aryanisation policies in a hostile environment. Despite Deutsche Bank belonging to the "Aryan" categorisation of business, the State did not extend its thanatopolitical imperative to the bank. Instead, it became increasingly imperative that the bank made no profit for the Aryanisation to be finalised. This did not stop Deutsche Bank from taking advantage of the labyrinth of bureaucracy that exemplified Nazi Germany in its attempts to remain profitable in spite of its *ban*, similar to its attempts to restore financial *bios* to the Mendelssohn family and for the Jewish owners of Adler & Oppenheimer.

Adler & Oppenheimer (Norddeutsche Lederwerke Aktiengesellschaft Berlin)

The Jewish-owned bank *Adler & Oppenheimer* (A&O) was one of the largest producers of leather in Germany (James, 2001, p. 90), with ownership held by the original founding families via a Dutch intermediary, N.V. Amsterdamsche Leder Maatschappij. Thus, any Aryanisation would have to be facilitated through Dutch shareholders (James, 2001, p. 91). Prior to the Aryanisation, Deutsche Bank began buying shares in A&O from its Jewish owners, who had been forced to emigrate, and by 1940 held shares worth RM 10,145,000 (James, 2001, p. 91). The Nazi Party, through representatives in the Reich Economics Ministry, remained "hostile to the idea that a major business (such as Deutsche Bank) might form the basis for an even larger concentration of economic power" (James, 2001, p. 91). Deutsche Bank continued to face firm State protectionist policies and the preconception of being a "Jewish" enterprise. The designation of the Deutsche Bank as an important, trusted implement of Nazi policy impeded making any serious profits from the Aryanisations. Therefore, the Nazis put the German Labour Front forward as a possible acquirer of A&O, an attractive option to the State because of its value as a major military supplier. Several other companies from all over Germany vied for the acquisition but were frustrated by the State's concern over oligopolisation. It was clear that centralisation fears would prevent any business from growing too big or too prosperous, contradicting the capitalist economic model present during the Weimar Republic. The laws designed to *ban* Jews had the corollary of *abandoning* the Aryan counterparts *(exception/example)*, leaving only the State protected.

In 1939, the inhibiting legislative moves to remove Jewish financial *bios* were almost at their nadir, with the *Reich Flight Tax* (1931) taxing at a rate of 90–96% of assets that were to leave Germany. Deals to acquire the bank were hindered by the State's insistence that the buyer be a German enterprise, which conflicted with the aims of the Dutch owners. It was not until the German invasion of the Netherlands and subsequent integration into the German New Order that the issue was overcome. Deutsche Bank seized the opportunity and purchased as many shares as permitted by the State. The State allowed the purchase, meticulously accounting for the purchase to ensure no profits were produced for the bank (James, 2001, p. 92). Repeatedly, the State altered the economic model to fit its ideology, even when this did not serve the interests of the Aryan firm seeking to make a purchase and was contrary to the Nazi's platform.

James (2001, p. 90) claims that A&O became "the largest and most complicated industrial 'Aryanisation' conducted directly by Deutsche Bank". The authorities, frustrated by the complexities of their task, tried to expedite the deal by placing further pressure on the remaining owners of A&O with a false bill for tax arrears (James, 2001, p. 85). The Deutsche Bank not only had to manage the Reich Economics Ministry, the numerous shareholders, and competing businesses but also "the occupation regime of the Netherlands, with the NSDAP 'Foreign Organisation,' and presumably (or at least indirectly) the SS over emigration permits" (James, 2001, p. 98).

The apparent lack of profits procured by Deutsche Bank appeased the Nazis. Deutsche Bank became a vehicle for their thanatopolitical policies under the guise of promoting the Aryan business by diminishing the presence of Jews. The accounts disguised the true profit Deutsche Bank managed to make when the bank sold their portion of shares at 140% of nominal value after being purchased at 106%. In numerical terms, the A&O Aryanisation was the most profitable for Deutsche Bank, despite the efforts of the State. Indeed, Deutsche Bank converted "special and one-off" equity into cash, deceiving the Reich Economics Ministry, thereby giving credence to Fleischman and

Tyson's (2004, p. 393) assertion that "accounting is much more constructive than reflective [and]...complicit in sustaining institutions". Deutsche Bank manipulated accounts in their financial statements to construct a narrative of little gain by concealing the transaction within the catch-all "special items and one-off transactions" account and later manoeuvring to ensure profits from Aryanisation despite contravening the numerous legislative sanctions that denied the bank from earning revenue under the corporative model.

The Annual Report of Deutsche Bank in 1941 did not mention the A&O Aryanisation, accounting instead serving National Socialism by concealing the Aryanisation process (Walker, 2000, p. 225). The bank used the Nazi-Deutsch practice of euphemism in its accounting reports to give the appearance of conforming to Nazi ideology by facilitating the thanatopolitical agenda of the State when it actively sought to thwart these intentions. Similar to the redirection of monies into differentiated accounts, such as the War Victim Aid account, Deutsche Bank utilised extraordinary accounts to facilitate Aryanisation and escape further taxation and profit requisitions by the State. Thus, Deutsche Bank used accounting to form "part of the structure of controls and practices ... contrived to deliver efficiency and effectiveness in the service of the State" (Funnell, 1998, p. 439), at least to outside observers.

For a large institution such as Deutsche Bank to deny a clear presence in their accounts for transactions related to the Aryanisation of A&O demonstrates how effectively they used accounting to dismiss the *bios* of Jewish victims. Similar to other silences in accounting, it sends a clear message that the Jewish people involved were not of value by rendering them invisible in the annual reports. Broadbent (1995, p. 4) claims that "it is this partiality in representation and its control potential which constitutes [accounting's] real social influence, as well as its social danger". Representations provided by Deutsche Bank's accounting failed to show the transaction of Aryanisation and, thus, the effect of this transaction, namely the loss of financial *bios* for the owners, thereby reiterating Goebbels's earlier claims that Jews "are to be silenced". The A&O families were eventually forced to immigrate to various regions, including the United States and South America (James, 2001, p. 98).

Abs, as the orchestrator of the deal on behalf of Deutsche Bank, was later accused by historian Eberhard Czichon (1995) of profiting from these Aryanisations after divesting the owners of their financial *bios*. Abs, however, claimed that "he had helped the original owners and delayed the 'Aryanisation'" (James, 2001, p. 90), which enabled them to emigrate before they were placed into a concentration camp. This was later confirmed by a member of the Adler family (McKale, 2011, p. 227). Deutsche Bank attempted to counter the efforts of the State to move beyond the removal of financial *bios* by "taking part in what was also a ransom operation, in which lives were to be exchanged for the consent to a financial transaction" (James, 2001, p. 98). This alludes to how human lives could only be bartered with currency, not ethical or moral considerations. Aryan businesses that sought similar exchanges could potentially have made a difference between the ultimate decisions over the life and death of Jews. As a vital part of the *ban* and *abandonment* of the law (Agamben, 1995), this may have motivated Deutsche Bank to give a sympathetic response to Aryanisations. Other studies have shown that not every Aryan business chose this action and had little regard for the fate of Jewish owners after Aryanisation (Hayes, 1987, 2004; Bajohr, 2002).

Conclusion

The process of Aryanisation demonstrated the tension between Nazi ideology, the capitalist model, corporatism, morality, and the culpability of both businesses and accounting practices to destroy financial *bios* within a state of exception. Importantly, Aryan banks, particularly Deutsche Bank as the *example*, were not supported by the State, thereby reinforcing how the Nazi ideology centred on Jewish extermination superseded all other considerations, including strengthening the Aryan economy. This saw accounting practices enmeshed in organisational and State-initiated violence that fulfilled the political ideology of the Nazi government (Dillard and Ruchala, 2005). In the use of Nazi-Deutsch euphemism, accounting statements, and financial reports hid the persecutory dimension of Aryanisations and, therefore, the loss of financial *bios*.

In examining specific Aryanisations, the takeover of Mendelssohn was shown to be a charade, with the Jewish owners agreeing that Deutsche Bank was to assume a caretaker, rather than owner, role. Holding Mendelssohn in this informal trust highlighted that not every participant in Nazi policy had malignant intentions or was an adherent to the underlying anti-Semitic, eliminationist ideology. This narrative defies the perception of businesses during the Holocaust (see Booth et al., 2007). Similarly, Deutsche Bank's acquisition of A&O demonstrates the threat to financial *bios* experienced by Aryan firms as well as Jewish firms, affirming Agamben's (1995, p. 179) theorisations on the indistinct nature of the state of exception where exclusion threatens all humanity because where there are people possibilities for losses of *bios* and *zoē* are apparent. Deutsche Bank's delays in the Aryanisation of A&O allowed the owners the brief opportunity to escape Germany before imprisonment within a concentration camp. Deutsche Bank helped the owners evade the state of exception and, therefore, death. The bank did so while still trying to profit from the policy of Aryanisation, thereby blurring the line of morality where both the act of seeking to profit and safeguarding Jewish lives required that the costs, both financially and socially, "of corporate actions be masked in order to increase the acceptability of such acts" (Chwastiak and Young, 2003, p. 534). As has been shown, neither act would demonstrate allegiance to the Nazi party, which would have imperilled Deutsche Bank.

The simultaneous act of profit-seeking and wilful neglect of the Nazi imperative to destroy Jewish financial *bios* indicates that where German businesses had the will and the capacity, Jewish families could be saved. Deutsche

Bank negotiated deals that enabled some members of the Mendelssohn, Hirschland, and A&O families to emigrate and start new lives away from the persecution they had endured in Germany. This is remarkable given that these were examples of compulsory Aryanisations when the option of emigration had been all but unavailable. However, despite these attempts to save Jewish financial *bios* and *zoē*, Deutsche Bank remains complicit in Nazi thanatopolitical policy, as evident in what was gleaned from the Nazi-Deutsch accounting records, which hid the human impact of Aryanisations. Despite its reluctance, Deutsche Bank was "a vital element in a chain of exploitation and theft" (James, 2001, p. 208) in fulfilling State policy. Aryan businesses instrumentalised Aryanisations, adopting accounting practices to obscure the true nature of the financial transactions and mask attempts to subvert Nazi policies that did not serve business interests.

Aryanisation was successful in denuding Jews of their financial *bios*, which then set them on the path to the eventual extermination of their actual life (*zoē*) (Twyford, 2021). Even the "lucky" families from Deutsche Bank's Aryanisations who managed to emigrate were forced to forge new lives in distant lands without financial means. The majority of Jews interned within the Nazi state of exception, and their subsequent fates prove that "seizure of property acts as an important catalyst in accelerating the downward spiral across the threshold to genocide" (Dean, 2008, p. 15). Other aspects of their lives were open to eradication by "killing" their financial *bios*. The study of the Aryanisation of the three banks by Deutsche Bank has disclosed the veiled role of accounting in this ultimately genocidal process.

While accounting operates surreptitiously, it nonetheless imparts human representation in accounting terms as the unifying language of economics (Lavoie, 1987). This representation in Nazi Germany facilitated the loss of financial *bios*, for which Lippman (2009, p. 76) faults the preparers of accounting statements when "their reports hid the human dimension of what occurred". Accounting is then intimately linked to the exercise of State power (Fourquet, 1980; Miller, 1986, 1990), used as a technique by the State to realise abstract political objectives (Hopwood, 1984, 1986; Miller, 1990; Radcliffe, 1998). Most importantly, this study has shown how the anti-Semitic ideology of the Nazis and Aryanisation processes were concealed by the accounting practices of Deutsche Bank. Accounting is shown to have been a critical component in the exclusion and *exception* creating process of thanatopolitics that resulted in the financial death of Jews, intruding upon the private sphere of citizens to deliver and enforce State directives, which held "severe ramifications" for people's lives (Lippman and Wilson, 2007, p. 299).

The Nazi-Deutsch-derived rhetoric of accounting would leave the fate of those Aryanised silenced or "non-valued", while the Nazis prioritised the careful rerouting of funds back to the State through levies and retroactive taxes. By uncovering how business decisions within a state of exception led to real consequences for the life and death of Jews, this study has also highlighted the understated yet salient role of accounting that concealed and mystified those consequences. Accounting practice disguised the persecutory ideology in collaborative complicity with Aryan businesses. Although Deutsche Bank, non-adherents to Nazism, attempted to protect the owners of the Aryanised businesses and made few profits from its involvement in Aryanisation, James (2001, p. 213) has observed that this does not make its actions any more justifiable. Indeed, it might be argued that transactions that fundamentally undermined trust in contracts and extended the arbitrary and capricious exercise of power are discreditable enough by themselves but even more discreditable when they cannot be legitimated in terms of the traditional logic of business decisions. Talk of simply going on with "business as usual" in the extraordinary circumstances of Nazi Germany is thus inherently implausible, for there was nothing very usual about German business at that time. While sympathetic to Jewish owners, Deutsche Bank was nevertheless an integral part of the apparatus that successfully delivered the Aryanisation of the German economy and the destruction of the financial lives of Jews.

This chapter is based on the paper by Erin Twyford and Warwick Funnell titled "Accounting for the Nazi Aryanisation of German banks", which originally appeared in *Accounting, Auditing & Accountability Journal* in 2023, vol. 36, no. 1, pp. 1–23. The authors would like to thank the publisher, Emerald, for permission to use this material.

Notes

1 An Aryan was a German who qualified to belong to a race of people originating in Nordic or northern European locations.
2 A list of financially persecutory legislation is provided in the Appendix.
3 Autarky was the policy of economic self-sufficiency pursued by the Nazi party as part of their Four-Year Plan with war as the ultimate goal.
4 NSDAP is the abbreviated form of The National Socialist German Workers' Party (Nazi Party).
5 Joseph and Abraham Mendelssohn were the sons of philosopher Moses Mendelssohn and uncle and father respectively of composers Felix Mendelssohn and Fanny Hensel. The Mendelssohn family was considered so influential that the Leo Baeck Institute held an exhibit in 2013 titled "The Mendelssohn's: A German Family of Scholars, Bankers, and Artists". The exhibit was opened by the German Ambassador who commented that "Few families have had a more profound impact on the shaping of German culture than the Mendelssohn's" (Leo Baeck Institute, 2013).
6 Other related legislation included the *Denaturalisation Law* (1933), *The Reich Citizenship Act* (1935), the *Executive Order on the Reich Tax Law* (1936), the *Decree Against the Camouflage of Jewish Firms* (1938), the *Order for the Disclosure of Jewish Assets* (1935), and the *Blood Protection Act* (1935) ("Nuremberg laws").

References

Primary sources

Enabling Act (1933).
Deutsche Bank (1933) *Geschäftsbericht 1933.*
Deutsche Bank (1934) *Geschäftsbericht 1934.*
Deutsche Bank (1935) *Geschäftsbericht 1935.*
Deutsche Bank (1936) *Geschäftsbericht 1936.*

Deutsche Bank (1937) *Geschäftsbericht 1937.*
Deutsche Bank (1938) *Geschäftsbericht 1938.*
Deutsche Bank (1939) *Geschäftsbericht 1939.*
Deutsche Bank (1940) *Geschäftsbericht 1940.*
Deutsche Bank (1941) *Geschäftsbericht 1941.*
Deutsche Bank (1942) *Geschäftsbericht 1942.*
Deutsche Bank (1943) *Geschäftsbericht 1943.*
Deutsche Bank (1944) *Geschäftsbericht 1944.*
German Stock Corporation Act (1937).
Grundsätze für Buchhaltungsrichtlinien (1937).
Reichstag Fire Decree (1933).

Secondary sources

Adler, H. (1939). "Neues Wirtschaftsrecht: VO. Über den Einsatz des jüdischen Vermögens vom 3.12.38. RGB1. I 1938 S. 1709", *Der Wirtschaftstreuhänder, Zeitschrift für deutsches Prüfungs-und Treuhandsweswn ed. Dr. Otto Mönckmeier*, *8*(1–2), 31.

Agamben, G. (1995). *Homo Sacer: Sovereign power and bare life.* Stanford, CA: Stanford University Press.

Agamben, G. (2005). *State of Exception.* Chicago, IL: The University of Chicago Press.

Arendt, H. (2000). *The Portable Hannah Arendt.* New York: Penguin Books.

Arrington, C., and Francis, J. (1993). Giving economic accounts: Accounting as cultural practice. *Accounting, Organizations and Society*, *18*(2/3), 107–124.

Bajohr, F. (2002). *"Aryanisation" in Hamburg: The Economic Exclusion of Jews and the Confiscation of Their Property in Nazi Germany.* New York: Berghahn Books.

Benjamin, W. (1942). On the concept of history. In: H. Eiland, and M. Jennings (Eds.). *Selected Writings 1938–1940.* Cambridge: Harvard University Press.

Billstein, R., Fings, K., Kugler, A., and Levis, N. (2000). *Working for the Enemy: Ford, General Motors, and Forced Labour in Germany during the Second World War.* New York: Berghahn Books.

Booth, C., Clark, P., Delahye, A., Procter, S., and Rowlinson, M. (2007). Accounting for the dark side of corporate history: Organizational culture perspectives and the Bertelsmann case. *Critical Perspectives on Accounting*, *18*(6), 625–644.

Broadbent, J. (1995). The values of accounting and education: Some implications of the creation of visibilities and invisibilities in schools. *Advances in Public Interest Accounting*, *6*, 69–98.

Broadbent, J., and Laughlin, R. (2013). *Accounting Control and Controlling Accounting: Interdisciplinary and Critical Perspectives.* Bingley: Emerald Group Publishing.

Burchell, S., Clubb, C., and Hopwood, A. (1985). Accounting in its social context: Towards a history of value added in the United Kingdom., *Accounting, Organizations and Society*, *10*(4), 381–413.

Chwastiak, M., and Lehman, G. (2008), Accounting for war. *Accounting Forum*, *32*(4), 313–326.

Chwastiak, M., and Young, J. (2003). Silences in annual reports. *Critical Perspectives on Accounting*, *14*(5), 533–552.

Claims Restitution Tribunal (2012). "In re account of Simon Hirschland", *Holocaust Victim Assets Litigation*, weblog post, viewed 2/4/2018. http://www.crt-ii.org/_awards/_apdfs/Simon_Hirschland_1.pdf

Cinquini, L. (2007). Fascist corporative economy and accounting in Italy during the thirties: Exploring the relations between a totalitarian ideology and business studies. *Accounting, Business & Financial History*, *17*(2), 209–240.

Czichon, E. (1995). *Die Bank und die Macht: Hermann Josef Abs, die Deutsche Bank und die Politik*. Cologne: Turtleback.

Dawidowicz, L. (1976). *A Holocaust Reader*. New York: Behrman House Inc.

Dean, M. (2008). *Robbing the Jews*. New York: Cambridge University Press.

Dillard, J., and Ruchala, L. (2005). The rules are no game: From instrumental rationality to administrative evil. *Accounting, Auditing & Accountability Journal*, *18*(5), 608–630.

Feldman, G., and Seibel, W. (Eds.). (2005). *Networks of Nazi Persecution: Bureaucracy, Business, and the Organisation of the Holocaust*. New York: Berghahn Books.

Fleischman, R., and Tyson, T. (2004). Accounting in service to racism: Monetizing slave property in the antebellum South. *Critical Perspectives on Accounting*, *15*(3), 376–399.

Fourquet, F. (1980). *Les Comptes de al Puissance*. Paris: Encres.

Friedlander, H. (1980). The manipulation of language In: H. Friedlander, and S. Milton (Eds.). *The Holocaust: Ideology, Bureaucracy and Genocide*. Millwood: Kraus International Publications.

Funnell, W. (1998), Accounting in the service of the Holocaust. *Critical Perspectives on Accounting*, *8*(4), 435–464.

Goldhagen, D. (1996). *Hitler's Willing Executioners: Ordinary Germans and the Holocaust*. London: Abacus.

Gray, R., Dey, C., Owen, D., Evans, R., and Zadek, S. (1997). Struggling with the praxis of social accounting: Stakeholders, accountability, audits and procedures. *Accounting, Auditing and Accountability Journal*, *10*(3), 325–364.

Grunberger, R. (1971). *The 12-Year Reich: A social history of Nazi Germany 1933–1945*. Canada: Hold, Rinehart and Winston.

Hayes, P. (1987). *Industry and Ideology: IG Farben in the Nazi Era*. New York: Cambridge University Press.

Hayes, P. (2004). *From Cooperation to Complicity: Degussa in the Third Reich*. New York: Cambridge University Press.

Hochstadt, S. (2004). *Sources of the Holocaust*. New York: Palgrave Macmillan.

Hopwood, A. (1984). Accounting and the pursuit of efficiency. In: A. Hopwood, and C. Tomkins (Eds.). *Issues in Public Sector Accounting*. Oxford: Philip Allan.

Hopwood, A. (1986). Management accounting and organizational action: An introduction. In: M. Bromwich, and A. Hopwood, (Eds.). *Research and Current Issues in Management Accounting*. London: Pitman.

Huber, C., and Scheytt, T. (2013). The dispositif of risk management: Reconstructing risk management after the financial crisis. *Management Accounting Research*, *24*(2), 88–99.

Humphreys, S. (2006). Legalizing lawlessness: On Giorgio Agamben's state of exception. *The European Journal of International Law*, *17*(3), 677–687.

James, H. (2001). *The Deutsche Bank and the Nazi Economic War Against the Jews*. Cambridge: Cambridge University Press.

Köhler, I. (2005). "Aryanisation" of the German private banks, presented at the 9th EBHA Conference, Frankfurt, Germany, 1–3 September 2005.

Lavoie, D. (1987). The accounting of interpretations and the interpretation of accounts: The communicative function of "the language of business". *Accounting, Organizations and Society*, *12*(6), 579–604.

Lehman, C., Annisette, M., and Agyemang, G. (2016). Immigration and neoliberalism: Three cases and counter accounts. *Accounting, Auditing & Accountability Journal*, *29*(1), 43–79.

Leo Baeck Institute (2013). LBI Focuses on Mendelssohn Family in Exhibit at German Ambassador's Residence. *Leo Baeck Institute*, accessed 28/06/2018, https://www.lbi.org/2013/05/lbi-focuses-on-mendelssohn-family-exhibit-at-german-ambassadors-residence/

Lippman, E. (2009). Accountant's responsibility for the information they report: An historical case study of financial information. *Accounting Historians Journal*, *36*(1), 61–79.

Lippman, E., and Wilson, P. (2007). The culpability of accounting in perpetuating the Holocaust. *Accounting History*, *12*(3), 283–303.

Lothar, G., and Underwood, J. (1999). Hermann Josef Abs and the Third Reich: "A man for all seasons". *Financial History Review*, *6*(2), 147–202.

McKale, D. (2011). *Nazis after Hitler: How Perpetrators of the Holocaust Cheated Justice and Truth*. Maryland, Virginia: Rowman & Littlefield Publishers.

Hayman, S. (Director). (2009). *Mendelssohn, the Nazis, and Me*, motion picture. Renegade Pictures.

Miller, P. (1986). Accounting for progress – national accounting and planning in France: A review essay. *Accounting, Organizations and Society*, *11*(1), 83–104.

Miller, P. (1990). On the interrelations between accounting and the State. *Accounting, Organizations and Society*, *15*(4), 315–338.

Miller, P. (1998). The margins of accounting. *European Accounting Review*, *7*(4), 605–621.

Miller, P., and O'Leary, T. (1987). Accounting and the construction of the governable person. *Accounting, Organizations and Society*, *12*(3), 235–265.

Morgan, G. (1988). Accounting as reality construction: Towards a new epistemology for accounting practice. *Accounting, Organizations and Society*, *13*(5), 477–485.

Newton, D. (1990). *Germany 1918–1945: From Days of Hope to Years of Horror*. Melbourne: Collins Dove.

Peukert, D. (1982). *Inside Nazi Germany: Conformity, Opposition, and Racism in Everyday Life*. New Haven, CT: Yale University Press.

Preston, A. (2006). Enabling, enacting and maintaining action at a distance: An historical case study of the role of accounts in the reduction of the Navajo herds. *Accounting, Organizations and Society*, *31*(6), 559–578.

Radcliffe, V. (1998). Efficiency audit: An assembly of rationalities and programmes. *Accounting, Organizations and Society*, *23*(4), 377–410.

Rose, N., and Miller, P. (1992). Political power beyond the state: Problematics of government. *The British Journal of Sociology*, *43*(2), 173–205.

Schmitt, C. (1922). *Political Theology*. Cambridge: MIT Press.

Schweitzer, A. (1964). *Big Business in the Third Reich*. London: Eyre & Spottiswoode.

Standish, P. (1990). Origins of the plan Comptable Général: A study in cultural intrusion and reaction. *Accounting and Business Research*, *20*(80), 337–351.

Spirito, U. (1932, 1 July). Dentro e fuori. *Critica Fascista*, *X*, 243–244.

Twyford, E. (2021). A thanatopolitical visualization of accounting history: Giorgio Agamben and the Holocaust. *Accounting History*, *26*(3), 352–374.

Walker, S. (2000). Encounters with Nazism: British accountants and the Fifth International Congress on Accounting. *Critical Perspectives on Accounting*, *11*(2), 215–245.

Appendix – List of Persecutory Legislation

Reich Flight Tax (1931).
Law Against Malicious Gossip (1933).
Law Against Betraying the German National Economy (1933).
Law for the Restoration of the Professional Civil Service (1933).
Law on the Admission to the Legal Profession (1933).
Law Against Overcrowding in Schools and Universities (1933).
Law for the Prevention of Progeny of the Genetically Unhealthy (1933).
The Denaturalization Law (1933).
Law for the Prevention of Hereditarily Diseased Offspring (1933).
The Law on Exchange Control (1935).
The Army Law (1935).
Law for the Protection of German Blood and German Honour (1935).
Reich Citizenship Law (1935) (Nuremberg law).
Hitler Youth Law (1936).
Executive Order on the Reich Tax Law (1936).
Executive Order on the Law on the Alteration of Family and Personal Names (1938).
The Decree against the Camouflage of Jewish Firms (1938).
Order for the Disclosure of Jewish Assets (1938).
Jewish Capital Levy (1938).
Decree on the Confiscation of Jewish Property (1938).
Decree on the Exclusion of Jews from German Economic Life (1938).
Ordinance on the Restoration of Street Scenery at Jewish Commercial Centres (1938).
Ordinance on the Registration of the Property of Jews (1938).
Ordinance on an Expiation Payments by Jews of German Citizenship (1938).
The Decree Concerning the Surrender of Precious Metals and Stones in Jewish Possession (1939).
Excess Profits Act (1939).
Decree of the Führer and Reich Chancellor on the Utilisation of the Requisitioned Property of Enemies of the Reich (1941).
Eleventh Ordinance of the Reich Citizen's Law (1942).
Audit of Dejewification Transactions (1942).

8 Accounting and expropriation of Jewish property in Fascist Italy 1939–1945

Valerio Antonelli, Raffaele D'Alessio, Roberto Rossi, and Warwick Funnell

Introduction

The attempted annihilation of European Jews by the German Nazis, which constituted a "gigantic, murderous operation" (Dawidowicz, 1975; Bauman, 1989; Muller-Hill, 1994, p. 68), was not exclusive to Nazi Germany in the 1930s and 1940s. After Mussolini entered into an alliance with Hitler in 1936, Fascist Italy embarked upon a program of anti-Semitism for which accounting practices made crucial contributions to a ministerial bureaucracy explicitly established for the persecution of Italian Jews. Race laws that the Italian Fascists promulgated in 1938–1939 resulted in restrictions on the rights of Italian Jews of which the expropriation of Jewish property by the Fascist Government became the prelude to the ultimate attempted annihilation of Italian Jews by the Nazis after the surrender of Italy. In Italy, the expropriation of Jewish property was mainly the responsibility of a new government body established in 1939, the *Ente di Gestione e Liquidazione Immobiliare*[1] (hereafter referred to as EGELI), that had exclusive authority for the expropriation, keeping, and auctioning of property owned by Jewish businesses and individuals.

EGELI was an independent organisation of the Finance Ministry with its own boards and staff who were specially selected from outside the Ministry, a very different practice to what generally happened in bureaucracies in dictatorial regimes (Mann, 2000). EGELI operated throughout the Fascist regime (1939–1943) and into the time of the Italian Social Republic, the *Repubblica di Salò* (1943–1945). It was still in existence when Italy was proclaimed a republic in 1946, surviving until 1997 to address ongoing litigation arising from expropriated but unsold real estate claims. This chapter focuses on the role of EGELI in the expropriation of Jewish property from the time that race laws were promulgated by the Fascist Government in Rome in 1938 until 1943 when EGELI was moved from Rome during the invasion of Italy by the Anglo-American allied forces. In the persecution of Italian Jews by EGELI, prior to and during World War II, accounting played a significant role in exposing and managing property in the expropriation process. Crucially, the language of accounting provided the means to disguise the nature

DOI: 10.4324/9781032685328-8

and brutality of the process and allow the bureaucrats of EGELI to be removed from the ultimate consequences of their actions. Although there is no evidence that the Italian Fascists sought to assist the Nazis in the annihilation of the Jewish race, the "Final Solution", the work of EGELI shows that there was a similar level of disengagement by Italian bureaucrats from any moral responsibility for their actions and similar claims of ignorance and innocence to those of German bureaucrats who implemented the Final Solution with great efficiency.

Bauman (1989) and Arendt (1964) have argued that the devastating extent of the Holocaust was mainly made possible by the unquestioning organisational efficiency of the bureaucracies involved. They emphasise that genocide of such proportions could not have been possible without a vast, fatally efficient organisational machine that involved many thousands of people who carried out their responsibilities without being impeded by any moral considerations other than their devotion to the Nazi's Aryanisation mission, irrespective of the consequences for a great number of victims (Goldhagen, 1996). Hitler believed that it was the responsibility of the State to protect the purity of German blood and that it was to act "without regard to understanding or lack of understanding, approval or disapproval" (Hitler, 1987, pp. 367–368). Hilberg (1980, p. 99) concluded that the scale of the Final Solution was "far too complex in its organisational build-up and far too pervasive in its administrative implementation to dispense with specialised bureaucrats in every segment of society". Rosenberg (1983, p. 13) has called these mostly anonymous technocrats "desk-killers" who killed "from behind a desk without wielding any weapons more lethal than a typewriter that issues reports dealing out death ... along deliberately anonymous channels or through a labyrinth of bureaucratic routines and apparatus" (Rosenberg, 1983, p. 13). According to Rosenberg (1983, p. 14) the Holocaust resulted in the "corruption of rationality into ideological forms of functional reasoning" whereby technologies of calculation, most importantly accounting, were used to

> reduce human beings to quantified objects, thus eliminating their troublesome qualities of humaneness.... Functional reason must treat people as objects, as things, as mere numbers that can be easily manipulated and casually disposed of ... It allows individuals to manipulate fellow human beings as things until they were done away with when no longer perceived as useful or needed.
>
> (Rosenberg, 1983, p. 12)

The moral aloofness[2] of the Nazi organisations responsible for the implementation of the Final Solution, most notoriously the Schutzstaffel (SS) under Heinrich Himmler, meant that they focussed on efficient routines and attention to outputs; the number of people processed and subsequently killed. According to this interpretation of the role of the Nazi bureaucracy, the

Final Solution was the routine product of bureaucratic procedures, means-ends analysis, budget balancing, and the application of universal rules rather than the moral deficiencies of particular individuals. Accordingly, the Holocaust was not an "intensive evil" made possible by a few people appearing in beastly forms but an "extensive evil" which, although not apparent at the time, was widespread and organised (Minnich, 2013). Arendt, therefore, emphasises the instrumental rationality of Nazi bureaucracy in a Weberian sense, encompassing the technologies necessary to allow it to do its work. Accounting provided the means to manage efficiently the resources required for both the collection and transportation of Jews and the management of the extermination camps, including the seizure and disposal of the prisoners' property. Although there was a close, indeed dependent, association between the contributions of accounting and the Nazi extermination process, Annisette (2009, p. 457) has claimed that "in realising the diabolical Nazi dream, the culpability of accountants and accountancy remains under-scrutinised".

At the same time that the Nazis sought to destroy all Jews, they took the opportunity that this provided to expropriate the property of persecuted Jews for racial and economic reasons (Browning, 1983; Funnell, 1998, 2013; Hilberg, 2003; Clegg, 2009). When the Third Reich began to confiscate property without paying compensation to the owners, many property owners, under extreme duress, tried to sell their assets for whatever they might be able to obtain (Hilberg, 2003). This meant that "accountants and bookkeepers ... could busy themselves with contracts that were products of pressure put on Jewish owners to sell their property ... The accountants could always say to themselves that acquisitions were acquisitions" (Hilberg, 1993, p. 65). This phenomenon was an especially prominent feature of the process of deportation to extermination camps when civilian government employees

> immediately confiscated and meticulously accounted for all property left by the Jews.... (T)he need to obtain an approved valuation and the final compilation of the asset lists would have entailed the assistance of professionals with accounting skills. Accounting, therefore, was involved in the spread of State surveillance and in the identification of resources in the possession of condemned Jews that could be made available to the State.
>
> (Funnell, 1998, pp. 454–455)

The Nazi's bureaucracies endeavoured to use accounting to purify their expropriation and disposal of the vast amount of property taken from Jews by using the identification and recording of property provided by accounting as a means to transform and "purify" what had been "defiled" when owned by Jews into property that could be at the service of the Aryan German State (Funnell, 2013).

Although Italian bureaucrats were committed to the Fascist cause, they did not take their role as a facilitator of Fascist anti-Semitic programs to the heinous extremes of the Nazis. There is, however, no evidence that they engaged in any attempts to thwart the seizure of Jewish properties. The process was organised to avoid direct contact between Italian Jews and public officers, ensuring that the impact of the bureaucrat's actions would not have been obvious to them. The expropriation was a judiciary act carried out by the local branch of the Ministry of Finance, the Ufficio Tecnico Erariale (Revenue Offices). Thereafter, the file of the property expropriated was transmitted to EGELI for evaluation and definitive requisition of the property. In this way, most public employees had no contact with Jews whose property had been expropriated; they were merely represented by a file.

The chapter first discusses the stages of discrimination and persecution of Jews in Italy during the twenty years of Fascist dictatorship. The institutional, organisational, and operational profile of EGELI is then examined. Subsequent sections develop the essential role of accounting in expropriating Jewish property and the rhetoric associated with accounting, which betrayed the anti-Semitic purposes of accounting practices. Particular emphasis is given to the nature of the discourse created by bureaucratic language and the way accounting as a technology of racist policies and programs helped to disassociate organisational processes from the "administrative evil".

Bureaucracy and the banality of evil

The common defence later of those who participated in the enactment of the Holocaust when accused of their complicity in the Nazi's heinous crimes against humanity would be that they had no knowledge of the ultimate consequences of their otherwise apparently innocuous actions when, for example, organising transport to take Jews to destinations across Europe at which the mass killings would take place. They managed to disjoin operationally, mentally, and morally their administrative actions from the homicidal outcome of their actions (Lippman and Wilson, 2013). Arendt (1964) refers to an "administrative evil" whereby the actions of human beings unjustly or needlessly inflict pain and suffering, and even death, on others (Adams and Balfour, 2009; Adams, 2011). The focus shifts from the extermination camp torturers to the hundreds of thousands of ordinary people involved in the organisation of the extraordinary logistical, statistical, financial, and productive processes that made the Holocaust both possible and efficient. These characteristics, concludes Arendt (1964), were embodied and epitomised by Adolf Eichman, an "ordinary man" prior to the rise of the Nazis. They also describe the work and attitude of Oskar Gröning, possibly the last Nazi extermination camp bureaucrat to be tried for their contributions to the efficiency of the extermination camps.

As an Auschwitz guard between September 1942 and October 1944, Gröning was mainly responsible for managing the money and other assets confiscated from Jews when they arrived at the camp and recording the information in a prescribed ledger. Hence, in the media at the time of his trial in Germany in 2015, he was widely referred to as the "accountant of Auschwitz" (*Guardian* 21 April 2015, 15 July 2015). The crimes with which he was charged related to the period 16 May to 11 July 1944, during which approximately 437,000 Jews from Hungary arrived in Auschwitz, of whom at least 300,000 were murdered soon after arriving. With the end of the war imminent, the aim was to kill as many Jewish prisoners as quickly as possible. Although he described himself as a "small cog in the machine", in a frank admission Gröning agreed that his undisputed work as a "bookkeeper", but not an active participant in the actual killing of the Jews, meant that "It is without question that I am morally complicit in the murder of millions of Jews through my activities at Auschwitz" but not criminally culpable (*Guardian* 15 July 2015). Gröning said that the process of extermination was "perfectly planned so that it had many different parts with the aim of making sure that no single person can be considered responsible for everything" (*Guardian* 15 July 2015).[3]

A government bureaucracy is meant to treat all citizens the same. If, however, equality of treatment is no longer a fundamental right of citizens, such as with the race-based discrimination suffered by European Jews, then bureaucrats will work as implements of legally sanctioned discrimination and oppression. The moral value of the consequences of organisational actions will then depend on the assumption that members of the population identified and vilified as different races have different rights (Shenhav, 2013). This requires that bureaucracies act only in a manner specified by laws and regulations, not moral imperatives, although exceptions and exemptions might be contrived in practice. Bureaucracies are known to reward and spread values such as self-sacrifice, obedience, docility, duty, and discipline (Bauman, 1989), that are meant to adapt actions and technologies to the rules prescribed by those in authority. The result is that morality is no longer a characteristic of individuals but a collective legitimation of an action (Bos, 1997).

Actions that in other contexts could be regarded as a crime, especially when carried out on a large scale, are legitimised as the exercise of State power by bureaucrats who are part of the civil service of a totalitarian regime that "merely" implement the regime's policies as required by law (Mann, 2000). All actions of the bureaucrats can be legitimised by political authority and routine through the division of labour and the development of procedures, instructions, and forms that result in the dehumanisation of the victims by turning them into numbers, statistical categories, and inventories (Kelman, 1973). Rose (1999, p. 26) believes that the strength of the Nazi extermination project lay in the "capacity to render itself technical, to connect itself up with all manners of technologies capable of implementing its nightmarish dreams into everyday existence". The development of technologies of total institutional power, notably accounting, is based on the construction of categories of individuals, the application of intrinsically instrumental and value-free science, the automatism of organised routines, and distancing oneself from the persecuted people (Clegg, 2009). The organisation and its members are removed from the decision, thereby separating their moral culpability from the morality of the decision.

The recognised authority on the Holocaust, Hilberg (2003, p. 1021), concludes that "the bureaucrats who were drawn into the destruction process were not different in their morals from the rest of the population.... (While) one may wish to draw the line of active participation the machinery of destruction was a remarkable cross-section of the German population" (Hilberg, 2003, p. 1021). Thus, rather than the extermination process being made possible by the inherent rationality of an organisation, that would work regardless of the goals it is used for, ultimately, it was the anti-Semitic attitudes of individuals (Goldhagen, 1996; Heinsohn, 2000). Every bureaucrat implementing the Final Solution depended on an inability to empathise with those they tormented and destroyed, an indifference to the moral question, and the organisation's inner workings being intent on rewarding those who accomplished its goals and punishing those who did not promptly pursue them.[4]

The bureaucratic mechanisms and the accounting practices of the Nazi bureaucracies to implement the Final Solution were also prominent features of the organisations set up by Mussolini's Fascist regime for the seizure of property owned by Italian Jews as part of their program of Jewish persecution. Although Fascism was a movement in search of a specific Italian race and therefore acquired racist characteristics, its rise was not built on racism, unlike Germany, where Nazi ascendency was based on racist, anti-Semitic roots (Israel and Nastasi, 1998).

Racial laws and the persecution of Jews in the Fascist era (1938–1945)

According to many historians, when Mussolini took power in 1922, he and his acolytes were indifferent to explicit racist ideologies (Gregor, 1974; Spinosa, 1994). Others, however, believe that the values of the Fascist movement and its leader had been derived from racist beliefs from the very beginning (Sabbatucci, 1979; Candeloro, 1981; Gentile, 2002, 2008), even though in the first few years of power the Fascist regime demonstrated no obvious antipathy towards Jews, nor did Jews appear to be opposed to Fascism. Indeed, many Jews, especially the working and middle classes who lived in the cities, had joined the Fascist March on Rome, while many Italian Jews joined the Fascist movement (De Felice, 1974, 1993). In addition, in the first 15 years of the Fascist dictatorship, Jewish citizens held many important public offices within the regime, including the Minister of Finance, Deputy Head of Police, colonial governor, head of the "Voluntary Militia for National Security" (the paramilitary groups in service of Mussolini), and membership of *Gran Consiglio del Fascismo* (Advisory Council of the Prime Minister). Many Jewish intellectuals had endorsed the Fascist intellectuals' manifesto drawn up in 1925 by Giovanni Gentile, philosopher and Minister of Education

(Turi, 1980). Remarkably, one of Mussolini's closest and most educated lovers, Margherita Sarfatti, whom he frequently relied on for advice, was Jewish (Wieland, 2010).

With the 1929 Concordat between the Fascist regime and the Holy See, Catholicism was appointed the State's official religion. The liberal principle of freedom of worship was retained, but the government more formally regulated the relationship between the State and other religions, including Judaism. Thus, under the so-called "Falco Law" of 1930 Jewish communities had to be grouped at a municipal level and coordinated by a National Union of Israelite Communities whose leader would liaise with the Minister of the Interior in any matter concerning relations with the State (Regno d'Italia (RdI), 1930). Many Italian Jews believed this law would bring relations with Fascism back to normal (De Felice, 1993). In September 1934, when speaking to the crowds in Bari, Mussolini stigmatised the racist and anti-Semitic attitude of Nazi Germany, which he contrasted with Italy's distinctive culture and values that were "above" such racist doctrines (Mussolini, 1934). Despite these assurances, the political and social conditions of Jews in Italy declined shortly thereafter, prompted mainly by economic problems.

The worsening situation of Jews was driven initially by the continuing depressive effects on the Italian economy of World War I, compounded by the 1929 world financial crisis, that led the Fascist regime and a large number of Italian business owners to seek someone to blame for their problems. This fuelled the negative myth of Jewish capitalism as predatory and damaging for the Italian middle classes (Leon, 1970). At the same time, the regime had also implemented a policy that discriminated against the native populations of the Italian colonies in Africa. This was justified by the emerging Fascist ideology, which proclaimed Italians to be a superior, pure race (Collotti, 1998; Cassata, 2008). Ultimately, the decision to promote an anti-Jewish racial policy was most powerfully driven by the international political isolation that followed the Ethiopian war (1935–1936) and the fines levied by the League of Nations (Del Prato, 1938). With Italy having lost its authoritative role among the European powers and no longer supported by them, Mussolini had to create stronger relationships with the Nazis. Even if not expressly forced to do so by the Führer, Mussolini embraced an anti-Semitic policy that, at least in theory, resonated with that of Germany so that he could demonstrate both his and Italy's commitment to Hitler's political and cultural positions (Cioffi, 1942; Michaelis, 1982; Sarfatti, 1994).

The first stage in the Fascist racial program began with the publication of the so-called "Manifesto of Race", hereafter the Manifesto, a 10-Article paper called "*Il Fascismo e i problemi della razza*" (Fascism and the Problem of Race) published in the newspaper *Il Giornale d'Italia* on 15 July 1938. The Manifesto, produced by a group of university scholars and intellectuals, defended the concept of a pure Italian race and claimed that Fascism had to have a racist attitude that was the ultimate expression of the actual traits of the Italian people (Anonymous, 1938a; Romano, 1941). The Manifesto was reported by other newspapers and republished in August of the same year by the recently founded journal "*La difesa della razza*" (Defending Race). The Manifesto provided Fascism with cultural and pseudo-scientific justifications for the discriminatory and segregationist claims it was developing and promoting (Costamagna, 1939; Gillette, 2002). Shortly after, on 19 September 1938, during a public speech in Trieste, Mussolini stated for the first time that Italy had a problem with the Jews. Mussolini described Jews as the enemies of Fascism who were involved in an international subversive plan that threatened the well-being and the very existence of Italy (Mussolini, 1938a).

The second stage in the development of the racial policy of the Fascist regime consisted of the promulgation of many laws and rules designed to discriminate against Jews in the economic and social life of Italy. The first racial laws, as seen in Table 8.1, targeted Jewish students, especially Jewish teachers, who were expelled from schools at all levels and banned from teaching (RdI, 1938c). Soon after, Jewish executives and clerks, both public and private, were forced to leave their jobs, as were Jews in the army and the police (RdI, 1938a; 1938d; Gentile, 2013). Legal protection was further restricted, which meant that Italian Jews could not work as self-employed professionals in trade or services (RdI, 1939a; 1939b; 1940b). In 1942, Jews were banned from the performing arts (Collotti, 2003) and they were also deprived of many other civil and political rights (Acerbi, 2011).

On 6 October 1938, a meeting of the Gran Consiglio del Fascismo pronounced that "Italian citizens of a Jewish race ... are not allowed ... to be owners of more than 50 hectares" of farmland (Sec. 5, d). This was followed soon after on 17 November by Decree 1728, Sec. 10, subsequently approved without debate by the Chamber of Deputies on 14 December[5] that set limits on the value of real estate that Jews could own. The limit for "Italian citizens of a Jewish race ..." was based on cadastral rent[6] and set at 5,000 lire for land and 20,000 lire for buildings (RdI, 1938c, Sec. 10, d, e). Initially, the only property that exceeded these limits was a target for expropriation. Thus, not all property was to be forfeited. To placate potential opposition, the Decree was justified with reference to the many houses allegedly owned by Jews as investments but which were left vacant when many Italians could not find a place to live. Thus, State intervention and public ownership of these buildings were said to be necessary (Anonymous, 1938a).

To ensure better access to property for the majority of Italians, Mussolini wanted Jews to have social and economic importance in proportion to their number. Accordingly, a "proportional criteria" was adopted by the Regime. At the time, Jews represented approximately 1/1000 of the Italian population. Therefore, according to the Fascists, their share of national wealth should not have exceeded 1/1000. However, the Fascists warned that this was well below the actual proportion of the property that Italian Jews owned and, thus, would mean that Jewish properties should be gradually sold to achieve the appropriate proportion (Anonymous, 1938b; 1938e; 1939d). To support

Table 8.1 Racial laws

Laws	*Main rules*	*Reference*
Royal Decree n. 1390, 5th September 1938.	Ban of Italian Jewish teachers in Italian public schools.	RdI (1938a)
Royal Decree n. 1539, 5th September 1938.	Institution of General Council on Race.	RdI (1938b)
Royal Decree n. 1728, 17th November 1938.	Definition of Jewish citizen; prohibition of mixed weddings; limits to Jewish property; ban of jaws clerks in Italian civil and military administrations; ban of Jewish students from Italian high schools and universities.	RdI (1938c)
Royal Decree n. 1779, 15th November 1938.	Prohibition of mixed classes in every public school; institution of Jewish-only classes.	RdI (1938d)
Royal Decree n. 2154, 21st November 1938.	Modification of National Fascist Party's charter in order to prohibit Jewish participation.	RdI (1938e)
Royal Decree n. 2111, 22nd December 1938.	Expulsion and jubilation of Jewish members of military forces, police and Royal Carabinieri	RdI (1938f)
Law n. 1054, 29th June 1939.	Limitation to Jewish citizens about the profession of lawyer, medical doctor, accountant, engineer, pharmacist, veterinarian, architect, chemist, agronomist, and industrial expert.	RdI (1939a)
Law n. 1055, 13th July 1939.	Limitation to testamentary transfers to Jewish citizens.	RdI (1939b)
Law n. 1403, 28th September 1940.	Abrogation of public funding to Jewish primary schools (kindergartens).	RdI (1940a)
Law n. 1459, 23rd September 1940.	Possibility to change the surname for citizens born from a Jewish mother and a non-Jewish father and their not belonging to the "Jews race".	RdI (1940b)
Law n. 517, 19th April 1942.	Exclusion of Jewish citizens by performing arts and entertainment.	RdI (1942)
Italian Social Republic, Duce Legislative Decree, n. 2, 4th January 1944.	Elimination of "discrimination" and Arian Jew definition. Absolute prohibition for all Jews to have any property, administrate firms, or practice a profession.	RSI (1944a)

the expropriation of Jewish property, the newspapers exaggerated the extent of property owned and controlled by Jews (Anonymous, 1938c). In one case, the Turin-based newspaper *La Stampa* published an article that proclaimed the existence of "The Jewish Octopus: 400 Jews own more than 1 billion lire real estate property" (Anonymous, 1938b; 1938c). Difficulties in implementing the "proportional criteria" meant that it was quickly abandoned, and a racial discrimination approach instead was adopted (Mussolini, 1938b).

To achieve the racist aims of the Fascists, a legal concept of race was required as the foundation of civil and economic rights. Thus, Section 1 of a "new" Civil Code provided with the 1938 Decree stated that "Legal capacity can be restricted with respect to the belonging to a race. Such restrictions are regulated by special laws[7]" (Royal Decree, 12 December 1938, no. 1852). This required the definition of the Jewish race to draw clear boundaries between Jews and the rest of the Italian population that was provided in Sec. 8 of the 17 November 1938 Decree 1728. The German definition of Jew was quite similar to that adopted by the Italians. In order to avoid a religious definition of the Jew, the Fascist Government adopted a racial pseudo-scientific definition based on a purported scientific paper published by the journal "*La difesa della razza*". The adoption of a pseudo-scientific definition that emphasised the existence of a Jewish race that originated with Semitic people who were spread throughout Mediterranean lands and maintained specific racial characteristics provided the means to discriminate against Jewish people even if they had converted to Catholicism and did not practice the Jewish faith.

The extent to which the Italian State bureaucracy was committed to the racial laws remains controversial. Some historians have sought to understate the actual pervasive effect of the oppressive measures introduced by the racial laws, claiming that the regime was only *seemingly* racist and that it introduced its racist policies to please Hitler without any real commitment or belief in what the new racial laws sought to achieve. According to this view, Italian bureaucrats did not effectively or widely enforce the racial laws (De Felice, 1993). Arendt (1964, p. 177) was strongly convinced that the condition of the Jews in Italy was not comparable to the suffering they endured in the other European countries that Nazi Germany either directly or indirectly controlled. She argues that Italian society and its institutions were indifferent, if not always openly hostile, to the anti-Semitic racial laws and that, unlike Germany, anti-Semitism had never been a prominent or recurring feature of the culture and history of Italy. In contrast, other historians find that the regime had clear racist beliefs and reject any attempt at exculpating the bureaucrats, police, teachers, and many other categories of public servants who were jointly responsible for the manner in which Jews were treated and the heinous consequences that followed under the Germans (Collotti, 2003; Sarfatti, 2007).

Despite the escalation of the laws, regulations, and bureaucratic measures of oppression, there was no attempt by large numbers of Italian Jews to leave the country, thus possibly confirming the indifference or resistance of the Italians to the persecution of their fellow citizens (Finzi, 1997; Toscano, 1998). The majority of Italy's Jewish population, still confident in the institutions and the legal system inherited from the liberal era, believed they would overcome what was assumed to be a short-lived adverse period and, therefore, chose to stay in Italy (Antonucci and Spizzichino, 2004; Livingston, 2014). Tragically, for many, their faith in Italian history and its people was to be finally and fatally betrayed when the Fascist regime, after Italy entered World

War II on 10 June 1940, collected in detention centres those who could be identified as Jewish. Unlike the detention centres operated by the German Nazis, there was no forced labour. A census conducted by the Fascists in 1938, which comprehensively recorded and classified nearly 48,000 Jewish inhabitants, thereby explicitly identifying and describing a Jewish race, was meant to provide the (pseudo) scientific basis to justify discrimination against Italians who were now categorised as Jewish and not part of an Italian race. This led to the formation of a special statistic-demographic office, the *DemoRazza*, to manage statistical data about Italian Jews (Cocchi and Favero, 2009).

On 4 September 1940, Mussolini signed a ruling that opened the first of 43 concentration camps in Italy for captured citizens from enemy countries, especially Jews, to expel them from Italy (Calimani, 2013). After the surrender of Italy to the Allies in September 1943, German forces quickly occupied northern and central Italy and began a major round-up of Jews. The census of 1938 provided the Germans with the means to round up Jews quickly for transportation to the extermination camps. It has been estimated that approximately 8,500 Italian Jews subsequently died in the Nazi extermination camps, mainly Auschwitz-Birkenau. The relatively small number of Italian Jews who were killed in the extermination camps when compared to other countries under German control has been attributed to both the general reluctance of Italian bureaucrats and the police to search for Jews and the preparedness of non-Jewish Italians to protect their neighbours and colleagues. Count Ciano, Foreign Minister of Fascist Italy from 1936 until 1943 and Mussolini's son-in-law, was criticised by Heinrich Himmler for not ensuring that more Jews were being sent to detention centres (Guerri, 1979). The reluctance of Italians to betray their neighbours, friends, and co-workers was also pronounced with the experience of the Jewish-Italian chemist and later famous writer Primo Levi, who was not betrayed and arrested until the last months of the war (Angier, 2011).[8]

EGELI and the seizure of property

The implementation of anti-Semitic policies by the Fascists required the creation of new bureaucratic institutions specifically designed to implement effectively the regime's racial policies. Accordingly, EGELI was created by Royal Decree 126 in 1939 (Anonymous, 1938d, 1938e; RdI, 1939c) as a body under the Ministry of Finance dedicated to the seizure and managing of the property of Jewish families and businesses until the property was sold. To carry out its work of expropriation and auctioning of Jewish property on a national scale, EGELI needed to work closely with other government institutions (Adams and Balfour, 2009), notably the Revenue Assessment Office and the Revenue Office, and banks (Naumann, 1966; Browning, 1992; Allen, 2005). EGELI did not commence its work until the last few months of 1939, becoming fully operational under the Act 1994/1940 in 1940 after

Italy entered the war. It also became responsible for expropriating and managing the real estate of citizens of enemy countries living in Italy (RdI, 1940). In addition, EGELI collected the so-called "*beni esattoriali*", the Italian taxpayers' assets that the Revenue Office could seize to satisfy a tax liability.

EGELI's governance system was centred on a Board of Directors chosen by the government. It was composed of ten members, three of whom had to be senators.[9] The first president of EGELI was Senator Asinari di Bernezzo,[10] who died shortly after his appointment. His successor, Dr Giovara,[11] a lawyer and senator, was appointed on 7 September 1939 and stayed in office until the end of World War II (EGELI, 1939c, p. 16). In its work, the Board of Directors was supported by a five-member Management Board (EGELI, 1939a) and a Board of Statutory Auditors. The rules governing the work of the Board of Statutory Auditors were contained in Article 12 of the EGELI charter (RdI, 1939d). Three auditors were appointed for three years by the Duce. The president of the Board had to be chosen among the judges of the Court of Auditors, while the other two members were proposed by the Ministry of Finance and the Ministry of Corporations. The first members of the Board of Statutory Auditors were Mario Pia, Giuseppe Frasca e Francesco Poncini (1940–1943), then Giovanni Turchini, Umberto Maculan e Giuseppe Dell'Orto (1944–1945) (EGELI, 1941b, 1944b). In addition to auditing financial statements, the auditors, whose fee was determined by the Ministry of Finance, were responsible for ensuring compliance of the Board of Directors' decisions with Fascist laws and regulations "in the same way as in the private companies".[12] Finally, the Board of Statutory Auditors had to present its audit report to the Ministry of Finance. In order to prevent a conflict of interests, according to Article 26 of the EGELI charter, the auditors (and the directors) were forbidden to buy properties from EGELI.

Initially, EGELI was to have been staffed by a head accountant, a chief legal officer who would be assisted by an Attorney General, two recordkeepers, two typists, and two bailiffs (EGELI, 1939a). EGELI developed associations with many banks, which helped to manage and sell the expropriated property. Although the banks, as noted in Table 8.2, were mainly small local banks, there were also some large banks that were publicly owned, including the *Istituto Bancario San Paolo di Torino, Banca Nazionale del Lavoro*, and *Banco di Napoli*. In return for expenses and commissions, the banks organised the auctions of expropriated Jewish property (RdI, 1939d, 1941).

The work of EGELI also played a crucial role in Fascist propaganda. Thus, as soon as EGELI commenced its operations, the press regularly reported its actions and gave particular prominence to any property that had been expropriated that exceeded limits set for the value of the property that Jews were now permitted to own (Anonymous, 1939a, 1939b). As early as the middle of 1939, *La Stampa* gave prominence and place to the work of EGELI and frequently gave specific details of the extent of Jewish ownership of property (Anonymous, 1939c, 1939d, 1939e).[13]

Table 8.2 Banks working with EGELI

Local banks	*National banks*
Istituto di Credito Fondiario di Verona	Credito fondiario dell'Istituto San Paolo di Torino
Credito fondiario della Cassa di Risparmio delle Provincie Lombarde	Sezione di Credito Fondiario della Banca Nazionale del Lavoro
Istituto Italiano di Credito Fondiario	Banco di Napoli
Istituto di Credito Fondiario delle Venezie	Istituto di credito fondiario del Monte dei Paschi di Siena
Credito fondiario della Cassa di Risparmio di Bologna	Banco di Sicilia
Istituto di credito fondiario di Roma	
Istituto di credito fondiario di Gorizia	

Sources: EGELI (1941a, p. 27, 1942a, p. 25).

Within ninety days of the issuance of the ruling in December 1938 for the approved limit to the value of the property that Jews could own, Jewish Italian citizens had to notify local agencies of the Ministry of Finance, the *Ufficio Tecnico Erariale* (Revenue Offices),[14] of the property that they owned. After receiving this information, the Revenue Offices determined if any property exceeded the specified limits and, if so, expropriated the property (Anonymous, 1939e, 1939f). Not all Jewish Italian citizens had to give up their property that exceeded the approved limits (Levi, 1995). Instead, on a case-by-case basis, many exceptions were made for "non-discriminated" Jews. The absence of anti-Semitism embedded in Italian culture and society, as noted earlier, meant that, unlike the Germans, there was no lethal obsession with eliminating the Jewish population only the necessity, according to the new race laws, to discriminate. The Royal Decree no. 1728 of 17 November 1938 stated that expropriations and limits on property did not apply to Jews and their relatives who either died or suffered as combatants in wars fought by Italy, notably the Italian-Turkish War (1911–1912), World War I (1915–1918), the Ethiopian war (1935–1936), and the Spanish Civil War (1936–1939), or who died or were injured for the Fascist cause. These measures introduced the so-called "Aryanised Jew", a qualification that could be conferred by the Minister of the Interior even when information in the public registries of births, deaths, and marriages said the opposite. In addition, Royal Decree no. 126/1939 ruled that Jewish property could be transferred to non-Jewish relatives, charities, or foundations (RdI, 1939c). These exceptions meant that EGELI had some discretionary power and that the rule was not consistently enforced across the country. Arendt (1964, pp. 178–180) observes that

> the result must have been that the great majority of Italian Jews were exempted. There can hardly have been a Jewish family without at least one member in the Fascist Party, for this happened at a time when Jews,

> like other Italians, had been flocking for almost twenty years into the Fascist movement, since positions in the Civil Service were open only to members.... The key to the riddle was, of course, that Italy actually was one of the few countries in Europe where all anti-Jewish measures were decidedly unpopular, since, in the words of Ciano, they "raised a problem which fortunately did not exist".

Expropriated property was subsequently transferred to EGELI, where it was accounted for as an asset. Unlike Nazi Germany, every owner of expropriated property was entitled to compensation prescribed by law as decided by the Revenue Assessment Office of the Ministry of Finance. The Jewish owners were paid by EGELI initially with 30-year government bonds at 4% interest (RdI, 1939c; Anonymous, 1939c). On expiration of the 30-year term, the government bonds were to be replaced by Treasury bonds of the same value. Any difference between the final price at which the property was sold by EGELI and the compensation paid was taken by the State, not the dispossessed owner.

In its first year of work, EGELI received, through the Provincial Tax Services, 726 notices from Jewish citizens about property that exceeded the approved property value limit and, thus, had been expropriated. By 31 December 1940, these notices and subsequent expropriations had increased to 1000, which meant a total property value of 675,115,395 lire was transferred to EGELI (1941a, p. 6) in preparation for the subsequent sale to non-Jewish Italians. As Italy entered the war, expropriations decreased significantly when the civil services were unable to meet demands now placed upon them and the owners either sold many Jewish or foreign properties before they could be valued and expropriated or the Jewish ownership of the property was disguised (EGELI, 1943a, p. 8). In 1941 the number of notices issued in the year reduced to 255, with the total assets expropriated and managed by EGELI since its inception approaching nearly 700,000,000 lire (EGELI, 1942c, p. 47). By the end of 1942, notices of property exceeding the approved value limit had again increased during the year to 395, while the value of the assets seized since the start of EGELI's operations then totalled 726,508,449 lire (EGELI, 1943c, p. 48). The compensation paid for property expropriated was still estimated on a fiscal basis, adopting an equation that related the value of lands and buildings to the taxable rent using a conventional multiple. This value was the basis for entering data in the accounting system of EGELI. Article 19 of the EGELI charter (RdI, 1939d) stated that the property should be recognised as assets and initially recorded at the net price estimated by the Revenue Office.

Table 8.3 shows that in December 1941, out of a possible 94 provinces, expropriated Jewish property came from just 17 Italian provinces where Jewish communities had traditionally lived (Sarfatti, 2007). All such provinces were in Northern Italy, with the only exception of Rome, home to the largest Jewish community, where racial persecution had the greatest financial impact (Procaccia, 2004).

Table 8.3 Provinces providing expropriated Jewish property (amounts in lire)

Real Estate Province	*Amount*	*Real Estate Province*	*Amount*
Cremona	18.700,00	Modena	94.640,00
Cuneo	27.000,00	Padova	557.044,40
Ferrara	43.416,00	Parma	427.950,00
Firenze	343.980,00	Roma	1.182.780,00
Genova	76.000,00	Rovigo	1.695.909,60
Livorno	410.446,80	Torino	1.808.566,60
Lucca	90.671,20	Trieste	5.277.871,80
Mantova	594.856,00	Venezia	279.517,00
Milano	2.276.520,00	***Total***	***15.205.869,40***

Source: EGELI (1942a, p. 12).

With the fall of Fascism in July 1943 and the proclamation of the Italian Social Republic in the northern part of the country, EGELI's headquarters were moved from Rome to San Pellegrino Terme, in the Italian Social Republic[15] (RSI, 1944b), from where it continued to manage the expropriation of the property of Jewish citizens who were now viewed as enemies (Anonymous, 1944; EGELI, 1944a, p. 5; RSI, 1944b, 1944c). According to a report from the Ministry of Finance dated 12 March 1945, the total assets expropriated by EGELI throughout the war amounted to 731,442,619 lire, with a total of 5,768 notices of expropriation (De Felice, 1993, pp. 610–611).

After World War II, EGELI was put under the control of an external commissioner to start "re-conveying" the unsold expropriated property, returning it where possible to individuals or their families from whom the property had been expropriated. Irrespective of these efforts, very little property was returned (PCM, 1948–1950). EGELI continued to operate until it was closed on 22 March 1957, even though there remained 66 properties that had not been returned, along with many other assets. Attempts to trace former property owners or their families to return property continued for another 40 years (GI, 2001).

The discourse of discrimination in EGELI's accounting records

The accounting and administrative records of EGELI provide consistent and compelling evidence of the manner in which accounting helped strengthen the identity and purposes of an organisation in charge of expropriating the private property of Italian citizens who were Jewish according to the racial laws. In the charter that governed the actions and authority of EGELI there were many rules about financial reporting, in particular, the need imposed by the law establishing EGELI (RdI, 1939c) to prepare financial statements about its operations (Article 11, par. 8). The annual report was prepared by the Board of Directors (Article 10) and audited by the Board of Statutory Auditors (Article 12). Even though EGELI was a government body, its annual report was quite similar to that prepared by private companies. According to the EGELI charter

(RdI, 1939d), the legal year coincided with the calendar year, unlike all other public sector accounting which was from 1 July to 30 June of the following year. Before 31 March the Board of Directors were required to send the financial report to the Ministry of Finance for its approval (Article 18).

The Annual Financial Statements that EGELI sent to the Ministry of Finance between 1940 and 1943 each year included a Director's Report, a balance sheet, an income statement, assorted tables, and the Board of Statutory Auditors Report. The Director's Report was usually about twenty pages long with a three-section introduction about managing the three main categories of property: Jewish property, assets of Italians who had not paid their taxes, and enemy property. The final sections of the Director's Report examined in detail the organisation and work of EGELI. EGELI's Jewish property balance sheet, as shown in Table 8.4, listed as its main assets the Jewish property that had been expropriated (EGELI, 1941b, 1942b, 1943b, 1944b). According to Article 1 of EGELI's charter, the "endowment fund" of the institution, that is, its capital awarded by the Ministry of Finance, was to be 20 million lire. Article 13 of the EGELI charter authorised the institution to issue "special bonds" with a 4% return to be paid as the consideration of the expropriated assets. In some cases, advances or prepayments could be made by the Board of Directors (Article 16 of the EGELI charter). Inexplicably, the total value of the bonds issued for the expropriated property was only approximately 50% of the total compensations paid to the Jewish owners. These different amounts are not accounted for either in the balance sheets or the accompanying tables. However, the accounts show that the amount of the "special bonds" issued by EGELI, which rose from 1,018 million in 1941 to 16,473 million in 1942 and 21,935 million in 1943, was to be listed among the liabilities in the balance sheet (EGELI, 1942c, p. 48; EGELI, 1943c, p. 47; EGELI, 1944c, p. 42). At the same time, any remaining amounts owed to the Jewish owners were included in the "Accounts Payable" and not in the "Bond" account (EGELI, 1941b, p. 33; EGELI, 1943c, p. 42).

Also shown in the balance sheet were "Mortgage Banks Receivables" and "Mortgage Banks Payable", loans made and received by the Mortgage Banks involved in managing the expropriated property. Between 1941 and 1943 the former rose from 460,000 lire to over 4.8 million lire, while the latter remained low throughout the period and was never above 300,000 lire.

By comparing sales prices with compensation paid for expropriation, the entries of the balance sheets provide a measure of the profits earned by the State through EGELI every year it operated during the war. As shown by Table 8.5, most sales occurred in 1941–1943. During this time, the gains from the sale of land and buildings sold were more than double the compensation paid.

Expropriated property was to be recorded at the cost, that is, the compensation paid for expropriation (Article 20), and revenues from the sale of property were to be recorded in separate accounts (Article 21). Rents and other incomes related to lands and buildings and costs were to be posted in

Table 8.4 EGELI's Jewish property balance sheet (lire)

Assets	*1940*	*1941*	*1942*	*1943*	*Liabilities*	*1940*	*1941*	*1942*	*1943*
State cash	475.469,10	85.336,00	2.414.073,99	548.532,00	Capital	20.000.000,00	20.000.000,00	20.000.000,00	20.000.000,00
Cash and cash equivalents		25.076,85	11.910,10	548.281,00	Mortgage banks payable	18.256,52	1.134,99	3.735,34	309.953,84
Plant and machinery	108.609,30	145.644,40	202.278,30	365.486,50	Accounts payable	59.940,20	14.544.727,85	34.365.400,49	32.638.550,36
Lands and buildings		15.205.869,40	43.993.532,24	45.838.094,64	Impairment	35.448,00	65.448,00	105.448,00	105.448,00
Cost of lands and buildings sold		265.266,20	4.932.580,80	9.794.122,80	Revenues from land and buildings sold		570.000,00	12.432.649,00	29.537.371,15
Securities	4.750.013,00	1.302.367,90	5.351.057,26	5.198.868,56	Cost		265.266,20		
Accounts receivable	14.002.040,00	14.002.435,30	14.187.523,94	9.231.313,38	Gain		304.733,80		
Deferred charges		1.295,60	786,10	3.664,25	Special bonds		1.018.900,00	16.473.600,00	21.935.800,00
Mortgage banks receivables		442.514,59	1.597.933,45	4.882.565,63	Mortgages			432.738,17	422.071,84
Bank deposits		11.236,65	9.568,55	11.541.587,21	Liabilities for lands and buildings				196.640,55
Property tax assessments	163.555,84	285.235,74	596.568,17	356.282,57	Other liabilities				13.421,70
Goods of enemies	309.650,95	3.864.999,23	8.593.370,38	12.096.168,26	Profit for the year			374.626,52	624.011,73
Inventory			145.917,30	327.559,88					
State treasury			1.587.718,36	4.862.436,03					
Carried forward losses	207.672,80	304.306,53	562.932,92	188.306,46					
Total assets	**20.017.010,99**	**35.941.584,39**	**84.187.751,86**	**105.783.269,17**					
Loss for the year	96.633,73	258.626,45							
Total	**20.113.644,72**	**36.200.210,84**	**84.187.751,86**	**105.783.269,17**	**Total liabilities and owners' equity**	**20.113.644,72**	**36.200.210,84**	**84.188.197,52**	**105.783.269,17**

Sources: EGELI (1941b, p. 30, 1942b, pp. 30–31, 1943b, Annex A, 1944b, Annex A/1).

Table 8.5 Income from property sales 1941–1943 (lire)

Gain calculation	*1941*	*1942*	*1943*
Lands and buildings	15.205.869,40	43.993.532,24	45.838.094,64
Prices of lands and buildings sale	570.000,00	12.432.649,00	29.537.371,15
Cost of lands and buildings sale	265.266,20	4.932.580,80	9.794.122,80
Gain on lands and buildings sale	304.733,80	7.500.068,20	19.743.248,35
Gain average %	53,46%	60,33%	66,84%

Sources: EGELI (1942b, pp. 30–31, 1943b, Annex A, 1944b, Annex A/1).

the income statement (Article 22). Any costs associated with maintenance of the property under EGELI's control were to be added to the value of the assets, while the cost of day-to-day or ongoing repair and maintenance was to be charged to the income statement as an expense (Article 23). Gains coming from property sales (as shown in Table 8.5) were not included in the income statements (see Table 8.6). According to Article 21 of the EGELI charter, the net revenues from the sales of properties on the free market were to be posted in separate accounts, and their amounts were paid in cash directly to the State Treasury every month. Consequently, the property sales themselves had no impact on the income of EGELI. The annual net profit was paid in cash to the State Treasury just after the approval of the annual report required by Article 22 of the EGELI charter (RdI, 1939d). The income statements for 1940–1943 (see Table 8.6) show total revenues rising from 234,000 lire in 1940 to 2.2 million lire in 1943, while over the same period, total expenses, apart from the compensation paid for the expropriated property, increased from 331,000 lire in 1940 to 2.27 million lire in 1943. In 1940 and 1941, as the war worsened for Italy, total losses amounted to 96,000 lire and 258,000 lire, respectively, while in 1942 and 1943, net profits amounted to 374,000 lire and 624,000 lire.

The annual report presented by EGELI to the Ministry of Finance was completed with the audit reports. The audit report consisted of four pages, although not in a standardised form, and was divided into four parts with a conclusion. In the first section, the auditors commented on the main annual report data, the sales, and the net profit. The second section was devoted to the Jewish property expropriated, including tables showing data about expropriations, sales and the total number and value of EGELI properties at the reporting date. The third and fourth sections of the audit report referred to the other activities of EGELI, such as dealing with the property of enemies and taxes. In the conclusions section, the Board of Statutory Auditors gave its (clean) audit opinion, addressing this to the Minister of Finance (EGELI, 1941c, 1942c, 1943c, 1944c).

The administrative banality of EGELI's accounts disguised the true nature of what had happened, the betrayal and dispossession of Italian Jews, by creating the impression that they reflected typical, unenforced commercial transactions. Throughout EGELI's existence, the annual Board of Directors'

Table 8.6 Income statements for 1940–1943

Costs	*1940*	*1941*	*1942*	*1943*	*Revenues*	*1940*	*1941*	*1942*	*1943*
Overheads	312.909,35	344.837,27	532.015,02	752.709,49	Revenues from buildings		46.481,65	1.340.383,38	1.785.218,04
Costs charged by land institutes	18.256,52	30.500,00			Revenues from other activities	234.501,32	85.952,52	162.243,06	486.273,42
Costs for managing buildings		13.003,35	595.984,90	894.770,24					
Costs of transactions		2.720,00							
Profit for the year			374.626,52	624.011,73	Loss for the year	96.633,73	258.626,45		
Total	**331.165,87**	**391.060,62**	**1.502.626,44**	**2.271.491,46**	**Total**	**331.135,05**	**391.060,62**	**1.502.626,44**	**2.271.491,46**

Sources: EGELI (1941b, p. 30, 1942b, pp. 30–31, 1943b, Annex A, 1944b, Annex A/2).

Report addressed to the Finance Ministry consistently referred to the expropriation, cataloguing, and upkeep of expropriated property as a patriotic, Fascist duty. The Board of Directors wanted to ensure that the financial and operational details in the accounts would be seen as confirmation of their loyalty and commitment to the Fascist cause. This interpretation of the financial performance of EGELI would highlight the significance of the numbers and their ideological meaning. The Board of Directors' 1940 Report notes that "At this time of harsh, tough fighting, the need was felt, deeper than ever, to fulfil our appointment as best as we could, while on the battlefields our fighters gloriously accomplish the sacred mission of giving Italy military victory, a bright future" (EGELI, 1941a, p. 3). The Board's determination to implement the racist policies of the regime without regard for the consequences for Jewish citizens was clearly evident in the cold bureaucratic language in the 1940 Report: "Under the applicable laws, in 1940 the Revenue Assessment Offices have kept collecting and processing certificates of Jewish ownership, reporting to the body concerned about the proceedings …" (EGELI, 1941a, p. 5). While the Board of Directors of EGELI emphasised its role as an uncompromising performer of the Fascist regime's politics, as noted earlier, there was not a consistent commitment to the racist agenda of the government throughout the rest of the Italian bureaucracy, especially the Ministry of Finance and the Ministry of the Interior, and incidents of corruption, or going against the government's wishes, were not uncommon.

In their 1940 Report, EGELI's Board of Directors, having discussed its performance and the problems it had encountered in expediting the expropriation of property, praised the banks working with EGELI, praise that was repeated in the 1941 and 1942 reports. EGELI's staff is also honoured: "The employees deserve the greatest praise for their abilities, diligence and efforts" (EGELI, 1941a, p. 18). To further confirm its devotion to the Fascist mission, EGELI's Board of Directors complains of two Finance Ministry departments, the Revenue Assessment Office and the Revenue Office, for their poor efforts that were said to show a lack of commitment to the racial priorities of the Fascists Government: "The Revenue Assessment Office should therefore take more care of the Jewish files … and the Revenue Office should be quicker in allocating surplus Jewish property to EGELI" (EGELI, 1941a, pp. 7–8). The Board of Directors mocks such laxity by assuming that "we should expect the files won't be fully dispatched until about 1946" (EGELI, 1942a, p. 9).

The bureaucratic procedures required to implement the applicable laws and regulations involved in the expropriation of property were often the source of complaints by the Board of Directors. In a report dated September 1940, the Board complains of the "current laws that give Jews a chance of implementing some delaying tactics …" (EGELI, 1940c, p. 58). The Board of Directors, using language which is clearly meant to communicate their commitment to the anti-Semitic priorities of the Fascist regime, complains that: "In this way, reporting Jews will keep all their properties until a conveyance ruling is issued. Such a long delay … is all to the detriment of EGELI and to the advantage of the Jews" (EGELI, 1941a, p. 10). In response, the Board of Directors proposed that the Finance Ministry make a few adjustments to the administrative procedure to expedite the expropriation of Jewish citizens' property, reiterating such proposals in the following year's Report (EGELI, 1942a, p. 11). The Board of Directors further complains about the Revenue Office conveying expropriated property to EGELI when the property had little value, was damaged or was located in a particularly inaccessible area, with few buyers willing to pay profitable prices. Accordingly, EGELI indicated that it would like to be allowed to judge the property before it was expropriated and, if necessary, reject it (EGELI, 1940a, p. 39; EGELI, 1940c, p. 59). The Act, which created EGELI, also specified a minimum value for Jewish property seizure in order to avoid lengthy and expensive procedures to take control of low value properties. EGELI had the authority to reject property seized by local agencies of the Ministry of Finance and the Revenue Offices when it was considered of poor value and not saleable (RdI 1939c, 1941).

The Board of Directors also complained about the way in which the law requiring the seizure of property was constructed, that allowed Jews to avoid too easily the forced sale of their property to the State. A 1940 Board of Directors Report reveals a "trick" used by Jews whose property was susceptible to expropriation, that possibly indicated a degree of sympathy among Italians for Jews to circumvent the seizure of property with the owner (Jewish) coming to an agreement with a creditor (not Jewish) to take over the property by foreclosure as collateral. The report states that "The Attorney General of the Court of Appeal of Turin ruled that such Jews cannot be formally prosecuted, but that such foreclosures, if on a large scale, would thwart the law and would reduce the assets of EGELI". Therefore, the report continues, the Board of Directors calls the Finance Ministry to address the weakness in the law (EGELI, 1940a, p. 33). In all these circumstances, EGELI's top management not only adheres as efficiently as possible to the government's instructions but also offers suggestions and even bills of law to make the expropriation of Jewish property more impactful, faster, and more certain.

With the Fascists in retreat in 1943 and EGELI relocated to northern Italy after the Anglo-American forces had occupied the south, the chair of the Board of Directors was eager to reassure their Fascist masters that although "Enemy occupation of a large area of the national territory has taken from EGELI the properties located in the southern provinces and on the islands, I am most confident that the situation may be reinstated and that, after so many painful events, the occupied areas too may be reunited and annexed to the Italian Social Republic" (EGELI, 1944a, p. 9). In the civil war between Fascists and non-Fascists that had been tearing Italy apart for months, combined with the relentless allied bombing of the main Italian cities, EGELI's Board of Directors boasts that the management of Jewish properties has provided, "despite the difficulties encountered ..., satisfactory profits" (EGELI, 1944a, p. 21). The Board of Statutory Auditors' Report consistently adopts the same Fascist rhetorical style as that of EGELI's top management. The 1941 Report, for example, notes how the Board "continue to accomplish the quite heavy and often uneasy tasks entrusted to EGELI ..." (EGELI, 1941c, p. 38) and "the fervent work of the Board of Directors and the illustrious Chairman turned out to unfailingly meet the purposes of the Board ..." (EGELI, 1943c, p. 48).

The style of language and the way events are recounted in the Board of Directors' confidential documents, that accompany the financial statements, also betray more than a concern for procedural efficiency. A key aspect of the dehumanisation of the victims and, therefore, the separation between the moral responsibility of the bureaucrats and the "administrative evil" was the words that identified the victims and the expropriation of their property (Kelman, 1973). Early reports of the Board of Directors use the phrase "Italian citizens of Jewish race" non-specifically (EGELI, 1939b, p. 9). In EGELI's accounting reports and related documents, such as the Board of Directors' minutes, the names of people whose property was expropriated were rarely mentioned. Individuals were mostly referred to as members of broad categories such as "the discriminated", "Jewish companies", and "the Jew", which in the singular form for Italians has a pejorative intention. In documents accompanying the accounts, where the text does mention the name of the individual being targeted, nothing else is said about them; nothing about their origin, their family, or their personal story at a time when Jews began to be arrested and deported. There is only reference to "files", "objects", "Jewish property", or legal status "of the discriminated person", which is enough to qualify for the attention of the Board the person who is mentioned. In a report dated July 1940 (EGELI, 1940b, p. 47), a list of figures about a bank's transactions merely refers to "Jewish property" and "property of the discriminated person" (p. 48).

At a meeting on 6 November 1940, when statistics about Jewish properties are presented, reference is made to "9 appeals", "9 files" served, and "15 files" yet to be served (EGELI, 1940d, p. 76). There are only isolated occurrences when specific individuals are mentioned by name, such as at a meeting on 27 February 1941 when 31 expropriations are listed, along with the names of the Jewish citizens whose property had been expropriated (EGELI, 1941d, pp. 94–99). Another exceptional example occurred in a meeting on 25 January 1942 when seven names were provided (EGELI, 1942d, pp. 6–7) and in a meeting on 25 February 1943, when nine names were disclosed. The phrase used to refer to those being targeted is: "File number 236 D. – First Name and Family Name[16] – Revenue Office of Ancona". This is followed by a detailed property description (EGELI, 1943d, pp. 7–8). The use of these descriptions was, and still is, very unusual in Italian bureaucratic processes and related documents, for it has long been the practice to specify the family name, the date and place of birth of the individuals concerned and where they lived.

The work of EGELI's management and staff was driven by instrumental rationality in the pursuit of the goals to be accomplished, not moral considerations (Browning, 1983; Mack, 2010; Minnich, 2013). Clegg (2009) has shown how the development of technologies of total institutional power, such as the accounting practices used by EGELI, is based on the building of categories of people, the automatism of the organisational routines and distancing oneself from the persecuted people, and the denial of their humanity (Funnell, 2015). While Arendt's views of the "Banality of Evil" give a glimpse of the racist character of bureaucracy,[17] the arbitrary nature of its functioning, if compared with the rule of law, and the peculiar aspect of racially based moral aloofness (Shenhav, 2013), in EGELI the principle of lawfulness was unfailingly adhered to, as were anti-Semitic attitudes. EGELI operated in a totalitarian regime that may have differed in many aspects from that of Nazi Germany but still exhibited most of the traits associated with bureaucratic organisations and the bureaucrats that Arendt refers to in *Eichman in Jerusalem*. EGELI reflected the functional picture described by Bauman (1989), where bureaucratic procedures ruled all administration and relied on means-ends analyses facilitated by accounting information, especially when the organisation's top management wanted to reject properties with little value. There is no evidence in the archival records that EGELI's top management ever questioned the morality of what they were doing. Instead, they would harshly criticise the poor efforts made by the other governmental institutions involved, which were suspected of abetting Jews to escape the expropriation of their property (Bos, 1997).

The Royal Decree no. 26 of 20 January 1944, issued in "Free Italy", established the restitution of property to Italian and foreign citizens who had formerly been declared or considered to be of "Jewish race". The issue was raised again immediately after the liberation of Rome, where a delegation of EGELI was still active with responsibility for the central regions and had continued its activities even after EGELI's transfer to the North of Italy. In September 1944, the Finance Minister (of the Kingdom of Italy under allied occupation) envisaged the imminent closure of EGELI because its objectives had ceased to exist. However, the idea of a rapid closure of EGELI would be short-lived. Although the Decree no. 252 of 5 October 1944 authorised the return of formerly sequestered Jewish property, after liberation it became increasingly difficult for EGELI to carry out the restitution of seized property in the Italian Social Republic. This was not only due to the vast amount of work and numbers involved but also the difficulty of getting an overall picture of the property situation. The organisation had to contend with chaos, dispersed documents, and abuse of power (PCM, 1948–1950). Moreover, from January 1945, EGELI also had to undertake the management of properties belonging to German subjects in Italy. In order to carry out the closure of EGELI, a special Liquidation Office was created.

Conclusion

In the expropriation of Jewish property, accounting used by the Italian Fascists was a key tool to manage the process of the seizure of Jewish property, its subsequent sale and the use of the monies received. It also provided the means for bureaucrats to separate and, thereby, absolve themselves from their immoral actions. Accounting practices and those who carried out these practices ensured that the attempted annihilation of European Jews by the Nazis was carried out with a level of efficiency and on a scale that had no precedents.

Far from being a neutral tool of management (Solomons, 1991), accounting, when set in the context of a racist-oriented dictatorship, was fully involved in the organisational work of the ministerial bureaucracy that was intent on the persecution of Jews in Italy. EGELI's accounting system allowed the identification of property exceeding the value specified for expropriation and carefully measured the performance of the expropriation process and sales of Jewish property. Not only had such work to be carried out on the basis of a race law but it also had to be profitable and accountable. This required accounting systems that would make the discrimination and persecution of Jews more efficient and visible to ensure that those responsible for the process knew that they would be held accountable for the success of the process (La Capra, 1994; Funnell, 1998; Fleischman and Funnell, 2007). Thus, the Annual Financial Statements of EGELI ensured they would be held accountable to the Finance Ministry for their commitment to Fascist values and aims.

Disclosing the profitability of expropriation in the Annual Financial Statements confirmed each year to the Ministry, and indirectly to Mussolini, that those who worked in EGELI were devoted to its mission as an agency of the Fascist State (EGELI, 1941a, p. 28). By making the expropriated and then sold property visible, the information provided in the Annual Financial Statements also supported the regime's propaganda that Jews were a threat to the State's financial stability. The Annual Financial Statements also hid the real effect of expropriation authorised by the Royal Decree no. 126/1939: the State's appropriation of the difference between the compensation paid and the actual selling price of the property expropriated. This confirmed the role of accounting as a technology to reveal what the regime had achieved and its priorities and to hide or disguise what it did not want to be known (Annisette, 2009; Funnell, 2013).

Those responsible for EGELI's role in the persecution of Italian Jews had moral culpability for their work, although to a different degree when compared to those in the Nazi bureaucracy who were at the very heart of the attempted annihilation of the Jewish race (Lovell, 1995; Lippman and Wilson, 2007). Despite the nature of their work, the language used in the Board of Directors' accounting records and reports was cold and neutral, rarely identifying the people affected. The emphasis was on transactions, prices, the value of property, and the timely manner in which the procedure was carried out. The inhumanity of the bureaucracies involved is again confirmed in EGELI's accounting practices by the silences, the omissions, and the replacement of the names of Jewish people with bureaucratic phrases or descriptions of the property.

This chapter is based on the paper by Valerio Antonelli, Raffaele D'Alessio, Roberto Rossi, and Warwick Funnell titled "Accounting and the Banality of Evil: Expropriation of Jewish Property in Fascist Italy (1939–1945)" which originally appeared in *Accounting, Auditing & Accountability Journal* in 2018, 31(8), 2165–2191. The authors would like to thank the publisher, Emerald, for permission to use this material.

Notes

1 Literally: Organization for Management and Liquidation of Property.

2 Arendt's interpretation of Eichman's motivations and moral culpability, which does not look for any other explanation of evil other than a bureaucracy driven by extreme circumstances, elicited a furious response. Horowitz (1982) believes that the implications of Arendt's conclusions, blaming instrumental rationality for the bureaucracy's permission to commit heinous crimes against humanity, underestimate the effects of efficiency and are based on ideology.

3 Gröning, at the age of 92, was sentenced to four years imprisonment.

4 For contrasting views, see Naumann (1966); Browning (1992); and Allen (2005).

5 Chamber of Deputies, CXLVIL 2a Tornata di mercoledì 14 dicembre 1938. Anno XVII, Resoconto stenografico, pp. 5609-5610.

6 In Italy, the base for taxes on land and on buildings was (and still is) related not to the market value or the price of the property actually paid but to a 'conventional' value, that is normally lower than the current market prices and it is related to the cadastral income listed in the registers held by the Land Registry Office. The conventional value is obtained by multiplying the cadastral income by a coefficient (generally between 33 and 100). This calculation was adopted also in the case of Jewish property expropriation.

As laid down by Act 126 of 1939, the following equations were used to calculate the conventional value of the land or the building:
Value of land = *80* × *Taxable rent as of February 1939.*
Value of building = *20* × *Taxable rent as of February 1939.*

7 These laws referred to categories of population.

8 Primo Levi survived and wrote the book *If This Is a Man* about his experience in the Auschwitz extermination camp.

9 Other members of the Board of Statutory Auditors included: representatives from the Ministry of Agriculture and Forestry; the General Manager of the Inspectorate for the Protection of Savings and Lending; the General Manager of Trade at the Ministry of Guilds, someone from the Fascist Confederation of Industrialists; the Inspector General of the Ministry of Agriculture and Forestry, and someone from the National Fascist Federation of landowners and farmers.

10 Marquis Demetrio Asinari di Bernezzo (1878–1939) was a regular cavalry colonel who received a silver medal for bravery in World War I. He was president of the publishing house of the Turin-based newspaper "La Stampa" from 1935 until his death.

11 Cesare Giovara (1878–1957) was an officer in the Italian-Turkish War, then prefect of Catanzaro, Ferrara, Piacenza, La Spezia, Livorno and Turin, where he was also mayor from 1938 to 1939. In 1938, he was also elected to the Senate, where he stayed in office until the fall of Fascism in 1943.

12 At the time, there were neither laws nor auditing standards regulating audit procedures.

13 La Stampa's interest in EGELI's work was not unexpected, given that Asinari di Bernezzo, the president of EGELI, was also president of the publisher of *La Stampa*.

14 The *Ufficio Tecnico Erariale* (UTE) was the local branch of the Ministry of Finance that searched and filed the registered ownership of property located within a province.

15 San Pellegrino Terme is a tiny village at the foot of the Alps, located about 100 km from what was then the capital of the Italian Social Republic, Salò, and about 690 km north of Rome.

16 Details of specific individuals have been omitted in accordance with a specific rule of the Central State Archives.

17 Recently, some authors have argued that while the "banality of evil" risks becoming a stereotype, a banality itself, such a concept may apply to many other monstrosities of our time, such as the genocides committed by Stalin, Pol Pot, Saddam Hussein and in Rwanda (Darley, 1992 Minnich, 2013).

References

Primary sources

Racial Laws and Rules

RdI (1930). RD 30 ottobre 1930 n.1731 Norme sulle Comunità israelitiche e sulla Unione delle Comunità medesime, Gazzetta Ufficiale del Regno d'Italia n.11, 15 gennaio 1931.

RdI (1938a). RD-L 5 settembre 1938, n. 1390. Provvedimenti per la difesa della razza nella scuola fascista, Gazzetta Ufficiale del Regno d'Italia n. 209, 13 settembre 1938.

RdI (1938b). RD-L 5 settembre 1938, n. 1539. Istituzione, presso il Ministero dell'Interno, del Consiglio superiore per la demografia e la razza, Gazzetta Ufficiale del Regno d'Italia n. 231, 8 ottobre 1938.

RdI (1938c). RD-L 17 novembre 1938, n. 1728. Provvedimenti per la difesa della razza italiana, Gazzetta Ufficiale del Regno d'Italia n. 264, 19 novembre 1938.

RdI (1938d). RD-L 15 novembre 1938, n. 1779. Integrazione e coordinamento in unico testo delle norme già emanate per la difesa della razza nella Scuola italiana, Gazzetta Ufficiale del Regno d'Italia n. 272, 29 novembre 1938.

RdI (1938e). RD 21 novembre 1938, n. 2154. Modificazioni allo statuto del Partito Nazionale Fascista, Gazzetta Ufficiale del Regno d'Italia n. 36, 13 febbraio 1939.

RdI (1938f). RD-L 22 dicembre 1938, n. 2111. Disposizioni relative al collocamento in congedo assoluto ed al trattamento di quiescenza del personale militare delle Forze armate dello Stato di razza ebraica, Gazzetta Ufficiale del Regno d'Italia n. 30, 6 febbraio 1939.

RdI (1939a). L 29 giugno 1939, n. 1054. Disciplina dell'esercizio delle professioni da parte dei cittadini di razza ebraica, Gazzetta Ufficiale del Regno d'Italia n. 179, 2 agosto 1939.

RdI (1939b). L 13 luglio 1939, n. 1055. Disposizioni in materia testamentaria nonché sulla disciplina dei cognomi, nei confronti degli appartenenti alla razza ebraica, Gazzetta Ufficiale del Regno d'Italia n. 179, 2 agosto 1939.

RdI (1940a). L 28 settembre 1940, n. 1403. Abrogazione del contributo statale a favore degli asili infantili israelitici contemplati dalla legge 30 luglio 1896, n. 343, Gazzetta Ufficiale del Regno d'Italia n. 245. 18 ottobre 1940.

RdI (1940b). L 23 settembre 1940, n. 1459. Integrazioni alla legge 13 luglio 1939-XVII, n. 1055, contenente disposizioni in materia testamentaria, nonché sulla disciplina dei cognomi, nei confronti degli appartenenti alla razza ebraica, Gazzetta Ufficiale del Regno d'Italia n. 256, 31 ottobre 1940.

RdI (1942). L 19 aprile 1942, n. 517. Esclusione degli elementi ebrei dal campo dello spettacolo, Gazzetta Ufficiale del Regno d'Italia n. 126, 28 maggio 1942.

Fascist Literature on Race

Cioffi, A. (1942). *Lo stato razziale e le sue guarentigie nel diritto italiano*, Noccioli, Empoli.

Costamagna, C. (1939). "Razza e diritto al Convegno italo-tedesco di Vienna". *Lo Stato*, *3*, 129–167.

Romano, P.A. (1941). I criteri legislativi per la qualificazione razziale. *Il diritto razzista*, *4*(1–4), 44–77.

EGELI Laws

RdI (1939c). Regno d'Italia. RD-L 9 febbraio 1939, n. 126. Norme di attuazione ed integrazione delle disposizioni di cui all'art. 10 del R. decreto-legge 17 novembre 1938 XVII, n. 1728, relative ai limiti di proprietà; immobiliare e di attività; industriale e commerciale per i cittadini italiani di razza ebraica. *Gazzetta Ufficiale del Regno d'Italia* n. 35, 11 febbraio 1939.

RdI (1939d). RD 27 marzo 1939, n. 665. Approvazione dello statuto dell'Ente di gestione e liquidazione immobiliare. *Gazzetta Ufficiale del Regno d'Italia* n. 110, 10 maggio 1939.

RdI (1940). L 19 dicembre 1940, n. 1994. Gestione dei beni dei cittadini di nazionalità nemica sottoposti a provvedimenti di sequestro.

RdI (1941). L 24 febbraio 1941, n 158. Autorizzazione all'Ente di gestione e liquidazione immobiliare a delegare agli Istituti di credito fondiario la gestione e la vendita degli immobili ad esso attribuiti. *Gazzetta Ufficiale del Regno d'Italia* n. 79, 2 aprile 1941.

RSI (1944a). DL 4 gennaio 1944, n. 2. Nuove disposizioni concernenti i beni posseduti dai cittadini di razza ebraica. *Gazzetta Ufficiale della Repubblica Sociale Italiana* n. 6, 10 gennaio 1944.

RSI (1944b). DLD 31 marzo 1944, n. 109. Nuovo statuto e regolamento dell'Ente di Gestione e Liquidazione Immobiliare. *Gazzetta Ufficiale – Repubblica Sociale Italiana* n. 81, 6 aprile 1944.

RSI (1944c). DM 30 dicembre 1944, n. 1036. Modifica dello Statuto dell'E.G.E.L.I. ed istituzione del posto di Direttore Generale. *Gazzetta Ufficiale della Repubblica Sociale Italiana* n. 58, 10 marzo 1945.

EGELI records – Archivio Centrale dello Stato, Piazzale degli Archivi, 27, Roma

EGELI (1939a). Verbale della giunta esecutiva, 5 giugno 1939, busta 47-bis.

EGELI (1939b). Verbale della giunta esecutiva, 22 giugno 1939, busta 47-bis.

EGELI (1939c). Verbale della giunta esecutiva, 7 settembre 1939, busta 47-bis.

EGELI (1940a). Verbale della giunta esecutiva, 23 gennaio 1940, busta 47-bis.

EGELI (1940b). Verbale della giunta esecutiva, 17 luglio 1940, busta 47-bis.

EGELI (1940c). Verbale della giunta esecutiva, 19 settembre 1940, busta 47-bis.

EGELI (1940d). Verbale della giunta esecutiva, 6 novembre 1940, busta 47-bis.

EGELI (1941a). Relazione al ministero delle finanze sull'esercizio 1940, busta 46-bis.

EGELI (1941b). Bilancio gestione beni ebraici 1940, busta 46-bis.

EGELI (1941c). Relazione dei sindaci, busta 46-bis.

EGELI (1941d). Verbale della giunta esecutiva, 27 febbraio 1941, busta 47-bis.

EGELI (1942a). Relazione al ministero delle finanze sull'esercizio 1941, busta 46-bis.
EGELI (1942b). Bilancio gestione beni ebraici 1941, busta 46-bis.
EGELI (1942c). Relazione dei sindaci, busta 46-bis.
EGELI (1942d). Verbale della giunta esecutiva, 25 febbraio 1942, busta 47-bis.
EGELI (1943a). Relazione al ministero delle finanze sull'esercizio 1942, busta 46-bis.
EGELI (1943b). Bilancio gestione beni ebraici 1942, busta 46-bis.
EGELI (1943c). Relazione dei sindaci, busta 46-bis.
EGELI (1943d). Verbale della giunta esecutiva, 25 febbraio 1943, busta 47-bis.
EGELI (1944a). "Relazione al ministero delle finanze sull'esercizio 1943", busta 46-bis.
EGELI (1944b). Bilancio gestione beni ebraici 1943, busta 46-bis.
EGELI (1944c). Relazione dei sindaci, busta 46-bis.

Other Official Sources

GI (2001). "Governo Italiano, Commissione per la ricostruzione delle vicende che hanno caratterizzato in Italia le attività di acquisizione dei beni dei cittadini ebrei da parte di organismi pubblici e privati. Rapporto generale", http://www.governo.it/Presidenza/DICA/beni_ebraici/
PCM (1948–1950). "Retrocessione beni immobili dall'EGELI ai proprietari che dovettero effettuarne il trasferimento coattivo", Archivio Centrale dello Stato, 3.2.2. fasc. 11472.4.

Newspapers

Anonymous (1938a). La piovra giudaica. 400 ebrei sono padroni per un miliardo di beni immobili. *La Stampa*, 15 November, page 6.
Anonymous (1938b). Gli ebrei e la proprietà edilizia. Quanto posseggono. *La Stampa*, Edizione della sera. 15 November, frontpage.
Anonymous (1938c). I beni immobili degli ebrei acquistati da un ente statale. *La Stampa*, 17th December, front page.
Anonymous (1938d). Le proprietà degli ebrei eccedenti i limiti concessi ai non discriminati saranno acquisite da un apposito ente. *La Stampa*, Edizione della sera. 17 December, frontpage.
Anonymous (1938e). Le proprietà ebraiche e la loro alienazione. *La Stampa*, 18 December, page 6.
Anonymous (1939a). Il trasferimento dei beni degli ebrei eccedenti la quota loro consentita. *La Stampa*, 12 February, page 5.
Anonymous (1939b). Le norme per le denuncie degli immobili e delle aziende di proprietà degli ebrei. *La Stampa*, 3 May, page 3.
Anonymous (1939c). Gli immobili ebraici. Certificati al 4% per i beni rilasciati. *La Stampa*, 11 May, last page.
Anonymous (1939d). La proprietà ebraica. Il lavoro di controllo da parte degli enti statali. *La Stampa*, 20 June, page 3.
Anonymous (1939e). Come avverrà la riduzione dei beni immobili degli ebrei. *La Stampa*, 12 August, page 2.
Anonymous (1939f). "e proprietà immobiliari ebraiche". *La Stampa*, 1 September, page 3.
Anonymous (1944). I beni degli ebrei. *La Stampa*, 30th January, front page.

Mussolini's Speeches and Writings

Mussolini, B. (1934). "Speech", 3rd September 1934, Bari, at: https://www.youtube.com/watch?v=m6j25ORorjE

Mussolini, B. (1938a). "Speech", 18th September 1938, Trieste, at: https://www.youtube.com/watch?v=3-mNqP7AT6g

Mussolini (1938b). "Informazione diplomatica n. 18", 5th August 1938.

Secondary Sources

Acerbi, G. (2011). *Le leggi antiebraiche e razziali italiane ed il ceto dei giuristi.* Milano: Giuffrè.

Adams, G.B. (2011). The Problem of Administrative Evil in a Culture of Technical Rationality. *Public Integrity*, *13*(3), 275–285.

Adams, G.B., and Balfour, D.L. (2009). *Unmasking Administrative Evil.* New York: M.E. Sharpe.

Allen, M.T. (2005). *The Business of Genocide: The SS, Slave Labour, and the Concentration Camp.* Chapel Hill, NC and London: University of North Carolina Press.

Angier, C. (2011). *The Double Bond: Primo Levi. A Biography.* London: Faber & Faber.

Annisette, M. (2009). Race and ethnicity. In J.R. Edwards, and S.P. Walker (Eds.). *The Routledge Companion to Accounting History* (pp. 451–469). London: Routledge.

Antonucci, S.H., and Spizzichino, G. (2004). Daily life during the racial laws and the Nazi occupation: Testimonies. In: M.I. Venzo, and B. Migliau (Eds.). *The Racial Laws and the Jewish Community of Rome 1938–1945* (pp. 33–36). Roma: Gangemi Editore.

Arendt, H. (1964). *Eichmann in Jerusalem. A Report on the Banality of Evil.* New York: The Viking Press.

Bauman, Z. (1989). *Modernity and the Holocaust.* Ithaca, NY: Cornell University Press.

Bos, R.T. (1997). Essay: Business ethics and Bauman ethics. *Organization Studies*, *18*(6), 997–1014.

Browning, C.R. (1983). The German bureaucracy and the Holocaust. In: A. Grobman, and D. Landes (Eds.). *Genocide: Critical Issues of the Holocaust* (pp. 145–149). Los Angeles: Simon Wiesenthal Center.

Browning, C.R. (1992). *Ordinary Men: Reserve Police Battalion 101 and the Final Solution in Poland.* London: Penguin Books.

Calimani, R. (2013). *Storia degli ebrei italiani nel XIX e nel XX secolo.* Milano: Mondadori.

Candeloro, G. (1981). *Storia dell'Italia moderna. IX. Il fascismo e le sue guerre.* Milano: Feltrinelli.

Cassata, F. (2008). *«La Difesa della razza». Politica, ideologia e immagine del razzismo fascista.* Torino: Einaudi.

Clegg, S. (2009). Bureaucracy, the Holocaust and techniques of power at work. *Management Revue*, *20*(4), 326–347.

Cocchi, D., and Favero, G. (2009). Gli statistici e la "questione della razza". Le leggi antiebraiche del 1938, le società scientifiche e la scuola in Italia. In: Accademia Nazionale delle Scienze detta dei XL (Ed.). *Scritti e documenti* (pp. 207–235). Roma: Biblioteca dell'Accademia Nazionale delle Scienze detta dei XL.

Collotti, E. (1998). Il razzismo negato. *Italia Contemporanea, 212*, 577–588.
Collotti, E. (2003). *Il fascismo e gli ebrei: le leggi razziali in Italia*. Bari: Laterza.
Darley, J.M. (1992). Social organization for the production of evil. *Psychological Inquiry, 3*, 199–218.
Dawidowicz L. (1975). *The War against the Jews 1933–1945*. London: Weidenfeld and Nicholson.
De Felice, R. (1974). *Mussolini il duce. Gli anni del consenso 1929–1936*. Torino: Einaudi.
De Felice, R. (1993). *Storia degli ebrei italiani sotto il fascismo*. Torino: Einaudi.
Del Prato, D. (1938). *Il conflitto con la Società delle Nazioni*. Roma: Unione Editoriale d'Italia.
Finzi, R. (1997). *L'università italiana e le leggi antiebraiche*. Roma: Editori Riuniti.
Fleischman, R.K., and Funnell, W.N. (2007) The relevance of the past. In: T. Hopper, D. Northcott, and Scapens, R.W. (Eds.). *Issues in Management Accounting* (pp. 377–398). Edinburgh: Pearson.
Funnell, W. (1998). Accounting in the service of the Holocaust. *Critical Perspectives on Accounting, 9*(4), 435–464.
Funnell, W.N. (2013). Accounting and the Holocaust. In: R.K. Fleischman, W.N. Funnell, and S.P. Walker (Eds.). *Critical Histories of Accounting: Sinister Inscriptions in the Modern Era* (pp. 57–68). New York: Routledge.
Funnell, W.N. (2015). The Holocaust, accounting and the denial of humanity. In: W.N. Funnell, and M. Chwastiak (Eds.). *Accounting at War: The Politics of Military Finance* (pp. 126–147). Abingdon: Routledge.
Gentile, E. (2002). *Fascismo: storia e interpretazione*. Bari: Laterza.
Gentile, E. (2008). *La via italiana al totalitarismo: il partito e lo Stato nel regime fascista*: Roma: Carocci.
Gentile, S. (2013). *La legalità del male. L'offensiva mussoliniana contro gli ebrei nella prospettiva storico-giuridica (1938–1945)*. Torino: Giappichelli.
Gillette, A. (2002). *Racial Theories in Fascist Italy*. London and New York: Routledge, London.
Goldhagen, D. (1996). *Hitler's Willing Executioners: Ordinary Germans and the Holocaust*. London: Abacus.
Gregor, A.J. (1974). *L'ideologia del fascismo. Il fondamento razionale del totalitarismo*. Milano: Lulucom.
Guerri, G.B. (1979). *Galeazzo Ciano: una vita (1903–1944)*. Torino: Bompiani.
Heinsohn, G. (2000). What makes the Holocaust a uniquely unique genocide?. *Journal of Genocide Research, 2*(3), 411–430.
Hilberg, R. (1980). The significance of the Holocaust. In: H. Friedlander, and S. Milton (Eds.). *The Holocaust: Ideology, Bureaucracy, and Genocide*. Millwood: Kraus International Publications.
Hilberg, R. (1993). *Perpetrators, Victims, Bystanders: The Jewish Catastrophe*. New York: Harper Collins.
Hilberg, R. (2003). *The Destruction of the European Jews*. New York: Yale University Press.
Hitler, A. (1987). *Mein Kampf*. Boston, MA: Hutchinson.
Horowitz, I.L. (1982). *Taking Lives: Genocide and the State Power*. New Brunswick: Transaction Books.
Israel, G., and Nastasi, P. (1998). *Scienza e razza nell'Italia Fascista*. Bologna: Il Mulino.

Kelman, H.C. (1973). Violence without moral restraints: Reflections on the dehumanization of victims and victimizers. *Journal of Social Issues*, *29*(4), 25–61.

La Capra, D. (1994). *Representing the Holocaust*. Ithaca, NY: Cornell University Press.

Leon, A. (1970). *The Jewish Question: A Marxist Interpretation*. New York: Pathfinder Press.

Levi, F. (1995). L'applicazione delle leggi contro le proprietà degli ebrei (1938–1946). In: F. Felice (Ed.). *Fascismo, antifascismo, democrazia a cinquant'anni dal 25 aprile* (pp. 845–862). Bari: Laterza.

Lippman, E.J., and Wilson, P.A. (2007). The culpability of accounting in perpetuating the Holocaust. *Accounting History*, *12*(3), 283–303.

Lippman, E.J., and Wilson, P.A. (2013). Accountants and Holocaust. In: R.K. Fleischman, W.N. Funnell, and S.P. Walker (Eds.). *Critical Histories of Accounting: Sinister Inscriptions in the Modern Era* (pp. 69–81). New York: Routledge.

Livingston, M.A. (2014). *The Fascists and the Jews of Italy. Mussolini's Race Laws (1938–1943)*. Cambridge: Cambridge University Press.

Lovell, A. (1995). Moral reasoning and moral atmosphere in the domain of accounting. *Accounting, Auditing and Accountability Journal*, *8*(3), 60–80.

Mack, M. (2010). Hannah Arendt's philosophy of plurality: Thinking and understanding *Eichmann in Jerusalem*. In: A. Schaap, D. Celermajer, and V. Karales (Eds.). *Power, Judgment and Political Evil: In Conversation with Hannah Arendt* (pp. 13–26). Burlington: Ashgate.

Mann, M. (2000). Were the perpetrators of genocide "ordinary men" or "real Nazis"? Results from fifteen hundred biographies. *Holocaust and Genocide Studies*, *14*(3), 331–366.

Michaelis, M. (1982). *Mussolini e la questione ebraica. Le relazioni italo-tedesche e la politica razziale in Italia*. Milano: Edizioni Comunità.

Minnich, E. (2013). The evil of banality: Arendt revisited, *Arts and Humanities in Higher Education*, *13*(1–2), 158–179.

Muller-Hill, B. (1994). The Final Solution and the role of experts. In: D. Cesarani (Ed.). *The Final Solution: Origins and Implementation*. London: Routledge.

Naumann, B. (1966). *Auschwitz*. New York: Praeger.

Procaccia, C. (2004). The Roman Jews from the Emancipation to the racial laws. Economic and social aspects. In: M.I. Venzo, and B. Migliau (Eds.). *The Racial Laws and the Jewish Community of Rome 1938–1945* (pp. 29–32). Roma: Gangemi Editore.

Rose, N. (1999). *Powers of Freedom*. Cambridge: Cambridge University Press.

Rosenberg, A. (1983). The philosophical implications of the Holocaust. In: R.L. Braham (Ed.). *Perspectives on the Holocaust*. Boston, MA: Kluwer-Nijhoff Publishing.

Sabbatucci, G. (1979). Fascist institutions, recent problems and interpretations. *The Journal of Italian History*, *2*(1), 92–100.

Sarfatti, M. (1994). *Mussolini contro gli ebrei: cronaca dell'elaborazione delle leggi del 1938*. Torino: Einaudi.

Sarfatti, M. (2007). *Gli ebrei nell'Italia fascista: vicende, identità, persecuzione*. Torino: Einaudi.

Shenhav, Y. (2013). Beyond "instrumental rationality": Lord Cromer and the imperial roots of Eichmann's bureaucracy. *Journal of Genocide Research*, *15*(4), 379–399.

Solomons, D. (1991). Accounting and social change: A neutralist view. *Accounting, Organisations and Society*, *16*(3), 287–298.

Spinosa, A. (1994). *Mussolini: razzista riluttante*. Firenze: Bonacci.
Toscano, M. (1998). *L'abrogazione delle leggi razziali in Italia (1943–1987). Reintegrazione dei diritti dei cittadini e ritorno ai valori del Risorgimento*. Roma: Senato della Repubblica.
Turi, G. (1980). *Il fascismo e il consenso degli intellettuali*. Bologna: Il Mulino.
Wieland, K. (2010). *Margherita Sarfatti: l'amante del Duce*. Torino: Utet.

9 Accounting for the Fossoli concentration camp

Warwick Funnell, Valerio Antonelli, Michele Bigoni, Emanuela Mattia Cafaro, and Raffaele D'Alessio

Introduction

The persecution of Italian Jews by the Fascist government of Mussolini, which began with Race Laws in 1938, entered a new phase with Italy's declaration of war against France and Britain in June 1940. Italians classified as Jewish according to the Race Laws were then hunted down and collected at numerous centres of detention installed throughout Italy. After the surrender of Italy in September 1943 and the Germans occupied the north and centre of the Italian peninsula, the German *Schutzstaffel* (SS) began preparations for implementing the "Final Solution" in Italy. From December 1943 to August 1944, the period that is the main focus of this chapter, the Fossoli concentration camp located in northern Italy, 6 km from the city of Carpi in the province of Modena, was the main centre for the collection of Italian Jews where more than a third of all Jews interned throughout Italy were sent (Gibertoni and Melodi, 1996; Sacchi, 2002). With the help of the Fascists and many private businesses, the Fossoli concentration camp became the major transit camp in Italy in March 1944 from where those imprisoned were sent by the Germans to be killed in the extermination camps, mainly at Auschwitz-Birkenau.

As noted by Marti and Fernandez (2013), Le Theule et al. (2020), and Stokes and Gabriel (2010), the Nazi's Jewish genocidal programmes, and other acts of genocide, have been dependent upon the willing participation of bureaucrats and the use of less obvious tools. Consistently, this chapter identifies the ways in which the calculative and reporting practices of accounting as ultimately "technologies of death" used by Italian Fascists and German Nazis provided a crucial means to reduce Italian Jews held captive in the Fossoli concentration camp to a life deemed to be without value and the culpability of those who practised these in the attempted annihilation of Italian Jews. The details in the concentration camp accounting reports of the resources and facilities provided for Jewish prisoners when firstly under the control of the Italians and then the Germans reveal more starkly than other reports associated with the camp the changing priorities and, thus, the ultimate intentions of the Germans in the treatment of Italian Jews. Accounting

DOI: 10.4324/9781032685328-9

practices were an important tool in the Nazi-Fascist machinery of death when they contributed to the creation of a "state of exception" (Agamben, 1998, 1999, 2000, 2005), a new juridical order that can suspend established law and allow specified individuals to be deprived of all rights and thereby to be reduced to a life with no value, a "bare life", when almost any murderous conduct is permitted.

Justifications for this new juridical order need to rely upon convincing interpretations of why there is a need for extreme responses that require the suspension of normal legal and political protections, to which purpose the apparently banal, objective practice of accounting can provide crucial contributions. The official documents related to the operations of the Fossoli camp in the form of invoices, letters, payment orders, financial reports, cost reports, and cost calculations of the daily diet of the inmates provide details about the way in which after the Germans took control accounting practices provided them with a means to deny the Jewish prisoners recognition of their humanity when it came time to leave for the Auschwitz-Birkenau extermination camp. Laws and regulations, ministerial accounts, and public records issued by the Fascist government regarding the discrimination, persecution, and deportation of Italian Jews further enriched understanding of how the Fossoli camp was part of a larger apparatus, the main goal of which was the extermination of the undesirable "Other".

The chapter proceeds firstly with a description of the concepts of "state of exception" and "bare life" that inform the work. The study then moves to a discussion of the political, cultural, and legal context of the persecution and deportation of the Jews in Italy and the importance of the Fossoli concentration camp in the Fascists' racial program and then later in the Nazi extermination process. This leads to an examination of the administrative organisation and budgeting systems implemented in the camp, emphasising the accounting practices that Italian civilian and military personnel used to support the Fossoli concentration camp when it was first under Fascist control and then when it was taken over by the Germans. Managing the costs and logistics of operating the camp became a key anti-Semitic tool and later a signifier of the intentions of the Germans.

Biopolitical control in the state of exception

Biopower, that is power exercised over life, recognises that individuals have a dual identity: a natural living being that has a "bare life", a mere existence, and a political identity given to an individual as a recognised member of a modern State. When humankind moved from a perilous existence that constituted bare life to political life, valueless life was turned into valuable or good life (Agamben, 1998, p. 8). This becomes the measure of what it means to be fully human, a "form or way of living proper to an individual or group" (Agamben, 1998, p. 166). In a state exercising biopower, it is only the political attributes of an individual, that is, the rights to which they are entitled as a citizen, that give their lives meaning and value that differentiates them from other living organisms (Foucault, 1990, p. 143; Agamben, 1998, pp. 8–9). By removing an individual's right to be recognised as a citizen of a State because they do not meet specified qualifications, most notoriously those that are derived from legally enforceable racial requirements, they are no longer entitled to the legal protections and rights that citizenship, their political life, provides. This allows them to be denied their humanity, the right to life, and to be accorded only the bare life of any living organism, which could be destroyed at any time by anyone without any consequences for the killer (Foucault, 1990, p. 143; Agamben, 1998, pp. 138–139). This will be accomplished most efficaciously by pronouncing a crisis that allows those in power to declare a "state of exception" when the normal law is suspended.

Agamben (1998, p. 18) emphasises that the "state of exception is … not the chaos that precedes order but the situation that results from its suspension". With the suspension of operative laws, the state of exception is not a "state of law" but a space without law, a "no-man's-land between public law and political fact …" (Agamben, 2005, p. 1) where an "exception is an element in law that transcends positive law in the form of its suspension" (Agamben, 1998, p. 17). Thus, in the state of exception that which in normal times was not a recognised practice becomes the rule, the "normal order" (Agamben, 2005, p. 39). Indeed, the state of exception becomes no longer provisional but "comes to be confused with juridical rule itself" (Agamben, 1998, p. 168). Declaration of a state of exception thereby provides the justification for extraordinary measures that "offers elites the opportunity to turn the exception into an enduring standard …" (Huber and Scheytt, 2013, p. 96), to become the norm. Therefore, subsequently activation of the extreme measures to enact a state of exception that exists both within and beyond the juridical structures of the state does not have to be a response to a situation that is specifically declared to be an emergency by the State.

The most threatening consequence of the enactment of a state of exception is the way in which it can be used to erase "any legal status of the individual, thus producing a legally unnameable and unclassifiable being" who is now at the mercy of those who institute the state of exception (Agamben, 2005, p. 3). Accordingly, declaration of a state of exception gives the sovereign the power to decide on "the value or the nonvalue of life" (Agamben, 1998, p. 142). Those who are valued become the "included", all others, the "excluded", can be condemned to being *homo sacer*, a condition of "sacred life" that in Roman law referred to anyone who "may be killed and yet not sacrificed" as a sacred being because they were not valued as life (Agamben, 1998, p. 8). In their plans to destroy all Jews, the Nazis created a category of individuals as *homo sacer* who, according to edicts and enactments by the Nazis, did not meet required racial qualifications and, thus, they had no right to exist and could be exterminated.

In a biopolitical State, the need to be able to penetrate the bodies and lives of subjects, that is, to provide a continuous all-encompassing control, becomes the focus of the mechanisms and calculations of modern power with the provision of the means to "qualify, measure, appraise, and hierarchize" (Foucault, 1990, pp. 140, 144; Agamben, 1998, p. 6). Biopower to be effective requires knowledge to be invested in human bodies to "subjugate them by turning them into objects of knowledge" (Foucault, 1991, p. 92). Indeed, emphasises Foucault (1991, p. 27), "power and knowledge directly imply one another ...". As a major source of this knowledge, accounting practices have become essential to creating structures and practices of biopolitical control that reflect and, most especially, constitute power relations (Hopwood, 1987; Napier, 2006; Cooper, 2015; Alawattage et al., 2019; Bigoni et al., 2020). This has required in the modern State the integration of techniques of individualisation with procedures of totalisation that allow the inclusion of natural life in the mechanisms and political calculations of State power (Agamben, 1998, p. 5).

According to Foucault (1990, p. 149), Nazi Germany was the first truly radical biopolitical State. A booklet produced by the Nazis on National Socialist ideology alluded to its biopolitical nature as envisaged by Hitler for whom the "new state knows no other task than the fulfilment of the conditions necessary for the preservation of the people" (quoted in Agamben, 1998, p. 147). This could only be secured "if the racial traits and hereditary health of the body of the people are preserved" (quoted in Agamben, 1998, p. 147). The result was that the "men, women and children who perished in the Holocaust died because an inexorable power had decreed that human beings with certain qualifications should, without exception ... be destroyed" (Zuccotti, 1987, p. 183). In Nazi Germany and Fascist Italy in 1944, Jews had become life without juridical value, merely "bare life", and thus could be killed without legal consequences (Agamben, 1998, p. 138). The killing of Jews, emphasises Agamben (1998, p. 114), constituted "simply the actualisation of a 'mere capacity to be killed' inherent in the condition of the Jew as such". In Italy, the qualifications that created the "excluded" Jew that were specified in 1938 in the new Race Laws had initially as their aim only the economic and social exclusion of Jews from Italian society and not, like the Germans, their annihilation. Ultimately, denying Italian Jews their right to a political life permitted condemning them to the extermination camps. Jews were "exterminated ... exactly as Hitler had announced, 'as lice ... as bare life'" (Agamben, 1998, p. 114). Thus, according to Agamben, unlike Foucault (1990, p. 137) and his association of biopower with improvement and a "plentitude" of life, the result of the modern hegemony of biopower is not the promotion of a positive existence. Instead, the Holocaust established that there is the potential for the deterioration of the quality of life to a condition of bare life and ultimately obliteration without consequence for the perpetrator for the "dimension in which the extermination took place is neither religion nor law, but biopolitics" (Agamben, 1998, p. 114).

Increasingly from the late 19th century concentration camps had become an implement of a state of exception, a space in which bare life seized by the State would be contained (Agamben, 1998, p. 170). Agamben (1998, p. 171), with reference to Foucault, refers to concentration camps as "the most absolute biopolitical space (founded solely on the state of exception) … ever to have been realized in which power confronts nothing but pure life, without any mediation". The camp is thus "the structure in which the state of exception …. is realized normally" (Agamben, 1998, p. 170). In the concentration camps, anything becomes possible, "life and politics become one", that makes the peril of bare life possible (Agamben, 1998, p. 149). In Nazi Germany, very early the concentration camp was given "absolute independence from every judicial control …" (Agamben, 1998, p. 169). Those condemned to the concentration camp could be killed by anyone without consequence for the killer, for according to the law, their killing was not murder. Stokes and Gabriel (2010, p. 462), in reference to the concentration camp, have shown that the way in which biopolitical genocidal programmes that can be permitted, even normalised, in a state of exception, are dependent upon "bureaucratic resources to initiate, sustain and, often cover it up" (see also Marti and Fernandez, 2013). This thereby enabled the Holocaust to be "constructed industrially- with systems of rules, impersonally applied, that made it as technically efficient as genocide could be" (Grey 2005 quoted in Stokes and Gabriel, 2010, p. 465).

Italian Jews as *homo sacer*

In Italy until 1937, the possibility of the establishment of specific spaces for forced detention according to racial criteria had not been a feature of either Italian Fascist beliefs or policies. Indeed, the Fascist regime installed after the March on Rome on 28 October 1922 showed little interest in racial stereotyping and the persecution of Italian Jews (Spinosa, 1994; Gillette, 2002). It was never Mussolini's intention prior to his removal from power to have Italy "turn into a cohort of Nazi-crazed racists, and he refused to release any Jews to the Nazis for deportation" (Burgwyn, 2018, p. 143). Although there had been historical instances of institutionalised anti-Semitism, such as during the Risorgimento, there had been no tradition in Italy of biological racism with Jews. Instead, Jews who had been living in Italy for centuries in major cities and towns such as Rome, Milan, Turin, and Trieste were widely assimilated (Calimani, 2015). One of the most prominent Fascist propaganda publications *Villari* proclaimed in 1934 that the Jews in Italy "have been completely absorbed into the body of the nation and regard themselves and are regarded by their neighbours as thorough Italians" (quoted in Michaelis, 1989, p. 192; Arendt, 1964, pp. 178–180; De Felice, 1993). This changed quickly with the invasion of Ethiopia in 1935.

After the invasion of Ethiopia, the resulting political isolation of Italy led Mussolini to seek a strong relationship with the Nazis. It also became the prelude to the effective declaration of a state of exception. Accordingly, Mussolini subsequently embraced an anti-Semitic stance in order to convince Hitler of the Italian commitment to his political and racial values (Fargion, 1989; Michaelis, 2003). This was to be confirmed with the publication of the so-called "Manifesto of Race" (*Manifesto della razza,* hereafter the Manifesto) on 15 July 1938. The Manifesto defined the concept of a pure Italian race, which closely mirrored that of the Nazis, and claimed that Fascism had to ensure the protection of this racial identity from what was seen to be Jewish contamination (Cuomo, 2005; Dell'Era, 2011). The Manifesto was followed by the publication of a journal promoted by the regime entitled "In Defence of Race" (*La difesa della razza*) (Cassata, 2008).

Implementation of the Fascist's new anti-Semitic program began in August 1938 with a census of the Jewish population living in Italy. The census, that was later to expedite the collection of Jews by the Germans, allowed the Italian Statistics National Bureau to officially identify and class 48,032 Italians as Jews according to the racial and religious criteria of the Manifesto (Sarfatti, 1993; Picciotto, 2005). Rome had the highest concentration of Jews with 12,494 in 1938 (Zimmerman, 2005). On 17 November 1938, a Royal Decree of King Victor Emmanuel III (Decree Law 1728/1938) gave a legal status to the race priorities of the Grand Council of Fascism. At the same time, numerous Race Laws were enacted to discriminate against Jews in the economic and social life of Italy (Regno d'Italia (RdI), 1938a, 1938b, 1938c, 1938d, 1938e, 1938f, 1939a, 1939b, 1940a, 1940b; Yael-Franzone, 2004; Gentile, 2013). Although the Race Laws were not genocidal in intent, they did create an administrative structure and legal priorities that required the collection of information about Italian Jews that would later expedite the Italian Holocaust. Enforcement of the race laws became the responsibility of newly formed special bodies to manage "Jewish affairs", most important of which was the *Direzione Generale per la Demografia e Razza* (Head Office for Demographics and Race), the *Demorazza*, that was given responsibility for investigating the "real" race of Italian citizens (Garofalo, 2013).

Inspired by the Duce's slogan, "discriminating, not persecuting" (Coen, 1988; De Felice, 1993), after the Royal Decree in November 1938 and subsequent Race Laws, the Fascist regime began a process that would lead to the progressive economic, social and political exclusion of the Jewish community in Italy and later their reduction to bare life in the concentration camps when taken over by the Germans. This, however, did not apply initially to all Jews. Unlike the Nazis, the Fascists allowed Jews who had fought for Italy in World War I or had supported the Fascist Party and its struggle to power to be legally designated as "the discriminated". This entitled them to escape the full impact of the Race Laws, including protection of their property from confiscation. When Italy went to war on 10 June 1940, the Fascist government began to intern in newly created concentration camps for foreign Jews and the "non-discriminated" Italian Jews who did not meet the conditions for protection from arrest. Management of the camps was given to the Ministry of the Interior (Division for General and Confidential Affairs), which then delegated responsibility to the next level of government, the Prefectures. Related financial matters were handled by the Central Accounts Department of the Ministry. During the final phase of the Fascist persecution of Italian Jews, in June 1943, the Fascist government decided to round up adult Jews to work in internment and labour camps, that now included those previously recognised as the "discriminated" and now the excluded (Zuccotti, 1987; De Felice, 1993; Zimmerman, 2005).

After the surrender of Italy in September 1943 the Germans quickly invaded Italy from the north and occupied it as far south as Rome (De Felice, 1997; Kogan, 2016). In the German occupied zone on 27 September, a state of exception was created when a new puppet State was established, the *Repubblica Sociale Italiana* (RSI), based in Salò, near Verona, with Mussolini as its token leader (Quartermaine, 2000). On 14 November, the congress of the RSI formally passed its Constitution (*Carta di Verona*), in which Article 7 stated that "Members of the Jewish race are foreigners. In this war, they are enemy citizens". Therefore, the Constitution of the RSI overtly defined itself as anti-Semitic (Calimani, 2015). The Constitution, in effect, was the means to declare a state of exception to allow suspension of the normal juridical order and, thereby, to legalise the removal of all rights for Italian Jews, although not yet their reduction to *homo sacer.*

In the German occupied zone, Jewish families were collected in the towns with larger Jewish communities by regular German and Italian troops, as well as by Fascist gangs led by Italian collaborators (Caracciolo et al., 1995; Calimani, 2015). The most infamous example occurred when 1,259 Jews were rounded up in the Roman *ghetto* on 16 October 1943 by the SS led by Colonel Kappler, of which 1,030 were soon after sent to Auschwitz and killed upon arrival. Himmler had previously written to Kappler calling for "a 'final solution' to the Jewish problem in Rome" (Michaelis, 1978, p. 352). Kappler was told by his superior that it was "the immediate and thorough eradication of the Jews in Italy which is the special interest of the present internal political situation" (quoted in Friedlander, 2007, p. 569). Thus, confirming their status now as *homo sacer,* all Jews were to be sent for "liquidation" (Michaelis, 1978, p. 352). On 16 December 1943, the Cabinet of the RSI confirmed that the transportation of Jews from the Italian concentration camps to the extermination camps had begun as the Germans extended to Italy the Final Solution to the "Jewish problem" (De Felice, 1993; Sarfatti, 2007; Picciotto, 2008). The Cabinet, therefore, now knew the ultimate fate of those who would be taken away from the camps. The Fascist authorities became "de facto accomplices in an unforgiveable way" in the extermination of thousands of Jews (De Felice, 2001, p. 444). The number of Italian Jews deported to the German extermination camps, mainly from the Fossoli concentration camp to Auschwitz, has been estimated to be 6,007, of whom 5,969 were killed, while another 322 died in Italy during detention or while trying to escape (De Felice, 1993, p. 465).

Fossoli concentration camp

Organisation and financial management

Fossoli concentration camp, located at the heart of the Po Valley in northern Italy, was opened by the Royal Italian Army in May 1942 as a place for the detention of British, Australian, and New Zealand prisoners from the North African battles (Baccino, 1961; Ori, 2007). When Italy surrendered in September 1943, and Germany occupied northern and central Italy, the Fossoli concentration camp then went through two different administrative episodes (Biondi et al., 1990). During the first period, from 5 December 1943 to 15 March 1944, the camp was run solely by the RSI through the *questura*, the Police Headquarters of Modena, with both Italian Jews and political opponents imprisoned at this time (Gasparotto, 2007). In the second period, between 15 March and 2 August 1944, the main focus of subsequent discussion, a section of the camp, known as "the new camp", *Campo Nuovo*, became a *Polizei und Durchgangslager*, a police and transit camp controlled by the Germans. Under Italian law, consistent with Agamben's concept of state of exception, the very existence of the Fossoli concentration camp was an arrangement that was at the same time created by the law but was outside the normal law. Italian Jews stayed at *Campo Nuovo* for a short time, rarely more than a few weeks, before they were sent by the SS to the extermination camps at Mauthausen, Dachau, Buchenwald, Flossenburg or Ravensbrück, but mostly Auschwitz-Birkenau. A second area of the Fossoli concentration camp known as "the old camp", *Campo Vecchio*, continued to be the responsibility of the RSI and held mainly non-Jewish Italian civilians (Gibertoni and Melodi, 1996). Italian Jews who survived the war and had been imprisoned in the Fossoli concentration camp when under the control of the Italians have consistently affirmed that their Italian guards and those who were responsible for managing the camp did not treat them harshly (Stille, 1991, p. 293). De Felice (2001, p. 444), confirming the experience of Elizabeth Szego who had been imprisoned at Fossoli (Herr, 2014, p. 160), concludes that the RSI "was without doubt more humane".

Operation of the Fossoli concentration camp required a sophisticated organisation of functions and logistics and highly attenuated, detailed, timely information. During the time that the Fossoli camp was under the control of firstly the RSI, the arrival of prisoners at the Fossoli concentration camp was managed with a detailed "filing" procedure that was specified by the Carpi police superintendent (Archivo del Comune di Carpi (ASCC), 1944, 161835). To ensure a meticulous round up of Jews using the information provided by the census of 1938 a file had to be prepared for every prisoner by recording all necessary details to identify an individual, including their name and address. The purpose was to ensure that each Italian Jew disclosed by the census had been removed (ASCC, 1944, 162354). After the camp came under German control from March 1944, the German forces working in the

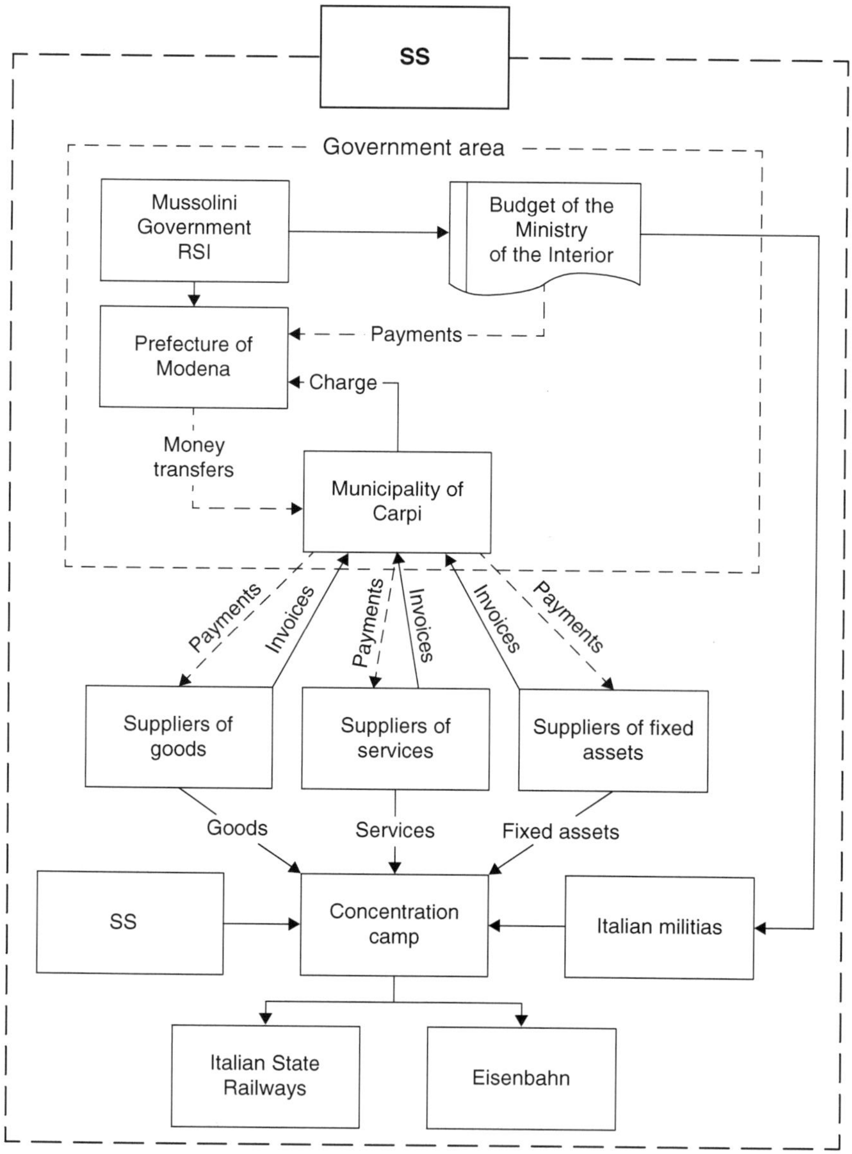

Figure 9.1 Financial relationships in the German-Italian Fascist network of institutions and organisations for the Fossoli concentration camp.

camp were, as shown in Figure 9.1, but one part, the more visible, involved in a very complex machinery of attempted annihilation.

Implementing what were to become the Italian contributions to the Final Solution would not have been possible without a wide, well-ordered involvement of the members of many Italian organisations, both public and private, who, from their desks, decided the fate of Jewish deportees even if they did not know the nature of the destination of those taken (Capogreco, 2004). After the German occupation, the financial relationships necessary for the operation of the Fossoli concentration camp extended to the central and local authorities of the RSI, in particular the Municipality of Carpi, and to the German Commander in Italy, as shown in Figure 9.1. Supreme authority over the camp was then exercised by the German military authorities, with the SS responsible for all matters related to camp security and escorting the trains to the extermination camps (Levis Sullam, 2015). The Municipality of Carpi was responsible for the overall daily administration of the camp while the Prefect of Modena was in charge of issuing policies and giving formal authorisations for the camp's operations as approved by the Germans (Picciotto, 2002).

The diverse nature and extent of the relationships between the many individuals and organisations involved in the operations of the Fossoli concentration camp made it difficult, especially under the increasing distress of war, to coordinate and manage the camp (Picciotto, 2002). In these circumstances, the camp budget and related accounting reports were especially important in providing the means to identify and control the organisations necessary for the camp to operate effectively and to monitor the conduct of the people involved. The first junction in the network of organisations responsible for the Fossoli camp budget, as seen in Figure 9.1, was Mussolini and the government of the RSI. It was at this level that financial resources were allocated to the RSI's Ministry of the Interior's budget to build, maintain, and operate all the concentration camps based in the RSI from which the Jewish prisoners would be transported later to the extermination camps (Herr, 2017). From the Ministry of the Interior's budget, the Prefecture of Modena was reimbursed for payments to the Municipality of Carpi. Evidence of these transactions had to be sent by the Municipality to the Prefecture of Modena to obtain reimbursement (see, for example, ASCC, 1944, 162004, 161753). The budget of the Ministry of the Interior thereby provided the means by which the RSI enforced its decisions about the Fossoli concentration camp and gave it the power to strictly monitor local authorities.

The responsibility of the Ministry of the Interior for the concentration camps in German occupied parts of Italy was clearly evident in the Ministry's budget. Ruling no. 167, dated 29 April 1944, one of many at the time (Archivo Centrale dello Stato (ACS), 2002, p. 577), referred to additions to the budgets of some Ministries for the fiscal year 1943–1944 for unforeseen circumstances due to the state of war called "Expenses for the installation and operation of concentration camps". On this occasion, these expenses required an additional 20,000,000 lire (RSI, 1944, p. 574) to be added to the Ministry of the Interior's budget. The ruling that approved payment was signed into law by the Minister of Finance, Pellegrini, and by the Minister of Justice, Pisenti. In the minutes of the session when payment was agreed there are no comments from those in attendance and no questions about the concentration camps, even though the budget of the RSI made it clear that these were expenses being incurred for the detention and transportation of the Jews in the concentration camps, most importantly Fossoli (ACS, 2002, pp. 577–578). Also, the conversion of the Fossoli camp into a transit point through which a large number of Jews now passed did not attract any explicit comments. With the camp now under German control, the Jews quickly descended to the condition of bare life with the quality of *homo sacer*: they had ceased to exist as individuals with the right to life.

The impact on the Municipality of Carpi of the large volume of transactions necessary to maintain the Fossoli camp is most obvious in its budgets, such as the budget dated 10 March 1944, shown in Table 9.1, for part of the period during which the Fossoli concentration camp was managed by them (Resolution of the *Podestà* No. 54, 10 March 1944). Most purchases of goods and services for both *Campo Vecchio,* under the control of the RSI, and later the SS controlled *Campo Nuovo,* were through the Municipality of Carpi. Thus, the central administration office of the Municipality of Carpi had specific authority for accounting for both sections of the camp (ASCC, 1944, 114835).

To fulfil its responsibilities with the concentration camp, the Municipality of Carpi used mainly local contractors for the maintenance of the camp and the provision of food and other supplies (Baccino, 1961). Herr (2014, p. 124) concludes that by "executing German orders, Italian officials helped transform Fossoli into a key juncture in the annihilation assembly line". These contributions from local businesses and the Municipality of Carpi, even on a small scale, "structured the normalisation of genocide" (Herr, 2014, p. 124) by helping to make possible the eventual killing of each Italian Jew when taken from the Fossoli concentration camp to the extermination camps. As an example, Figure 9.2 shows an invoice of Autolinee Cav. P. Valenti &

Table 9.1 The budget of the Municipality of Carpi (10 March 1944)

Description	*Amount (lire)*
Ordinary revenues	5,320,227.18
Extra-ordinary revenues	2,924,925.00
Total revenues	**8,245,152.18**
Special accounts	1,965,078.10
Total	**10,210,230.28**
Ordinary mandatory expenses	5,713,268.73
Extra-ordinary mandatory expenses	1,812,906.00
Ordinary optional expenses	232,378.00
Total expenses	**7,788,352.73**
Investments	456,799.45
Special accounts	1,965,078.10
Total	**10,210,230.28**

Source: ASCC (1944, 163256, pp. 95–99).

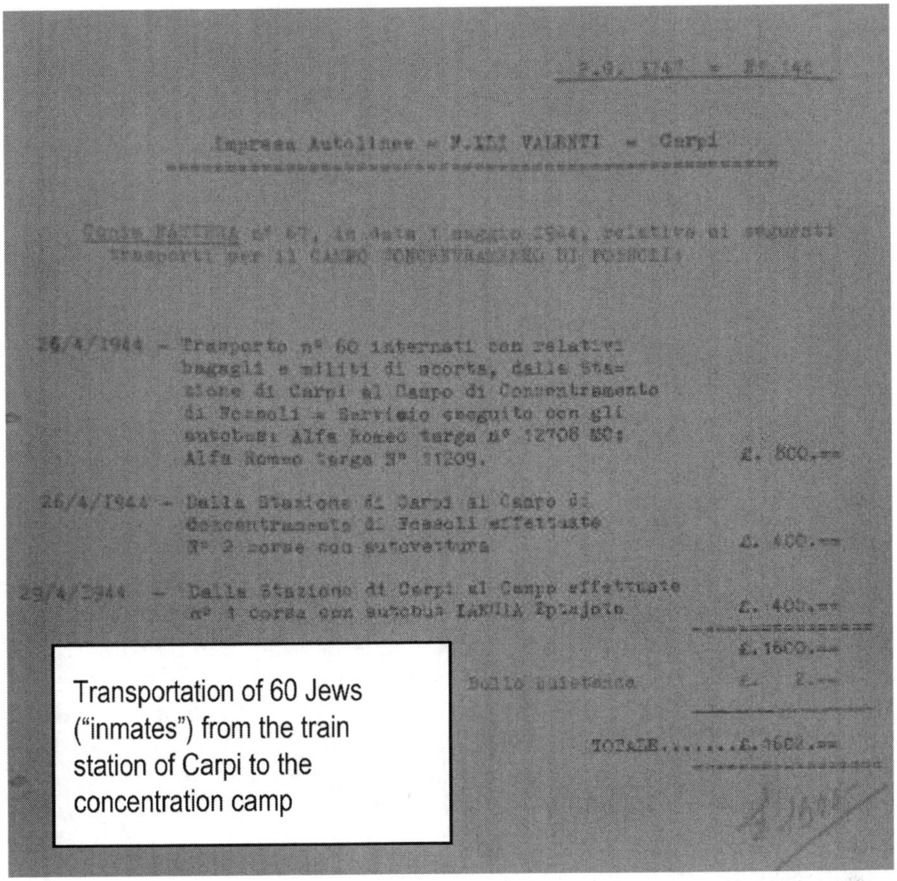
Impresa Autolinee = F.LLI VALENTI = Carpi

Copia FATTURA n° 67, in data 1 maggio 1944, relative ai seguenti trasporti per il CAMPO CONCENTRAMENTO DI FOSSOLI:

26/4/1944	Trasporto n° 60 internati con relativi bagagli e militi di scorta, dalla Stazione di Carpi al Campo di Concentramento di Fossoli = Servizio eseguito con gli autobus: Alfa Romeo targa n° 12706 MO: Alfa Romeo targa N° 11209.	£. 800.==
26/4/1944	Dalla Stazione di Carpi al Campo di Concentramento di Fossoli effettuate N° 2 corse con autovettura	£. 400.==
29/4/1944	Dalla Stazione di Carpi al Campo effettuate n° 1 corsa con autobus LANCIA Eptajota	£. 400.==
		£. 1600.==
	Bollo quietanza	£. 2.==
	TOTALE......	£. 1602.==

Figure 9.2 Invoice for the transportation of Jews to Fossoli concentration camp. ASCC (1944, 155033). Reproduced with permission of the Archive of the Municipality of Carpi.

Fratelli (Valenti Bros Bus Company), in which the service that they are providing, transporting the Jews the 6 km from Carpi to the Fossoli concentration camp, is clearly named "Jews Transport Service". In addition to the cost of the service, the table in the invoice lists the number of Jews carried (ASCC, 1944, 155033, 154713). In the invoices, they are never referred to as Jews but, instead, more cryptically, as "*internati*", inmates.

The object of the work of the firms contracted by the Municipality of Carpi, the internment of Italian Jews, was irrelevant to them. They were merely engaged in a commercial transaction. The results of the work of those who carried out their responsibilities in connection with the Fossoli concentration camp indicate commitment with no apparent moral concerns for the incarceration of Italian Jews. According to Zuccotti (1987, p. 174), while some high level Italian bureaucrats "may not have been certain" about what was to happen to the deportees once they left Fossoli, now an "ante-chamber of death", "they did not know because they did not want to know". However, Herr (2014, p. 107) concludes that by March 1944, Carpi officials would have known "how Fossoli supported the Reich's annihilation machine". Indeed, the most senior political and administrative authorities of the RSI, most especially Mussolini and Buffarini-Guidi, who was the Minister of the Interior, were very much aware of the results of their betrayal of Italian Jews (Fargion, 1989, p. 285).

Accounting for bare life

Managing the complex dealings between the many organisations, both public and private, that were involved in the operations of the Fossoli concentration camp in the Municipality of Carpi required the RSI to create a highly developed set of accounting mechanisms and reporting structures. Unlike the Carpi municipal budget and related reports sent to Modena, the detailed accounts of the Fossoli concentration camp were not accessible to the wider public. Thus, any matters related to the camp could be given specifically named accounts and precise details provided. When the camp was still controlled by the Italians, the costs for the Jewish prisoners included, as shown in Table 9.2, basic bedding, a good array of food types that included non-essentials such as milk and coffee, some heating materials and token healthcare (ASCC, 1944, 121205). The cost of the Italian security staff for *Campo Vecchio*, that included the Republican Police, *Carabinieri*, soldiers, and Blackshirts, came directly from the budget of the Ministry of the Interior and the War Ministry, as allocated by the government of RSI (1944).

Despite the purpose of the costs incurred, the same accounting practices used in the normal operations of the Municipality of Carpi were adopted for

Table 9.2 Cost categories in the accounting system of Fossoli concentration camp when under Italian control

Categories of costs	*Types of expenditure*
Tools costs	Napkins, cutlery, glasses, cups, plates, saucepans
Fuel costs	Coal, electricity, firewood, methane tanks
Maintenance work	Locks, handles, brickwork, nails, plates, shovels, hoes, scythes, hammers, screwdrivers, pliers, saws, paint
Food costs	Oil, pasta, rice, flour, cheese, legumes, potatoes, other vegetables, preserves of tomatoes, butter, milk, bread, sugar, salt, coffee, bacon, meat, bran
Drugs costs	Drugs
Stationery costs	Paper knives, rubbers, ink, black pencils, block notes, paper
Spare parts	Fuel, fuel tank, copper pipes, labour
Furnishings	Glass, light bulbs, beds, pillows, stools, blankets, tables
Transport costs	Jewish transport service
Medical service costs	Medical service

Source: ASCC (1944, 153756, 153833, 153923, 154257, 154348, 163433).

the Fossoli concentration camp. The one prominent exception was the way in which the financial details of the Fossoli concentration camp were kept apart from other functions of the municipality, as clearly suggested by its 10 March 1944 budget in which the camp was also not specifically identified (ASCC, 1944, 163256, pp. 95–99). Instead, as shown in the Municipality of Carpi budget for 10 March 1944, provided previously in Table 9.1, a "Special Accounts" entry in both the revenues and expenses sections of the Carpi budget, amounting to 1,965,078.10 lire, related to transactions for the Fossoli concentration camp. The individual accounts that constituted the Special Accounts of the Municipality of Carpi for transactions involving the Fossoli concentration camp included the calculation of a cost figure known as "Cost for the upkeep of the Jews" (ASCC, 1944, 121205, 122059). The description of the expenditure for the camp as Special Accounts, that would have disguised the purpose of the expenditure to anyone not immediately responsible for the preparation of the budget, confirmed that members of the Carpi Municipal Government and the bureaucrats who implemented its decisions were aware that identifying the purpose of these expenditures to the local community by giving the concentration camp a clear presence in the accounting reports might not be well received. The position of many Carpi citizens was clearly evident by the way in which they would line the streets to give food and other essential items to the Jewish prisoners as they were herded through the town to be taken by train to Verona (Ori, 2007).

A municipal clerk appointed as the accountant for the camp was fully employed with duties at the camp. Throughout the reports and records of the camp, the clerk was specifically referred to as "*economo del campo*" (the accountant of the concentration camp). He had to report directly to the *Podestà* of Carpi, Tranquillo Federici Zuccolini, the executive who acted on behalf of the RSI government at the local level, thus confirming the importance and sensitive nature of his responsibilities. The *economo del campo* contributed significantly to facilitating the operations conducted at the Fossoli concentration camp, both when it was controlled by the Italians and the Germans. He signed all expense reports, managed supplier relationships, and drew up the food budgets (ASCC, 1944, 114835, 145532, 145547). Most of the records passing across the accountant's desk were clearly marked as "*Campo di concentramento degli ebrei*" (Jews' concentration camp) (see, for example, ASCC, 1944, 122939).

The amoral, bureaucratically benign manner in which the *economo del campo* carried out their duties characterised the way in which the Germans were able to extend to Italy their lethal anti-Semitic racial priorities. The subject of the calculations and other information provided by the numerous accounting reports, the condemned Jews, was readily accommodated by the prosaic discourse of accounting. This was especially obvious in the expenses account book, where every page of the book was marked at the top as "*Rendiconto spese del campo di concentramento di Fossoli*" (Expenses report for the Fossoli concentration camp) (ASCC, 1944, 123723). From the details

Table 9.3 Male daily food plan of Fossoli concentration camp, early 1944

Food	*Weight*
Bread	225 g
Pasta	66 g
Vegetables	100 g
Fats	5 g
Sugar	17 g
Salt	3 g
Tomato	3 g
Meat	10.5 g

Source: ASCC (1944, 145547).

contained in the expense accounts, total expense reports were prepared and transmitted to the Prefecture of Modena, which could, if they wished, demand to see the details of the spending for which reimbursement was sought (ASCC, 1944, 121632). Reimbursement of expenses depended on the Carpi administrators demonstrating through the accounts that expenditures were strictly controlled and only for the most basic essentials, primarily food rations, appropriate for the *excluded*. Therefore, Carpi officials would have been aware of the function of the Fossoli concentration camp, including when it became a transit camp with the Germans (Herr, 2014, p. 182).

Accounting practices as a biopolitical tool also provided a less obvious means to penetrate and give visibility to all aspects of the lives of Jewish internees, most especially their diet, thereby to discipline them. The amount and type of these rations were recorded in a daily food plan for every adult Jewish prisoner at the camp, an example of which is shown in Table 9.3 for males in early 1944 while the camp was still substantially under Italian control. The daily food consumption plan mentioned even the smallest details of how much salt and sugar had to be added to each type of food.

After the Italians relinquished control of the Fossoli camp, non-essential components of the diet, such as sugar, salt, butter, and coffee, were no longer provided. Thus, as shown in Table 9.4, the diet allowed to Jewish prisoners by the Germans became just enough to sustain life during the prisoners' brief

Table 9.4 Food expenses (lire)

Date	*Vegetables*	*Sugar*	*Salt*	*Coffee*	*Milk*	*Cheese and butter*	*Bread*	*Pasta and rice*
From 5th December 1943 to 15th March 1944	210.00	589.30	83.00	816.50	6,591.20	11,877.45	18,379.59	11,714.50
From 16th March 1944 to 2nd August 1944	10,254.00	0.00	0.00	0.00	63,866.60	8,260.00	118,894.56	19,816.00

Source: ASCC (1944, 114835, 114845, 114851, 114858, 114927, 114942, 114953, 115008, 115359, 151816, 152015, 152102, 152858, 154348).

stay at the camp, consistent with them being condemned to the position of bare life as *homo sacer*. The SS, who knew the ultimate fate of the Jews in the camp, wanted to avoid any potential complications with the Italians that a large number of deaths at the camp might provoke. Thus, although the Jews might be severely emaciated when leaving the Fossoli concentration camp they mostly would not die in the camp but instead were to die "scientifically" at the extermination camps. Table 9.4 also shows how after the Fossoli concentration camp became a transit camp expenditures on basic food requirements underwent a very considerable increase. This reflected a sharp rise in the number of Jews now required to be collected in the camp to ensure that each train that left for the extermination camps would be fully loaded.

The manner in which conditions in the camp deteriorated immediately after the Germans took control and that showed that the Jews had now become bare life was clearly evident when, as shown in the accounts in Table 9.5, medical services and sanitary products were no longer provided.

The clear identification of the purpose of the expenditures and their treatment by the *economo del campo* as merely financial transactions to be thoroughly documented betrayed their immoral consequences. However, the detailed records of the ever rising number of Jews arriving at the camp and leaving soon after would have meant that the *economo del campo*, possibly more than any other Italian bureaucrat who was also involved, would have been fully aware of the nature of the facility as a transit camp; a place where Jews would soon leave on German trains. The *economo del campo*, working in close contact with the *Podestà*, would also have known the destination of these trains, if not exactly what happened to the Jews after they arrived at their destination, the extermination camps. This was also the experience of many other Italian officials at the Fossoli concentration camp.

The progression of the Jews to a state of bare life when they came under the control of the Germans became especially obvious in the accounts submitted by the Carpi municipality to the Prefecture of Modena at the time that the prisoners were transported by the Germans to the extermination camps. Previously, when the Fossoli camp was under Italian control Jewish inmates still had a personal identity, even though when they arrived at the Fossoli concentration camp they were given a number. This was clearly in evidence with the funerals still allowed for those who died before the Germans took full control of the Fossoli concentration camp and in the accounts provided

Table 9.5 Medical and sanitary needs (lire)

Date	*Medicine*	*Soap and cleaning*
From 5 December 1943 to 15 March 1944	1,181.20	6,678.00
From 16 March 1944 to 2 August 1944	0.00	0.00
Total	**1,181.20**	**6,678.00**

Source: ASCC (1944, 114835, 114845, 114851, 114858, 114927, 114942, 114953, 115008, 115359, 151816, 152015, 152102, 152858, 154348).

for funeral expenses where those who died were identified by their name (ASCC 1944, 114835, 114845, 114851). The small number of funerals also confirms that Jewish existence had not yet approached that of bare life. When the condemned Jews were leaving the Fossoli concentration camp with the Germans their names and personal details were used for the last time (ASCC, 1944, 162601) to ensure that each prisoner would be precisely accounted for, that none would escape and that the Final Solution would be complete. Should any Jewish prisoner not appear for transportation the Germans would select a number of others who would be immediately executed.

When they were later deported to the death camps, the Jewish prisoners were transported by train from Carpi to Modena and then from Modena railway station to the Polish death camps by the German railways, the *Eisenbahn* (Herr, 2014). During the period under which the Fossoli concentration camp was under SS control, eight trains crammed with prisoners left Fossoli, the last on 1 August 1944. Primo Levi was taken to Auschwitz on the second train. At the time of departure from the Fossoli concentration camp, the number that each prisoner had been given when arriving at the camp was tattooed on their arms. They no longer existed as human beings with a right to life, they had become *homo sacer*. This was reinforced with the entries in a special "Transport Account Book" that was kept at the Fossoli concentration camp to monitor the people coming to the camp from the Italian regions that were still under Nazi-Fascist control and then taken from Fossoli to Carpi train station and loaded on the freight trains bound mostly for the Auschwitz extermination camp. The "Transport Account Book", such as that provided in Figure 9.3, showed the distance that had to be covered, the agreed fare and the total cost (ASCC, 1944, 144535). The number of Jews to be transported was then converted into kilos, thereby recognising very explicitly their reduction to bare life. They were no longer people but quantifiable objects, the only feature of which that was recognised like any other object transported by train was their weight. This confirmed that the identity that those who were being transported now had was something that had to be moved from one place to another.

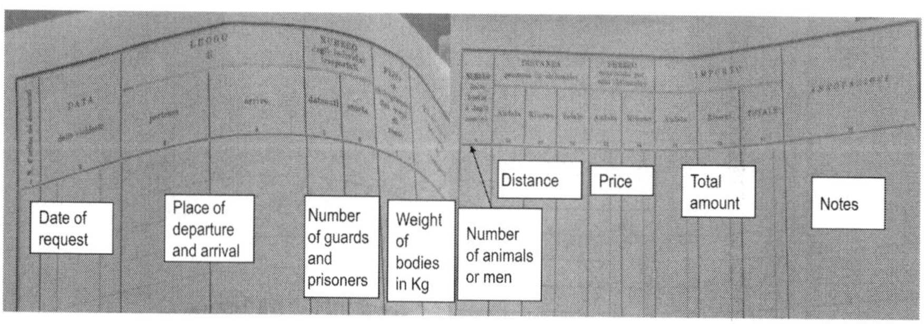

Figure 9.3 Accounting for transportation. ASCC (1944, 144535). Reproduced with permission of the Archive of the Municipality of Carpi.

The only presence that those being transported had as living beings was when the "Transport Account Book" was required to show the total number of "animals and men" carried. People and animals that travelled in the same space were equated and shown as one entry, thus confirming that the process of dehumanisation as the prelude to extermination was the object of bureaucratic procedures (Bauman, 1989). This was immediately obvious with the conditions on the trains that would take them to the extermination camps. For the five days journey to the extermination camps in Poland, a train consisted of ten cars, each crammed with at least 60 people, with nothing to eat or drink and one bucket in which everyone was to relieve themselves (Levi, 1996, p. 22; Levi, 1959; Picciotto, 2010). In the rail car in which Primo Levi was placed there were two mothers with children who "groaned night and day, begging for water" (Levi, 1996, p. 18). Upon his arrival at Auschwitz, Levi realised that it was "not possible to sink lower than this ... Nothing belongs to us anymore; they have taken away our clothes, our shoes, even our hair ... They will even take away our name ... (We become) a man whose life or death can be lightly decided with no sense of human affinity ..." (Levi, 1996, p. 27). As *homo sacer* now, they had descended to the ultimate fate that accounting practices had helped to ensure.

Conclusion

The roles performed by accounting practices in the management of the Fossoli concentration camp, most especially when under German control, confirm their fatal contributions to the abhorrent intent and scale of the Holocaust. In the Italian state of exception, Jews became merely an entry in a file, they were no longer sentient human beings with legal rights and protections. The social and political exclusion of Italian Jews was complete when, in the various accounting reports, they were made invisible as human beings in the concentration camps under German control by substituting their human, political identity with measurable attributes such as the number of "objects" to be transported on the trains to the extermination camps. They had become merely *home sacer* with a bare life. This allowed the Fossoli concentration camp to operate as an ante-chamber of death for Italian Jews. This consequence of accounting practices confirms Foucault's warning that in a biopolitical regime, "power is tolerable only on condition that it mask a substantial part of itself. Its success is proportional to its ability to hide its own mechanisms.... (Secrecy) is indispensable to its operation" (Foucault, 1990, p. 86). Accounting practices used in the management of the Fossoli concentration camp were very effective in masking the ultimate genocidal intent of the use of the information produced.

In the Fossoli concentration camp prior to the arrival of the Germans, the information provided by accounting practices was primarily used as a mechanism of financial accountability. To ensure that the Municipality of Carpi would receive payment from the Prefecture, there needed to be meticulous recording of all transactions and the reasons for the transactions. The accounting records of both the Prefecture and the Municipality of Carpi, that expressly mentioned internment and transportation from the Fossoli camp, would have made obvious to all those who had responsibilities for the camp how the Jews were being treated, if not the ultimate consequences of the Race Laws when Jews were eventually taken from Fossoli to the extermination camps. The extensive accounting records and the network of bureaucratic bodies and suppliers in Italy that revolved around the Fossoli concentration camp also confirm the importance of an efficient, cooperative bureaucracy in the internment and deportation of the Jews to the extermination camps.

In stark contrast to when the Fossoli concentration camp was under Italian control and they provided a wide range of products and services, such as medical services, habitable accommodation, and heating, the only expenditures that were permitted by the Germans were for transporting the Jews to their deaths and to provide just enough food to sustain life to allow this to occur. In this process, accounting practices were imbued with an ethical and moral significance derived from racial beliefs that belied their apparent banality (Funnell, 1998, p. 436). Accounting practices in the service of biopolitical imperatives that condemned Jews provided an important means to isolate and deprive those imprisoned of any subjective feature that would identify them as human. In particular, "accounting as an instrument of the bureaucracy provided the 'centres of calculation' with new quantitative visibilities" (Miller, 1990, p. 318) that were able to supplant the qualitative dimensions of the Jews as individuals by commodifying and dehumanising them as *homo sacer* with bare life, thereby, for all intents, making them invisible as people (Funnell, 1998, p. 439).

During times of biopolitical disempowerment in a state of exception, certain forms of knowledge are privileged over others to ensure total control without, if necessary, previously enacted legal requirements. Foucault (1991, p. 91) also reminds us that with biopower, "there is no power relation without the correlative constitution of a field of knowledge". The effectiveness of biopower, the ability to penetrate all aspects of human interactions and intentions for the purpose of exercising control, is dependent on the "growing inclusion of man's natural life in the mechanisms and calculations of power" (Agamben, 1998, p. 120). It brought life "into the realm of explicit calculations and made knowledge-power an agent in the transformation of human life" (Foucault, 1990, p. 143). In the operation of the Fossoli concentration camp, most especially when under German control, accounting practices that involved the collection of financial and non-financial information allowed visibility to be given to particular actions and to deny a presence to others, most notably the number of deaths, thereby making the unaccounted effectively invisible. The invisible disciplinary power of accounting as a technology of surveillance that was experienced everywhere in the concentration camps was emphasised by functioning "permanently and largely in silence" (Foucault, 1991, p. 177).

The deceptive abilities of accounting that have allowed genocidal practices to occur and to possibly go undetected have prompted Stokes and Gabriel (2010, p. 461) to remind researchers and others of the need to "unlock the organisational and managerial processes that make it possible". This also confirmed the conclusions of Alawattage et al. (2019, p. 53) that to be effective biopolitics will need to use disciplinary technologies. The reports and details provided by accounting for the management of the Fossoli concentration camp were forms of knowledge that were given a privileged place that also denied a presence to other forms of knowledge, in particular details that would have allowed each individual to be specifically identified. Thus, describing expenditures in the budget of the Municipality of Carpi as "Special Accounts" was in effect a *violent act*, an unchallenged and unchallengeable attack on Italian Jews whereby other knowledge of their identity was supplanted with dehumanised numerical representations that under the Germans had fatal intentions.

Through the process of "typification", which was essential to the perpetration of the Nazi's Final Solution, when the Fossoli concentration camp was under German control accounting practices allowed Italian Jews eventually to become known only with "categorical attributes, not as passionate, feeling individuals" with a right to life (Schultz, quoted in McPhail, 1999, p. 858). Jewish prisoners sent to the extermination camps to be killed became mere numbers, data to be processed (Bauman, 1989). Possessing now only bare life, they became people who were "not known" but "merely known of", a mere number that was part of a tally of "objects" on the train and then in the extermination camps. This made it possible for those involved in this process to "feel little or no moral obligation towards them" as they were crammed onto railway cars without even the most basic amenities (McPhail, 1999, pp. 858–859). The brutality of this was very obvious at the time that Primo Levi was being transported from Fossoli to Auschwitz when as the inmates were being loaded by a German officer onto buses to be taken to the train station at Carpi he "held the roll-call. At the end the officer asked '*Wieviel Stuck*? (How many pieces?)'. The corporal saluted smartly and replied that there were six hundred and fifty 'pieces'" (Levi, 1996, p. 16). When they arrived at the railway the men, women, and children were crammed into wagons, "pressed together without pity, like cheap merchandise, for a journey towards nothingness, a journey down there, towards the bottom" (Levi, 1996, p. 17).

The way in which accounting practices can be used to help construct legitimacy for the creation of a state of exception with the suspension of the normal laws and the imposition of penetrating controls over the population, allows the possibility that this control by the state will become no longer the exception but the norm. The legitimacy that accounting practices help to create, both the need for the declaration of a state of exception and the apparent success of the policies implemented, provide the potential for the state of exception to become the accepted normal response, indeed the expected response, to alleged crises that are portrayed as threatening a state. Thus, subsequently, the propagation of similar information from these now trusted sources allows the state of exception to assume almost seamlessly the status of the norm; the norm "becomes indistinguishable from the exception" (Agamben, 1998, p. 170). Technologies "for the calculation and measurement of death" are "prefabricated" to produce favourable calculations and measurements to communicate an impression of successful responses by governments that "justifies or even normalizes exceptional measures and procedures" (Yu, 2021, p. 2).

This chapter is based on the paper by Warwick Funnell, Valerio Antonelli, Michele Bigoni, Emanuela Mattia Cafaro, and Raffaele D'Alessio titled "Accounting for Jewish 'Bare Life' in the Fossoli Concentration Camp, 1943–44" that originally appeared in Critical Perspectives on Accounting in 2022, article number 102323. The authors would like to thank the publisher, Elsevier, for permission to use this material.

References

Primary Sources

Gazzetta Ufficiale del Regno d'Italia – Gazzetta Ufficiale d'Italia

RdI (1938a), RD-L 5 settembre 1938, n. 1390. Provvedimenti per la difesa della razza nella scuola fascista, Gazzetta Ufficiale del Regno d'Italia n. 209, 13 settembre 1938.

RdI (1938b), RD-L 5 settembre 1938, n. 1539. Istituzione, presso il Ministero dell'Interno, del Consiglio superiore per la demografia e la razza, Gazzetta Ufficiale del Regno d'Italia n. 231, 8 ottobre 1938.

RdI (1938c), RD-L 17 novembre 1938, n. 1728. Provvedimenti per la difesa della razza italiana, Gazzetta Ufficiale del Regno d'Italia n. 264, 19 novembre 1938.

RdI (1938d), RD-L 15 novembre 1938, n. 1779. Integrazione e coordinamento in unico testo delle norme già emanate per la difesa della razza nella Scuola italiana, Gazzetta Ufficiale del Regno d'Italia n. 272, 29 novembre 1938.

RdI (1938e), RD 21 novembre 1938, n. 2154. Modificazioni allo statuto del Partito Nazionale Fascista, Gazzetta Ufficiale del Regno d'Italia n. 36, 13 febbraio 1939.

RdI (1938f), RD-L 22 dicembre 1938, n. 2111. Disposizioni relative al collocamento in congedo assoluto ed al trattamento di quiescenza del personale militare delle Forze armate dello Stato di razza ebraica, Gazzetta Ufficiale del Regno d'Italia n. 30, 6 febbraio 1939.

RdI (1939a), L 29 giugno 1939, n. 1054. Disciplina dell'esercizio delle professioni da parte dei cittadini di razza ebraica, Gazzetta Ufficiale del Regno d'Italia n. 179, 2 agosto 1939.

RdI (1939b), L 13 luglio 1939, n. 1055. Disposizioni in materia testamentaria nonché sulla disciplina dei cognomi, nei confronti degli appartenenti alla razza ebraica, Gazzetta Ufficiale del Regno d'Italia n. 179, 2 agosto 1939.

RdI (1940a), L 28 settembre 1940, n. 1403. Abrogazione del contributo statale a favore degli asili infantili israelitici contemplati dalla legge 30 luglio 1896, n. 343, Gazzetta Ufficiale del Regno d'Italia n. 245, 18 ottobre 1940.

RdI (1940b), L 23 settembre 1940, n. 1459. Integrazioni alla legge 13 luglio 1939-XVII, n. 1055, contenente disposizioni in materia testamentaria, nonché sulla disciplina dei cognomi, nei confronti degli appartenenti alla razza ebraica, Gazzetta Ufficiale del Regno d'Italia n. 256, 31 ottobre 1940.

RSI (1944), Decreto ministeriale 29 Aprile 1944-XXII, n. 167. Maggiori assegnazioni agli stati di previsione della spesa di taluni Ministeri per l'esercizio finanziario 1943–1944 per occorrenze straordinarie dipendenti dallo stato di guerra (pp. 573–575). Roma: Gazzetta Ufficiale d'Italia, 4 maggio 1944.

Archivio Centrale dello Stato – Piazzale degli Archivi 27, Roma

ACS (2002), Verbali del Consiglio dei Ministri della Repubblica Sociale Italiana, settembre 1943 – aprile 1945. I, Roma, Ministero per i Beni e le Attività Culturali.

Archivio del Comune di Carpi – Fondo miscellanea Fossoli – Palazzo del Pio – Piazzale Re Astolfo, 1 – Carpi (MO)

ASCC (1944) 114835. Liquidazione note del campo di concentramento di Fossoli.

ASCC (1944) 114845. Liquidazione note del campo di concentramento di Fossoli.

ASCC (1944) 114851. Liquidazione note del campo di concentramento di Fossoli.

ASCC (1944) 114858. Liquidazione note del campo di concentramento di Fossoli.

ASCC (1944) 114927. Liquidazione note del campo di concentramento di Fossoli.

ASCC (1944) 114942. Liquidazione note del campo di concentramento di Fossoli.

ASCC (1944) 114953. Liquidazione note del campo di concentramento di Fossoli.

ASCC (1944) 115008. Liquidazione note del campo di concentramento di Fossoli.

ASCC (1944) 115359. Elenco delle fatture che si trasmettono al Sig. Economo del campo di concentramento Ebrei di Fossoli per il visto di controllo e il nulla osta al pagamento.

ASCC (1944) 121205. Spesa mantenimento Ebrei in campo di concentramento.

ASCC (1944) 121632. Rendiconto spese.

ASCC (1944) 122059. Spese del campo di concentramento di Fossoli.

ASCC (1944) 122939. Rendiconto delle spese del Campo di Concentramento di Fossoli.

ASCC (1944) 123723. Rendiconto delle spese del Campo di Concentramento di Fossoli.

ASCC (1944) 144535. Conto dei trasporti carcerari.

ASCC (1944) 145532. Costo di mantenimento del campo di concentramento di Fossoli.

ASCC (1944) 145547. Budget del cibo.

ASCC (1944) 151816. Distinta delle fatture per generi forniti al campo di concentramento Ebrei.

ASCC (1944) 152015. Fornitura del latte.

ASCC (1944) 152102. Fattura per generi forniti al campo di concentramento Ebrei dal 7 al 31 gennaio 1944.

ASCC (1944) 152858. Forniture di pane.

ASCC (1944) 153756. Copia Fattura medicinali forniti al campo di concentramento Ebrei.

ASCC (1944) 153833. Copia Fattura del 20 gennaio 1944. Forniture al campo di concentramento Ebrei.

ASCC (1944) 153923. Copia Fattura meccanico Tirelli Francesco.

ASCC (1944) 154257. Fattura n. 229: Ditta Enzo Mailli.

ASCC (1944) 154348. Fattura Enzo Mailli. Impianti elettrici.

ASCC (1944) 154713. Fattura n. 67 1 maggio 1944, per il trasporto ebrei al campo di concentramento.

ASCC (1944) 155033. Fattura per il trasporto ebrei al campo di concentramento.

ASCC (1944) 161753. Fondi per le spese di mantenimento del campo di concentramento di Fossoli.

ASCC (1944) 161835. Questura di Modena. Ebrei internati.

ASCC (1944) 162004. Acconto per le spese del campo di concentramento di Fossoli.

ASCC (1944) 162354. Questura di Modena. Ebrei in arrivo da altre province per essere internati al Campo di Concentramento di Fossoli.

ASCC (1944) 162601. Lista di Ebrei deportati dal Campo di Concentramento di Fossoli.

ASCC (1944) 163256. Bilancio preventivo del Comune di Carpi, 10 Marzo 1944.

ASCC (1944) 163433. Servizio sanitario per il Campo di Concentramento di Fossoli.

Secondary sources

Agamben, G. (1998). *Homo Sacer. Sovereign Power and Bare Life*. Stanford, CA: Stanford University Press.

Agamben, G. (1999). *Remnants of Auschwitz: The Witness and the Archive*. New York: Zone Books.

Agamben, G. (2000). What is a camp?. In S. Buckley, M. Hardt, and B. Massumi, (Eds.) (2000). *Means without Ends. Notes on Politics* (pp. 37–48). Minneapolis, MN: University of Minnesota Press.

Agamben, G. (2005). *Homo Sacer II: State of Exception*. Chicago, IL: University of Chicago Press.

Alawattage, C., Graham, C., and Wickramasinghe, D. (2019). Microaccountability and Biopolitics: Microfinance in a Sri Lankan Village. *Critical Perspectives on Accounting*, 72, 38–60.

Arendt, H. (1964). *Eichmann in Jerusalem. A Report on the Banality of Evil*. New York: The Viking Press.

Baccino, R. (1961). *Fossoli*. Modena: Cooperativa Tipografi.

Bauman, Z. (1989). *Modernity and the Holocaust*. Ithaca, NY: Cornell University Press.

Bigoni, M., Antonelli, V., Cafaro, E. M., D'Alessio, R., and Funnell, W. (2020). Accounting for the "Deviant" in 19th Century Italian Prisons. *Critical Perspectives on Accounting*, 66, 102087.

Biondi, E., Liotti, C., and Romagnoli, P. (1990). Il Campo di Fossoli: Evoluzione d'Uso e Trasformazioni. In G. Leoni (Ed.). (1990). *Trentacinque Progetti per Fossoli* (pp. 35–49). Milano: Electa.

Burgwyn, H. (2018). *Mussolini and the Salo Republic, 1943–1945: The Failure of a Puppet Regime*. Cham: Palgrave Macmillan.

Calimani, R. (2015). *Storia degli Ebrei Italiani nel XIX e nel XX Secolo*. Milano: Mondadori.

Capogreco, C.S. (2004). *I Campi del Duce: L'Internamento Civile nell'Italia Fascista, 1940–1943*. Torino: Einaudi.

Caracciolo, N., Koffler, F. R., and Koffler, R. (1995). *Uncertain Refuge: Italy and the Jews during the Holocaust*. Urbana, IL and Chicago, IL: University of Illinois Press.

Cassata, F. (2008). *«La Difesa della Razza». Politica, Ideologia e Immagine del Razzismo Fascista*. Torino: Einaudi.

Coen, F. (1988). *Italiani ed Ebrei, Come Eravamo. Le Leggi Razziali del 1938*. Genova: Marietti.

Cooper, C. (2015). Entrepreneurs of the Self: The Development of Management Control Since 1976. *Accounting, Organizations and Society*, *47*, 14–24.

Cuomo, F. (2005). *I Dieci: Chi erano gli Scienziati Italiani che Firmarono il Manifesto della Razza*. Milano: Baldini and Catoldi, Milano.

De Felice, R. (1993). *Storia degli Ebrei Italiani Sotto il Fascismo*. Torino: Einaudi.

De Felice, R. (1997). *Mussolini, l'Alleato*. Torino: Einaudi.

De Felice, R. (2001). *The Jews in Fascist Italy*. New York: Enigma Books.

Dell'Era, T. (2011). *Il Manifesto della Razza. Luglio 1938: Il Decalogo del Razzismo Italiano*. Torino: Utet.

Fargion, L.P. (1989). Le Informazioni sulla «Soluzione Finale» Circolanti in Italia nel 1942–1943. *La Rassegna Mensile di Israel*, *55*(2/3), 331–336.

Foucault, M. (1990). *The History of Sexuality*. London: Penguin Books.

Foucault, M. (1991). Governmentality. In G. Burchell, C. Gordon, and P. Miller (Eds.) (1991). *The Foucault Effect: Studies in Governmentality* (pp. 87–104). Chicago, IL: University of Chicago Press.

Friedlander, S. (2007). *The Years of Extermination: Nazi Germany and the Jews 1939–1945*. London: Weidenfeld and Nicolson.

Funnell, W.N. (1998). Accounting in the Service of the Holocaust. *Critical Perspectives on Accounting*, *9*(4), 435–464.

Garofalo, L. (2013). La Demorazza: Storia di un Archivio. *Italia Contemporanea*, *272*, 374–401.

Gasparotto, L. (2007). *Diario di Fossoli*. Torino: Bollati Boringhieri.

Gentile, S. (2013). *La Legalità del Male. L'Offensiva Mussoliniana contro gli Ebrei nella Prospettiva Storico-Giuridica (1938–1945)*. Torino: Giappichelli.

Gibertoni, R., and Melodi, A. (1996). Il Campo di Fossoli e il Museo Monumento al Deportato di Carpi. In T. Matta (Ed.) (1996). *Un Percorso della Memoria. Guida ai Luoghi della Violenza Nazista e Fascista in Italia* (pp. 99–119). Milano: Electa.

Gillette, A. (2002). *Racial Theories in Fascist Italy*. London and New York: Routledge.

Herr, A. (2014). *Fossoli di Carpi: The History and Memory of the Holocaust in Italy*. PhD Thesis, Worcester: Clark University.

Herr, A. (2017). *The Holocaust and Compensated Compliance in Italy: Fossoli di Carpi, 1942–1952*. New York: Palgrave McMillan.

Hopwood, A.G. (1987). The Archaeology of Accounting Systems. *Accounting, Organizations and Society*, *12*(2), 287–305.

Huber, C., and Scheytt, T. (2013). The Dispositif of Risk Management: Reconstructing Risk Management after the Financial Crisis. *Management Accounting Research*, *24*(2), 88–99.

Kogan, N. (2016). *8 Settembre 1943. L'Italia allo Sbando e gli Alleati*. Milano: Res Gestae.

Laqueur, W. (2001). *The Holocaust Encyclopaedia*. New Haven, CT: Yale University Press.

Le Theule, M.A., Lambert, C., and Morales, J. (2020). Governing Death: Organizing End-of-Life Situations. *Organization Studies*, *41*(4), 523–542.

Levi, P. (1959). *If This Is a Man*. New York: The Orion Press.

Levi, P. (1996). *Survival in Auschwitz: The Nazi Assault on Humanity*. New York: Collier Books.

Levis Sullam, S. (2015). *I Carnefici Italiani. Scene dal Genocidio degli Ebrei 1943–1945*. Milano: Feltrinelli.

Marti, I., and Fernandez, P. (2013). The Institutional Work of Oppression and Resistance: Learning from the Holocaust. *Organization Studies*, *34*(8), 1195–1223.

McPhail, K. (1999). The Threat of Ethical Accountants: An Application of Foucault's Concept of Ethics to Accounting Education and Some Thoughts on Ethically Educating for the Other. *Critical Perspectives on Accounting*, *10*(6), 833–866.

Michaelis, M. (1978). *Mussolini and the Jews: German-Italian Relations and the Jewish Question in Italy 1922–1945*. Oxford: Clarendon Press.

Michaelis, M. (1989). The Duce and the Jews. An Assessment of the Literature on Italian Jewry under Fascism (1922–1945). In M. Marrus (Ed.) (1989). *The Nazi Holocaust: Historical Articles on the Destruction of European Jews*. London: Meckler.

Michaelis, M. (2003). L'Influenza di Hitler sulla Svolta Razzista Adottata da Mussolini. *Rassegna Mensile di Israel*, *69*(1), 257–266.

Miller, P. (1990). On the Interrelations between Accounting and the State. *Accounting, Organizations and Society*, *15*(4), 315–338.

Napier, C.J. (2006). Accounts of Change: 30 Years of Historical Accounting Research. *Accounting, Organizations and Society*, *31*(4/5), 445–507.

Ori, A.M. (2007). Il Campo di Fossoli. In F. Pizzul, A.M. Ori, and M. Franzinelli (Eds.) (2007). *Fossoli. Memoria Privata, Rimozione Pubblica* (pp. 15–42). Milano: Ambrosinum.

Picciotto, L. (2002). *Il Libro della Memoria. Gli Ebrei Deportati dall'Italia (1943–1945)*. Milano: Mursia.

Picciotto, L. (2005) The Shoah in Italy: Its History and Characteristics. In J.D. Zimmerman (Ed.) (2005). *Jews in Italy under Fascist and Nazi Rule, 1922–1945*. Cambridge: Cambridge University Press.

Picciotto, L. (2008). La Macchina Anti-Ebraica della RSI e l'Ispettore Generale per la Razza Giovanni Preziosi. In M. Sarfatti (Ed.) (2008). *La Repubblica Sociale Italiana a Desenzano: Giovanni Preziosi e l'Ispettorato Generale per la Razza* (pp. 17–44). Firenze: Giuntina.

Picciotto, L. (2010). *L'Alba ci Colse come un Tradimento: Gli Ebrei nel Campo di Fossoli 1943–1944*. Milano: Mondadori.

Quartermaine, L. (2000). *Mussolini's Last Republic: Propaganda and Politics in the Italian Social Republic (RSI), 1943–45*. Exeter: Elm Bank Publications.

Sacchi, D. (2002). *Fossoli: Transito per Auschwitz. Quella Casa davanti al Campo di Concentramento*. Firenze: Giuntina.

Sarfatti, M. (1993). Il Censimento degli Ebrei del 22 Agosto 1938 nel Quadro dell'Avvio della Politica Antiebraica di Mussolini. In V. Colorni, F. Pusceddu, G. Sermoneta, and S. Simonsohn (Eds.) (1993). *Italia Judaica. Gli Ebrei nell'Italia Unita 1870–1945. Atti del IV Convegno Internazionale (Siena, 12–16 giugno 1989)* (pp. 358–413). Roma: MIBAC.

Sarfatti, M. (2007). *Gli Ebrei nell'Italia Fascista: Vicende, Identità, Persecuzione*. Torino: Einaudi.

Spinosa, A. (1994). *Mussolini: Razzista Riluttante*. Firenze: Bonacci.

Stille, A. (1991). *Benevolence and Betrayal: Five Italian Jewish Families under Fascism*. New York: Penguin Books.

Stokes, P., and Gabriel, Y. (2010). Engaging with Genocide: The Challenge for Organization and Management Studies. *Organization*, *17*(4), 461–480.

Yael-Franzone, G. (2004). La Normazione Antiebraica in Italia tra il 1938 e il 1943. Alcune Annotazioni di Natura Giuridica ed Economica. In Collegio Rabbinico Italiano, Corso di Laurea in Studi Ebraici and Archivio Storico della Comunità Ebraica di Roma (Eds.) (2004). *Gli effetti delle leggi razziali sulle attività economiche degli ebrei nella città di Roma (1938–1943)* (pp. 23–47). Roma: CCIAA.

Yu, A. (2021). Accountability as Mourning: Accounting for Death in the Time of COVID-19. *Accounting, Organizations and Society*, *90*, 101198.

Zimmerman, J.D. (2005). *Jews in Italy under Fascist and Nazi rule, 1922–1945*. Cambridge: Cambridge University Press.

Zuccotti, S. (1987). *The Italians and the Holocaust: Persecution, Rescue, and Survival*. New York: Basic Books.

10 The culpability of accounting in perpetuating the Holocaust

Ellen Lippman and Paula Wilson

Introduction

The Holocaust was an event unprecedented in the history of man. Never before had a people been systematically and deliberately hunted and gathered from many different countries by one country for the sole purpose to annihilate them. This was not a disagreement of peoples within a country or even a disagreement between countries. This was an organized hatred by one country against a people who lived disbursed among many countries. Germany's efficient organization was organized and focused to wipe Jews and other targeted groups from the earth. The implementation of the Holocaust could not have been possible without the widespread complicity of business people, lawyers, doctors, engineers, churchmen and women, public officials, military, police, as well as millions of ordinary citizens (Jones, 1999).

This chapter identifies how accounting facilitated the injustices experienced by the concentration camp victims. As support, the chapter provides common financial analysis tools and accounting information used in the slave labor operations that either failed to adequately measure the true costs of Nazi crimes or served as aids for decisions that contributed to the genocide. By analysis of the use and misuse of these tools, the study contributes to the understanding of accounting and its ability to inform and affect decisions, including the decision to eliminate a distinct group of people. In addition, the chapter extends the study of the German accounting profession by Markus (1997) by examining the profession immediately prior to and during the war years, considering how the profession itself may have facilitated the Holocaust.

The chapter first considers slave labor operations managed by private corporations and Nazi State-run entities. It then identifies accounting information and common financial analysis tools used in the management of these operations and considers how they assisted in the management of these operations. This is followed by an examination of the German accounting profession in the years preceding and during the war and considers whether the state of the German accounting profession explains accountant complicity with the Holocaust. Finally, the chapter considers the culpability of accounting and accountants in perpetuating the Holocaust.

DOI: 10.4324/9781032685328-10

Slave labor operations

During World War II, many German corporations, including I.G. Farbenindustries (IG Farben), Krupp, Union Metallendustrie, Bishmarchkhutte, Oberschlesische Hyderwerke, Siemens-Schuchert, Herman Goering Werke, and Volkswagen manufactured items using the labor of prison slaves. The laborers included Jewish workers transported from their home States to various concentration camps maintained by the Nazis, and local workers from the countries in which the camps were located (Gutman and Berenbaum, 1994; Allen, 2002). The workers were employed in facilities owned by the corporations and in facilities built within the concentration camp compounds.

German corporations willingly made use of cheap slave labor. The historian Mark Spoerer examined 33 known case histories of companies that employed concentration camp slave labor and found only one case where evidence exists that the State "forced a firm to use slavery against its will" (Allen, 2002, p. 170). Moreover, often, the German business leaders negotiated partnerships with the Schutzstaffel (SS), an important client during the war years. I.G. Farben, a leading manufacturer of explosives, light metals and chemical warfare agents, began using slave labor in 1941. The company used 10,000 persons as slave laborers in 1941 and increased its reliance on slave labor to approximately 100,000 persons by 1945, foreigners and prisoners of war (*Trials of War Criminals Before the Nuremberg Military Tribunals under Control Council Law No.10, Nuremberg, 1946–1949*, 1953, p. 54). Krupp, a company that manufactured armaments and tanks, made extensive use of slave labor, both inside its own plants and in plants established inside the concentration camps. As early as 1942, Krupp used slave labor in its own plants, and by 1943 it had established a manufacturing plant inside the Auschwitz concentration camp, where concentration camp laborers made parts for automatic weapons. Although exact measurements do not exist, estimates of prison labor usage by Krupp range from a low of 75,000 slave workers to a high of 100,000 slave workers in Germany alone (*Trials of War Criminals Before the Nuremberg Military Tribunals under Control Council Law No.10, Nuremberg, 1946–1949*, 1950b, p. 115).

State owned and operated enterprises also made extensive use of slave labor. The entire slave labor operation was run by a small group of engineers, accountants and managers who worked in the SS Wirtschaftsverwaltungshauptamt (Business Administration Main Office, hereafter referred to as the WVHA). The WVHA controlled many economic enterprises that used concentration camp labor for the German State and supplied slave labor to private corporations. German corporations negotiated slave labor contracts with the WVHA. These contracts specified both the lease payment for the slave laborers and the provisions to be provided to them. Unlike ancient slaves, who were provided with adequate food and housing as a means to protect their value, German corporations and State-controlled enterprises provided little to protect the concentration camp slaves. For example, Krupp provided each of its slave laborers one blanket, one set of eating utensils, one drinking cup, and food costing 70 pfennig per day (approximately 18 cents in today's value) (Muhlen, 1959, p. 168). In a 1941 meeting, I.G. Farben negotiated a contract with the SS to pay between 1.5 and 3 Reichsmarks (RM) per day for each worker leased, with the price dependent upon the age and skill of the worker (Borkin, 1978, p. 117). This price was discounted from that paid to a free worker, as IG Farben management anticipated that the condition of concentration camp inmates would hinder their efficiency, making them only a third as efficient when compared to free workers (Borkin, 1978).

Yet, even with the built-in inefficiency of the slave laborers, use of these workers yielded extraordinary returns to investors. Neither State owned and operated entities nor corporations maintained reasonable working conditions,[1] considered the health of the laborers, provided protective clothing, or accrued future pensions to slave laborers,[2] conditions that were required for civilian workers (Gutman and Berenbaum, 1994). Thus, unusually large returns were earned by these corporations. "Slave labor did not satisfy any deep aggressive instincts" of the corporations; rather "it satisfied the shareholders" (Wertham, 1978, p. 21).

Accounting for operations and slave labor

Employment of slave laborers was big business. In 1942, revenue to the SS from the lease of slave laborers totaled 13.2m RM (Black, 2001, p. 362), and corporations and Nazi enterprises used sophisticated accounting techniques to track the results. Oswald Pohl, head of the SS Business Administration Main Office, the division responsible for the extensive slave labor operations, "molded informal and amateurish accounting practices into a standardized, homogeneous system so that the SS could stand up to public audit" (Allen, 2002, p. 27). I.G. Farben's accounting system provided board members with reports detailing company labor usage, with slave labor reported separately from other labor (Borkin, 1978). The Gustloff Works, formerly a Jewish owned business called the Suhler Weapons and Vehicle Works until it was taken over by the Nazis in 1935 (Allen, 2002), maintained reports that cataloged each prisoner's output (Hacket, 1995). A textile and garment works called The Textile and Leather Utilization GmbH (TexLed), founded by the SS, employed "sophisticated technical management in slave-labor supervision" (Allen, 2002, p. 73) that tracked production statistics including "unit costs, labor costs, and depreciation rates on machinery and combined aggregate statistics to yield calculations of production minutes per unit product and unit labor costs" (Allen, 2002, p. 73). TexLed maintained steady production with its employment of unskilled women of Ravensbrück, a women's concentration camp. Although TexLed was an SS entity that used slave labor, it was a viable factory operation run by competent management, generating real profits estimated at 18 percent (Allen, 2002, p. 78), and "achieved productivity rates close to those of civilian workers" (Allen, 2002, p. 74).

To prepare financial statements of SS businesses that used the free prison labor, the SS needed to determine an appropriate wage scale to assign to prison labor. The SS determined a standard wage rate, as any good cost accounting system would do, "on the basis of the elaborated system ... to establish labor costs. Thus, the norm wage for the Jewish prisoners employed can be exactly accounted for on the plant account sheet, with the daily average rate serving a basis" (*Trials of War Criminals Before the Nuremberg Military Tribunals under Control Council Law No.10, Nuremberg, 1946–1949*, 1950a, p. 585). This enabled the preparation of a profit and loss statement "from the employment of Jewish prisoners" (*Trials of War Criminals Before the Nuremberg Military Tribunals under Control Council Law No.10, Nuremberg, 1946–1949*, 1950a, p. 586). As an example of information produced that tracked revenues and labor costs, an income statement from Buchenwald, a German prison camp in existence between 1937 and its liberation in 1945, is reproduced in Table 10.1.[3] This statement reports the estimated net profits to the SS from the leasing of a single prisoner. At the top of the statement, the estimated net revenue per prisoner per day is presented. Next, expenses related to leasing prisoners and including estimates for food and clothing amortization are presented. An estimate for the expected number of working days for the prisoner appears next. Prisoners were expected to work 30 days each month with no apparent time off for vacation or weekend rests. The statement then estimated the revenue for only nine months per laborer. This was not because the laborer was reassigned after the nine-month period. Rather, nine months was the life expectancy of the prison laborer, the result of the harsh working conditions and insufficient food allotment (Ferencz, 1979; Rubenstein and Roth, 1987).

Even death through labor was a measured financial decision, as extermination of potentially employable prisoners in gas chambers would deprive the Reich of revenue from the lease program. A significant revenue stream could be generated by allowing the prisoners to work until they died from exhaustion or starvation (Black, 2001). Upon death, the prisoner still generated profit. The income statement included an estimate of revenue at death

Table 10.1 Income statement

Revenue	**6.00**
Less food	0.60
Less amortization for clothes	0.10
Net revenue	**5.30**
Times – expected life span in months	9.00
– days worked per month	30.00
Total revenue for period (9 × 30 × 5.30)	**1,431.00**
Plus revenue at death	200.00
Net profit per prisoner	**1,621.00**

Source: Translated from the original. Reproduction from Buchenwald (Kogon, 1950, p. 269). Amounts are in Reichsmarks.

from the value of the deceased's personal clothing, valuables, currency, gold extracted from the teeth of the deceased and sales of hair, fat (for soap) and ashes for fertilizer (Shirer, 1960; Feig, 1981) less the cost of cremation that averaged two marks per person (Kogon, 1950). This operating statement included standard accounting concepts such as estimates on life expectancy, which are used today in determining post-retirement benefits, and amortization which was used to report the systematic expensing of intangible assets. The income statement also included information quite foreign to income statements today; the explicit limited life expectancy of prison laborers due to harsh working conditions. Estimating the useful life of the slave laborers at nine months is an accounting procedure that ignored the value of life. As other chapters in this book have repeatedly shown, accounting can reduce individuals to numbers to "render the human side invisible" (Fleischman and Tyson, 2004, p. 383), masking the suffering of the victims who were worked to death.

Cost benefit analysis represents another common financial tool used to support decision-making. In Nazi Germany, accountants used a cost benefit analysis to compare the cost of killing children with gas and then burning their bodies, to the alternative of burning the children to death (Greenberg, 1975). Both options required an expenditure for burning, but the second option would use less gas, thereby reducing the costs. Gas cost 975 RM for 195 kilos. For every 1,500 persons gassed, approximately 5.5 kilos were required. By not gassing the children first, the State could save 10 cents per child (Fleischner, 1977). Gassing was by no means humane. After prisoners were told that the gas chambers were showers they panicked once they realized the truth. While gassing was painful, the pain from being burned alive was certainly worse. Nonetheless, the Nazis elected to burn the children alive, and their screams could be heard throughout the camp (Fleischner, 1977).

As the extermination efforts continued, gas supplies decreased. In response, the Nazis elected to decrease the amount of gas used for each killing. This prolonged the time to death increasing the suffering of the prisoners as they died (Fleischner, 1977). Time for the onset of death increased from an average range of 3–7 minutes of gas time to an average range of 15 to 20 minutes (Greenberg, 1975). The Nazis' decision to reduce the amount of gas used for killing appears motivated by economic considerations. In this analysis, the Nazis considered the costs of killing but did not consider the cost of human suffering associated with the killing method or the individual human lives lost. A well-prepared cost benefit analysis may be mathematically correct; however, it is not value neutral. Personally held values affect the information prepared, and, depending upon the values embedded in the task, the analysis may be flawed even when the computations are accurate. Such was the case in the cost benefit analysis used to support decisions about gassing the children to death.

One information system used during the Holocaust identified the flow of laborers and the supervision of production (Allen, 2002). As part of this information system, the category "unfit" was used to distinguish between prisoners who were fit to work from those incapacitated. This latter category "became a standard tool for the systematic liquidation of prisoners" (Allen, 2002, p. 124).

While accounting information may have masked some of the horrors of Nazi Germany, accountants preparing the information must have been aware of the operations. The information prepared by accountants was not limited to that expected during war, costs of prisoner of war camps, or conventional weapons. Rather, accounting information detailed the concentration work camps and extermination costs of prisoners, war costs unique to Germany. In certain circumstances, the accountants at individual factories were Jews required to record the transactions (*Trials of War Criminals Before the Nuremberg Military Tribunals under Control Council Law No.10, Nuremberg, 1946–1949*, 1950a). As the Jewish bookkeepers were exterminated, German accountants took their place. Some recorded transactions and others performed audits of the factory results. "I have examined the entries of the capital accounts and found these to be in order" (*Trials of War Criminals Before the Nuremberg Military Tribunals under Control Council Law No.10, Nuremberg, 1946–1949*, 1950a, p. 520). The accountants doing this work, while sometimes SS officers, were often civilians (*Trials of War Criminals Before the Nuremberg Military Tribunals under Control Council Law No.10, Nuremberg, 1946–1949*, 1950a). Surely, they understood the magnitude of what they reported. For instance, Dr Max Horn, a university educated accountant and SS officer assigned to Globocnik's industries, noted mistreatment of the prison laborers and the resultant negative impact on production. He identified starvation as the key problem with low production and protested the conditions. Horn stated that "if the SS wished to exploit prisoners, some modicum of preservation of life had to take precedence over the denigration of the work Jews, and – with the genocide in full swing – over their wholesale murder" (Allen, 2002, p. 248). It is impossible to know with certainty the true motive for Horn's protests, but it is doubtful that a humanitarian motive existed. Horn was the "business manager" (*Trials of War Criminals Before the Nuremberg Military Tribunals under Control Council Law No.10, Nuremberg, 1946–1949*, 1950a, p. 513) for OSTI, SS run factories that used Jewish labor. Without a labor force he could not maintain his factories. Thus, it was in his best interest to maintain a healthy workforce. In November 1943, when OSTI was deprived of Jewish workers, Horn was placed in charge of liquidating the factories.

Accountants, whether they worked directly for the State or for private corporations that leased slave labor from the State, were aware of the slave labor operations and likely had access to information about these operations and the mistreatment of the workers. Although accountants were not directly responsible for the killing, they have been called "desk-killers" for issuing reports that detailed the killing machine (Rosenberg and Marcus, 1988, p. 213). Rather than apply a sweeping blame to accountants as killers and accomplices, this chapter considers the profession of accountancy during this time and the potential impact of the professional accounting organization upon accountants' actions during the Holocaust.

Accountancy profession in Germany

In countries influenced by Anglo-American interests, professionalism in accounting was driven by the accountants, as personal status was achieved through professional classification. Prior to 1931, German accountants felt no compelling need to establish themselves as a profession. Instead, their status was obtained through education (Evans, 2003). Official professional status was conferred upon German accountants when, in 1931, the German government required statutory audits of firms with a stated capital in excess of 3,000,000 RM. By the following year, such audits were required for companies with capital of at least 500,000 RM. The audits were to be prepared by publicly commissioned accountants.

When the German government introduced the requirement that mandated statutory audits, Germany was in the midst of economic and political turmoil, still recovering from the loss in World War I. The country required significant capital investment as part of its recovery plan. However, foreign investors would not accept the audits of German corporations that were performed by German accountants. It was hoped that a newly established accounting society would introduce professionalism to accounting and increase foreign acceptance of German audits. In many countries, including the USA, Canada, England and Scotland, organization of an accounting society entailed struggles between competing organizations and interests. In Germany, the accounting society was created by the government, thereby short-circuiting struggles between competing groups. Germany could not afford the time for the various competing accounting organizations to resolve their differences within the private sector, as was done in other countries. Rather, the German government intervened, establishing the professional accountant, the publicly commissioned Wirtschaftsprüfer, and the accounting society Institut der Wirtschaftsprüfer (IdW) (Meisel, 1992).

The IdW was formed by the merger of various organizations, including those of consulting economists, academic experts, small accounting organizations whose members lacked graduate degrees, highly qualified graduate members, associations providing bookkeeping services, trust and audit companies and other associations. They became a comprehensive, self-contained professional organization of accountants. The IdW provided standardized protocols, uniform authorization and testing for publicly commissioned accountants called Wirtschaftsprüfers (WPs), within the unified German State. To become certified as a WP, applicants needed to meet various requirements including German residency, an orderly financial and personal life, a minimum age of 30 years, 6 years of professional practice including at least 3 years of auditing, successful completion of a written exam, and demonstrated knowledge of the accounting discipline (Meisel, 1992, p. 191). While the certified accountants were to be commissioned only after passing an exam, a transition period from 1931 through 1935 existed when candidates with relevant experience and personal aptitude could become certified without testing (Meisel, 1992, p. 186). With these requirements, the profession of accountancy was elevated from discrete specialties into a new profession that had a monopoly on the examination of public entities and possessed credibility throughout the country.

Initially, the profession set goals to establish laws of professional practice, form a discipline newspaper, provide professional assurance duties and work with related professionals. The IdW had not yet begun to consider ethical questions of professional practice and the organization itself was only in its infancy when Hitler was appointed Chancellor of Reich in January 1933. In national elections held on 5 March 1933, the National Socialists received 43.9 percent of the vote. By 23 March 1933, Hitler had obtained the majority of support from the other parties and the government passed the Enabling Law (Ermachtigungsgesetz), which permitted dictatorial power by the National Socialists. Thus began the systematic dehumanization and persecution of Jews. As Germany began to change under Hitler's leadership, so did the IdW. A general meeting of the IdW membership held in February 1933 became the last meeting of this organization until after the war, as the IdW would lose its independence in the intervening years. An advisory council of the IdW continued to meet and on 4 April 1933, the council expressed support for the National Socialist government. Two of the Jewish members of the council, previously elected at the February 1933 meeting, were asked to resign. Beginning on 6 April 1933, Jews could no longer serve as authoritative tax representatives (Meisel, 1992). In September 1934, the IdW changed its statutes and adapted the profession to the National Socialist principles "Führerprinzip", the Institute of the Führer. The IdW became a professional accounting organization administered by loyal party members. Candidates and other professionals were required to produce proof of their Aryan heritage. A party member became the "führer" of the IdW, and administrative functions were given to a non-WP party member, Dr Otto Mönckmeier (Meisel, 1992).

The National Socialist government prohibited Jews and others not friendly to the new regime from working as approved auditors, although exceptions were made for Jewish veterans of World War I or those Jews whose father or son was killed during World War I. The National Socialists reaffirmed the need for WPs but believed that the profession would best be served by the government's oversight rather than the oversight by an independent professional organization. As stated in June 1934 by Dr Elmar Michel, a representative of the Reich's Economic Minister, "Although not an official invested with the power of the State, the WP has become in a certain sense the executor of a state function.... Due to the importance of the WP's work, assigned to it by legislation, it stands to reason that state's management must influence decisively the management of the profession" (Meisel, 1992, p. 211).

With the adoption of Führerprinzip, democratic processes in the IdW had essentially ended as the IdW lost its independence as well as its function as an independent representative of accountants' professional interests (Meisel, 1992). Thus, the IdW had become an instrument of the State and the self-governing accounting societies of each province in Germany were either assimilated or dissolved. Members acquiesced to the changes to its statutes when the entire membership approved, by a vote of 612 to 0 with two abstentions, the adoption of Führerprinzip. At the time of the vote, 55 Jews were members of the IdW (Markus, 1997, p. 78). They, therefore, either did not vote, abstained, or voted with the majority to essentially limit their own rights. While only 38 percent of the membership of the IdW were then members of the National Socialist party, nonetheless the members did not object as the National Socialists began to assume control of the organization.

The hope was expressed that no additional Jews were to be admitted to the IdW, although six additional Jews were admitted (five in Berlin and one from Munich), all veterans of World War I (Markus, 1997, p. 5). In November 1938, three days before Kristallnacht, the burning of Jewish businesses and homes, and the arrest of thousands of Jews, the remaining 28 Jewish IdW members (others having dropped their membership or emigrated) had their membership revoked (Markus, 1997, p. 250).

With the transfer of oversight to the government came a shift in the focus of the WP. Previously, the auditor's responsibilities addressed the needs of the corporation for which it worked and the public for which it audited. With the introduction of government intervention, auditing became a mechanism to force advancements for the public's good (Meisel, 1992) and auditors became beholden to the interest of the public economy. The focus of the auditors changed again in 1937 when an oath of allegiance to Hitler was added to WPs' certification requirements. The original oath, "I swear that I will fulfill the duties and obligation of a publicly commissioned accountant knowledgeably and impartially and that I will fulfill them with the desired expert opinion knowledgeably and impartially" (Meisel, 1992, p. 186), was amended to read "I swear by God that I will exercise absolute obedience to the Führer and Reichs-Chancellor Adolf Hitler and that I will carry out my duties and responsibilities of a publicly appointed Wirtschaftsprüfer conscientiously and impartially, that I will preserve professional secrecy and that all reports requested of me will be prepared conscientiously and impartially" (Markus, 1997, p. 89). Thus, in 1937 WPs became primarily responsible to Hitler and began carrying out the policies of the Nazi party.

Under the leadership of Mönckmeier, the IdW used its official accounting magazine to educate accountants about specific rules that discriminated against Jews. For instance, in 1939, the official accounting magazine outlined directives about Nazi regulations required of WPs in their interactions with Jews in business (Mönckmeier, 1939). Accountants were forbidden from offering professional advice to Jews without expressed official permission in writing from appropriate Nazi officials. When representing Jews, accountants were to work for the good of the Party over the personal benefit of a Jewish client. Business laws requiring the dissolution of Jewish businesses were detailed in the magazine. Among the laws described was a law ordering Jewish businesses to sell or liquidate within an appointed time period as part of the process of Aryanization of Jewish companies (Reich Law Sheet Register RGBI, I, 1938, cited in Genschel, 1966). The 12 March 1938 article by Dr H. Adler on New Business Laws in the accounting magazine describes this new order and the additional business for accountants who will be appointed as attestors of value in the dissolution of the Jewish businesses (Adler, 1939). The law also required the Jewish business owners to bear the cost of the audits. Thus, discrimination within Germany had become further institutionalized and the WPs, the German accountants, were actively engaged in the formation and implementation of the laws that discriminated against Jews.

The IdW relinquished its autonomy to the National Socialist Party without significant dissent. One possible explanation for the IdW's ready acceptance of Hitler's regime relates to the accounting organization itself. The IdW was a new organization; it did not have a professional history upon which to rely. Indeed, the profession was still learning what professionalism meant. For instance, in 1933, the advisory committee to the IdW reported unsatisfactory performance of WPs, questioning whether additional, specific supplemental discipline tests of competence should be implemented (Meisel, 1992). The IdW did not have the fully developed loyalty of members that comes only with long-lived organizations. WPs could easily give up what they did not yet value. Additionally, consideration of ethical responsibilities of accountants had not become a part of accounting competency in Germany.

Accounting professionals from the international community appeared to show support for Germany's accounting body, even after the Nazis took office. The Fifth International Congress on Accounting was held in Germany in 1938 and enrollment of foreign representatives to the conference, while below the 500 expected, still totaled 315 foreign participants (Markus, 1997, p. 106) from 33 countries (Walker, 2000, p. 232), with the largest number of foreign delegates from Britain. Walker argues that British delegates attended this conference, despite widespread knowledge of persecution of the Jews, in order to protect their business interests and the British chartered accountants who were already working in Germany.[4] After the conference, accounting articles that appeared in the journal *The Accounting Review* praised Germany and its efficient accounting methodology (Matz, 1938, 1940). The publication *Standardized Accountancy in Germany* (1943) published in England during the war also touted Germany's regulatory system of standardized accounting, a result of the German "talent for organization" (Singer, 1943, p. 10). Singer stated that the accounting system aided the Germans in accounting for its war economy. Neither Singer nor Matz acknowledged that the accounting system reported about the horrors of the operation of the concentration camps.

In other countries such as the USA, Great Britain, and Canada, where self-imposed professionalism required more active participation and where individual rights of citizens were paramount, accountants may have more actively opposed the takeover of their accounting society by the State. In Germany, however, the view of the State as guide was prevalent throughout society, where German communal responsibility was the primary focus and individual rights were secondary to societal goals. "German individualism, tempered by a strong nationalistic and paternalistic tradition, enjoined everyone to work for the communal good" (Harston, 1993, p. 148). Accepting current conditions for the good of society was the norm. German accounting emphasized compliance with laws and regulations and not representational faithfulness. Moreover, secrecy in financial transactions was preferred over financial disclosure. These characteristics, therefore, would set a tone in financial reporting that discouraged the questioning of State actions, particularly since the State was the ultimate client as opposed to the corporation (Neal and Morgan, 2002). It was State policy, as articulated by Heydrich and first made public at the Wannsee Conference, to use slave laborers, to under-provide for the workers, to work some concentration camp inmates to death, and to kill the remaining others who did not die working (Shirer, 1960, p. 965).

Although little evidence exists that accountants, as a group, formally questioned the new management of the IdW, there exists evidence of individual efforts to resist the dictates of the government. For instance, Dr Elmar Michel, a civil servant in the Ministry of Economics, continually clashed with Mönckmeier, pushing for the continued independence of the IdW from the government and the protection of Jewish members. In 1937, when Mönckmeier moved to exclude persons with Jewish mothers or wives from membership in the IdW, Michel intervened (Markus, 1997). Other accountants resisted the changes of Führerprinzip as well. In 1933, six members of the Der Verband Deutscher Bucherrevisoren (VDB) (Association of German Auditors), one of the founding groups of the IdW, were reprimanded for criticizing the new leadership (Markus, 1997, p. 69). Of the 1,100 members of the VDB in April 1933, 74 resigned by January 1934. In 1942, a professional accounting disciplinary committee reprimanded an accountant for using language considered too respectful when corresponding with Jewish clients (Markus, 1997). In another instance, one accountant protested when the Nazis took over the management of a previously Jewish-owned business for which she worked. She quit her job stating that "she'd rather die" than work for the Nazis (Jones, 1999, p. 219). She was not punished for her comments or actions, although her later active resistance led to her death.

It is likely that other accountants performed individual, undocumented efforts of resistance related to their work with the Nazis. State-wide, WPs were not active in opposing the changes in the IdW. Within only a few years after

Hitler came to power, the accounting organization had ceased acting as an independent board to which concerned accountants could look for guidance. WPs were to serve the State, and if accountants disagreed with the State, they had no professional recourse as their organization was controlled by the State. Thus, accountants, individually, needed to have the moral courage to resist. If they did not (as most did not), were they culpable in perpetrating the genocide through their accounting of the slave operations?

Culpability of accountants and accounting

Researchers have suggested that accounting supports illegal or immoral activities of institutions. For example, Fleischman and Tyson (2004, p. 393) examined the use of accounting on slave plantations in the antebellum south and concluded that "accounting is far more complicit in sustaining slavery and its institutions than many other accounting scholars or historians have acknowledged". In the slave trade, accounting commodified and objectified human lives by converting human attributes into categories of age, sex, and color, which were then used to assign monetary values to the slaves. These monetary values facilitated slave trading while also ignoring the human dimensions of slavery or even masking the degree to which atrocities occurred (Oldroyd et al., 2005). This also happened during the Holocaust when accounting reports did not convey the human dimension of the victims. In cost benefit analyses, operating statements, and worker efficiency computations, the human cost from the policies of the Holocaust was ignored in the accounting data.

Accounting information does not exist independent of persons engaged in generating that information or persons using that information for immoral or illegal acts. Fleischman et al. (2004) argued that accountants should be held accountable for the misdeeds of slave owners due to the severity of the slave mistreatment. They stated that a basic standard of justice exists for the "treatment of humans against which accounting and accounting practitioners can be judged culpable" (Oldroyd et al., 2005, p. 5). Oldroyd et al. (2005, p. 5) argued that accountants "were contributing to genocide in the sense that slavery, with its high mortality rates, created a perilous demographic situation, and thus it is legitimate to adjudge its collaborators guilty of crimes against humanity". The authors held the accountants responsible for the consequences of slavery despite the wide use of slavery during that period. Using this standard of justice, German accountants would likewise be held responsible for the consequences of their information despite Germany's wide usage of slave labor.

Oldroyd et al. (2005) considered whether accountants are culpable for the support of slavery in the absence of a professional organization and code of professional ethics to guide accountants' behavior. The authors argued that legality provides a framework for professional ethics in accounting. Since slavery was legal in the British Empire until 1834 and in the USA until

1863, "involvement in slavery would not have been judged professionally unethical by the standards of today, had an organized profession existed" (Oldroyd et al., 2005, p. 10). In Germany, an independent professional accounting organization did exist but was only in its infancy, having been created in 1933. It did not have a professional code of conduct, and by 1934 it had lost its independence and became State controlled. Thus, accountants neither had a formalized code of ethics to govern their behavior nor an organization to turn to for independent, professional advice. Other than personally held values, accountants could only rely on the laws of the country for guidance. Since discrimination, slave labor, and annihilation were State authorized, under Oldroyd et al.'s argument, accountants would not be culpable. These behaviors were clearly illegal in other Western countries and did not conform to laws or values held in Germany either prior to or after the Holocaust. Because genocide, slavery, and discrimination were unacceptable in the Western world yet widely practiced in Germany, it is unclear whether complicit German accountants would be culpable under the terms of Oldroyd's standard.

In the International Military Tribunal Trials held after the war, lower and senior-level accountants were tried for crimes against humanity. Many high-level SS accountants of the Holocaust acknowledged what they did but argued that their actions were not wrong. These individuals believed they were acting within the bounds of acceptable behavior at the time and felt no additional responsibility for moral reflection (Krens, 1988). Additionally, some felt they were made a scapegoat for others' transgressions. "Men like Himmler, Gluecks … these men are dead and I believe that I can say that if this dozen men would be sitting here in the defendants' dock today, then the bookkeepers of Amtsgruppe A would not be sitting in the first row of the defendants' dock" (*Trials of War Criminals Before the Nuremberg Military Tribunals under Control Council Law No.10, Nuremberg, 1946–1949*, 1950a, p. 761).

In the Tribunal's rulings, the court differentiated accountants' responsibility for the Holocaust dependent upon the ability of the accountant to affect change or change jobs. The court convicted Dr Hans Hohberg, the top SS accountant, of crimes of war and crimes against humanity and sentenced him to ten years imprisonment (History of the UN War Crimes Commission and the Development of the Laws of War, 1948, p. 530). Due to Hohberg's high level of responsibility, the court held him responsible for the information he, and those who reported to him, produced. In contrast, lower-level accountants were not held culpable for the genocide. Even some higher-level accountants were exonerated if their level of knowledge was remote or if their association with the concentration camps was only sporadic. However, those who directed accountants, who had information about the killing learned from the preparation of financial information, and who were in a position to affect change or find an alternative job were held responsible for the information they helped prepare and were convicted of crimes against humanity (*Trials of War Criminals Before the Nuremberg Military Tribunals under Control Council Law No.10, Nuremberg, 1946–1949*, 1950a).

The Tribunal introduced a new standard for accountant responsibility, holding accountants culpable if in a position to affect change or if possessing the ability to change employment. The standard used at the Tribunal acknowledges the responsibility of accountants while also acknowledging that certain circumstances may make decisive action by accountants difficult. "Mere knowledge of crime without the power to interfere carries no moral or legal condemnation. But knowledge of crime and participation in the system that makes that crime possible dissipates the concept of unblemished innocence" (*Trials of War Criminals Before the Nuremberg Military Tribunals under Control Council Law No.10, Nuremberg, 1946–1949*, 1950a, p. 1159).

Implications

The Holocaust represents an unprecedented genocide against a people simply because of race. This chapter has shown the failure of accountants and professional accounting organizations to respond to the Holocaust. Although neither accounting nor accountants initiated the Holocaust, accounting practices involved in the slave labor operations contributed to the genocide, as the accounting information disregarded basic human rights of the laborers. Slave laborers were not treated even as productive assets. Rather, in most cases, these humans were treated as commodities to be used up in the production process.

The chapter has provided examples of analyses prepared by accountants that were used to inform and facilitate decision-making during the genocide. However, the motivation of the accountants to disregard the value of human life when preparing the analyses is unknown; whether individuals chose to ignore the information and the implications of that information or whether German accounting profession's emphasis on professional competence rather than moral considerations were responsible for the behavior of accountants who prepared and used accounting information to support the elimination of the Jews.

Few accountants today prepare accounting information detailing atrocities on the scale of that in Germany and few accountants are confronted with a State government that has as its key strategy the elimination of a race of people. Perhaps a strong and independent German accounting profession would have positively affected accountants' response to the Holocaust. However, at the time, the accounting profession was only beginning to develop. Consideration of ethical issues was not a skill mandated for prospective WPs. Test questions on the WP exam did not include any ethical issues (Meisel, 1992), and the certifying board's qualifying personal characteristics only required that candidates lead an orderly life, personally and financially. Today, ethics are a focus of professional certifying organizations. A strong code of ethics and an equally strong accounting professional organization that takes an active role in managing accountant work may provide a moderating influence to illegal or immoral pressures. As seen in this chapter, accounting information can have severe ramifications and holding accountants responsible for such information can change the way accountants work and ultimately the decisions made.

The authors gratefully acknowledge the research assistance provided by Donald Beebe, who translated key references from German into English. This chapter is based on the paper by Ellen Lippman and Paula Wilson titled "The culpability of accounting in perpetuating the Holocaust" which originally appeared in *Accounting History* in 2007, vol. 12, no. 4, pp. 283–303. The authors would like to thank the publisher, Sage, for permission to use this material.

Notes

1 Prison laborers endured horrendous working conditions. They slept in crowded quarters on hard floors. No clothes were issued (Shirer, 1960). They were not permitted to converse during working hours (Borkin, 1978). Prisoners worked from dawn to dusk, seven days a week.
2 Recently, corporations have acknowledged their financial and moral obligations to slave laborers.
3 The primary source for this financial statement is Eugen Kogon, an Austrian imprisoned by the Nazis from 1938 until his liberation, by the Allies, in April 1945. Kogon was then enlisted to help prepare a report for the Supreme Headquarters, Allied Expeditionary Forces that would detail the operations of a concentration camp. The 450-page report, finished one month later in May 1945, became the basis for Kogon's book, first originally written in German and then translated into English. In the financial statement, Kogon writes, "Let it not be thought that this calculation is my own handiwork. It comes from SS sources" (Kogon, 1950, p. 269).
4 Despite these efforts, British accountants were asked to leave Germany by 1939 (Markus, 1997).

References

Adler, H. (1939). Neues Wirtschaftsrecht: VO. über den Einsatz des jüdischen Vermögens vom 3.12.38. RGBl. I 1938 S. 1709. In O. Mönckmeier (Ed.) (1939). *Der Wirtschaftstreuhänder, Zeitschrift für deutsches Prüfungs- und Treuhandswesen, Volume 8* (p. 31). Leipzig: G.A. Gloeckner Verlagsbuchhandlung.

Allen, M.T. (2002). *The Business of Genocide: The SS, Slav Labor and the Concentration Camps.* Chapel Hill, NC: The University of North Carolina Press.

Black, E. (2001). *IBM and the Holocaust.* New York: Crown Publishers.

Borkin, J. (1978). *The Crime and Punishment of IG Farben.* New York: The Free Press.

Evans, L. (2003), Auditing and Audit Firms in Germany Before 1931. *Accounting Historians Journal, 30*(2), 29–64.

Feig, K. (1981). *Hitler's Death Camps: The Sanity of Madness.* New York: Homes & Meier Publishers.

Ferencz, B. (1979). *Less Than Slaves: Jewish Forced Labor and the Quest for Compensation.* Cambridge: Harvard University Press.

Fleischman, R.K., and Tyson, T.N. (2004). Accounting in Service to Racism: Monetizing Slave Property in the Antebellum South. *Critical Perspectives on Accounting*, *15*(3), 376–399.

Fleischman, R.K., Oldroyd, D., and Tyson, T. (2004). Monetizing Human Life: Slave Valuations on U.S. and British West Indian Plantations. *Accounting History*, *9*(2), 35–62.

Fleischner, E. (Ed.). (1977). *Auschwitz: Beginning of a New Era*. New York: Cathedral Church of St John the Divine.

Genschel, H. (1966). *Die Verdrangung der Juden aus der Wirtschaft im Dritten Reich, Göttingen Meisterschmidt-Verlag* (Reich Law Sheet Register RGBI, I, 1938, p. 1709).

Greenberg, I. (1975). *Confronting the Holocaust and Israel*, booklet of speech given to UJA Study Conference.

Gutman, Y., and Berenbaum, M. (1994). *Anatomy of the Auschwitz Death Camp*. Bloomington, IN: Indiana University Press.

Hacket, D. (1995). *The Buchenwald Report*. Boulder, CO: Westview Press.

Harston, M. (1993). The German Accounting Profession – 1931 and Before: A Reflection of National Ideologies. *The Accounting Historians Journal*, *20*(2), 139–162.

History of the UN War Crimes Commission and the Development of the Laws of War (1948). Noteworthy War Criminals. Second World War-Europe. SS. UN War Crimes Commission, London: HMSO, p. 53. Available at: http://www.ess.uwe.ac.uk/WCC/warcrimindss.htm.

Jones, D. (1999). *Moral Responsibility in the Holocaust: A Study in the Ethics of Character*. Oxford: Rowman & Littlefield Publishers.

Kogon, E. (1950). *The Theory and Practice of Hell, The German Concentration Camps and the System Behind Them*. New York: Farrar, Straus & Co.

Krens, G. (1988). The Holocaust Moral Theory and Immoral Acts. In A. Rosenberg and G. Meyers (Eds.) (1988), *Echoes from the Holocaust, Philosophical Reflections on a Dark Time* (pp. 245–261). Philadelphia, PA: Temple University Press.

Markus, H. (1997). *The History of the German Public Accounting Profession*. New York: Garland Publishing.

Matz, A. (1938). The Position of the German Accountant. *The Accounting Review*, *13*(4), 392–395.

Matz, A. (1940). Accounting as a Tool for Economy in German Business. *The Accounting Review*, *15*(2), 177–185.

Meisel, B. (1992). *Geschichte der deutschen Wirtschaftsprüfer: Entstehungs – und Entwicklungsgeschichte vor dem Hintergrund einzel – undgesamtwirtschaftlicher Krisen*. Köln: Verlag Dr. Otto Schmidt.

Mönckmeier, O. (Ed.). (1939). *Der Wirtschaftstreuhänder, Zeitschrift für deutsches Prüfungs- und Treuhandswesen*. Leipzig: G.A. Gloeckner Verlagsbuchhandlung.

Muhlen, N. (1959). *The Incredible Krupps: The Rise, Fall, and Comeback of Germany's Industrial Family*. New York: Holt.

Neal, M., and Morgan, J. (2002). The Professionalization of Everyone?: A Comparative Study of the Development of the Professions in the United Kingdom and Germany. *European Sociological Review*, *16*(1), 9–26.

Oldroyd, D., Fleischman, R.K., and Tyson, T.N. (2005). The Culpability of Accounting in the Practice of Slavery in the British Empire and Antebellum U.S. Paper presented at the 17th Accounting, Business, and Financial History Conference, Cardiff.

Rosenberg, A., and Marcus, P. (1988). The Holocaust as a Test of Philosophy. In A. Rosenberg, and P. Marcus (Eds.) (1988). *Echoes From the Holocaust, Philosophical Reflections on a Dark Time* (201–222). Philadelphia, PA: Temple University Press.

Rubenstein, R., and Roth, J. (1987). *Approaches to Auschwitz: The Holocaust and Its Legacy*. Atlanta, GA: John Knox Press.

Shirer, W. (1960), *The Rise and Fall of the Third Reich*. New York: Simon and Schuster.

Singer, H.W. (1943). *Standardized Accountancy in Germany. Occasional Papers V.* London: Cambridge University Press.

Trials of War Criminals Before the Nuremberg Military Tribunals under Control Council Law No.10, Nuremberg, 1946–1949 (1950a), Vol. 5, Washington, DC: United States Government Printing Office.

Trials of War Criminals Before the Nuremberg Military Tribunals under Control Council Law No.10, Nuremberg, 1946–1949 (1950b), Vol. 9, Washington, DC: United States Government Printing Office (Mazal Library) (http://www.mazal.org/archive/nmt/09/).

Trials of War Criminals Before the Nuremberg Military Tribunals under Control Council Law No.10, Nuremberg, 1946–1949 (1953), Vol. 7, Washington, DC: United States Government Printing Office (Mazal Library) (http://www.mazal.org/archive/nmt/07).

Walker, S.P. (2000). Encounters With Nazism: British Accountants and the Fifth International Congress on Accounting. *Critical Perspectives on Accounting*, *11*(2), 215–245.

Wertham, F. (1978). *The German Euthanasia Program*. Cincinnati, OH: Hayes Publishing.

11 To live or to die

Experiences of Jewish accountants and auditors in Italy 1938–1945

Valerio Antonelli, Raffaele D'Alessio, and Stephen P. Walker

Introduction

This chapter focuses on the persecution of individual Jewish accountants and auditors in Fascist Italy. It represents a companion piece to the analysis of the Fascist state's expulsion of Jews from the accounting profession contained in chapter 6. Whereas the story told in the earlier chapter essentially focused on the perpetrators of persecution and extermination (Hilberg, 1993), here, the emphasis is on the experience of their victims. The chapter shows how Jewish accountants and auditors in Italy attempted to survive, taking advantage of the opportunities provided by the law to adapt and defend their professional careers as well as the lives of their families. Unfortunately, for some, especially those resident in the Nazi-controlled Republic of Salò from September 1943, such strategies failed and culminated in arrest, deportation, and murder.

Historical insights of the everyday experience of anti-Semitic racial laws are gained by constructing a collective biography of a significant number of lives from a defined community (Jordanova, 2000, p. 215); in the chapter the individual Jewish accountants and auditors who were persecuted under Fascism. Micro-histories are provided of five Jewish accountancy practitioners who survived the persecution and five who did not. Such research depends on utilising a wide range of primary and secondary sources (Previts et al., 1990, p. 137).

Data relating to the birth, parentage, university education, professional registration and office location of accountancy professionals were collected from the official lists of practitioners and from the *Demorazza* files relating to Jewish accountants who applied for "discrimination" (see the following section). The board minutes of the Local Fascist Branches of Doctor of Commerce also provided information about the status of individual Jewish practitioners. Of particular importance were documents contained in the State Archives of Verona and Turin, which contained the results of investigations into individuals and their families.

Italian Companies' Yearbooks were consulted in order to identify the appointment of the individuals studied as auditors and to boards of directors.

DOI: 10.4324/9781032685328-11

Information about those appointed as forensic accountants by the courts was available in lists published by the Ministry of Justice. It was possible to trace details of those who held academic appointments in university records. An important attribute in determining the treatment of Jewish professionals under the race laws was whether they possessed a record of military service. The Ministry of War produced a yearly bulletin of all Army officers in service and those who resigned. This source provided information about the military careers of the focal community of this chapter. Newspapers contained obituaries on a number of individuals and some also received mentions in professional journals during their lifetimes. Attempts were also made to locate relevant visual materials.

Biographical information on a number of Jewish accountants and auditors was available online. In one case, a biography written by the accountant's nephew was published in a book. For a number of those transported to Auschwitz, "stumbling stones" (*Stolpersteine* or *Pietra d'inciampo*) were located in Italian cities. These monumental inscriptions contain information such as year of birth and dates of arrest, deportation, and death. Their installation has often been accompanied by websites containing more detailed biographical information about the individual. An example of a stumbling stone installed in Florence for one of those presented in this chapter who was never to return from Auschwitz, Enrico Dalla Volta, is shown in Figure 11.1 below.

The dataset of the *Fondazione Centro di Documentazione Ebraica Contemporanea*, available online,[1] listed all Italian Jews deported by the Nazis and provided some information about their fate. This source allowed location of those Jewish accountants and auditors who were known to have been deported and killed in concentration camps.

Figure 11.1 A "stumbling stone". Author's photograph

The chapter is structured as follows. Firstly, the legislative and bureaucratic framework is provided that relates to the accountancy profession under the Fascist Racial Laws and the subsequent deportation of Jews following the Nazi occupation of Northern Italy. The chapter then provides details of five Jewish accountants and auditors who survived persecution and five professionals who were deported to Auschwitz.

Accounting profession under Fascism

In Fascist Italy, professional accountants were perceived as a privileged class due to their education, income and wealth, and elevated lifestyle (Maida, 1997; Tonelli, 2013). During the 1930s, the profession comprised three occupational categories: accountants (Royal Decree 552/1929), doctors of commerce (Royal Decree 588/1929), and auditors (Royal Decree 1548/1936). These statuses were restricted to those whose names appeared in official registers. The registers were overseen by public bodies. Hence, the local Fascist Branches of Doctors of Commerce kept the registers of accountants and doctors of commerce, while the Ministry of Justice maintained the register of auditors (Cantagalli, 1996). Admission to the registers depended on satisfying moral, legal, and educational criteria. From 1938, membership of the National Fascist Party was also required (Royal Decree 743/1938).

Statutory measures to expel Jews from economic and social life commenced in November 1938 with the "Laws in Defence of the Race" (Royal Decree 1728/1938) (Coen, 1988; Acerbi, 2011; Livingston, 2014). In 1939, expulsion from the professions was mandated by Law 1054/1939. This contained specific provisions relating to the professions of accountant, doctor of commerce (Article 1), and auditor (Article 23).

Since the exercise of the accountancy profession was restricted to those whose names appeared in the registers (Law 897/1938), the official lists of practitioners were central to the expulsion and marginalisation of Jews. Removing a name from the register could end a professional career. However, outright cancellation of the right to remain on the register was only one of a number of degradations applied to Jewish practitioners. Law 1054/1939 identified different categories of Jewish professionals. It was possible to apply for the more favourable legal status of "discriminated". Article 14 of Royal Decree 1728/1938 established that "discrimination" might be applied to those who could claim merits in respect of the Fascist regime. Such merits were defined as follows:

> (a) Members of families of those who fell in the Libyan War, the World War, the Ethiopian War, and the Spanish Civil War, and of those who fell for the Fascist cause.
> (b) Those who meet one of the following conditions: 1) Those who were mutilated, disabled or wounded, war volunteers, and recipients of decorations for valour in the Libyan War, World War, Ethiopian

War and Spanish Civil War; 2) Combatants in the Libyan War, World War, Ethiopian War and Spanish Civil War who have received at least the Cross for War Merit; 3) Those who were mutilated, disabled or wounded for the Fascist cause; 4) Members of the National Fascist Party in the years 1919, 1920, 1921, 1922, and the second half of 1924; 5) Legionaries of Fiume; 6) Those who have earned exceptional merits, to be evaluated.

The names of "discriminated" professional accountants appeared in "Additional Lists", which were printed as an appendix to the official list of practitioners. Discriminated status meant that a Jew could continue in practice, but there were limitations. These ensured that it was not possible to perform tasks that implied the function of a public official (such as an insolvency administrator), be appointed as a judicial trustee or as a consultant to the courts. Moreover, it was not possible to collaborate with non-Jewish professionals. Accountants who were not eligible to apply for "discriminated" status were classified as "non-discriminated". This meant that they were removed from their professional organisations and ceased to be members of the Fascist associations. However, the names of "non-discriminated" professional accountants could be included on "Special Lists". Those so identified were able to continue to practice with all the limitations applicable to "discriminated" accountants, but also, crucially, with the proviso that they exercise the profession "exclusively for people belonging to the Jewish race" (Article 21). Such "non-discriminated" professional accountants were also compelled to pay a contribution to financing the bureaucracy associated with operating the racist procedures in the professional realm. A ministerial decree dated 30 July 1940 fixed this contribution at 200 lire (equivalent to *c*.150 Euros today). This was payable at the time of application for registration. An annual fee of 100 lire was also imposed. Both "discriminated" and "non-discriminated" professional accountants were also required to declare their status as Jews.

It was the *Demorazza* and the Race Court that determined whether a citizen was Jewish and, if so, whether they were "discriminated" or classed as "non-discriminated" (Royal Decree No. 1539 of 5 September 1938). If a professional accountant was recognised as a "discriminated Jew", their activity (registration, discipline, controls) remained with the local Fascist Branch of Doctors of Commerce, as for non-Jewish professional accountants (SNFDC, 1939). If, however, the professional accountant was classed as a "non-discriminated Jew", their activity fell under the auspices of the Court of Appeal, a board of magistrates. In relation to auditors, the distinction between "discriminated" and "non-discriminated" was irrelevant because Law 1054/1939, (Article 23) prevented all Jews from taking audit engagements. Decrees issued by the Ministry of Justice in February 1940 removed Jewish professionals from the official register of auditors (Ministerial Decree 3 February 1940 and 27 February 1940).

The experiences of Jewish accountants and auditors under this regimen varied and also altered significantly as World War II progressed. Fascist Italy had entered the war on 10 June 1940, but following a series of military defeats, Mussolini's government fell on 25 July 1943. In September 1943, Italy surrendered when the Armistice of Cassibile was signed. Once the armistice was announced Hitler gave orders to occupy Italy, free Mussolini and set up a puppet State (the Italian Social Republic) under direct German control (Oliva, 1997). With the Nazi occupation of central and northern Italy and the restoration of the Kingdom of Italy in the South under the protection of the Allies, the position of the Jews changed radically in each half of the country (De Felice, 1993, p. 440; Calimani, 2013, p. 624). In Southern Italy, the end of Fascist rule resulted in the dismantling of the racist state. On 20 January 1944 the Badoglio Government abolished the racial laws, including Law 1054/1939, thereby restoring all rights and prerogatives to Jewish accountants and doctors of commerce (Toscano, 1998). In central and northern Italy, by contrast, the position of Jews deteriorated markedly. Indeed, among the first actions of the Italian Social Republic was to declare itself a racial State (Calimani, 2013). All Jews, including those previously "discriminated", were unconditionally expelled from the professions (Italian Social Republic Decree N° 2 of 4 January 1944, Article 1).

The government of the Italian Social Republic facilitated the extermination of Jews resident in the territory under its control. Jews there were rounded up, sent to Italian concentration camps, and then transported to extermination camps in Germany and Poland, Auschwitz-Birkenau in particular (Di Sante, 2001, p. 200; Mayda, 2002, p. 243; Picciotto, 2002, p. 89). Following the end of the war, all the rights and goods stolen under the racial laws were restored to Italian Jews.

To live: Professional accountants and auditors who escaped the Final Solution

Bruno Pincherle (1895–1967)

Bruno Pincherle was born in Trieste on 21 October 1895. Pincherle had volunteered for service in World War I and began military life as a lieutenant. He was wounded in battle, awarded the War Merit Cross, and was promoted to Army Captain as a reservist in 1928 (Ministero della Guerra, 1928, p. 2229). After graduating in Economics and Business Sciences from the University of Trieste in 1924 (University of Trieste, 1935, p. 46), he moved to Verona in August 1926 and married Itala Prister. They had a son, Manlio. Pincherle resided at Lungadige Campagnola in an elegant neighbourhood of Verona (Zappi, 1936, p. 365). He had professional engagements in public companies, such as the auditor of the tax collector *Società Anonima Gestione Appalti Dazi ed Esattorie* in Catania (Anonymous, 1935, p. 800). In 1936,

Pincherle was enrolled in the register of the Fascist Branch of Doctors of Commerce (Albo Veneto, 1942).

Pincherle applied for "discrimination". On 11 January 1939, the Prefect of Verona ordered an investigation by the Fascist Police with a twofold aim. First, to gather extensive information on the moral, civil and political conduct of the applicant and members of his family. Second, to ascertain "whether the aforementioned and his family profess the Hebrew religion and if they belong or have belonged to a Jewish community or have embraced the Catholic religion and, if so, since when" (Archivio di Stato di Verona (ASVr), 1938–1945a). The Fascist Police report on Pincherle was forwarded by Trieste Police Headquarters on 19 January 1939. It stated that Pincherle had been a member of the Fascist National Party since 1 September 1926 and was of "regular moral and political conduct, of Jewish religion and race and a member of a Jewish community". To verify this information, the Fascist National Party provided a "certificate of registration" dated 27 January 1939. Verona Police Headquarters forwarded the documents on Pincherle to the Prefecture in Verona on 15 March 1939 and to the *Demorazza*. Pincherle was "discriminated" by a "discreet" communication on 22 June 1939 (ASVr, 1938–1945a). "Discrimination" status allowed Pincherle to join the Fascist Branch of Doctors of Commerce, which included his name on the "additional list" on 28 February 1940 (Sindacato Fascista del Dottori in Economia e Commercio (DISFDEC), 1940c; Albo Veneto, 1942).

Insights to the realities of domestic life under the Fascist regime were revealed by Pincherle's battles with the authorities to retain his employment of an "Aryan domestic maid" and to prevent his radio from being confiscated during the war. Law 1728/1938 stated that "Members of the Jewish race cannot employ Italian Aryan nationals as their servants" (Article 12). However, following a favourable report from Verona Police Headquarters dated 21 August 1939, which had investigated the conditions of the Pincherle family and the "poor health" of his wife, the Prefect of Verona authorised Pincherle, "on a provisional basis", to keep the "Aryan domestic maid" in his service. Three years later, on 26 November 1942, the police sent a new report on the Pincherle family. On 27 November 1942, the chief of police questioned the continued engagement of the maid as Pincherle and his wife were in good physical health and their son Manlio had been sent to Switzerland for treatment despite having been called up for military service. On 30 November 1942, the Prefect of Verona revoked the authorisation permitting the employment of the maid. On 8 December 1942, Pincherle challenged this decision by presenting a medical certificate attesting to his wife's continuing illness. Pincherle was unsuccessful and was forced to dismiss the maid (ASVr, 1938–1945a).

The Pincherle family owned a radio. In wartime, radio was perceived by the authorities as a potential vehicle for receiving anti-Italian propaganda. On 23 October 1941, Pincherle was notified that he had to surrender the appliance. In an attempt to keep it, Pincherle, arranged for a technician to block access on the radio to all frequencies except the station in Rome controlled by the regime (Ministry of the Interior, Circular of 4 November 1941, 442/30228). On 28 November 1941 the Prefect of Verona requested that the Ministry of the Interior permit the return of the radio to Pincherle. The Ministry of the Interior responded favourably and on 22 December 1941 the Verona Police ordered that the radio, with frequencies limited to one station, be released. A year later, Pincherle sold the appliance to a private individual for 4,000 lire, the invoice for which was submitted to the Fascist Police (ASVr, 1938–1945a).

Little is known about Bruno Pincherle and his family after 8 September 1943, when Nazi Germany occupied Northern Italy. On 20 March 1944, a search order for the Pincherle family was issued by the Fascist Police in the Republic of Salò. Evidently, this order aimed to seize and then deport them to an extermination camp. On 13 September 1944, a Fascist Police report noted that Pincherle and his family had fled and could not be traced (ASVr, 1938–1945a).

Soon after the War, on 5 December 1945, the Prefect of Verona ordered an investigation into Bruno Pincherle in order to gather "information on the moral and political conduct of the person in question, and also to ascertain whether he had become compromised with the former regime". Ironically, the Prefect of Verona was anxious to discover whether Pincherle had collaborated with the Republic of Salò. On 16 December 1945, the Police reported that: "Dr. Bruno Pincherle ... is of regular moral and political conduct and has no previous convictions. He was not compromised by the former regime but, rather, was persecuted because he was of the Jewish race, as is clear from the records of this office" (ASVr, 1938–1945a).

Bruno Pincherle died in Verona on 6 April 1967.[2]

Attilio Reichenbach (1894–1981)

Attilio Reichenbach was born in Verona on 4 January 1894. He served as a lieutenant in the cavalry during World War I and was promoted to captain as a reservist on 1 January 1930 (Regio esercito, 1938, p. 12). He graduated in Economics and Business Sciences at Bocconi University, Milan. Reichenbach became a member of the board of directors of the most important local bank, *Banca Mutua Popolare di Verona* (Anonymous, 1935, p. 854). In 1925, he married Marcella Jenna, and they had two children: Giancarlo and Gian Giacomo. The family resided at Via Emilia, 36, an elegant neighbourhood in Verona (Zappi, 1936, p. 365). In 1932 Reichenbach was enrolled on the Verona register of the Fascist Branch of Doctors of Commerce (Albo Veneto, 1942).

Soon after the racial laws were enacted, on 2 December 1938, the Fascist Police showed interest in Reichenbach. An initial report found the following: "Political conduct: regular; member of the Fascist National Party since 3 November 1934. Moral conduct: regular. Criminal record: none ... Maid: Maria Pizzini, Catholic" (ASVr, 1938–1945b). Reichenbach presented an application for "discrimination" based on his record of military service. On 13 January 1939, the Prefect of Verona ordered a further investigation. The Fascist Police reported that Reichenbach was of the "Jewish race and religion". Attached to the report was a document dated 24 May 1937 regarding his son Gian Giacomo, where he was described as "Head of the '*Balilla Moschettieri*' Maniple in the Seventh Legion. Decorated with the cross of merit". The latter was one of the highest awards that could be given in the Fascist youth. On 26 January 1939 Verona Police Headquarters formally initiated a preliminary investigation for "discrimination" in which the Federal Secretary of the National Fascist Party of Verona also became involved. On 8 February 1939 the Verona Police Commission submitted its final report. Reichenbach was described as follows:

> A veteran of the First World War, in which he served as a cavalry officer. He took part in the campaigns of 1915, 1916, 1917 and 1918, earning the War Merit Cross. He is a member of the Fascist Branch of Doctors of Commerce and is on the Roll of auditors. He has been an effective member of the District Commission for Direct and Indirect Taxation since 23 October 1937. He has been a senior director of the *Banca Mutua Popolare di Verona* since 1934.

It was also reported that during the war, Reichenbach's wife had been "a volunteer nurse in the Italian Red Cross, earning a silver medal for military merit and a bronze medal". Also referred to were the merits achieved by Gian Giacomo. On 15 March 1939, the Federal Secretary of the National Fascist Party expressed a favourable opinion on Reichenbach's "discrimination". Shortly thereafter, the Prefect of Verona forwarded the file to the Ministry of the Interior. On 22 June 1939 the *Demorazza* granted Reichenbach the right to "discrimination".

Like Bruno Pincherle, Reichenbach employed a domestic servant. On 3 December 1938, Reichenbach petitioned the Verona Police Headquarters to keep his non-Jewish maid, Maria Pizzini, citing as reasons the absence of his wife, who was with their eldest son (Giancarlo), and the need to care for their youngest child (Gian Giacomo) who lived on his own in Verona. The Prefect of Verona considered the matter. To support his case, Reichenbach produced a medical certificate confirming that his wife was ill, and on 12 June 1939, the Prefect granted a temporary authorisation to retain the services of the maid. However, the Fascist Police argued that this decision contravened the law, which prevented Jews from employing Italian Aryans as maids in any circumstances. On 9 December 1942, the Fascist Police questioned the Prefect of Verona's authorisation (ASVr, 1938–1945b).

Some concessions were secured. In July 1941, following a series of written applications evidenced by medical certificates, the Reichenbach family was permitted to travel to Bosco Chiesanuova in the Province of Verona for medical treatment. An application to visit the seaside at Miramare to seek a cure for his sons was also successful (ASVr, 1938–1945b). Attempts to keep a radio were less successful. On 30 October 1941, Verona Police made enquiries about Reichenbach's device. On 6 December 1941, Reichenbach applied to the Ministry of the Interior for permission to keep the radio in his home. Although the Ministry granted authorisation on 12 February 1943, the Fascist Police seized the radio. Subsequent attempts to secure its return proved fruitless (ASVr, 1938–1945b).

After 8 September 1943, when Nazi Germany occupied northern and central Italy, Reichenbach fled to Switzerland with his wife and children, remaining there until the end of the war.[3] His wife's family was captured and deported. The family's escape was described by Reichenbach's son Gian Giacomo. The Reichenbachs had moved from Verona to Cerro, a village in the foothills of the Veneto Alps. The local boys, including Reichenbach's sons, played a weekly football match in Erbezzo (IVRR, 2013, p. 28). At the end of one match, aided by teammates and adults from the village, the family made their escape. Travel was arranged by a bank manager that Reichenbach knew. The family moved first to a village on Lake Maggiore and from there to the Swiss border (Zambaldo, 2017). During his years of exile, Reichenbach practiced as an accountant in Lugano.[4] In the Republic of Salò, the Fascist Police searched for all Jews with a view to ensuring their deportation to an extermination camp. In the case of the Reichenbachs, this search proved futile. A police report dated 18 March 1944 acknowledged the disappearance of the family and the consequent impossibility of securing their arrest (ASVr, 1938–1945b).

After World War II, the Reichenbachs returned to Verona. In November 1945, the Civil and Penal Court of that city enrolled Attilio Reichenbach, at his request, on the register of technical consultants to the court (ASVr, 1938–1945b). He also requested that his name be re-entered on the official list of auditors, and this was achieved in 1946 (Ministero della Giustizia, 1946). Reichenbach subsequently led the newly established Local Council of Chartered Accountants of Verona, serving as its president from 1948 to 1964 (Borghini, 2016). His son, Gian Giacomo, graduated in Economics, and in 1949, his name was added to the Official List of Chartered Accountants in Verona (CNDC, 1994, p. 1100). Attilio Reichenbach died in 1981 and was buried in the Jewish cemetery in Verona.[5]

Rodolfo Colombo (1894–1952)

Rodolfo Colombo was born in Vercelli, Piedmont on 14 January 1894. He graduated in Economics and Business Sciences at the University Bocconi in Milan on 19 July 1920. He then moved to Vercelli where he married Elvira Ancona. They had a son, Dario, who narrated Colombo's personal and family history in a long interview which was published online.[6]

Rodolfo Colombo was enrolled on the Official List of Doctors of Commerce of Vercelli on 15 December 1929 (Albo Piemonte, 1938). His office was located on Via Piero Lucca 25 in that city (Archivio di Stato di Torino (ASTo), 1940–1943a). He also held a number of auditor appointments. In 1929, these included entities such as *Officine Morandi & Mighetti, Luzzatti & Muggia* (Anonymous, 1929, p. 201) and *Società Anonima SESAC* (Anonymous, 1931, p. 230). Colombo was also appointed as a member of the board of directors of joint-stock companies, such as the pasta manufacturer *Società Anonima Milanese di Pastificio e Prodotti Affini Frumens* (Anonymous, 1935, p. 284). In 1932, Colombo was also enrolled in the register of judicial administrators held by the Ministry of Justice (Ministero della Giustizia e degli Affari di Culto, 1932, p. 1158).

His successful practice ensured that the Colombo family enjoyed a comfortable standard of living. However, with the enactment of the racial laws in 1938, their domestic staff were required to leave. The family was aligned to Fascist organisations. Colombo was a member of the National Fascist Party, Elvira attended Fascist women's meetings, Dario was in the Balilla fascist youth organisation and the Federal Secretary of the National Fascist Party and Gazzotti was a frequent guest in the Colombo household.

When Law 1054/1939 was passed, Rodolfo Colombo's accountancy career was severely impacted. As Dario Colombo recalled:

> My father was expelled from the professional register although he had the right to be 'discriminated' in accordance with certain exceptions to the law for having taken part in the March on Rome, wearing the fascist scarf, things that my father did not do, although he was a decorated veteran and an officer in the First World War (...). As my father did not want to be discriminated, he was no longer able to exercise his profession (...). He had the requisites to do so and perhaps, unlike the others, had the means to support himself but, out of pride, he did not want to be 'discriminated' (...). But I was a kid and maybe all I thought about was riding my bike as fast as I could. My father closed the office permanently, did the occasional consultancy job (...) until a certain time in 1943.

Following the Royal Decree of 3 February 1940, Colombo's name was also deleted from the official list of auditors maintained by the Ministry of Justice.

As shown above, "non-discriminated" professional accountants could be included on "special lists". Inclusion was by a specific request that was subject to the scrutiny of a special district commission.[7] Rodolfo Colombo presented his request to the Appeal Court of Turin on 8 February 1940 (ASTo, 1940–1943a). On 12 February 1940, the Fascist Branch of Doctors of Commerce became involved. It sent the Appeal Court of Turin a certificate stating that "Mr. Colombo Rodolfo, son of Giuseppe is registered as no. 59 on the Piedmont Regional Official List of Doctors of Commerce. He will be expelled at the end of the current month in compliance with the recently issued racial laws". On 9 February 1940, the Appeal Court of Turin had asked the Royal Police of Vercelli for information about Rodolfo. The Police sent a report stating that Rodolfo "has no criminal records. Colombo has been registered with the National Fascist Party since 28 October 1932, and was subsequently expelled due to the racial laws. He has not been acting against the regime or the national interest. He took part in the Great War as a lieutenant" (ASTo, 1940–1943a). Although Dario Colombo recalled that his father was reluctant to pursue "discrimination", he appears to have made an application "but the Ministry never replied" (ASTo, 1940–1943a). The District Commission of Turin made the decision to include Rodolfo Colombo on the "Special List" of Doctors of Commerce on 8 June 1940. Complying with the ministerial decree of 30 July 1940, Rodolfo regularly paid the registration tax for inclusion on the special list. This was only levied on Jewish professional accountants (ASTo, 1940–1943a).

The years of World War II saw an escalation of tension in Vercelli, with conflicting views about the racial laws within the local middle classes and even within the Fascist hierarchy. The Colombo family became increasingly marginalised. With the Nazi occupation from September 1943, the Colombos realised that they could no longer remain in Vercelli. Colombo contacted people smugglers who organised their escape to Switzerland. Following a long walk through the mountains, the family reached the Swiss gendarmerie station at Stabbio. They subsequently travelled from one Swiss fugitive camp to another (Broggini, 2003, p. 483). Dario was sent to a boarding school for boys and, later, stayed with a Swiss family until the end of the war.[8]

The Colombo family returned to Vercelli in July 1945 to resume their former life. Rodolfo Colombo applied to the Ministry of Justice for the reinstatement of his name to the register of auditors (Ministero della Giustizia, 1945b). On 13 January 1946, he was elected as a member of the Vercelli Branch of Chartered Accountants.[9] Colombo gained new clients such as the real estate company *Società An. Immobiliare Ponente Sanremo*, the clinic *Ospedale Maggiore degli Infermi di Vercelli*, the farm *Cascina Laione*, and the *Società S.I.T.E.S* (Comunità ebraica di Vercelli, 2012, p. 224). Rodolfo Colombo died in Vercelli on 2 March 1952 (Obituary, 1952).

Attilio Fubini (1894–1968)

Attilio Fubini was born in Turin on 4 May 1894. He graduated in Economics from the University of Turin in 1914 (Albo Piemonte, 1938, p. 11). He married Linetta Colombo and they had a daughter, Franca. Fubini served as an officer in the Italian Royal Navy during World War I. He demonstrated his support for the Fascist cause as a Legionnaire of Fiume in 1919 and as a participant in the Ethiopian War in 1935-36 (Fubini, 2010, p. 35).

Attilio Fubini commenced his career as a lawyer. He was enrolled on the National List of Supreme Court Attorneys in October 1923 and also appeared on the Official List of Lawyers of Turin (Ministero di Grazia e Giustizia, 1929, p. 50). He also appeared on the Official List of Doctors of Commerce, being enrolled as no. 33 on the list of Turin professionals dated 15 December 1929 (Albo Piemonte, 1938, p. 3). His office was located at Via XX Settembre, 62 in Turin. Fubini's clientele included local companies. For example, he was an auditor to the wool manufacturer *Società Anonima Lanificio Tedeschi & C.* (Anonymous, 1935, p. 449). From 1932 Fubini was also enrolled in the register of judicial administrators held by the Ministry of Justice (Ministero della Giustizia e degli Affari di Culto, 1932, p. 1157).

With the advent of the racial laws, Fubini, like Rodolfo Colombo, sought inclusion on the "Special List" maintained by the Court of Appeal of Turin. Fubini submitted his application to the First President of the Court of Appeal. The application was successful, and, like Colombo, he was compelled to pay tax for the privilege (ASTo, 1940–1943b). As a Jew, Fubini's name was expunged from the Official Register of Turin Lawyers on 29 February 1940 (Ministero di Grazia e Giustizia, 1940, p. 478).

Following the occupation of northern and central Italy by the Nazis, Fubini and his family moved from Turin to Milan, residing at a guesthouse on Via Melzo under a false name. On visiting Turin with his daughter on 12 December 1944, he was apprehended by the Political Investigation Police and taken to Lamarmora Barracks, where the torture of anti-fascist political prisoners took place. He was identified as "Lawyer Fubini" by the tenant of his house in Moncalieri Street, Turin. Fubini, showing a genuine identity card issued by the municipality of Milan but bearing a false name, claimed to be "Accountant Querci" (Fubini, 2010, p. 36). Fubini spent eighteen days in jail. Officially, Fubini was released from prison because his wife was Aryan. However, a sum of 100,000 liras was paid to Gastone Serloreti, the director of the barracks. Favourable testimony from Fubini's Turin tenant and the intervention of a police brigadier may also have facilitated his release. Fubini returned to Milan. He avoided deportation to a concentration camp by changing his name again, but thereby lost clients who had known him as "Accountant Querci" (Fubini, 2010, p. 49). After World War II, Fubini returned to Turin, where he resumed his professional life. He died there on 12 March 1968 (Obituary, 1968).

Luciano Jona (1897–1979)

Luciano Jona is one of the best known Jewish professional accountants. He was born in Chieri, Piedmont, on 24 March 1897, into a family of textile entrepreneurs. His grandfather, Colonel Giacomo Segre, was esteemed as the leader of the assault by the Italian *Bersaglieri* at Porta Pia when Rome, the capital of the Papal States, was conquered in 1870. Luciano Jona became an accountant in 1913, but his career was stalled by military service in World

War I as an officer of the *Alpini* regiment. On 14 January 1918, he was awarded a medal for his role in the Battle of Mount Asalone. He married Giuditta and they had three children.

Jona graduated with a degree in Economics from the University of Turin in November 1920. From 1919, he worked in the prestigious practice of Vittorio Valletta who was also a lecturer in Economics. When Valletta was recruited as a manager of an accountant for the Fiat motor company in 1921 Jona took over as head of his accounting firm (Calligaris and Allio, 2009).

In 1926, Jona joined the National Fascist Party (Albo Piemonte, 1942, p. 21). His name appears on the Official List of Doctors of Commerce in Turin from its foundation on 15 December 1929 (Albo Piemonte, 1938, p. 3). Jona also appeared on the Official List of Auditors. He was appointed auditor to businesses such as the paper manufacturer *Società Anonima Cartonaggi, Impresa Ing. Luigi Bertelè*, estates company *Società Anonima Piemontese Immobiliare* (Anonymous, 1929, p. 360), building contractors *Borini & Bros* (Unione Fascista Industriali, 1937, p. 242), and the *Società Anonima Veneta Gas* (Anonymous, 1935, p. 549), the Milan-based branch of the chemical company Boston Blacking Company (Unione Fascista Industriali, 1937, p. 573). He also audited a number of smaller companies, most of which were owned by municipal or provincial government (Anonymous, 1931, p. 435; Anonymous, 1935, p. 549). From 1932, Jona's name also appeared on the register of judicial administrators (Ministero della Giustizia e degli Affari di Culto, 1932, p. 1156). Jona also pursued an academic career at the University of Turin, working alongside Giuseppe Broglia, an eminent Professor of Management. Jona initially assisted Broglia in his banking and commerce courses, but later he became a Lecturer in Commercial and Banking Techniques (Ministero dell'Educazione Nazionale, 1934, p. 375).

Jona's status with the regime was such that in 1938 he received a professional assignment from the Fascist *Podestà* of Turin (Cantaluppi, 2017, p. 84). Shortly thereafter, Jona's career was halted by the imposition of racial laws. On 16 October 1938, his service as a Lecturer at the University of Turin was suspended, and on 14 December, he was dismissed.[10] When Law 1054/1939 was passed, Jona lost much of his professional practice. In 1940, he was "discriminated", and his name entered the "Additional List" of the Doctors of Commerce of Jewish Race "discriminated" in Piemonte (Albo Piemonte, 1942, p. 21). Jona was also removed from the Official List of Auditors on 3 February 1940.

With the Nazis' occupation in September 1943, Jona changed his family name to "Celesia" in order not to be recognised. Conti (1979, p. 4) reported that at this time Jona was

> Persecuted by the fascists as a Jew and forced to live a clandestine existence in which he had 'to disperse his family and disguise his face as much as possible'. From 15 October 1943 to 20 February 1944 Jona

lived in the house of Penango. His wife was hospitalized in the house of Diana d'Alba, with Salesian nuns, the children found refuge in the religious institute of Lombriasco (Bo, 1999, p. 175). Jona participated in the Resistance without ever losing his pride or his confidence in the future.

After World War II, Jona resumed his professional activity as an auditor of numerous companies having been reinstated to the register of auditors following the Ministerial Decree of 17 August 1945 (Ministero della Giustizia, 1945a). Jona was reinstated to his position at the University of Turin on 1 May 1945 (Regia Università di Torino, 1945). Jona also began a political career, becoming a municipal councillor and, briefly, Mayor of Turin. He was President of the *San Paolo di Torino Banking Institute* from 1959 to 1979 (Borio, 1980). In the final months of his life, he was president of the *Lariano Bank* (Anonymous, 1979). Following Jona's death in Turin on 11 February 1979, a square in the city was named after him (Anonymous, 1986) and the *aula magna* of the Department of Management of the University of Turin was dedicated to his memory (Calligaris and Allio, 2009).

To die: Professional accountants and auditors exterminated during the Final Solution

Giuseppe Parenzo (1886–1944)

Giuseppe Parenzo, the son of Libero and Anita Praga, was born in Rovigo, Veneto on 12 December 1886.[11] He married Elda Vigevani of Parma in 1915 (Anonymous, 1915). She died at 35 in 1923, leaving a six-year-old son, Renato. Giuseppe subsequently lived with his brother Italo in Corso del Popolo 14 in Padua.

Parenzo served as a lieutenant in the infantry during World War I (Ministero della Guerra, 1918, p. 4561). After the war, Parenzo practiced as an accountant; his office was located at Via Eremitani 7, in Padua (Anonymous, 1922, p. 191). In 1929 his name was entered in the Register of Doctors of Commerce of the Veneto Region (Albo Veneto, 1942). In addition to practicing as an accountant, he was also a judicial administrator of the District Court of Padua (Ministero della Giustizia e degli Affari di Culto, 1932, p. 1160).

Parenzo was removed from the register of Doctors of Commerce on 1 March 1940, following a resolution to that effect on 28 February denouncing his "belonging to the Jewish race" (DISFDEC 1940c). He was included in the "additional list" due to his being "discriminated" on the basis of his war merits (Albo Veneto, 1942). Practicing from his office, now in Via Zabarella 30A, Padua, Parenzo continued professional activity that was permitted within the Jewish sphere.

Parenzo was arrested by the Nazi-Fascists on 29 July 1944 while a patient at the Civil Hospital in Padua. Two days later, he was placed on a train in

Trieste. Together with his brother Italo, Giuseppe Parenzo arrived at Auschwitz on 3 August 1944. On failing the initial selection of prisoners for internment, he was immediately sent to the gas chambers.[12]

Ugo De Benedetti (1893–1943)

Ugo De Benedetti was born in Turin on 17 August 1893, the son of Abramo and Carolina Carmi. He married Maria Antonietta Reinach, who was descended from a family of entrepreneurs in the industrial lubricants sector. They had two children: Pietro (born in 1929) and Giancarlo (born in 1931). De Benedetti was a lieutenant in the artillery during World War I (Regio Esercito, 1921, p. 815) and was subsequently promoted to the rank of captain (Regio Esercito, 1938, p. 120).

De Benedetti appeared on the official list of auditors and held numerous auditor appointments. These included the *Società Anonima Molini Albani*, a grain company in Milan; *Società Anonima Telefonica Tirrena*, a telephone operator in Florence; *Società Anonima Finanziaria Zaccaria,* a finance company in Pisa; and *Società Anonima Hotel Cavour*, a hotel chain (Anonymous, 1935). De Benedetti was also a successful lawyer for large companies in Milan and Turin. He was an associate of Toeplitz, the founder of the *Banca Commerciale Italiana*. With the passing of the racial laws, De Benedetti was removed from the register of auditors on 1 March 1940 (Ministero della Giustizia, 1940).

De Benedetti had previously purchased property in San Felice del Benaco, on the western shore of Lake Garda, comprising cultivated land and a number of buildings. In December 1942, the De Benedetti family left Milan to take up residence there. Rather than move to the manor house, they occupied a less conspicuous property on the estate intended for a sharecropper. Unfortunately, the presence of the De Benedetti family was known to the local law enforcement agencies as their names appeared in the "Register of Displaced People – Temporary Immigrants from Other Municipalities". Their choice of refuge also proved unfortunate. San Felice del Benaco was only four kilometres from Salò, which was the capital of the Italian Social Republic following Nazi occupation in September 1943.

On 31 October 1943, the family, accompanied by De Benedetti's 80-year-old father-in-law, Ernesto Reinach, attempted to escape to Switzerland. On reaching Torriggia on Lake Como, they were arrested while attempting to cross the border in a car. The family was then sent to the Jewish section of San Vittore prison in Milan. On 6 December 1943, they were placed on a train that departed from the infamous "Track 21" at Milan Central Station for Auschwitz. Ernesto Reinach died during the journey. Ugo De Benedetti, his wife Maria Antonietta, and their son Pietro were sent to the gas chambers a few days after their arrival. Their other son, Giancarlo, evaded the same fate because he had been sent to a school in Switzerland. He later filed an application for the restitution of the family's real estate that had been seized by the Republic of Salò (Anonymous, 2022).

Giorgio Ottolenghi (1909–1944)

Giorgio Ottolenghi, the son of Benedetto Ottolenghi and Emilia Lattes, was born in Acqui Terme, Piedmont, on 4 October 1909. His elder brother Giacomo[13] was a lawyer and a textile entrepreneur. In his early career, Giorgio Ottolenghi worked as a consultant to the family pharmaceutical company (Ministero delle Corporazioni, 1930, p. 875). Ottolenghi graduated from the University of Turin with a degree in Economics in October 1931. In 1933, he enrolled as a student in the Faculty of Law, being admitted to the third year of the course.[14] Ottolenghi was admitted to the Piedmont Register of Doctors of Commerce on 1 March 1934 (Albo Piemonte, 1938, p. 15). His office was in Via Sacchi 28-bis, in downtown Turin. He was a member of the National Fascist Party.

Ottolenghi was arrested in Turin on 11 December 1943 along with his brother Giacomo, his sister Michelina and his nephew Sergio. At the time, they were preparing to escape. The plan was for all four to gather at Giacomo's office and proceed to Porta Nuova, the main railway station in Turin. From there, they would travel first to Milan, then to Como. After a couple of days, they would cross the border into Switzerland, assisted by a people smuggler. The plan soon unravelled. On walking past the *Hotel Nazionale*, the headquarters of the SS in Turin, two men wearing civilian clothes apprehended Giorgio and Giacomo Ottolenghi. Sergio and Michelina managed to escape.[15] Giorgio was imprisoned first in Turin and then in Milan. On 30 January 1944, he was placed on a train in Milan bound for Auschwitz. He arrived on 6 February and died in the extermination camp sometime during the following months.[16]

Riccardo Sezzi (1907–1945)

Riccardo Sezzi, son of Augusto and Adriana Levi, was born in Piacenza, Emilia-Romagna on 28 December 1907. After graduating in Economics and Business Studies, he was enrolled in the Milan Register of Doctors of Commerce. His office address was Via Sammartini 15 in Milan (Fontana, 1940, p. 2005). Sezzi was removed from the register on 24 February 1940 (DISFDEC, 1940b). On 31 December 1943, he was arrested and sent to Milan prison and then to the Fossoli concentration camp. On 2 August 1944, he was placed on what was to be the last transport from Fossoli before its closure. The destination was Auschwitz, where he arrived on 6 August 1944. Sezzi died at an unknown location sometime after January 1945.[17]

Enrico Dalla Volta (1894–1944)

Enrico Dalla Volta, the son of Riccardo and Amalia Finzi, was born in Florence on 27 February 1894. His father was a lawyer and a Professor of Economics at the University of Florence. From 1927 to 1936, Riccardo Finzi was Rector of the newly established Higher Institute of Economic and Commercial

Sciences in Florence, subsequently, the Faculty of Economics and Commerce. From 1933 Finzi also sat on the Board of Directors of the Institute for Industrial Reconstruction (IRA), an organisation strongly supported by Mussolini.

Dalla Volta fought in World War I as an artillery officer and received a medal of merit having been wounded in one of the Battles of the Isonzo River (Ministero della Guerra, 1916, p. 2615). He was promoted to lieutenant on 28 October 1917 (Ministero della Guerra, 1921, p. 847). Enrico Dalla Volta followed his father into the law, but after graduating in Economics and Business Studies, he was also enrolled in the Florence Register of Doctors of Commerce. Under the racial laws, Enrico Dalla Volta was "discriminated" on the basis of his war merits. He was included in the "additional list" by the Board of the Florence Branch of Doctors of Commerce on 7 February 1940 (DISFDEC, 1940a).

When the persecution of the Jews commenced, Enrico Dalla Volta moved with his wife Lidia from the family home in Via Leone X to a boarding house near the Basilica of Santa Croce in Florence (Baiardi, 2022, p. 195). The family was well known in Florence. They were easily identified by the fascist police. Enrico Dalla Volta was arrested in Florence on 8 February 1944, together with his father Riccardo and his younger sister Margherita (Collotti, 2007, p. 91). They were first sent to the Fossoli concentration camp. On 22 February 1944, they were transported to Auschwitz (as was Primo Levi, who later documented his experiences as a deportee and survivor of Auschwitz in his book *If This Is a Man*), arriving on 26 February. Enrico Dalla Volta was sent to the gas chambers on the same day.[18]

Conclusion

This chapter has augmented accounting histories of the persecution of Jews under Fascism and Nazism by providing insights from the experiences of individuals who experienced it (Antonelli et al., 2018, 2023; Funnell, 1998, 2013, 2015; Lippman, 2009; Funnell et al., 2022; Twyford, 2021; Twyford and Funnell, 2023).

The micro-level stories presented have indicated the strategies pursued by Jewish professionals to survive in increasingly adverse legal, economic, and social conditions and, in some cases, to escape the horrors of the Final Solution (Bauman, 1989; Jacobsen and Marshman, 2008). A number, aware of the danger brought by Nazi occupation of northern and central Italy in 1943, assumed false identities and/or attempted to take flight across the border to Switzerland in particular. The consequences of capture could be disastrous. Some, such as Jona, joined the resistance movement.

Their loss of all auditor appointments and inclusion on the "Additional List" or the "Special List" of practitioners resulted in drastic reductions in the clientele of Jewish accountants. Labels such as "discriminated" and "non-discriminated" affirmed their status as the "Other" as members of a different, inferior race (Mussolini, 1938). In their home lives, accounting practitioners also suffered the loss of domestic employees, the seizure of devices, and social exclusion, including from local Fascist *élites* in which some (such as Colombo, Ottolenghi, and Dalla Volta) had built networks. Only Pincherle appears to have maintained a reputation with the regime sufficient to secure concessions from local officials, but this too was disrupted by the Nazi occupation in September 1943.

Bauman (1989, p. 112) observed that when unable to collectively improve their position persecuted Jews might individually seek out "positions and roles deemed favoured or privileged" and by invoking rights to exemptions or special treatments (Bauman, 1989, p. 109). In relation to Jewish accountants, the most obvious pathway here was to exploit the meagre opportunities provided to avoid total exclusion from the accountancy profession by attaining "discriminated" status. Most of the individuals examined had a case for "discrimination" based on military service during World War I and beyond. Despite this, not all pursued "discrimination". Reichenbach, Pincherle, Jona, and Dalla Volta decided to undergo the indignities of that process and the possibility of inclusion in a separate "additional list" of Jewish practitioners. Others, such as Colombo, Fubini, and Sezzi, did not.

It is acknowledged that the lives of numerous Jewish professional accountants have gone unrecorded and that the survival or otherwise of source material results in varying degrees of depth in the ten biographies provided. However, the stories told provide valuable insights into the diverse experiences of Jewish members of a particular professional community under Fascism and Nazism.

Notes

1 https://digital-library.cdec.it
2 https://catalogo.beniculturali.it/detail/HistoricOrArtisticProperty/0500230863
3 http://digital-library.cdec.it/cdec-web/persone/detail/person-cdec201-153/reichenbach-attilio.html
4 http://wwwkatiadipietrantonio.blogspot.com/2012/07/piccoli-ebrei-come-pelenel-film-una.html?m=1
5 https://catalogo.beniculturali.it/detail/HistoricOrArtisticProperty/0500230911
6 http://www.storia900bivc.it/pagine/editoria/merlo104.html
7 In order to be registered in the special list it was necessary: to be an Italian citizen; be of good moral conduct and not to have carried out any action contrary to the interests of the regime and the nation; be resident in the district of the Court of Appeal; and, be in possession of the other requirements established by the professional regulations in force (Law 1054/1939, Article 9).
8 http://www.storia900bivc.it/pagine/editoria/merlo104.html
9 https://www.odcecvercelli.it/it/web/la-nostra-storia-38
10 https://scienzaevergognaunito.wordpress.com/2018/10/30/luciano-jona-1897-1979/
11 http://www.lepietredinciampoapadova.it/
12 https://digital-library.cdec.it/cdec-web/persone/detail/person-5505/parenzo-giuseppe.html
13 http://www.chieracostui.com/costui/docs/search/schedaoltre.asp?ID=25625
14 https://www.asut.unito.it/studenti/web/index.php?r=studenti%2Fview&id=27058

15 https://giorgiolevi.com/2017/01/20/pietre-dinciampo-a-torino-il-ritorno-a-casa-degli-zii-giorgio-e-giacomo-ottolenghi-uccisi-nel-1944-ad-auschwitz-ci-sono-voluti-73-anni/
16 http://digital-library.cdec.it/cdec-web/persone/detail/person-5854/ottolenghi-giorgio.html
17 http://digital-library.cdec.it/cdec-web/persone/detail/person-7283/sezzi-riccardo.html
18 http://digital-library.cdec.it/cdec-web/persone/detail/person-1837/dalla-volta-enrico.html

References

Primary sources

Ministerial decrees

Ministero della Giustizia (1940). Decree 3rd February 1940.

Ministero della Giustizia (1945a). Decree 17th August 1945.

Ministero della Giustizia (1945b). Decree 12th October 1945.

Ministero della Giustizia (1946). Decree 24th August 1946.

Ministerial yearbooks

Ministero dell'Educazione Nazionale (1934). *Annuario 1934-XII.* Roma: IPS.

Ministero della Giustizia e degli Affari di Culto (1932). *Bollettino Ufficiale*, 31 December 1932, n. 53.

Ministero della Guerra (1916). Bollettino Ufficiale. Ottavo elenco di ricompense al valore militare ai morti in combattimento o in seguito a ferite nella campagna di guerra 1915–1916. 2 May.

Ministero della Guerra (1918). Bollettino ufficiale delle nomine, promozioni e destinazioni negli uffiziali dell'esercito italiano e nel personale dell'amministrazione militare. 6 July.

Ministero della Guerra (1921). Ruoli di anzianità per il 1919 degli ufficiali in congedo. Roma: SPAG.

Ministero della Guerra (1928) Bollettino ufficiale delle nomine, promozioni e destinazioni negli ufficiali e sottufficiali del R. esercito italiano e nel personale dell'amministrazione militare, n. 31.

Ministero delle Corporazioni (1930) Bollettino dei marchi di fabbrica e di commercio, 18 (13–14).

Ministero di Grazia e Giustizia (1929). Albo Ufficiale degli Avvocati. Bollettino, Supplemento al n. 41.

Ministero di Grazia e Giustizia (1940). Bollettino Ufficiale, 1940, n. 33.

Sindacato Fascista dei Dottori in Economia e Commercio (SNFDC) e Direttorio Interprovinciale (DISFDEC)

DISFDEC (1940a). Firenze. Verbale di direttorio. 7 February 1940. *Il Commercialista 13*(3), p. 122.

DISFDEC (1940b). Milano. Verbale di direttorio. 24 February 1940. *Il Commercialista 13*(3), p. 125–129.

DISFDEC (1940c). Venezia. Verbale di direttorio. 28 February 1940. *Il Commercialista*, *13*(3), 133.
SNFDC (1939). Circolare n. 114, 8 October 1939. *Il Commercialista*, *12*, 389.

Regional Branches of Chartered Accountants – Official Lists

Albo Piemonte (1938). Albo degli esercenti in materia di economia e commercio per le provincie del Piemonte, aggiornato a tutto agosto 1938.
Albo Piemonte (1942). Albo professionale esercenti di economia e commercio, aggiornato al 30 giugno 1942.
Albo Veneto (1942). Albo professionale esercenti di economia e commercio, aggiornato al 30 giugno 1942.

State Archive Records

ASTo (1940–1943a). Archivio di Stato di Torino, Fondo Corte d'Appello di Torino, primo versamento, b. 1612, fasc. "Commercialisti", sottofascicolo "Rodolfo Colombo".
ASTo (1940–1943b). Archivio di Stato di Torino, Fondo Corte d'Appello di Torino, primo versamento, b. 1612, fasc. "Commercialisti", sottofascicolo "Attilio Fubini".
ASVr (1938–1945a). Archivio di Stato di Verona, Prefettura, Gabinetto, Ebrei. "Dott. Pincherle Bruno di Erminio e di Emma Luzzatto. Gabinetto serie 3, classe 8".
ASVr (1938–1945b). Archivio di Stato di Verona, Prefettura, Gabinetto, Ebrei. "Reichenbach Attilio fu Leopoldo. A-1 40".

Miscellaneous

Anonymous (1915). Avvisi. *Rivista dei ragionieri*, p. 335.
Anonymous (1922). *Guida di Padova, amministrativa, commerciale, industriale.* Padua: SCT.
Anonymous (1929). *Biografia finanziaria italiana*. Roma: Macciocchi & Orlandi.
Anonymous (1931). *Biografia finanziaria italiana*. Roma: Armani.
Anonymous (1935). *Biografia finanziaria italiana*. Roma: Laboremus.
Anonymous (1979). Jona passed away, he was 82. *La Stampa*, 12th February 1979, p. 5.
Anonymous (1986). A square to remember Luciano Jona. *La Stampa*, 5th December 1986, p. 34.
Anonymous (2022). *Etta. Da San Felice ad Auschwitz.* Comune di San Felice del Benaco.
Comunità ebraica di Vercelli (2012). Archivio Storico. Inventario, at the URL https://inventari.san.beniculturali.it/inventari/665/pdf
Conti, S. (1979). Jona, a life in the flag of honesty. *La Stampa*, 13th February 1979, p. 4.
IVRR (2013), Ebrei a Verona. Mostra storico-documentaria, at the URL: http://resistenza.univr.it/materiali/ebrei_a_verona_mostra_2013.pdf
Fontana, G. (1940). *Guida di Milano e provincia*. Milano: Savallo.

Mussolini B. (1938). Discorso a Trieste, 18 settembre 1938. At the URL: https://www.youtube.com/watch?v=IsoQdrnKDK4

Obituary (1952). Dott. Rodolfo Colombo. *La Stampa*, 3 Mars 1952, p. 2.

Obituary (1968). Dott. Attilio Fubini. *La Stampa*, 12 Mars 1968, p. 16.

Regia Università di Torino (1945). Estratto del verbale del Consiglio di Facoltà di Economia e Commercio, August 20.

Regio Esercito (1921), Annuario ufficiale delle forze armate del Regno d'Italia. 1, Regio esercito, Roma, IPS.

Regio Esercito (1938). *Annuario ufficiale delle forze armate del Regno d'Italia. 1, Regio esercito*, Roma, IPS.

Unione Fascista Industriali (1937). *Annuario industriale della provincia di Milano 1937-XV*, Milano: DeSilvestri.

University of Trieste (1935). *Guida dello student.* Trieste: Tipografia PNF.

Zambaldo, V. (2017). The escape for life of Reichenbachs, Jews from Verona. *L'Arena*, 19 November 2017, p. 21.

Zappi F. (1936) *Guida generale della Provincia di Verona*, Verona, La Nazionale.

Secondary sources

Acerbi, G. (2011). *Le leggi antiebraiche e razziali italiane ed il ceto dei giuristi.* Milano: Giuffrè.

Antonelli, V., D'Alessio, R., Rossi, R., and Funnell, W. N. (2018). Accounting and the banality of evil: Expropriation of Jewish property in Fascist Italy (1939–1945). *Accounting, Auditing & Accountability Journal, 31*(8), 2165–2191.

Antonelli, V., D'Alessio, R., and Walker, S. P. (2023). Operationalizing expulsion. Jewish accountants in Fascist Italy, 1938–1943. *Critical Perspectives on Accounting, 94*, 102462.

Baiardi, M. (2022). *Le tavole del ricordo. Guerre e Shoah nelle lapidi ebraiche a Firenze (1919–2020).* Roma: Viella Editrice.

Bauman, Z. (1989). *Modernity and the Holocaust.* Ithaca, NY: Cornell University Press.

Bo, V. (1999), *Cattolici, ebrei ed evangelici nella guerra vita religiosa e società, 1939–1945.* Milano: Franco Angeli.

Borghini, G. (2016). *I professionisti dell'economia a Verona, dal calculator al commercialista.* Milano: Egea.

Borio, F. (1980). *I sindaci della libertà: Torino dal 1945 ad oggi.* Torino: EDA.

Broggini, R. (2003). *Frontier of Hope. Jews from Italy Seek Refuge in Switzerland 1943–1945.* Milano: Hoepli.

Calimani, R. (2013). *Storia degli ebrei italiani nel XIX e nel XX secolo.* Milano: Mondadori.

Calligaris, G., and Allio, R. (2009). La storia della ragioneria a Torino. In *Ricordando Giovanni Ferrero* (pp. 3–108). Torino: Giappichelli.

Cantagalli, A. (1996). La professione del dottore commercialista. In M. Malatesta (Ed.). *Storia d'Italia. Annali 10: I professionisti* (pp. 225–258). Torino: Einaudi.

Cantaluppi, A. (2017). Le carte di Luciano Jona e Francesco Rota nell'archivio della Segreteria generale dell'Istituto Bancario San Paolo di Torino. *Archivi, 12*(1), 79–96.

CNDC (1994). *Annuario Nazionale dei Dottori Commercialisti.* Milano: Ipsoa.

Coen, F. (1988). *Italiani ed ebrei, come eravamo. Le leggi razziali del 1938.* Genova: Marietti.

Collotti E. (2007). *Ebrei in Toscana tra occupazione tedesca e RSI: Saggi*. Roma: Carocci.

De Felice, R. (1993). *Storia degli ebrei italiani sotto il fascismo*. Torino: Einaudi.

Di Sante, C. (2001). *I campi di concentramento in Italia: dall'internamento alla deportazione, 1940–1945*. Milano: Franco Angeli.

Fubini, G. (2010). *L'ultimo treno per Cuneo. Pagine autobiografiche (1943–1945)*. Aosta: Le Chateau.

Funnell, W.N. (1998). Accounting in the service of the Holocaust. *Critical Perspectives on Accounting*, *9*(4), 435–464.

Funnell, W.N. (2013). Accounting for the Holocaust. In R.K. Fleischman, W.N. Funnell, and S.P. Walker (Eds.). *Critical Histories of Accounting: Sinister Inscriptions in the Modern Era* (pp. 67–78). Abingdon: Routledge.

Funnell, W.N. (2015). The Holocaust, Accounting and the Denial of Humanity. In W.N. Funnell, and M. Chwastiak (Eds.). *Accounting at War: The Politics of Military Finance*. Abingdon: Routledge.

Funnell, W.N., Antonelli, V., Bigoni, M., Cafaro, E.M., and D'Alessio, R. (2022). Accounting for Jewish "bare life" in the Fossoli Concentration Camp, 1943–44. *Critical Perspectives on Accounting*, *88*, 102323.

Hilberg, R. (1993). *Perpetrators Victims Bystanders: The Jewish Catastrophe 1933–1945*. New York: Harper & Collins.

Jacobsen, M.H., and Marshman, S. (2008). The four faces of human suffering in the sociology of Zygmunt Bauman-continuity and change. *Polish Sociological Review*, *161*, 3–24.

Lippman, E.J. (2009). Accountants' responsibility for the information they report: An historical case study of financial information. *Accounting Historians Journal*, *36*(1), 61–79.

Livingston M.A. (2014). *The Fascists and the Jews of Italy. Mussolini's Race Laws (1938–1943)*. Cambridge: Cambridge University Press.

Maida, B. (1997). Classi medie e fascismo. Per uno studio sui piccoli commercianti nella crisi del regime. *Studi Storici*, *38*(3), 793–833.

Mayda, G. (2002). *Storia della deportazione dall'Italia: 1943–1945: militari, ebrei e politici nei lager del Terzo Reich*. Torino: Bollati Boringhieri.

Oliva, G. (1997). *La Repubblica di Salò*. Firenze: Giunti.

Picciotto, L. (2002). *Il Libro della Memoria. Gli ebrei deportati dall'Italia (1943–1945)*. Milano: Mursia.

Previts, G.J., Parker, L.D., and Coffman, E.N. (1990). An accounting historiography: Subject matter and methodology. *Abacus*, *26*(2), 136–158.

Tonelli, A. (2013). Fascismo e classi medie: un dibattito storico ancora aperto. *Società Mutamento Politica*, *4*(7), 115–128.

Toscano, M. (1998), *L'abrogazione delle leggi razziali in Italia (1943–1987). Reintegrazione dei diritti dei cittadini e ritorno ai valori del Risorgimento*. Roma: Senato della Repubblica.

Twyford, E. (2021). A thanatopolitical visualisation of accounting history: Giorgio Agamben and Nazi Germany. *Accounting History*, *26*(3), 352–374.

Twyford, E.J., and Funnell, W.N. (2023). Accounting for the Nazi Aryanisation of German banks. *Accounting, Auditing & Accountability Journal*, *36*(1), 1–23.

12 Knowing the Holocaust

Erin Twyford, Warwick Funnell, and Michele Bigoni

Accounting for the Holocaust has shown how the Nazi oppression of Jews who were condemned as the "Other", an "unequal" race and culture that purportedly threatened the Aryan race, resulted in their dehumanisation and the denial of their fundamental human right to life; their descent to a condition of "bare life". Eyewitness evidence of individuals involved, especially Jewish victims, provides the most potent physical and documentary evidence for confirming the Nazis' attempt to exterminate European Jews. The books, diaries, and other written testimonies created by both those who survived, such as the Italian writer Primo Levi, and by those who were murdered have been able to provide eyewitness accounts of the systematic, merciless manner in which this genocide was carried out across Europe and elsewhere. Evidence of the intent and extent of the Holocaust was also given by senior Nazis who were captured and later tried at Nuremberg after the war. Albert Speer, Hitler's personal architect and later Minister of Armaments, provided damning first-hand evidence at the Nuremberg trials of a systematic State-sponsored policy of Jewish extermination. This was given disturbing confirmation when Adolf Eichmann, the senior Schutzstaffel (SS) officer responsible for organising the transportation of Jews to the extermination camps, testified at his trial in 1961 to the intent and extent of the killing and the absence of any feeling he had of culpability when he boasted that:

> I did not take on a job as a senseless exercise. It gave me uncommon joy ... I found it fascinating to deal with these matters.... My job was to catch these enemies and transport them to their destination ... To be frank with you, had we killed all of them ... I would be happy to say, alright, we managed to destroy an enemy.... (When) I suggested these words "Final Solution", at the time I meant by this the elimination of Jews, their marching out of the German Nation. Later ... these harmless words were used as a camouflage for the killing.
>
> (Bauer, 1982, p. 207)

To achieve the "Final Solution" that Eichmann proposed, "forms of knowledge affiliated with domination" are required (Said, 1994, pp. 8, 93).

DOI: 10.4324/9781032685328-12

Accounting for the Holocaust has demonstrated how a primary source of this knowledge was the information provided by a vast number of accounting and management reports containing financial and non-financial information. These constituted, in effect, another type of eyewitness evidence. The devastating detail recorded in these reports that arose from the procedures and facilities which were created to identify, capture and then murder Jews gives even more significant impact and authority to the evidence of the experiences of those who became the victims of the Nazis.

Throughout *Accounting for the Holocaust,* it has been consistently confirmed in a variety of situations and forms how accounting practices, broadly defined as "calculations and techniques which mediate the relations between individuals, groups, and institutions as well as the accountability relationships that result from these social relations" (Neu, 2000, p. 270), were used to give the murderous actions of the Nazis not only the ability to be carried out with great efficiency but also with a moral credibility according to Nazi beliefs. The detailed reports required from those who either carried out or assisted with the actual killing at the extermination camps were to be an ever-present reminder to them that their actions were always to be for what the Nazis proclaimed was a high moral purpose, protecting the Aryan race, and that they would be held accountable according to these higher motives, not any possible personal material gains. Thus, the contributions of accounting practices as a moral agent in the management of the concentration camps and extermination camps enforced the fatal oppression of Jews. Accounting reports and related practices provided a means to give legitimacy to racial justifications for the way in which Jews were treated in the concentration and extermination camps. This was particularly obvious with details of the minimal food and other items to meet essential needs that confirmed their treatment as condemned Jews.

Qualitative matters of life and death were not given a presence with accounting information and so were rendered invisible. The accounting reports and other statistics that were required for the implementation of the Final Solution allowed exposure primarily of only specific aspects of the conditions to which Jews were condemned, such as food allowances, not the increasingly fatal impact that these conditions permitted. By emphasising knowledge that did not allow any consideration of Jews as sentient human beings, accounting practices could be described as a "method of barbarism" (Said, 1994, p. 93). The apparent ordinary, routine numerical representations and calculations in accounting reports also provided the means to allow the fatal consequences of the way in which the camps were managed to be largely hidden from the outside world, even though the Nazis were determined to maintain very detailed, highly regulated records of their actions. Most infamously were the details of personal possessions seized and the hair and teeth removed when those who were to be killed entered the gas chambers. Later, much to the regret of many senior Nazis who survived the war, this was to be the evidence upon which they were convicted at the Nuremberg trials.

The apparent amoral, prosaic nature of the reports used to manage the Final Solution gave them a deceptive banality that contributed to the survival of this enormous amount of documentation despite well-organised, concerted attempts by the Germans to destroy anything that might implicate them in the genocide that they had perpetrated. These documents, as confirmed throughout this book, provide further irrefutable confirmatory evidence of the actions that led to the programmed murder of more than 6 million Jews and others, despite attempts by those, such as the historian David Irving,[1] who have sought to deny that this occurred.

There is still so much to be uncovered about the role and culpability of accounting practices in enabling the Holocaust and a need for more interdisciplinary approaches that will complement and augment the studies in this book. Also, to broaden and introduce new trajectories and domains to Holocaust studies, a greater presence should be given to many more locations such as Greece and the Greek Islands, Norway, Denmark, and Croatia. On the tiny island of Rhodes in Greece, for example, the Germans rounded up 1,650 Jews, of which only 150 returned.

The ramifications of the Holocaust permeate society today, with continuing conflict, diaspora, court cases, and reparations sought by survivors and their families. It remains important to consider the context of these contemporary issues and draw attention to the practices that enable human suffering. It is hoped that *Accounting and the Holocaust* has illuminated the many ways accounting, accountants, and calculative practices inherently hold social and moral implications for people. It is only through this illumination that we can critique these practices to ensure we learn the lessons from history; otherwise, we are doomed to repeat the mistakes and thus engender the complicity of the profession in further instances of violence, degradation, and even death.

Note

1 In 2000, David Irving sued the author Deborah Lipstadt for publishing the book *Denying the Holocaust* in which Irving believed he had been defamed. The court supported Lipstadt and ruled that Irving had deliberately falsified historical facts about the Holocaust.

References

Bauer, Y. (1982). *A History of the Holocaust*. London: Franklin Watts.

Neu, D. (2000). Accounting and accountability relations: Colonization, genocide and Canada's first nations. *Accounting, Auditing and Accountability Journal*, *13*(3), 268–288.

Said, E. (1994). *Culture and Imperialism*. London: Vintage Books.

Index

Note: Page references in *Italics* for figures and **bold** for tables.

9781032685274